RONAN BOUROULLEC

RONAN BOUROULLEC

DAY AFTER DAY

DAY AFTER DAY   6
JOUR APRÈS JOUR   7

2014   8
2015   12
2016   28
2017   108
2018   184
2019   240
2020   282
2021   331
2022   388

LIST OF WORKS   417
LISTE DES ŒUVRES   435

I don't have a defined work method; I work instinctively, by successive strokes. I like to repeat, start over, accumulate, to work simultaneously on several subjects. I like to bring models of current projects back from the studio, place them on my table and study them, searching for the right *impression*. In this permanent state of flow, where improvisation is part of research, it is through a sketch or a makeshift rendering in cardboard that the solutions suddenly appear.

I also draw all the time, everywhere. On the train, at night, in the morning, on a boat, on the corner of a table, in a park, at a café, at home. Drawing without constraint, without aim, without premeditation, free from the pressure to solve anything. Drawing for its own sake.

I take photographs daily, on a mobile phone, of my drawings, my works, the light in the studio, an object that we designed several years ago spotted in a shop window, our chairs on the terrace of a café, the morning sun on a ceramic vase.

About ten years ago, I started to post the occasional picture on Instagram. Then I began posting daily images of my research, documenting my doubts, the joy of certain projects, and sometimes also their dead ends. Colourful impressions, blossoming shapes, perfect moments, emotions. It became a journal.

This book, which contains images of my own research as well as work carried out in collaboration with my brother Erwan and the wonderful team around us, follows the thread of these photographs as they were posted, day after day.

As we progress picture by picture, projects are gradually revealed. In this kaleidoscope of images, urban projects rub shoulders with a tiny drawing, a large-format print, the sea near the studio, a maquette in modelling clay, a flower, a cat, a bronze prototype, the silhouette of a friend...

It is a library of details, colours, collages and atmospheres collected over time. It is a manifesto of the elements at the heart of my work and my life: precision, confusion, passion, accumulation, the need for disorder, which gives rise to energy, and the need for emptiness.

It is a self-portrait.

Je n'ai pas de méthode de travail définie, je fonctionne à l'instinct, par touches successives. J'aime répéter, recommencer, accumuler, travailler simultanément sur plusieurs sujets. J'aime remonter de l'atelier les maquettes des projets en cours, les poser sur ma table, les observer, à la recherche de la bonne *impression*. Dans ce flux permanent où l'improvisation fait partie de la recherche, c'est au détour d'un croquis, d'un bricolage en carton que les solutions apparaissent soudain.

Je dessine aussi partout, tout le temps. Dans le train, la nuit, le matin, sur un bateau, un coin de table, dans un parc, au café, à la maison. Un dessin sans contrainte, sans objectif, sans question à résoudre, libre de toute préméditation. Un dessin pour lui-même.

Je photographie quotidiennement avec mon téléphone portable, mes dessins, mes travaux, la lumière dans l'atelier, un objet que nous avons dessiné il y a plusieurs années rencontré dans la vitrine d'un magasin, nos chaises à la terrasse d'un café, le soleil du matin sur un vase en céramique.

Il y a une dizaine d'années, j'ai commencé à utiliser Instagram pour diffuser quelques images. Puis j'ai partagé quotidiennement mes recherches, mes doutes, la joie de certains projets, parfois aussi leurs impasses. Des impressions colorées, des formes qui éclosent, des moments parfaits, des émotions. C'est devenu un journal.

Ce livre, constitué de mes recherches personnelles, ainsi que de recherches et de projets réalisés avec mon frère Erwan et la belle équipe qui nous entoure, suit le fil de l'organisation de ces photographies, postées jour après jour.

On y avance image par image. Les projets se révèlent au fil des pages. Dans ce kaléidoscope se côtoient des projets urbains, un dessin minuscule, un très grand format, la mer près de l'atelier, une maquette en pâte à modeler, une fleur, un chat, un prototype en bronze, la silhouette d'un proche...

C'est une bibliothèque de détails, de couleurs, d'assemblages, d'atmosphères, qui se constitue alors que passe le temps. C'est un manifeste des éléments qui sont au cœur de mon travail et de ma vie : la précision, la confusion, la passion, l'accumulation, la nécessité du désordre, qui fait naître l'énergie, et la nécessité du vide.

C'est un autoportrait.

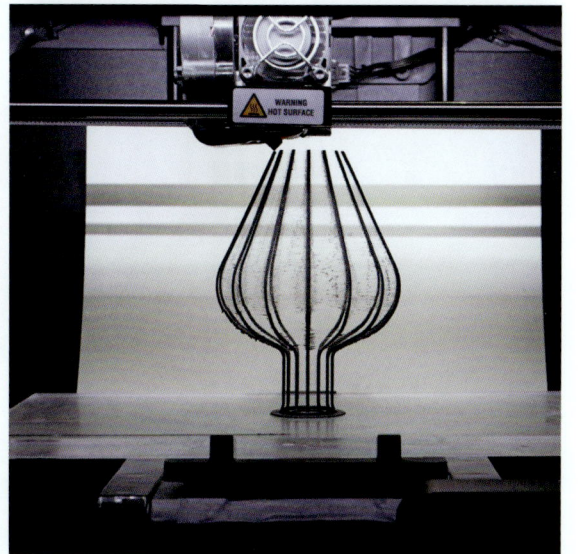

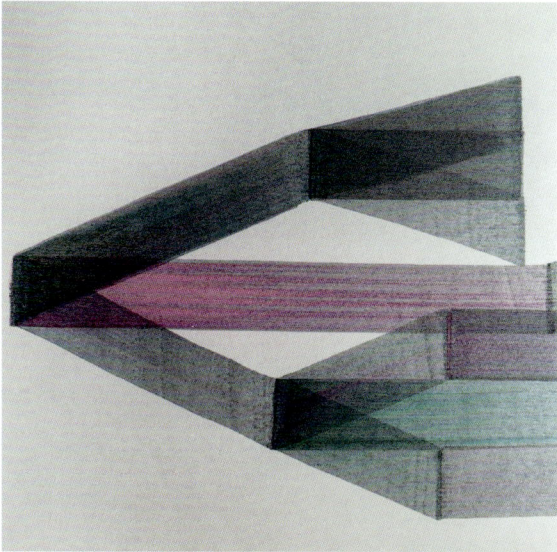

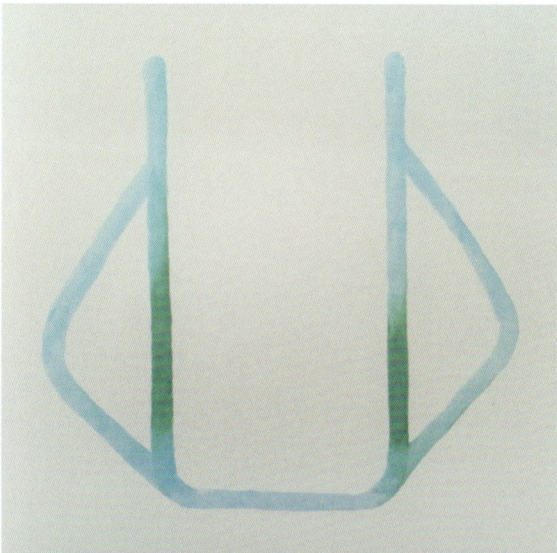

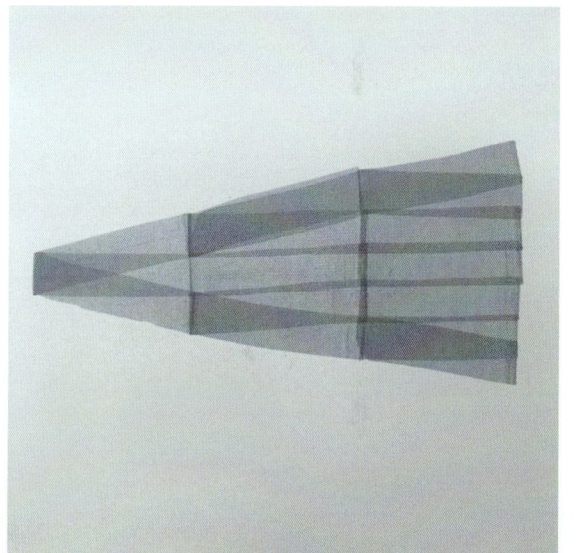
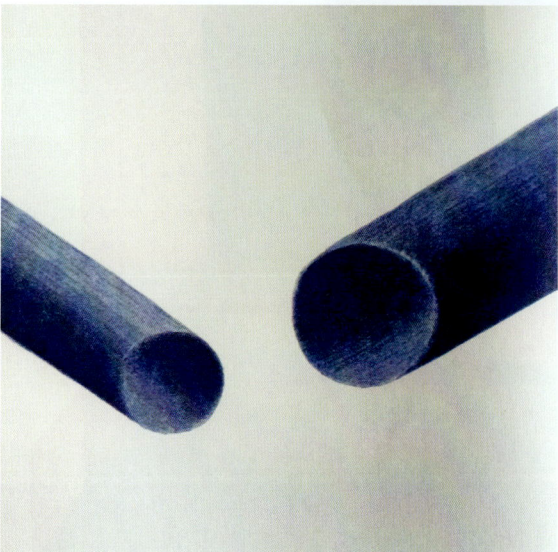

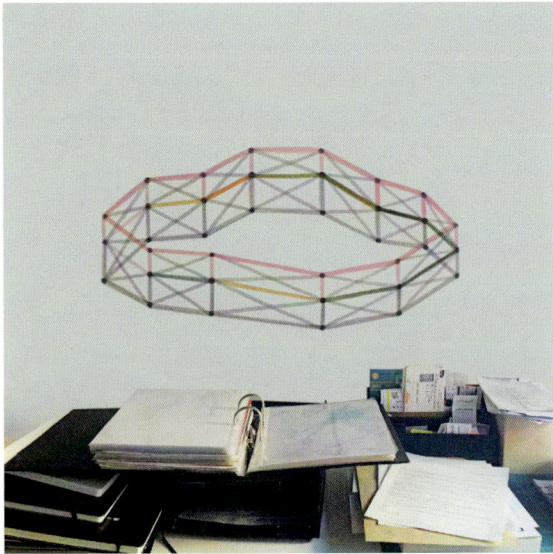

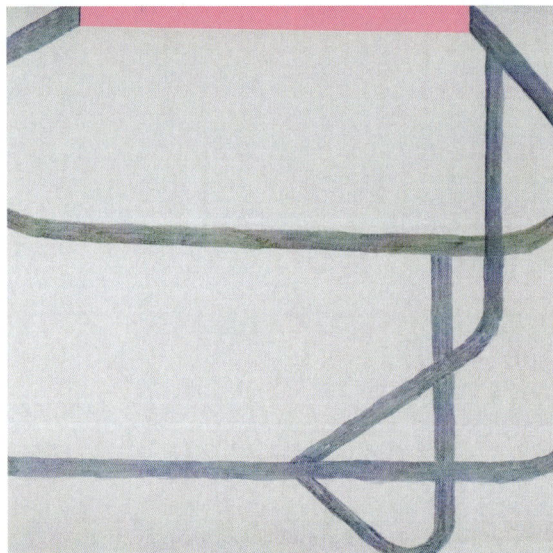
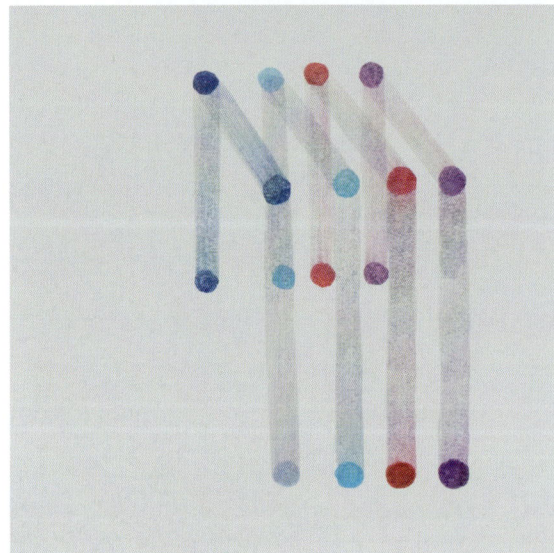
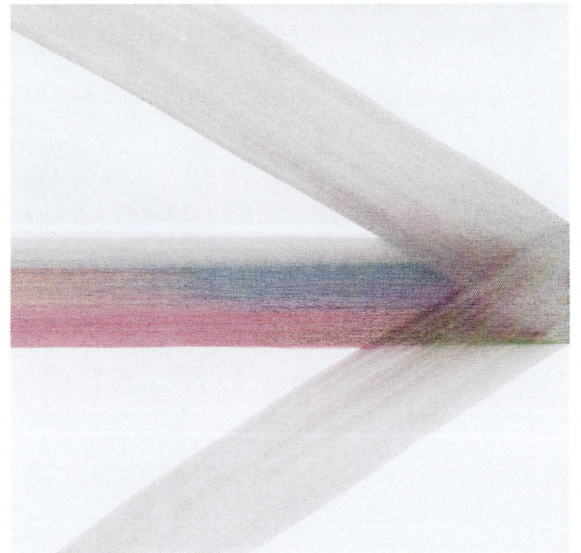

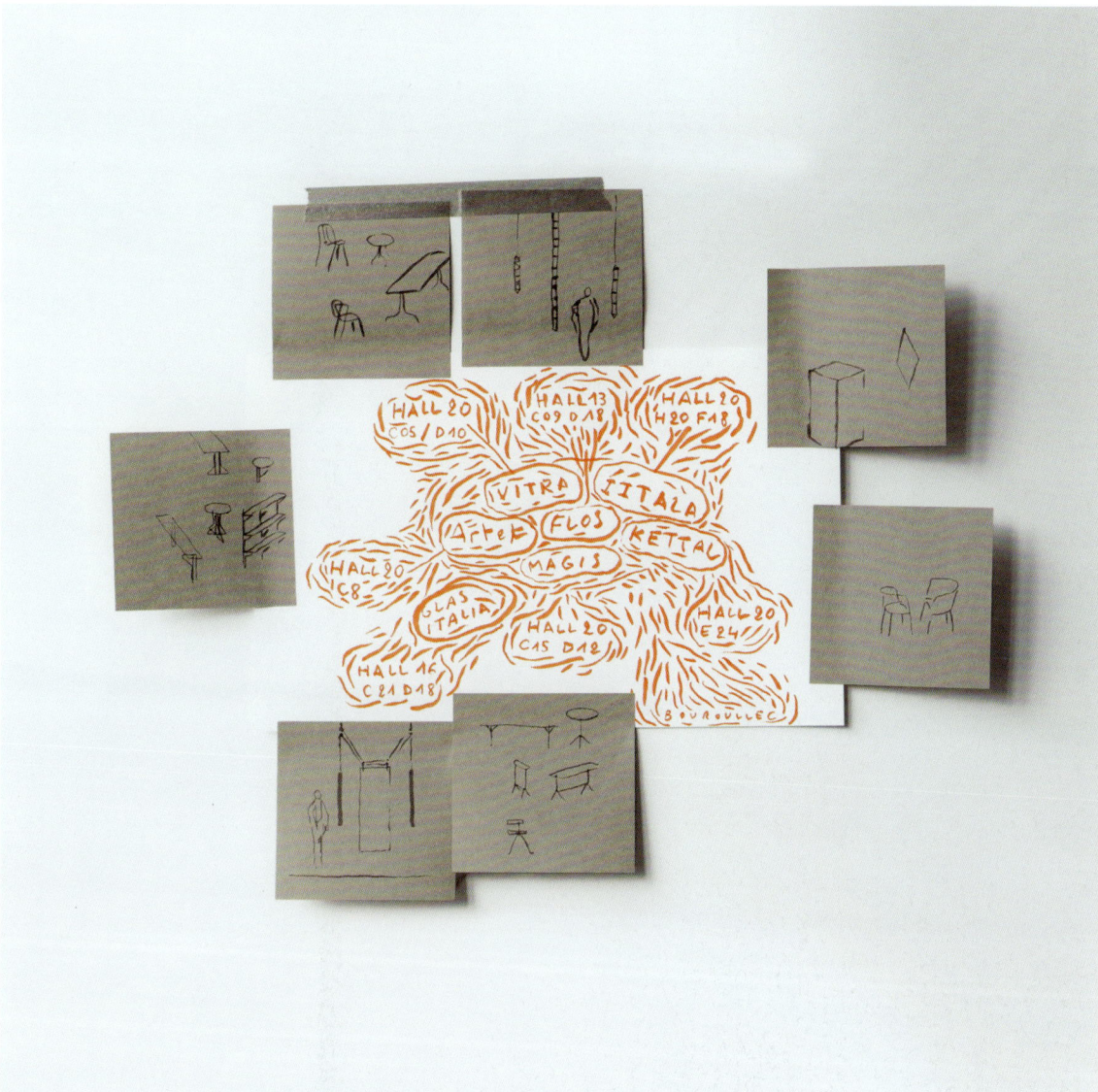

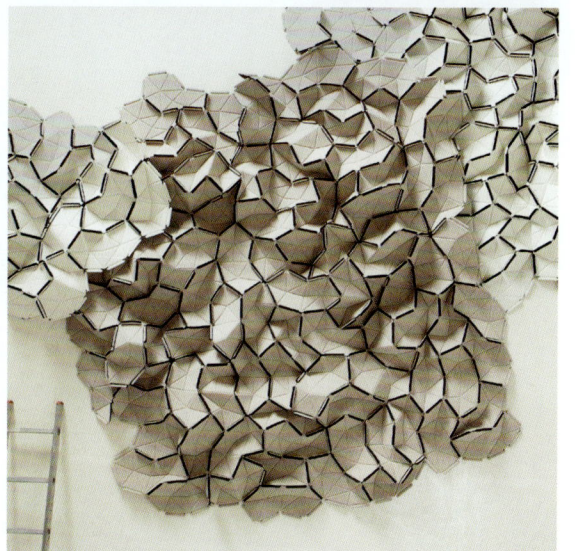

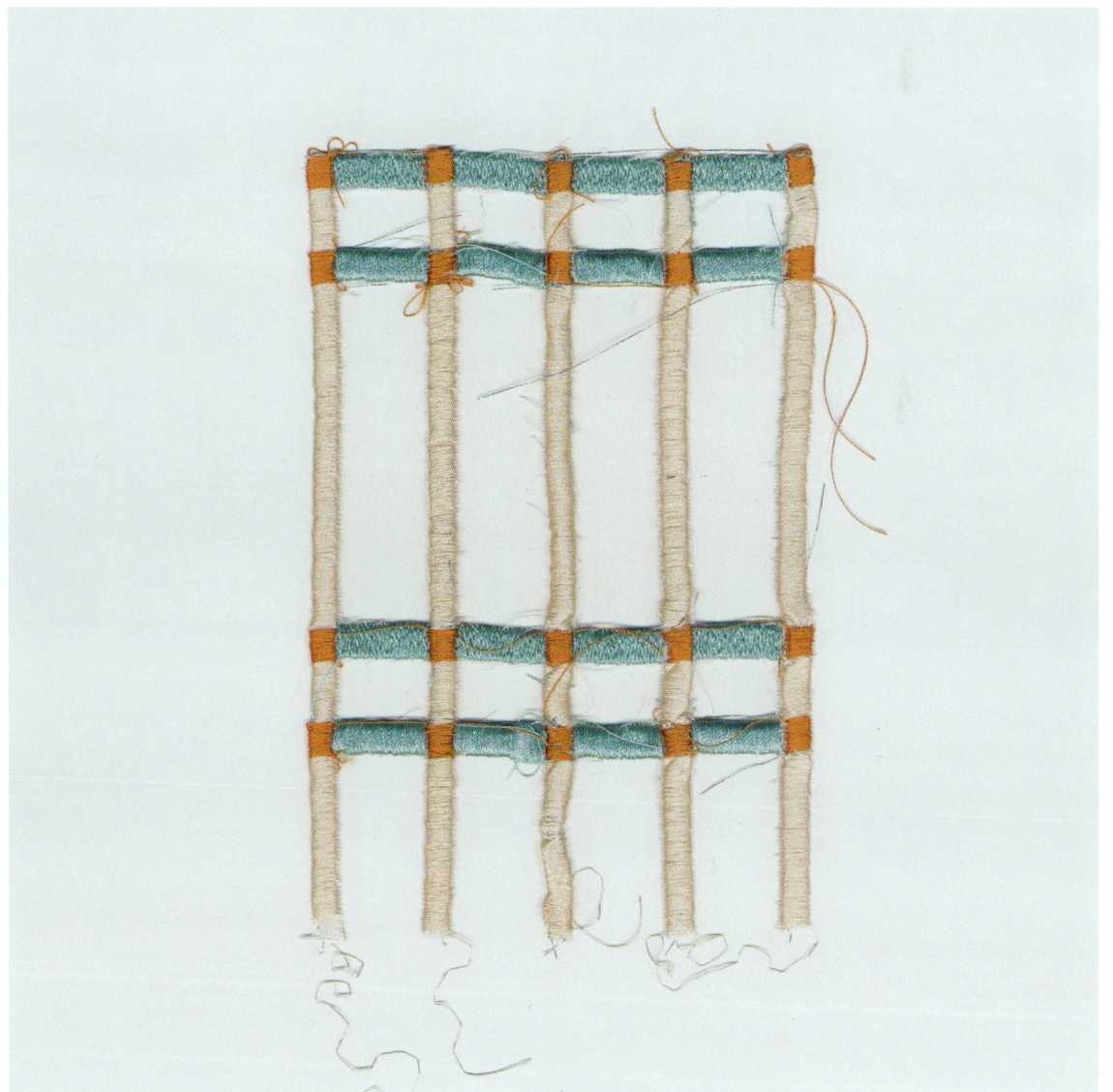

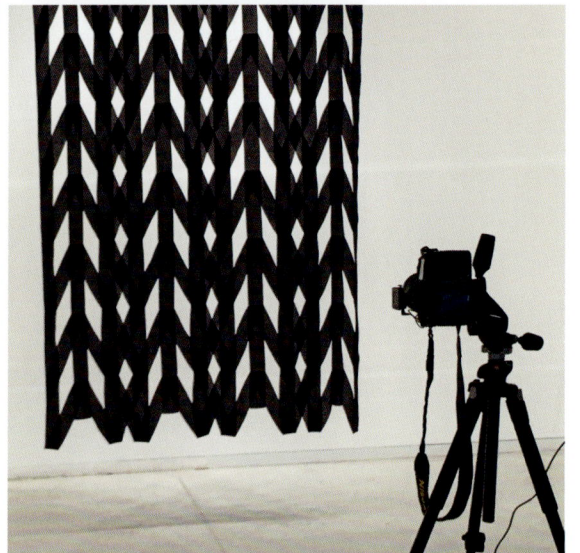

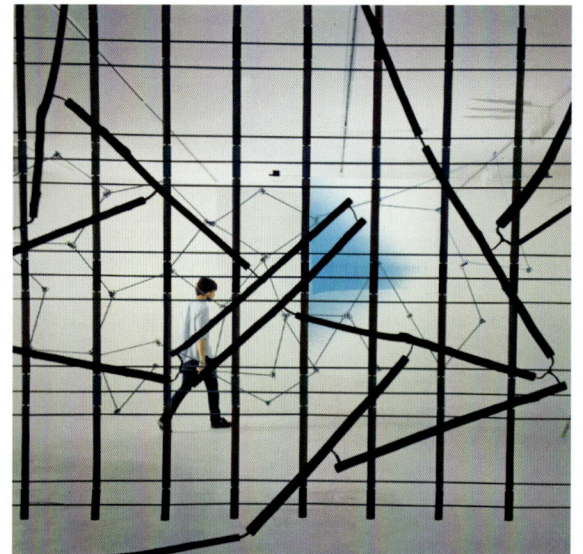

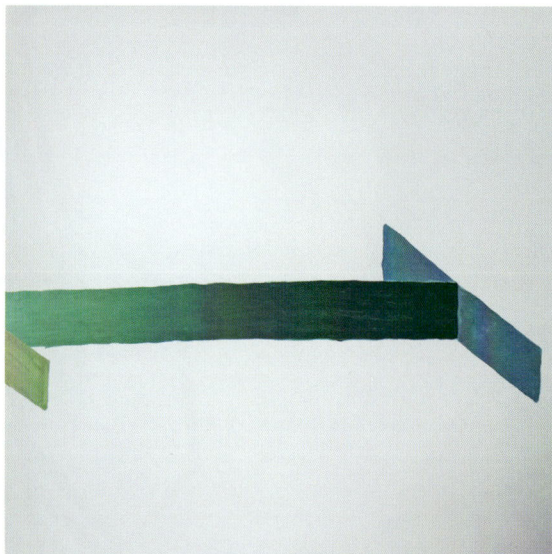

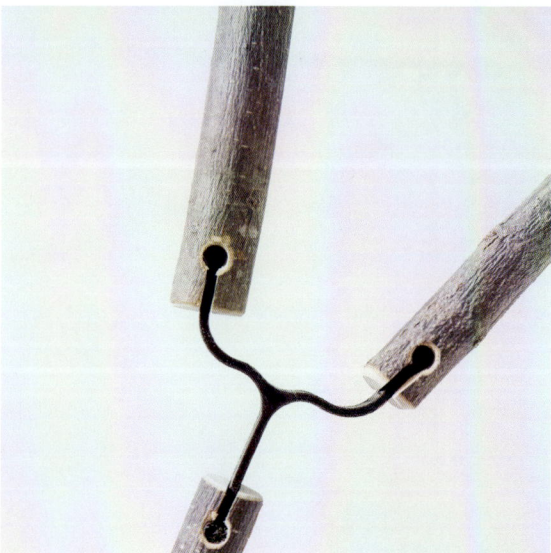
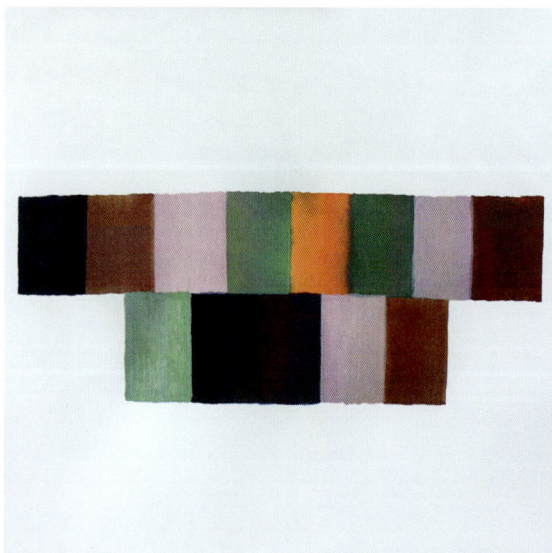
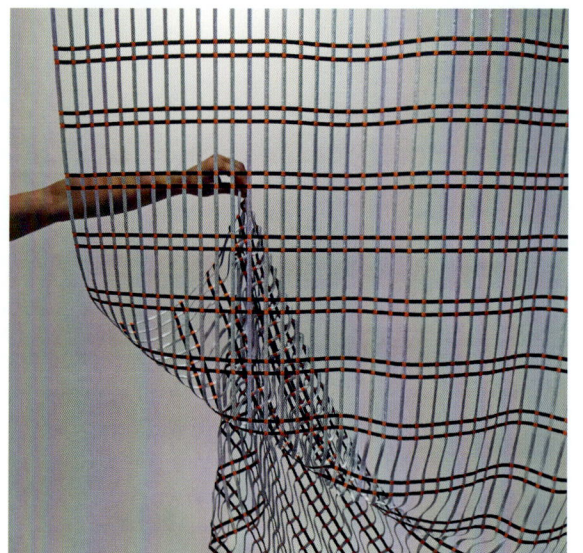

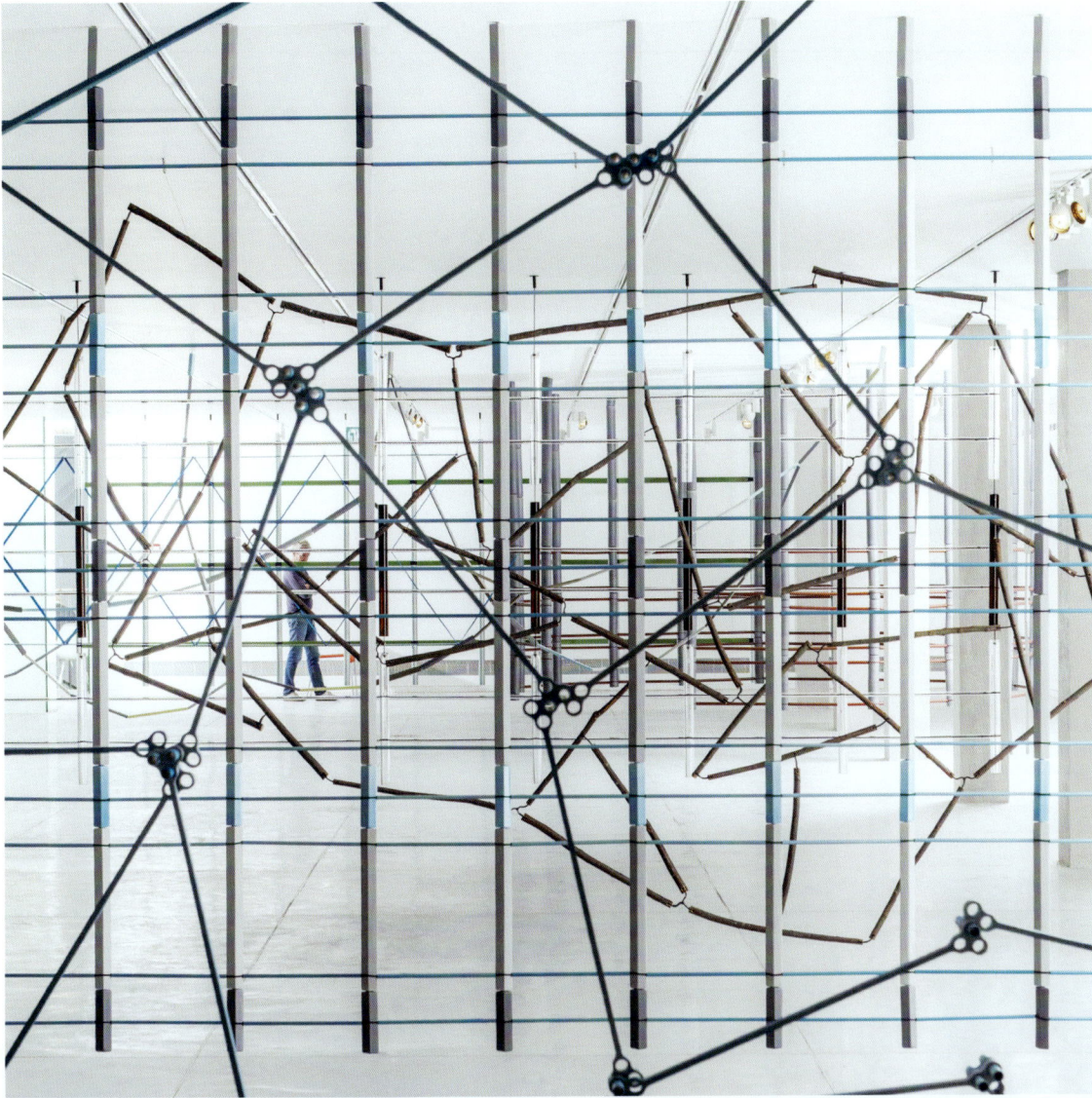

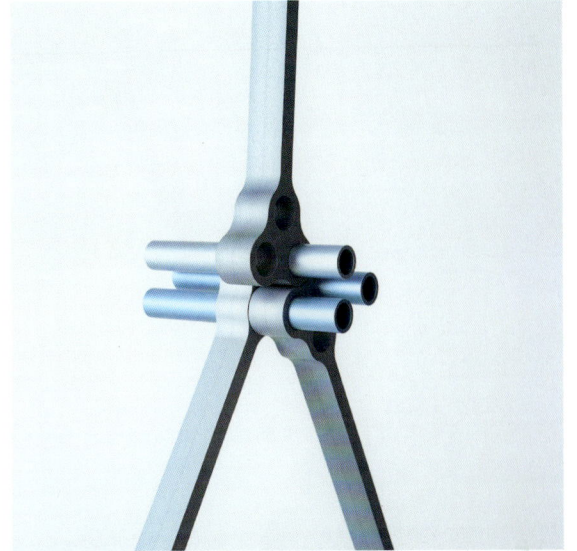

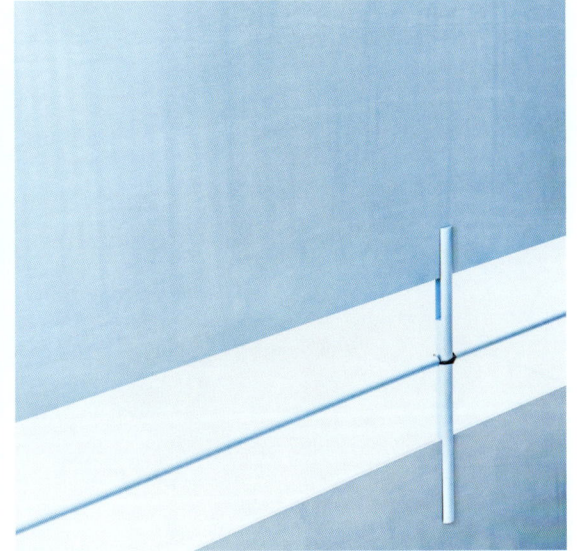

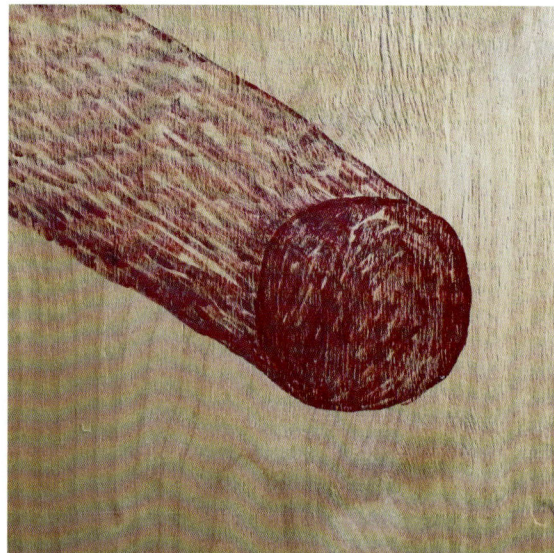

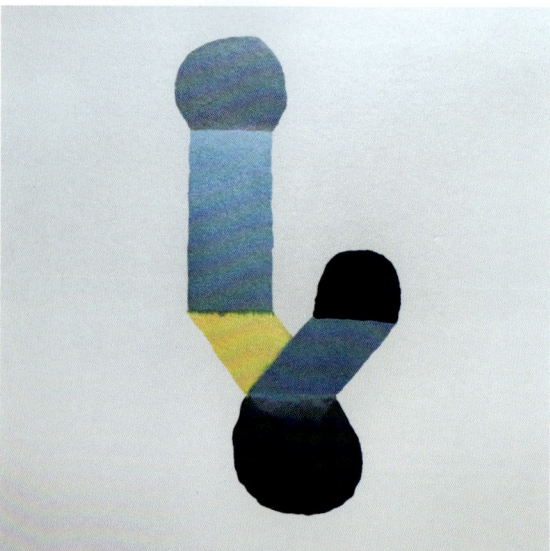

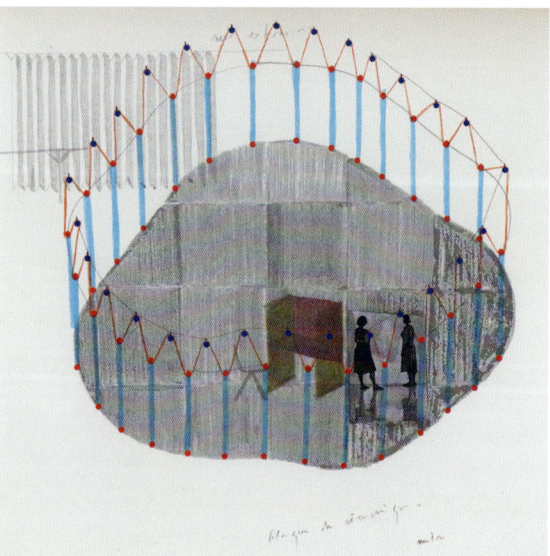

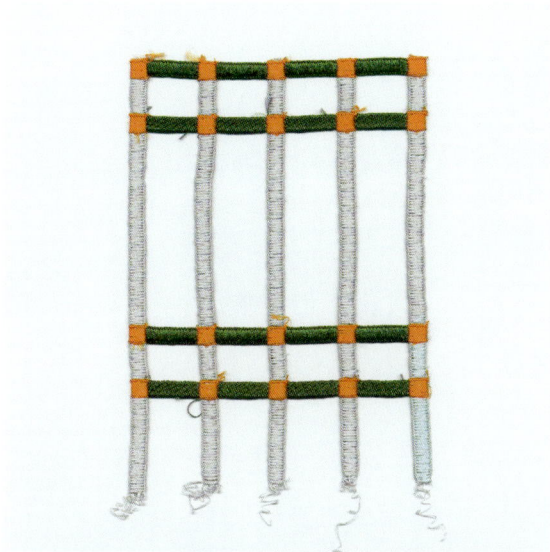

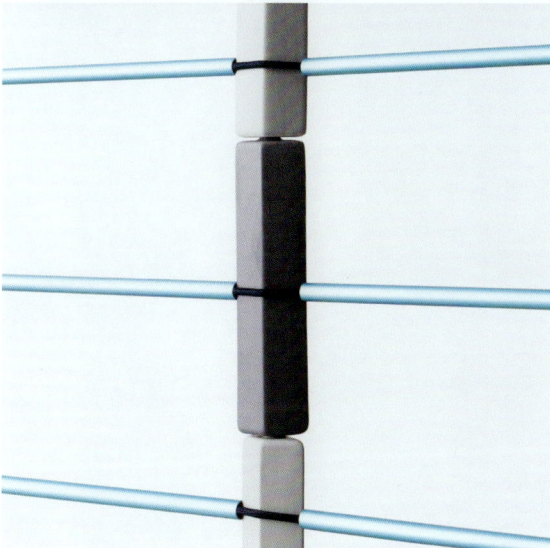

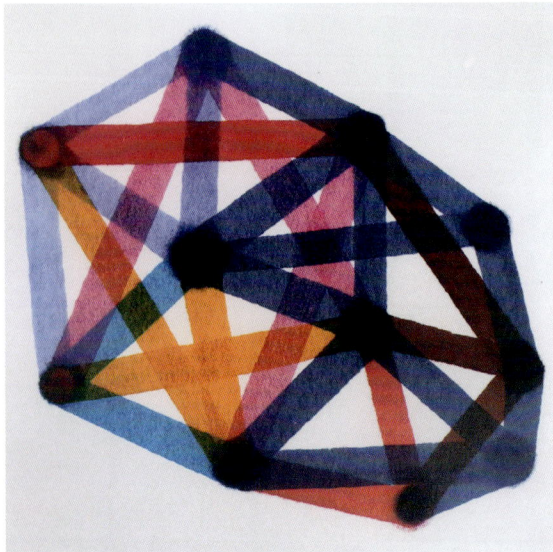

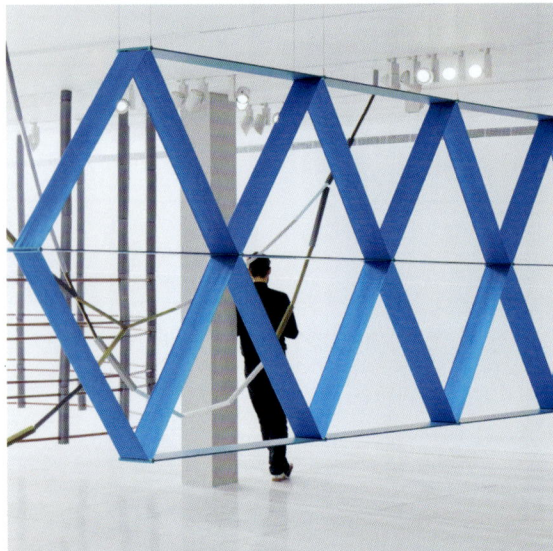

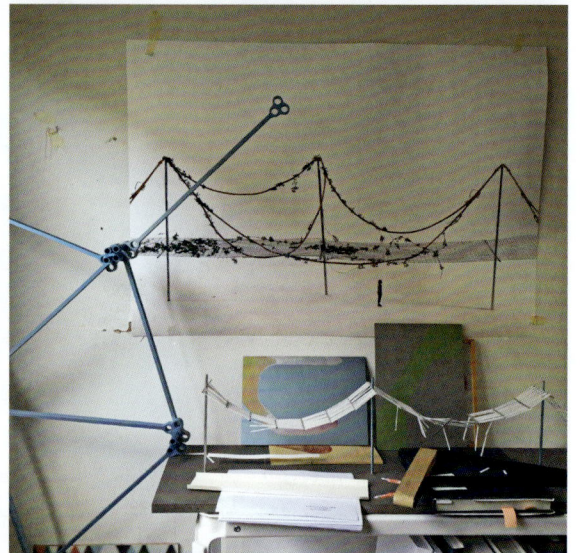

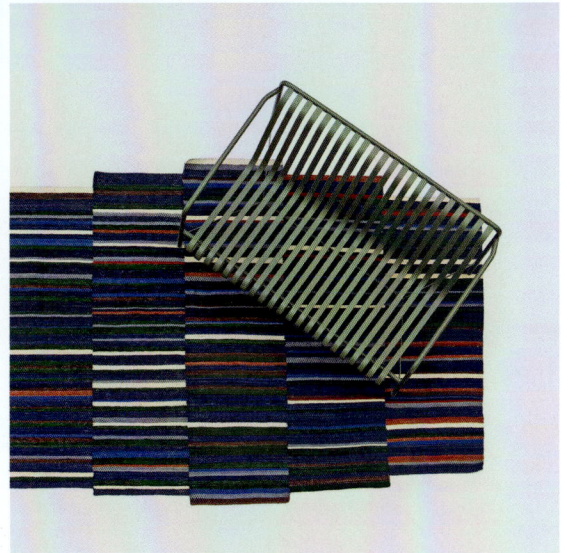

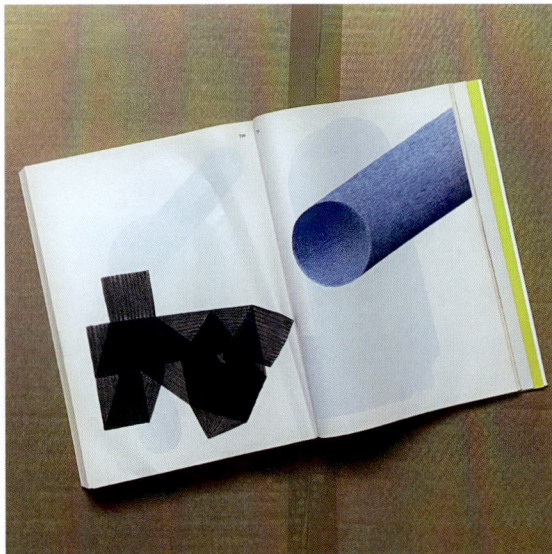

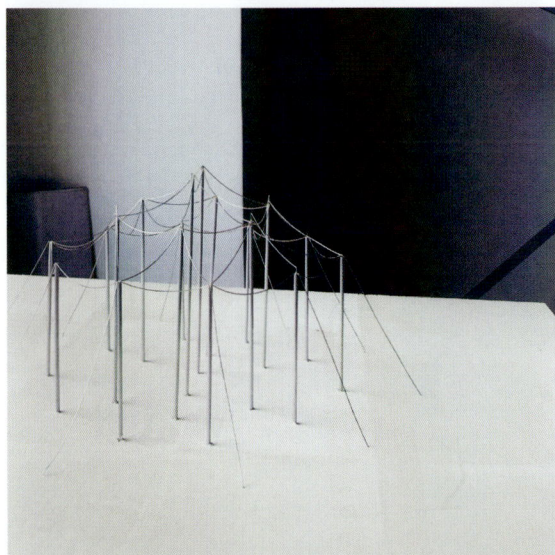

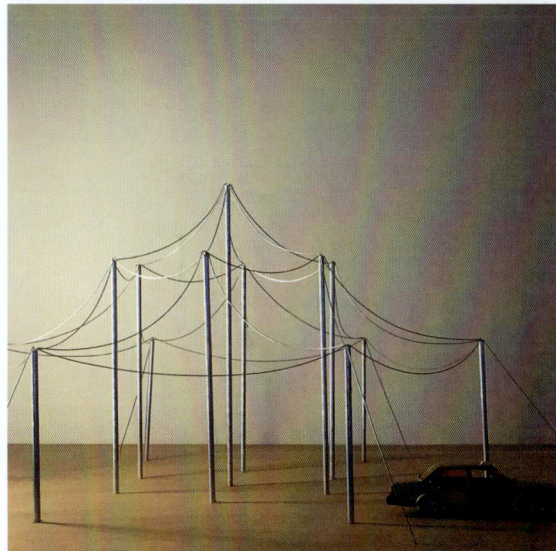

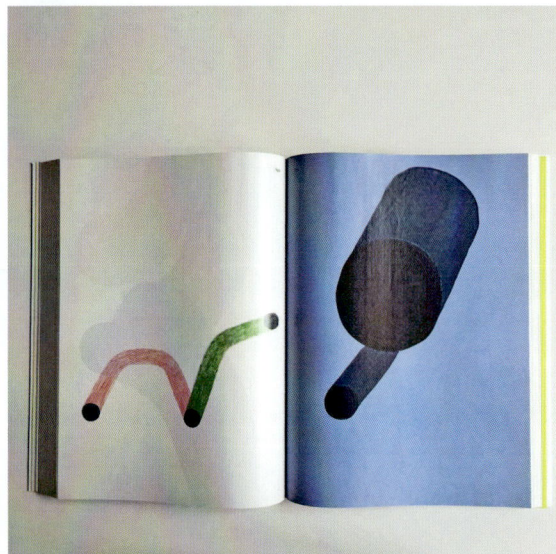

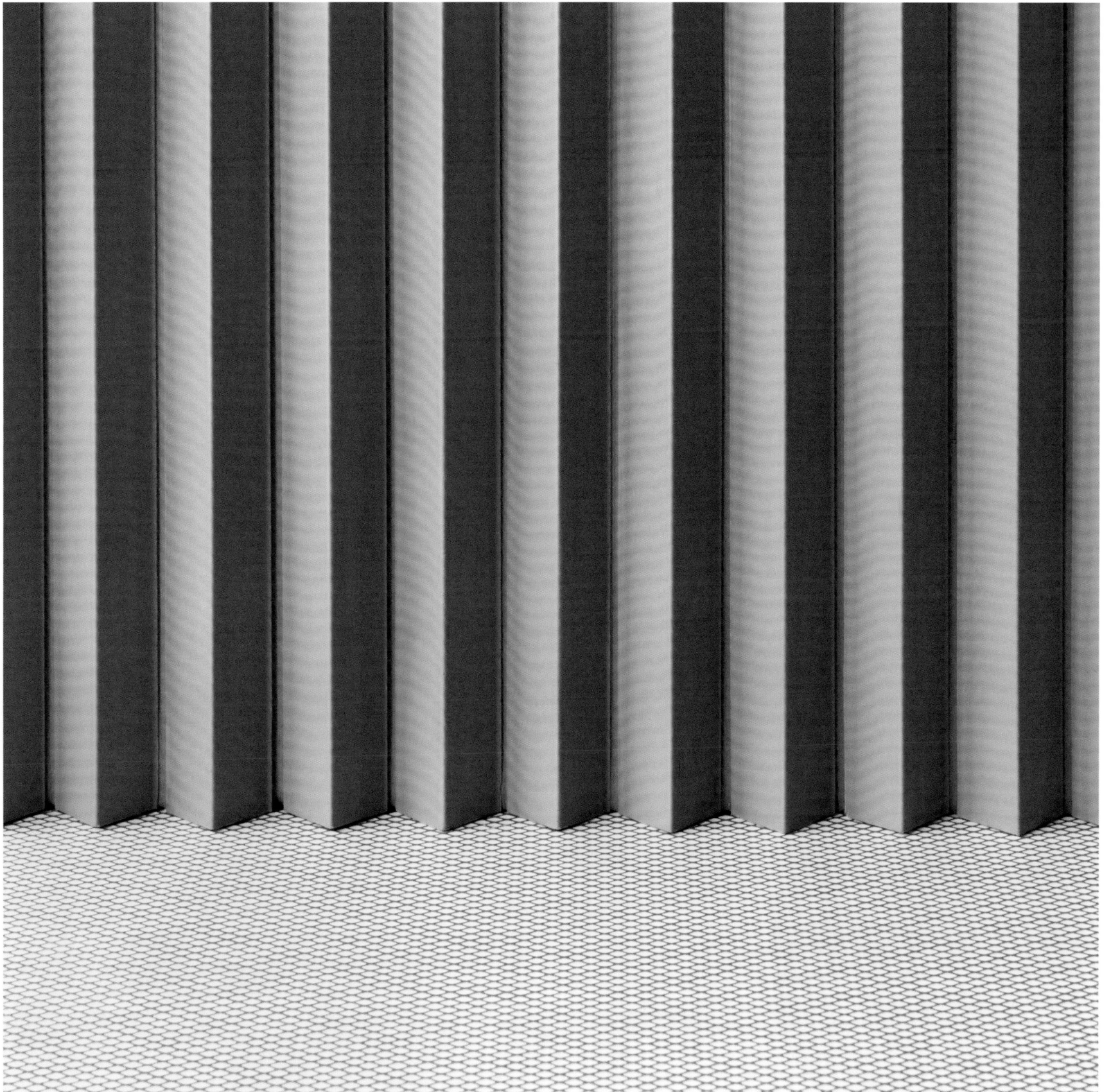

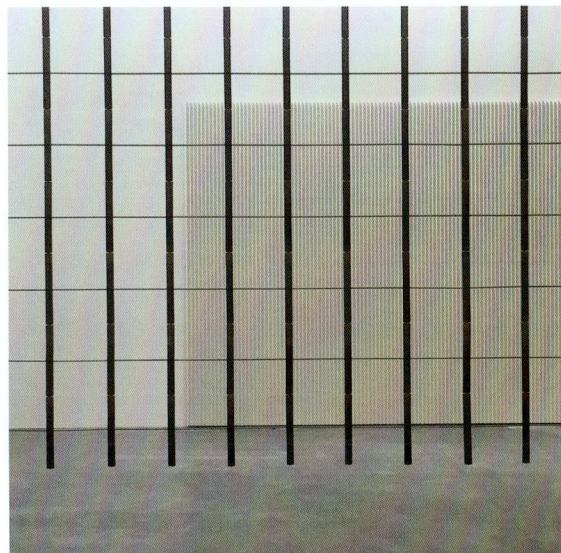

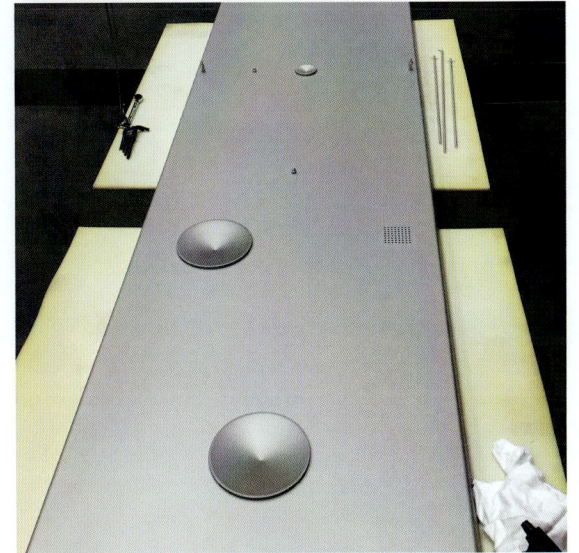

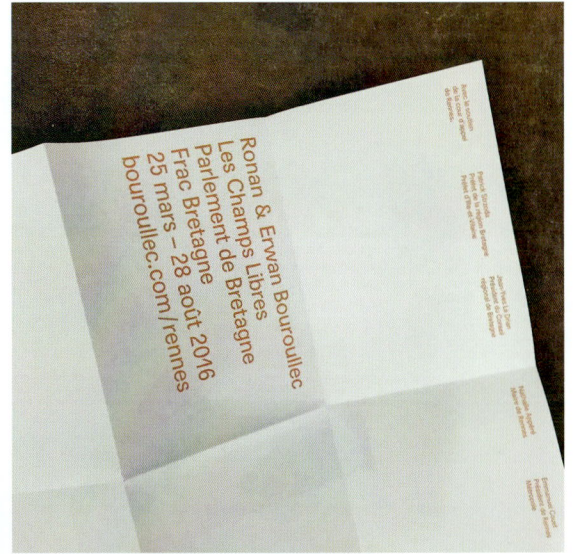

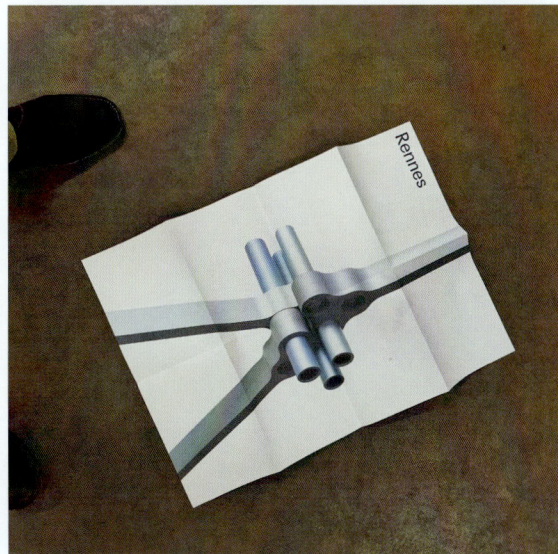
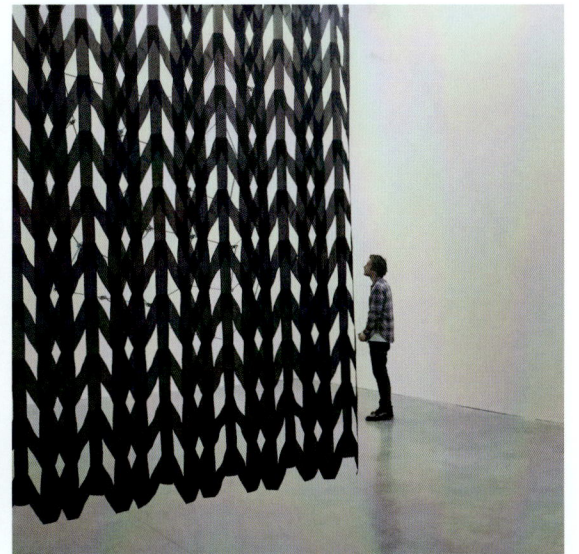

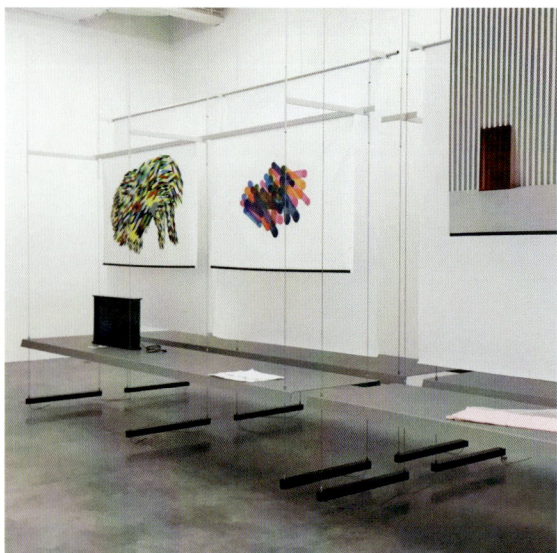

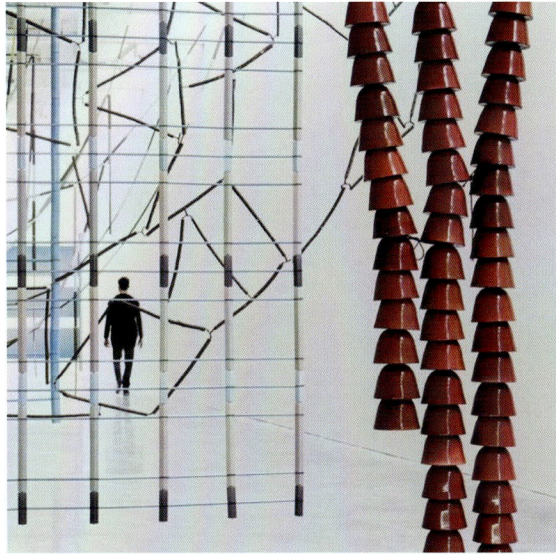

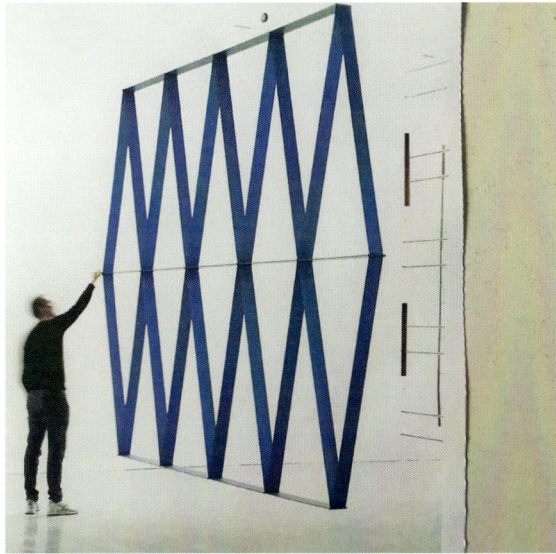

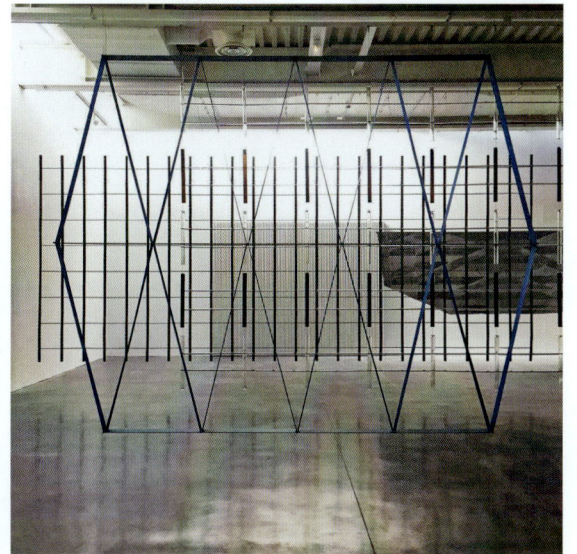

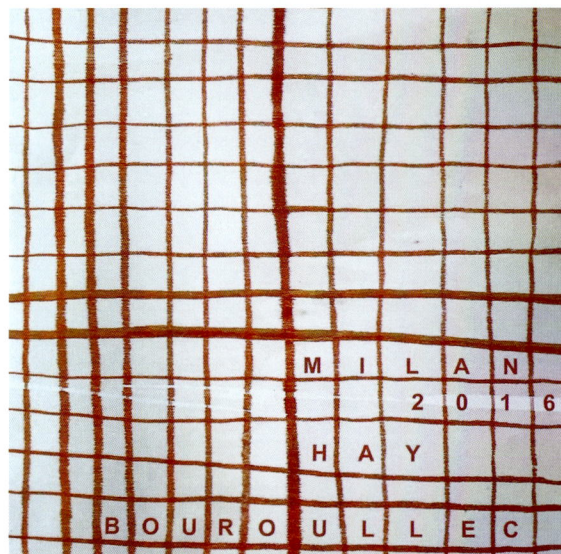

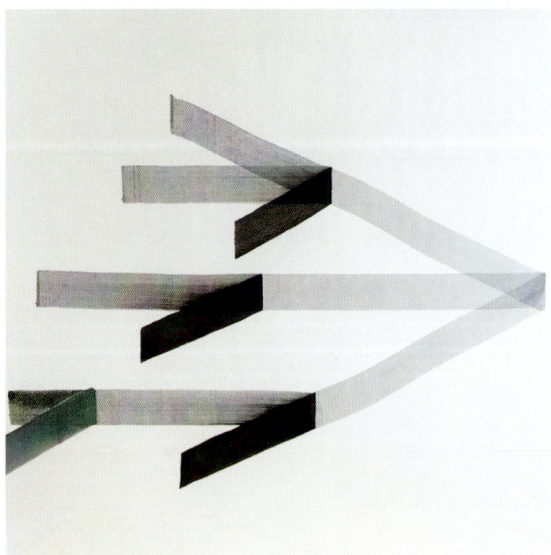

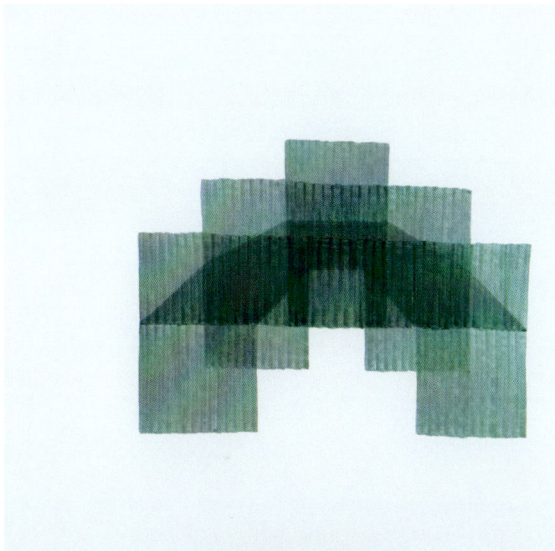

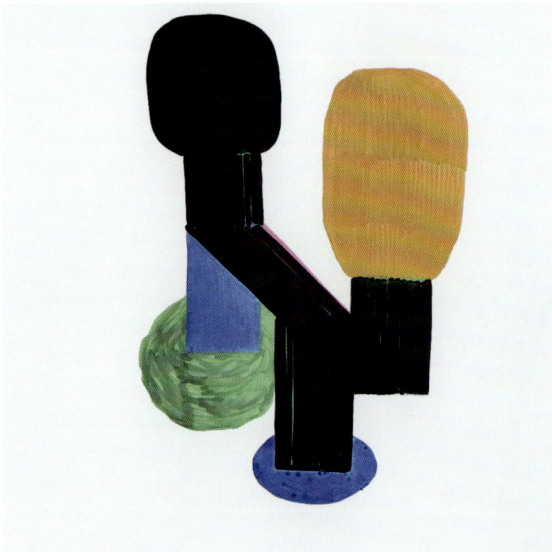

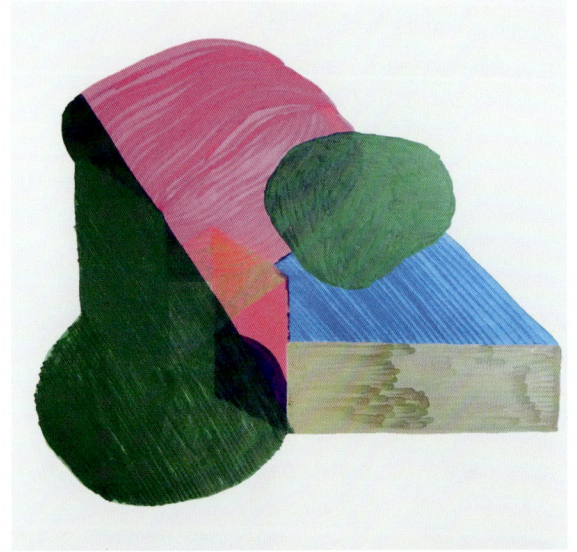

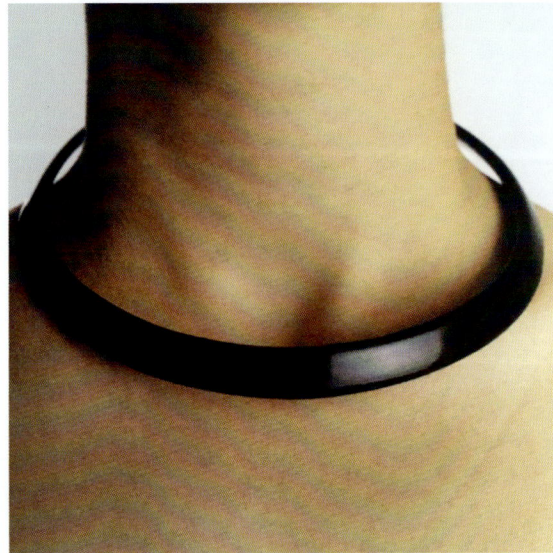

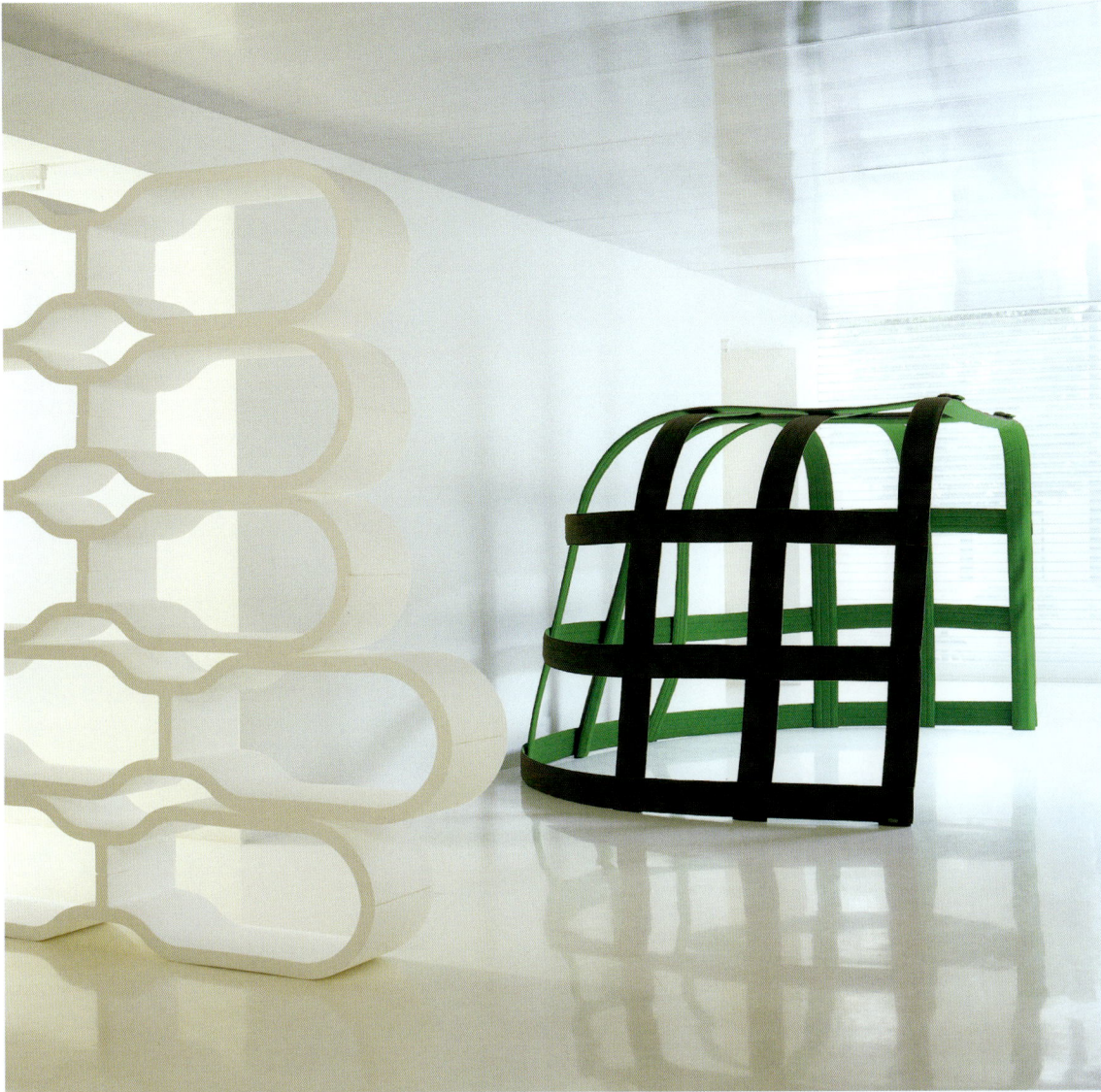

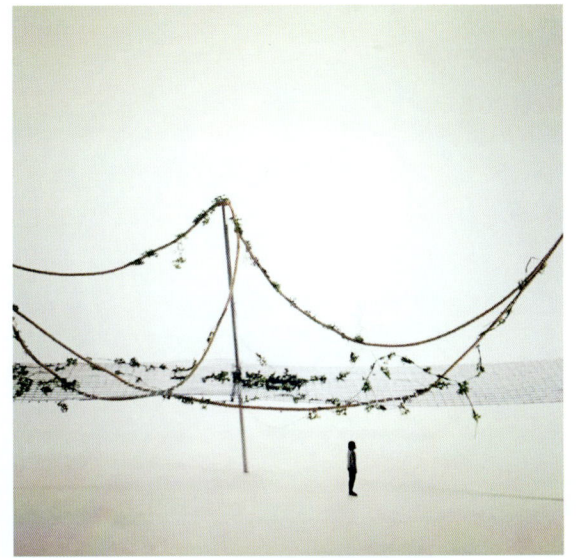

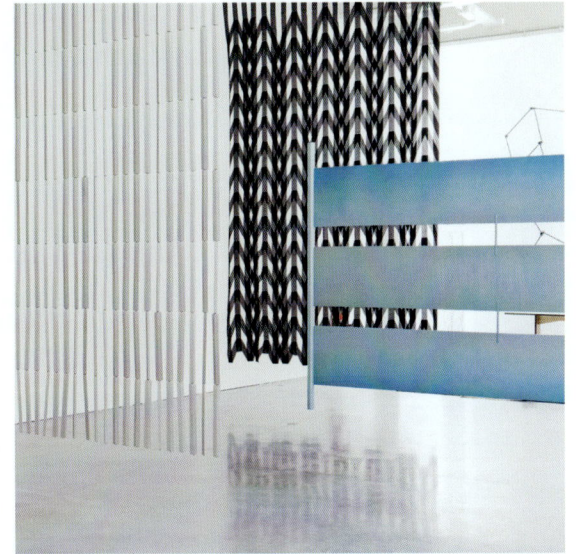

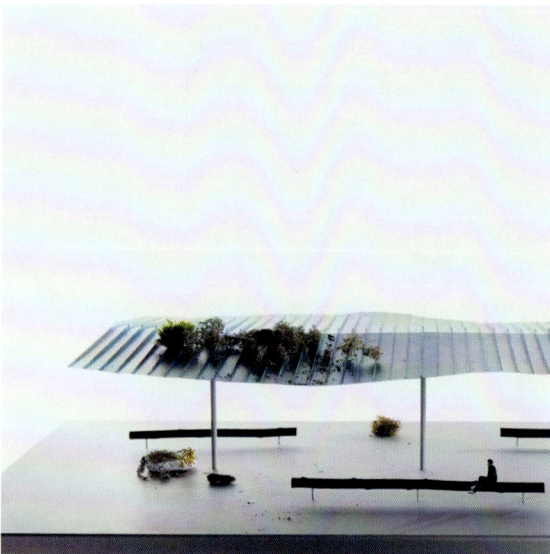

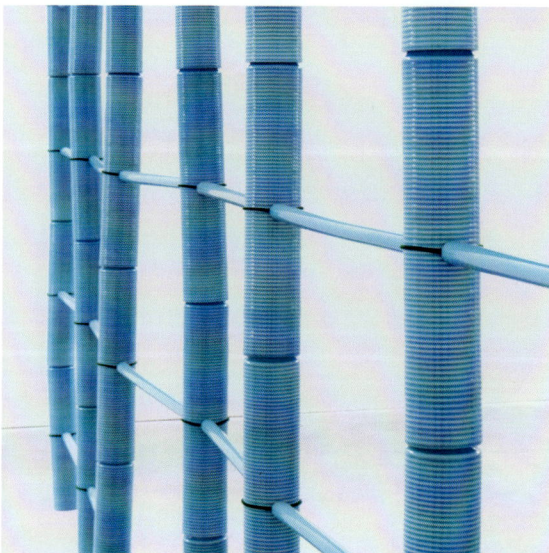

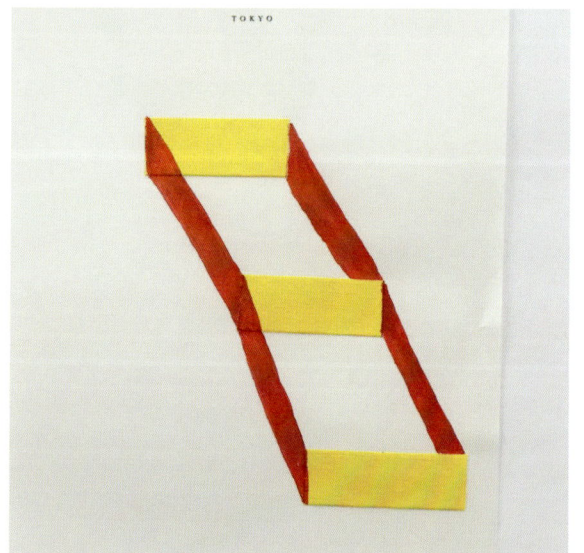

TOKYO

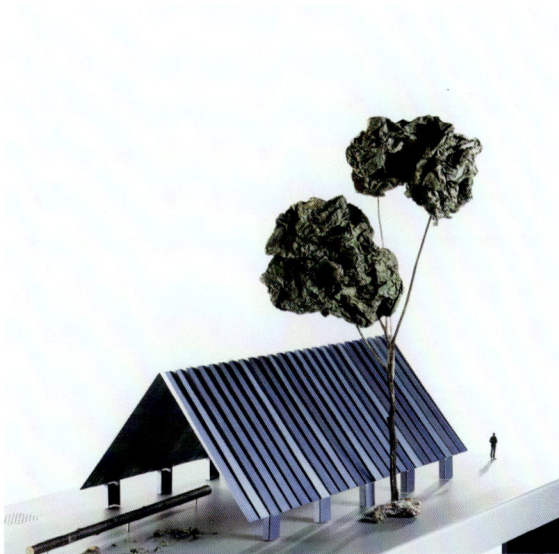

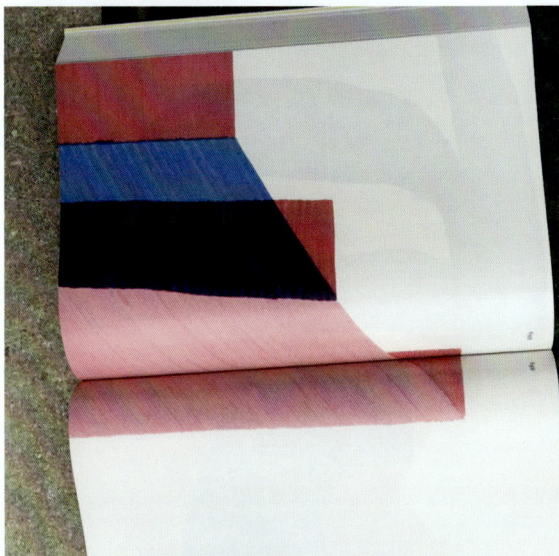
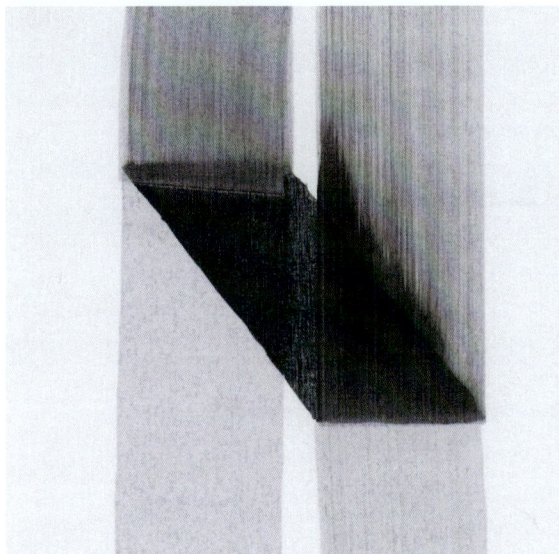

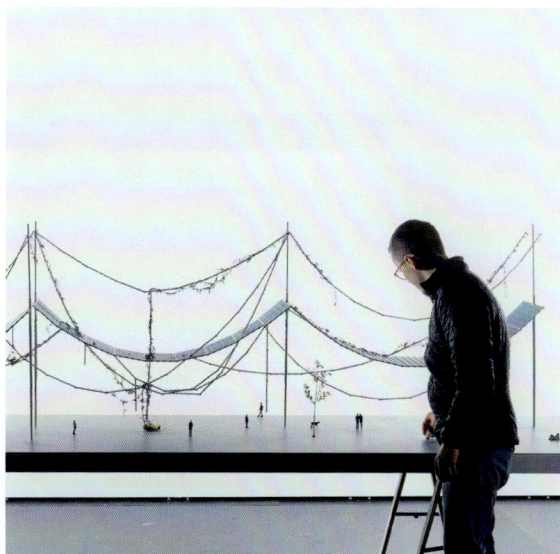

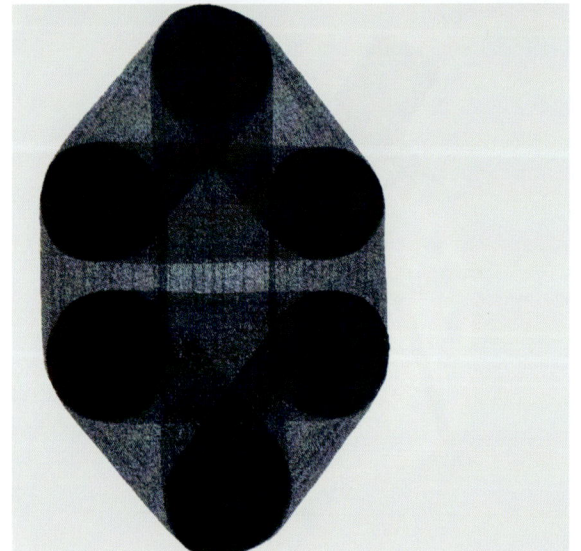

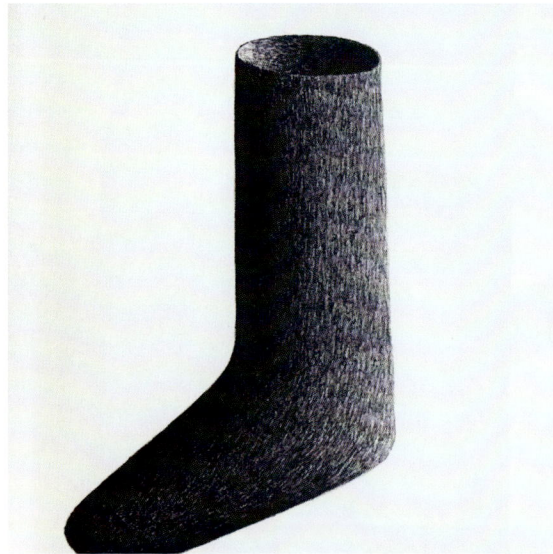

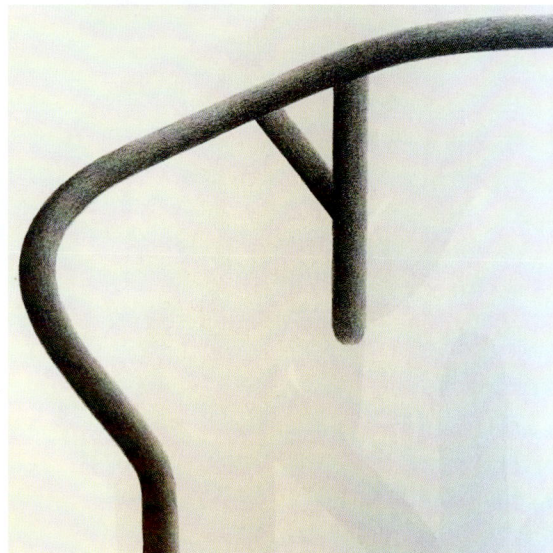
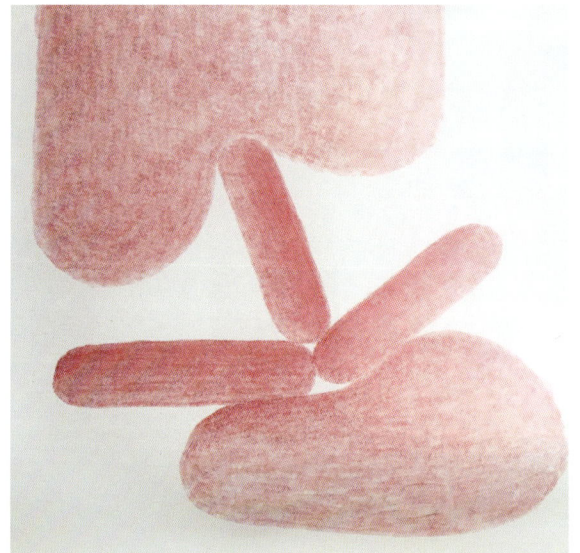

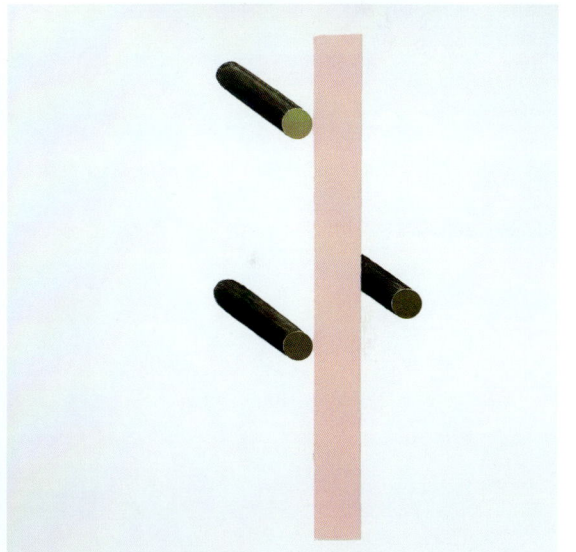
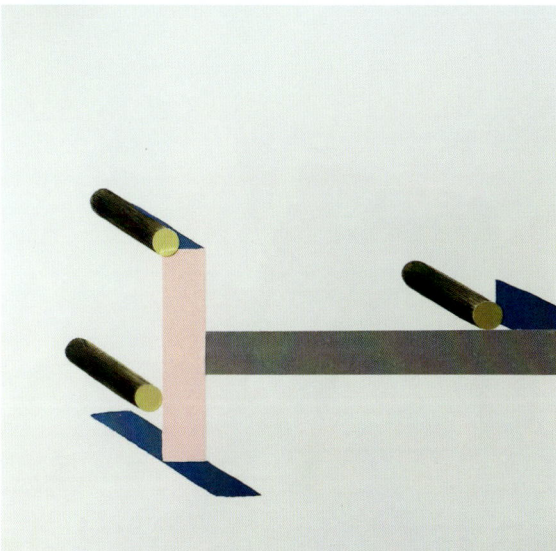

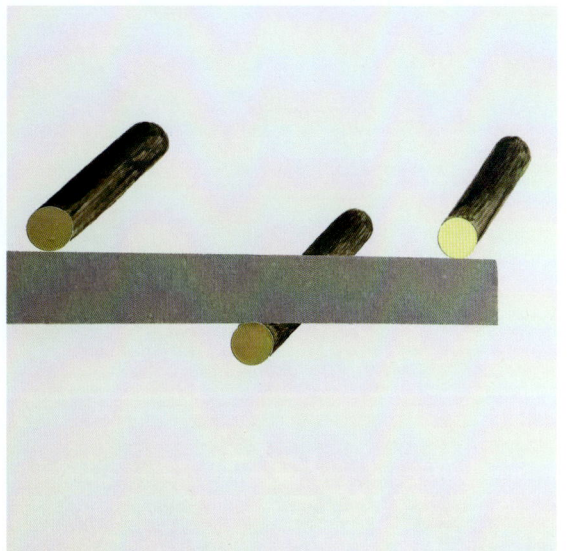

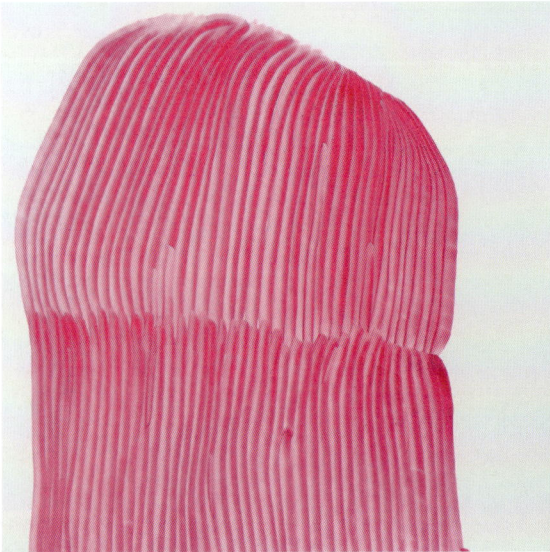

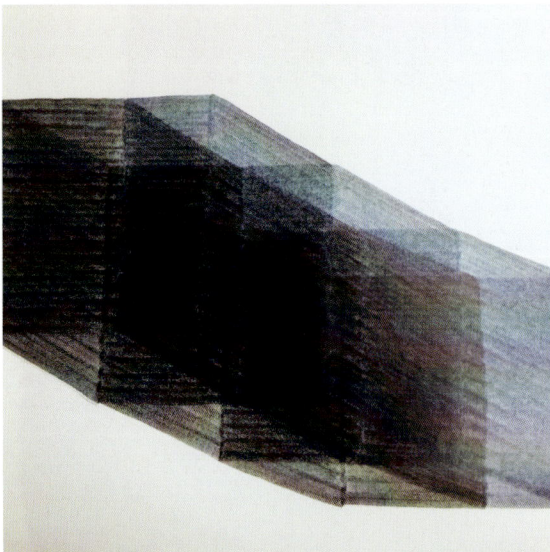

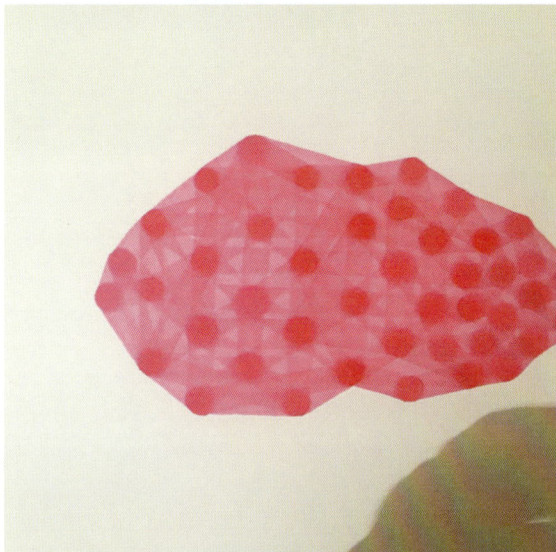

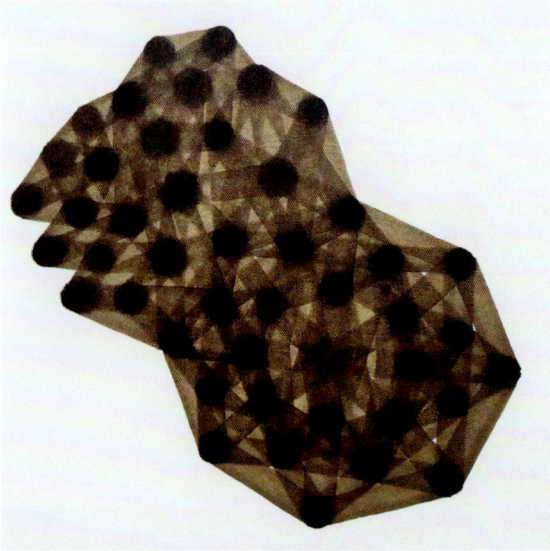

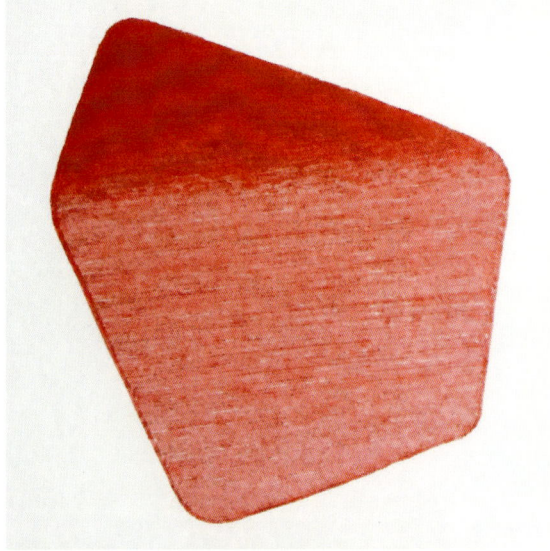

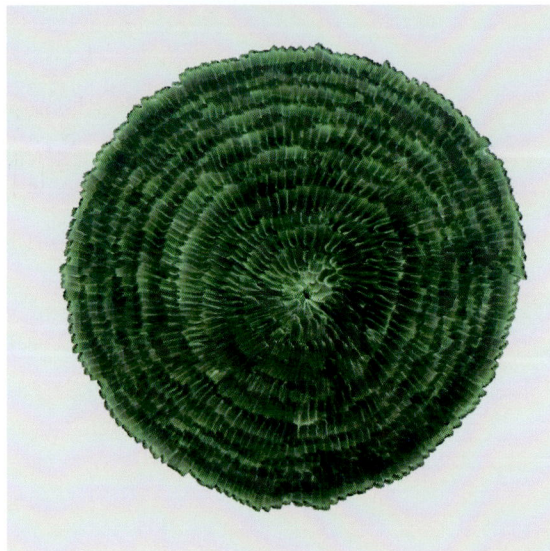

 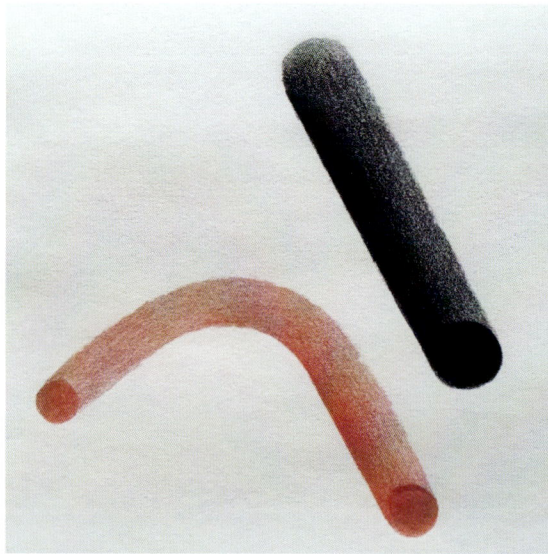 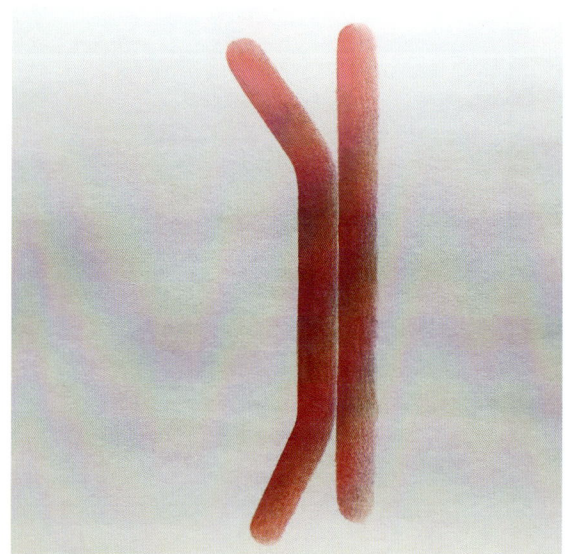

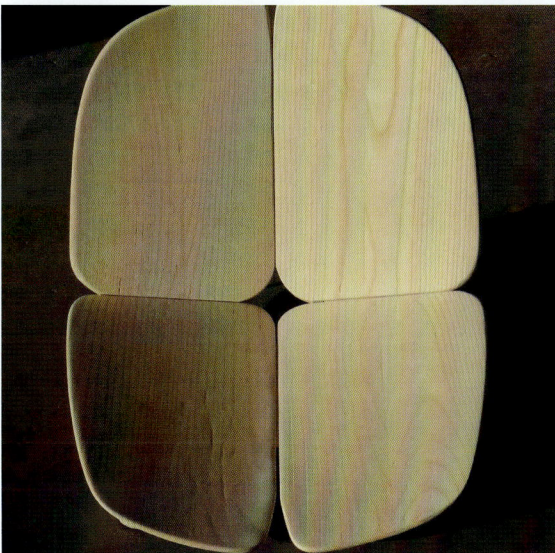

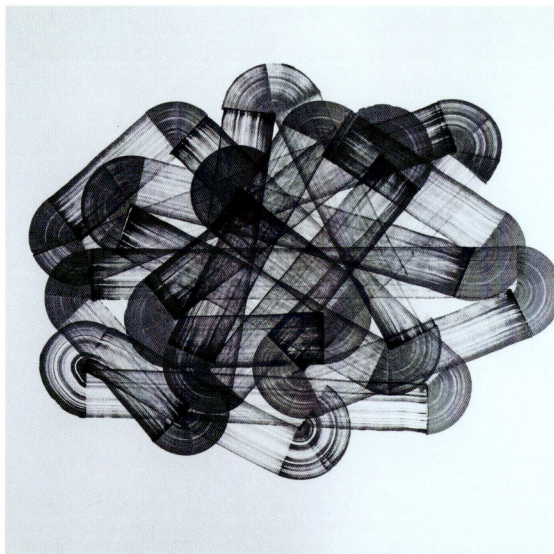

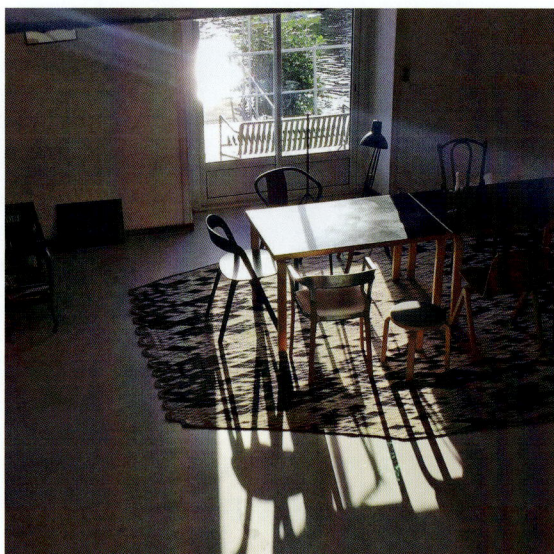

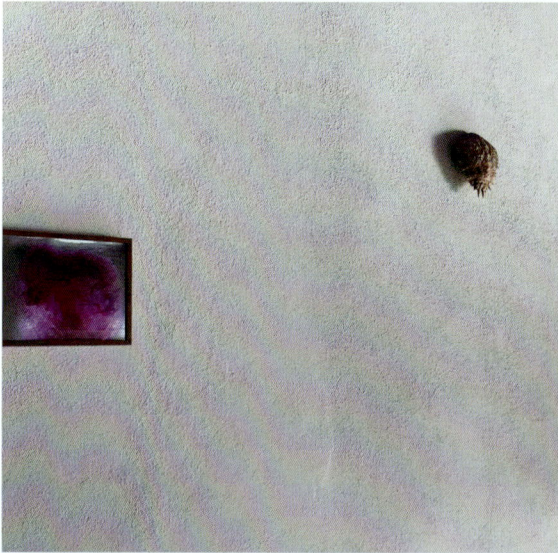

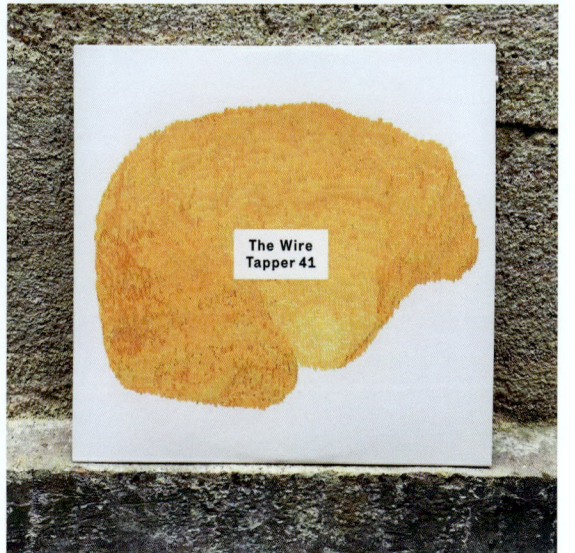

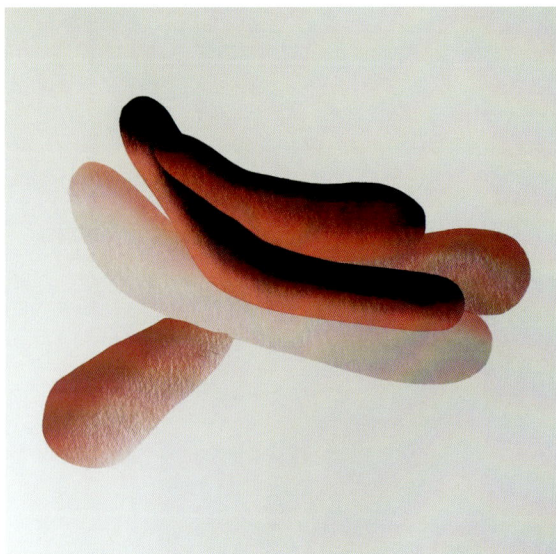

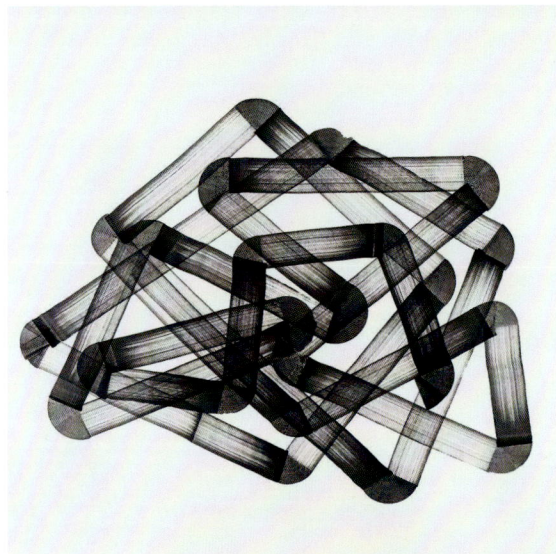

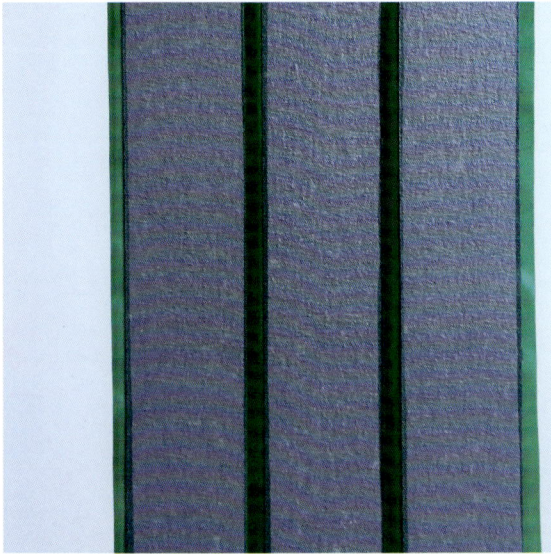
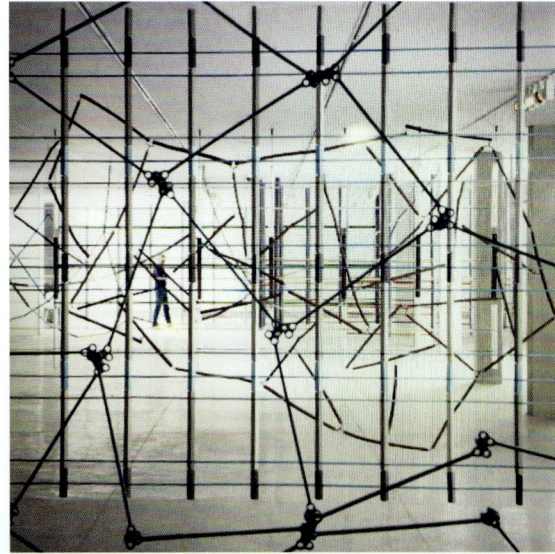

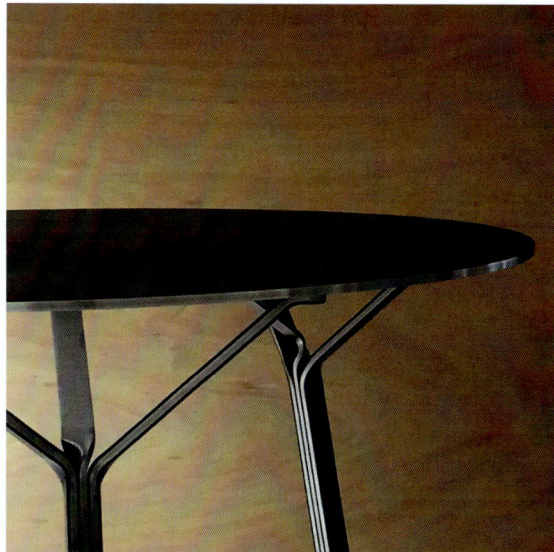

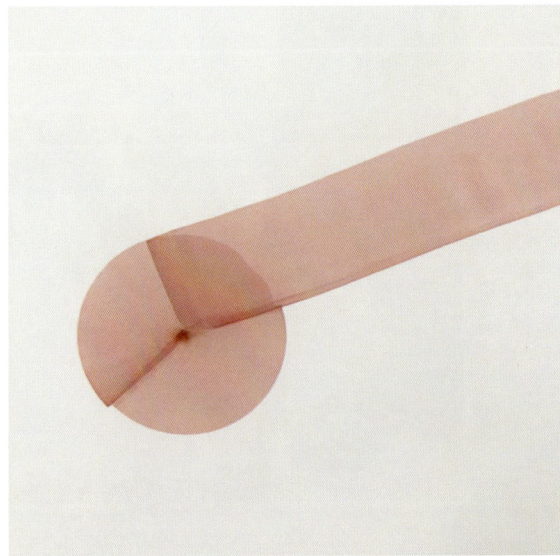

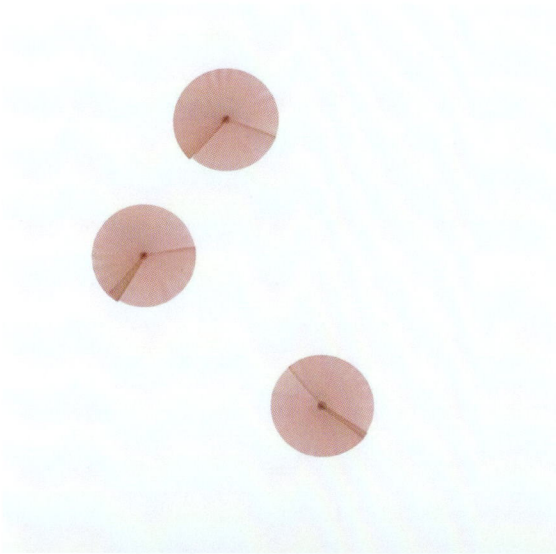

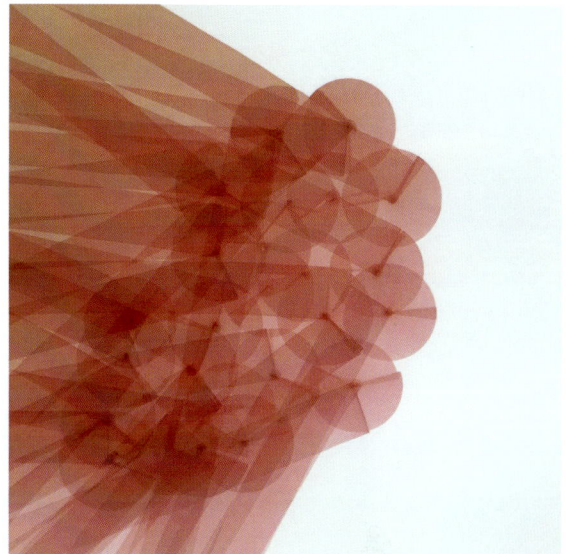

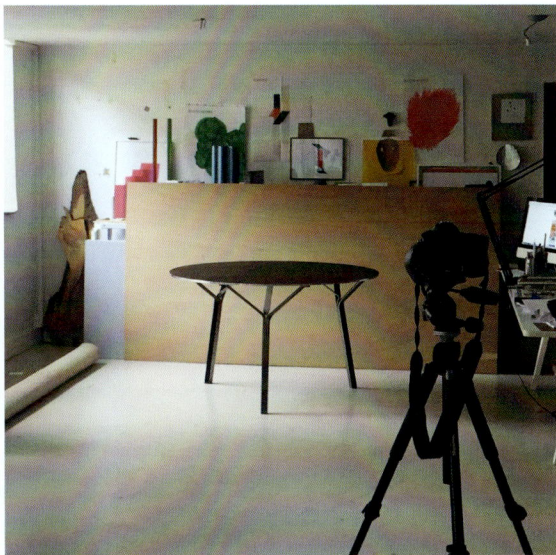

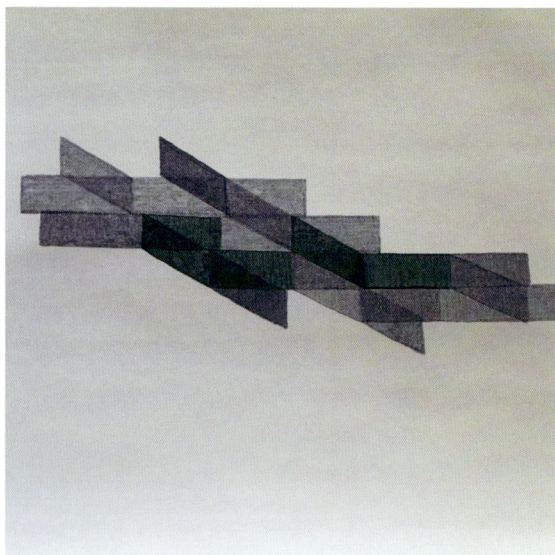

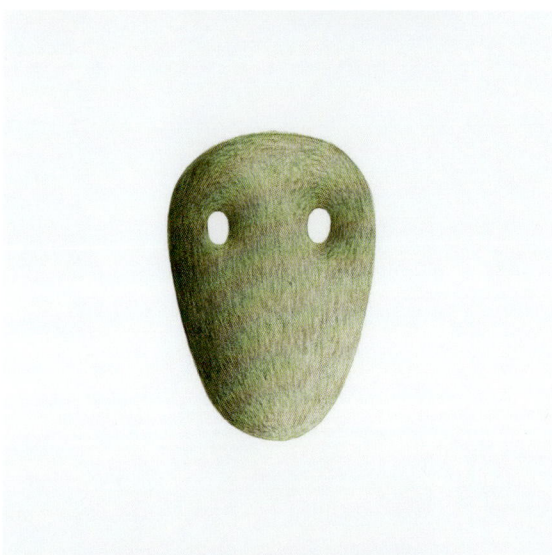
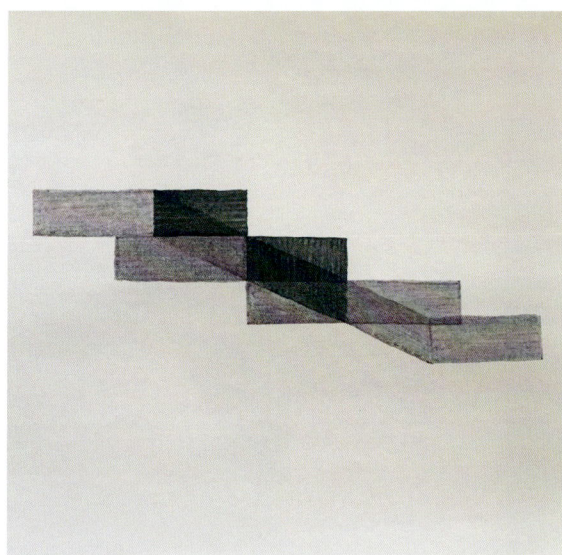

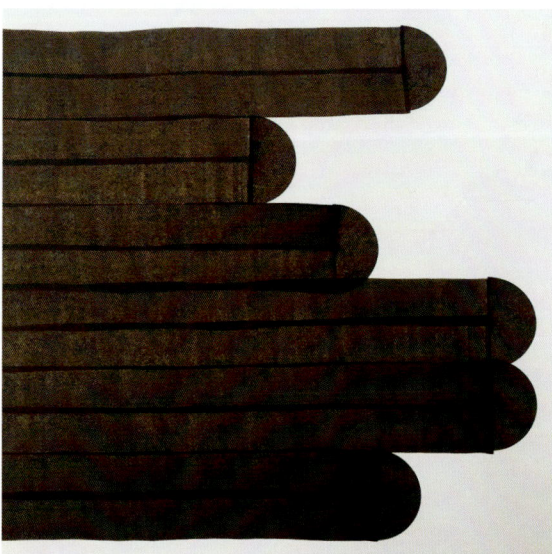

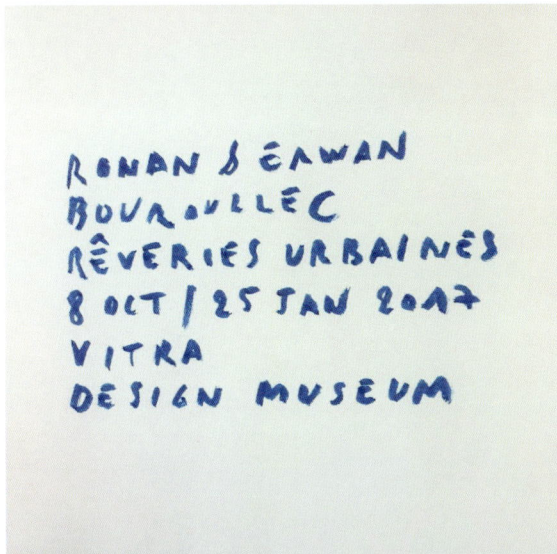

RONAN & ERWAN
BOUROULLEC
RÊVERIES URBAINES
8 OCT / 25 JAN 2017
VITRA
DESIGN MUSEUM

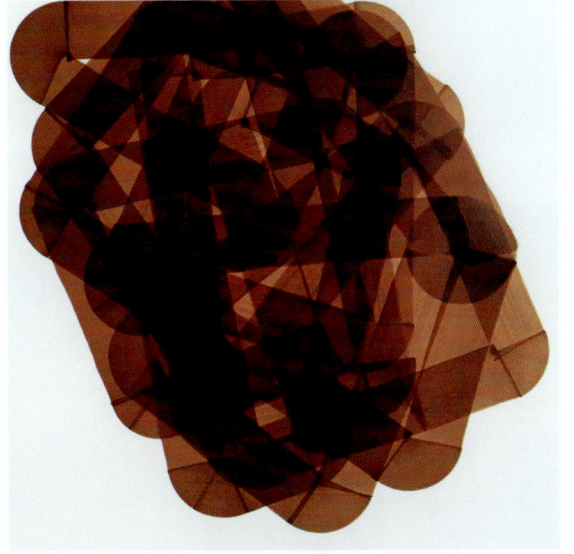

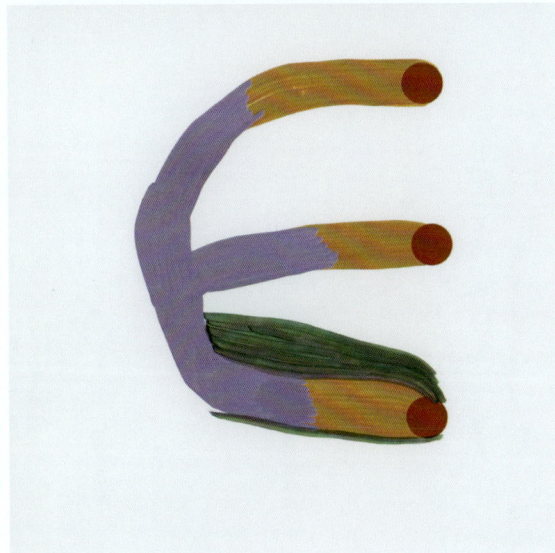

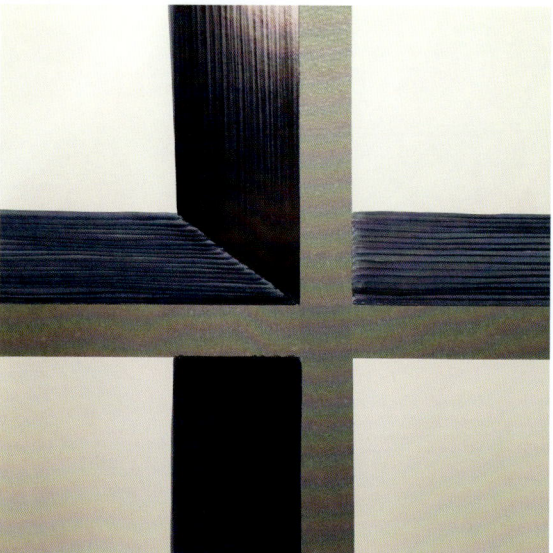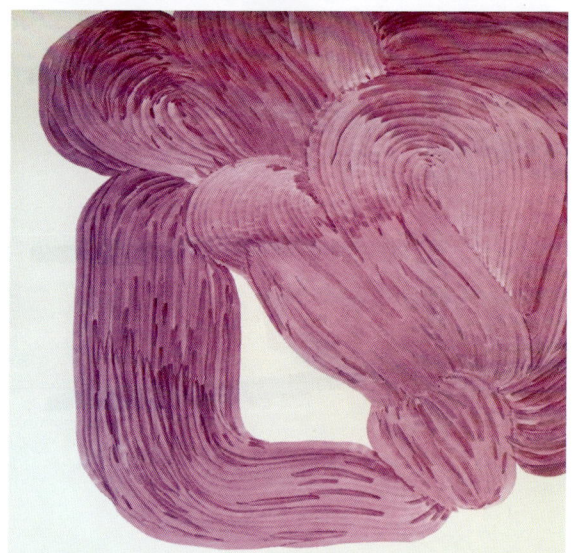

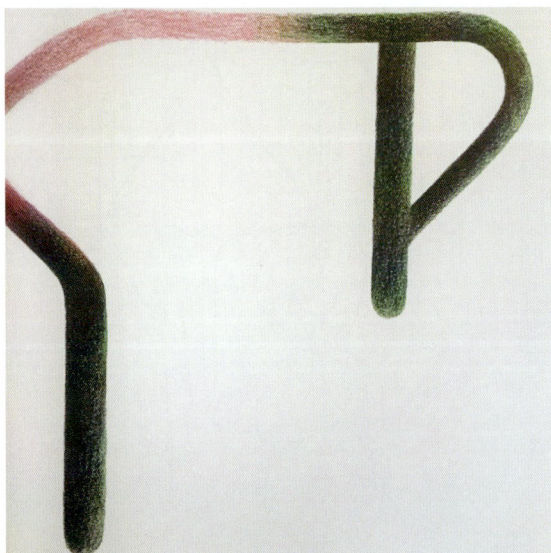

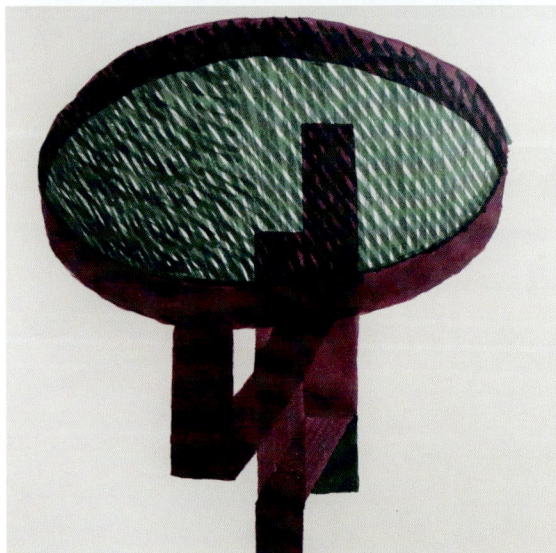

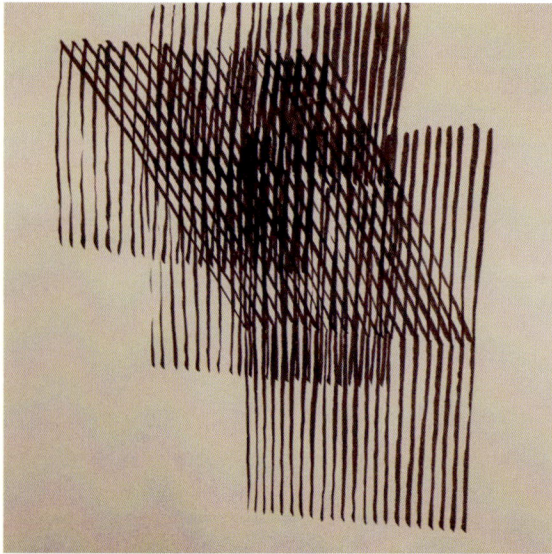

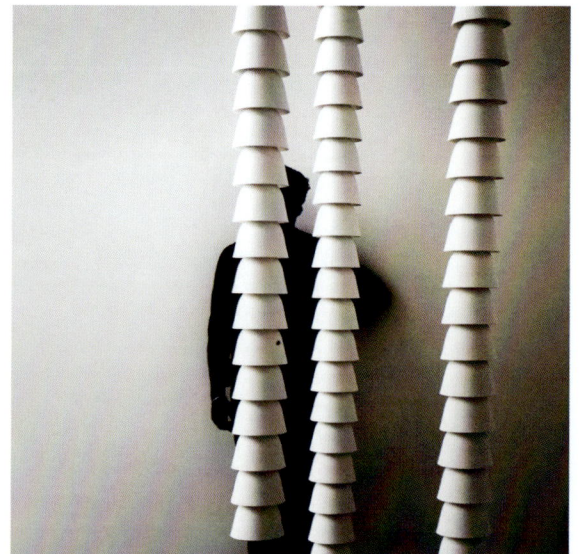

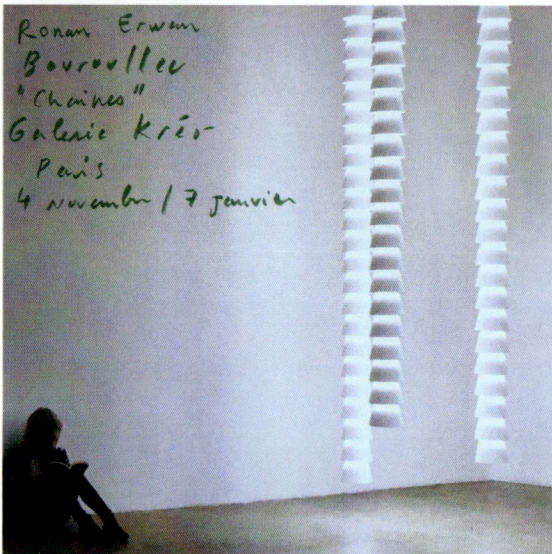

Ronan Erwan
Bouroullec
"Chaînes"
Galerie kréo
Paris
4 novembre / 7 janvier

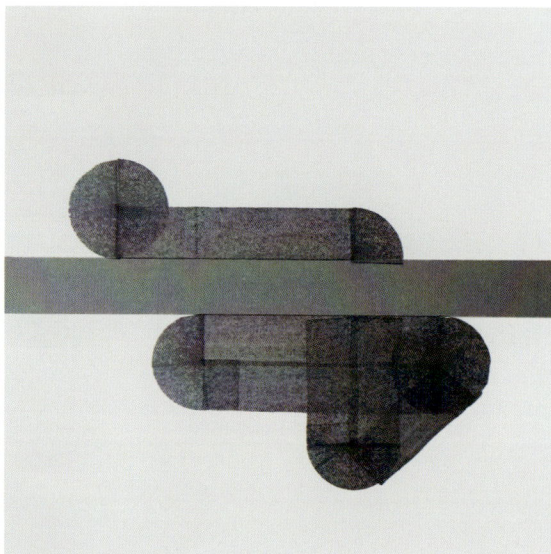

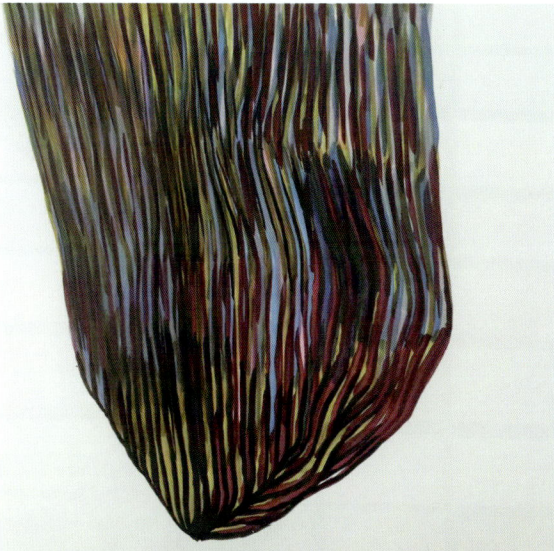

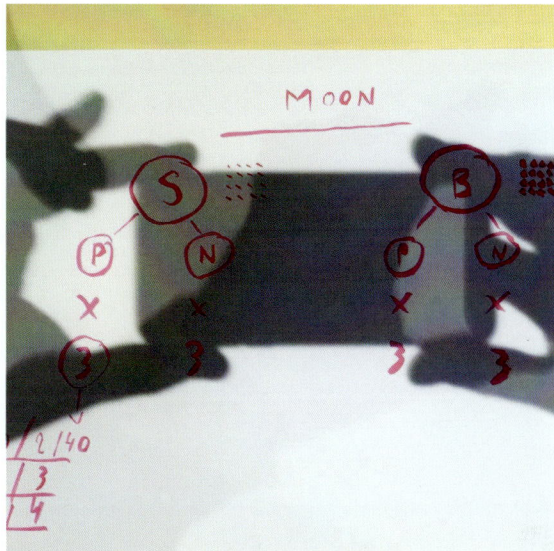

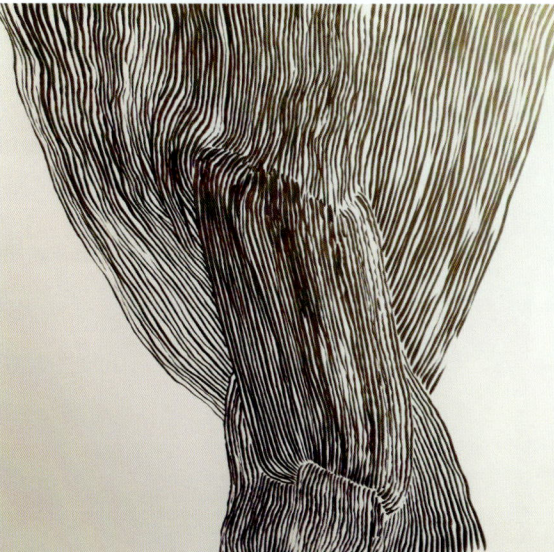

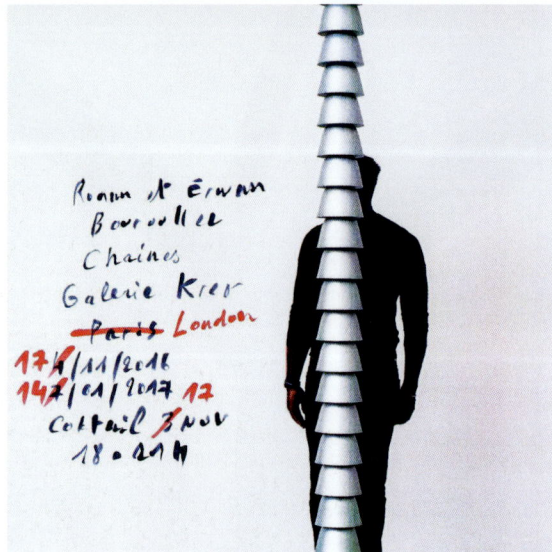

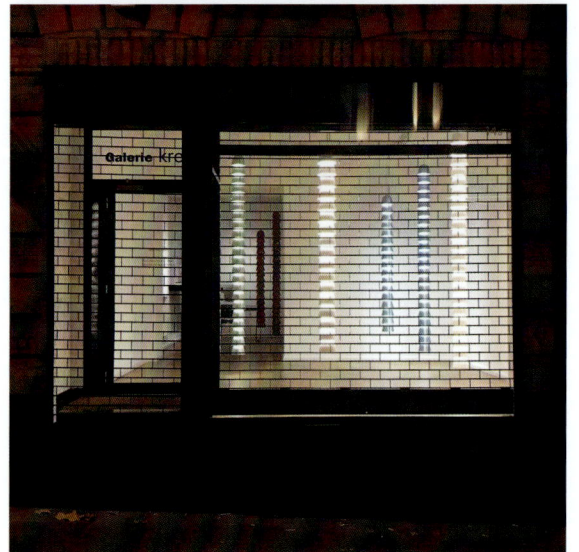

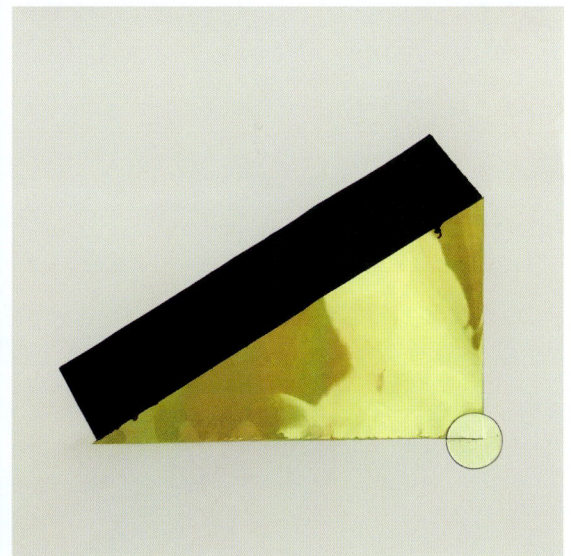

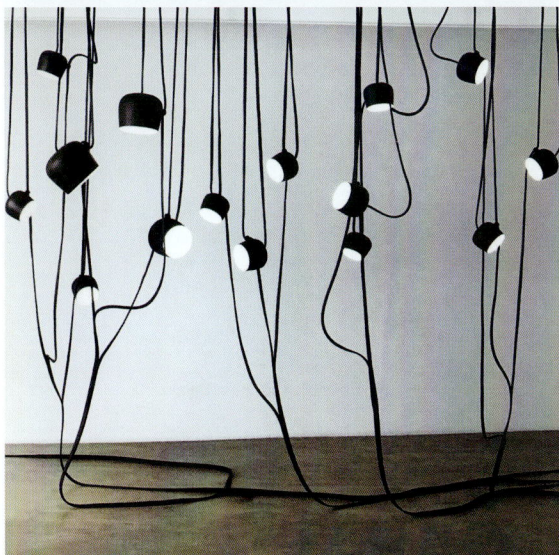

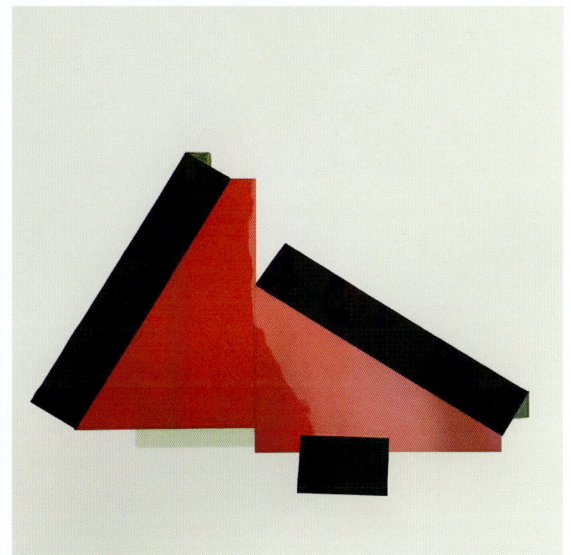

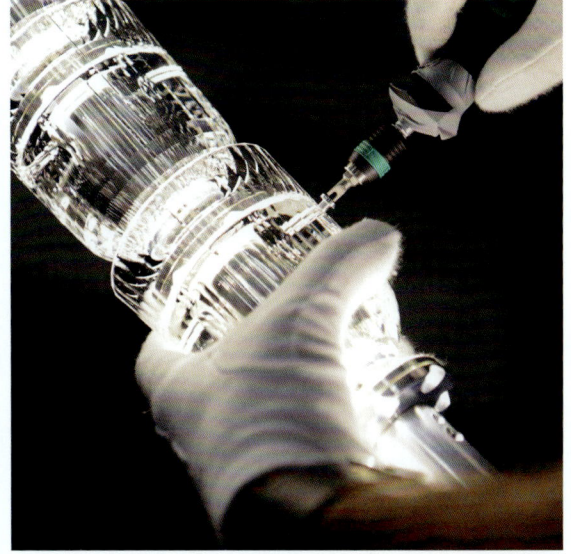

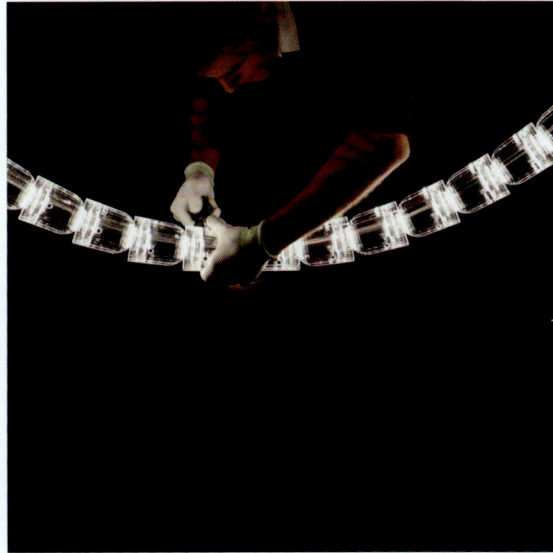

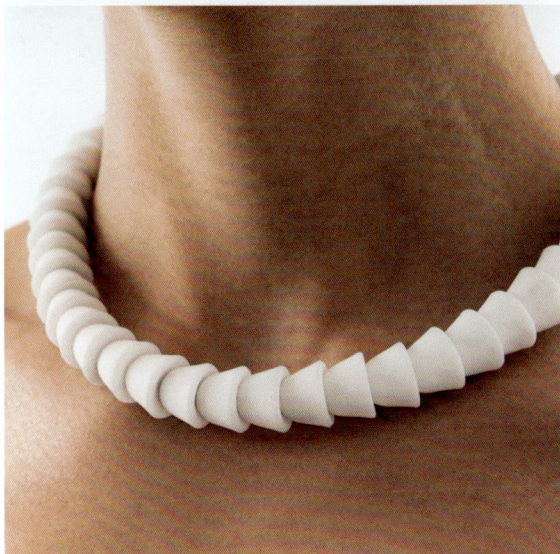

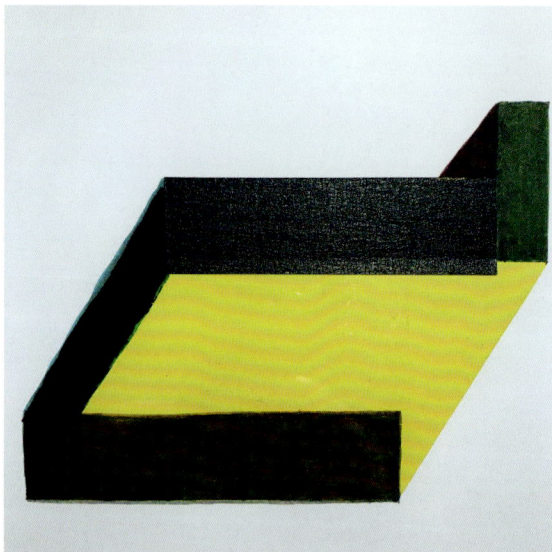
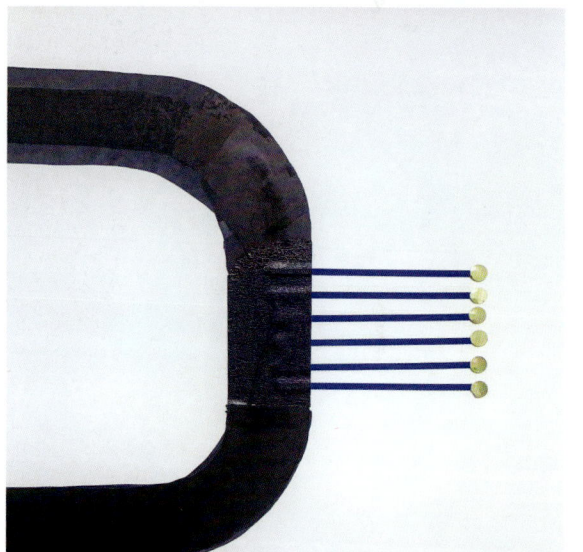

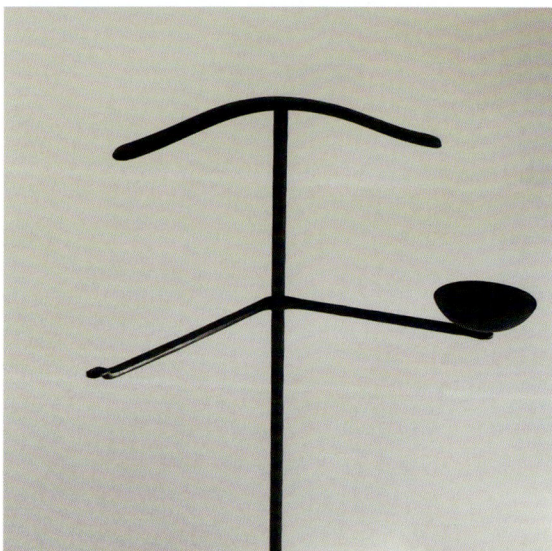
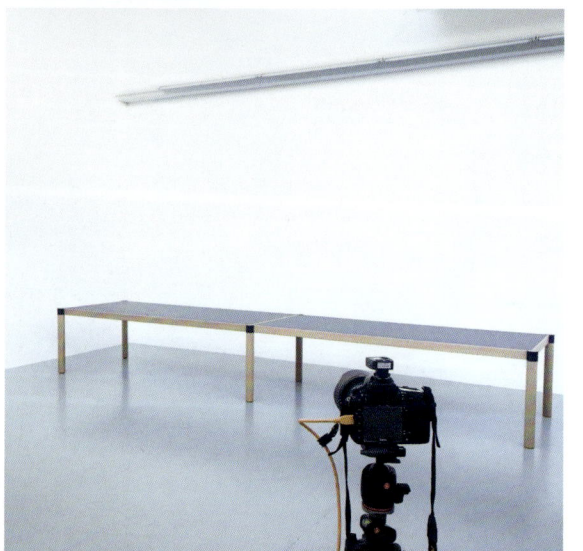

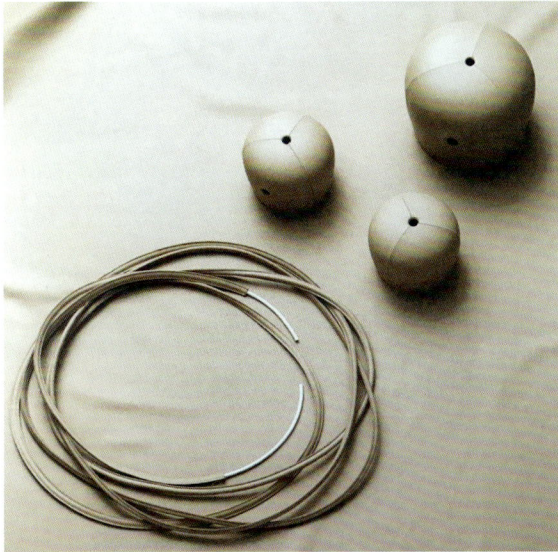

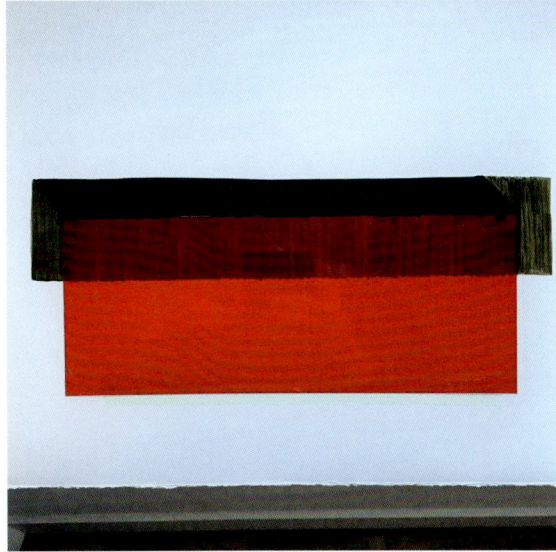

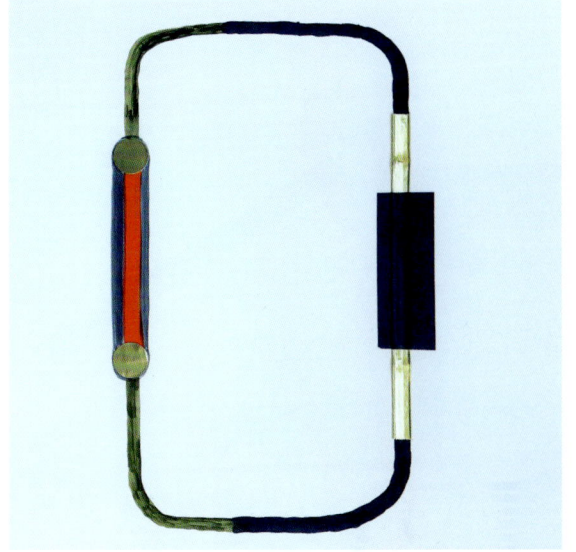

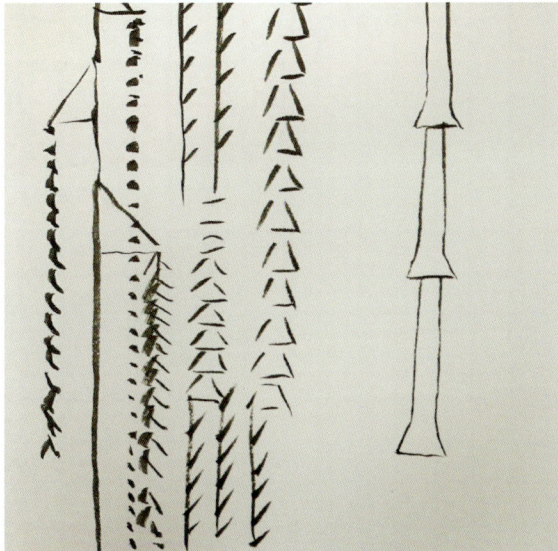

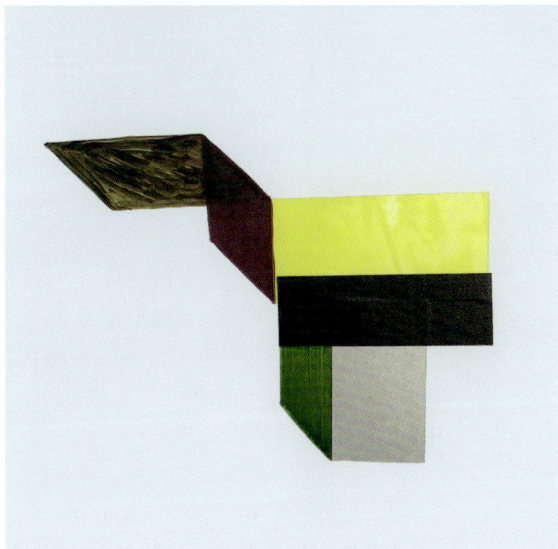

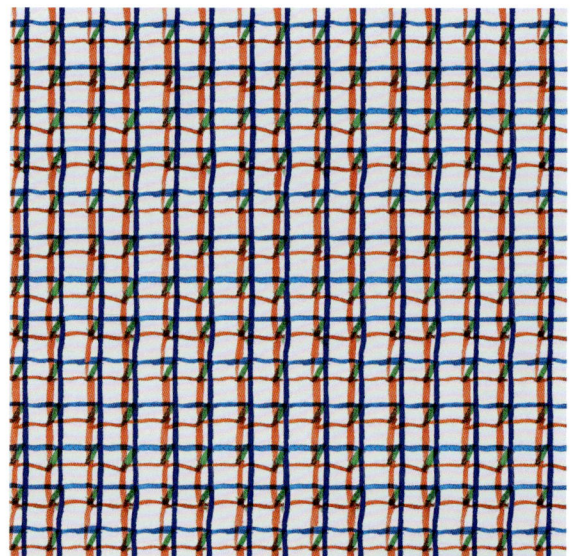

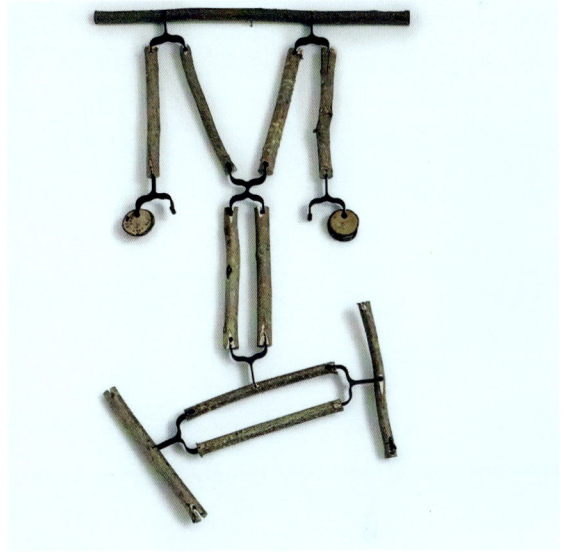

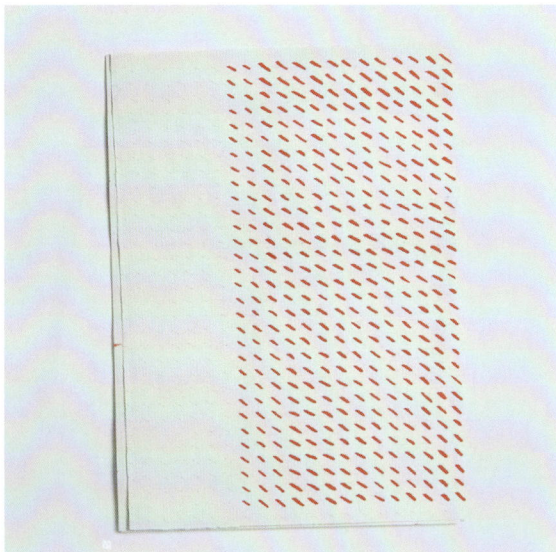

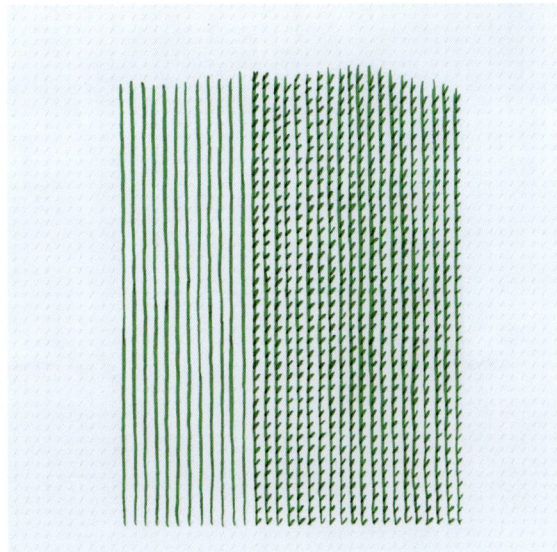

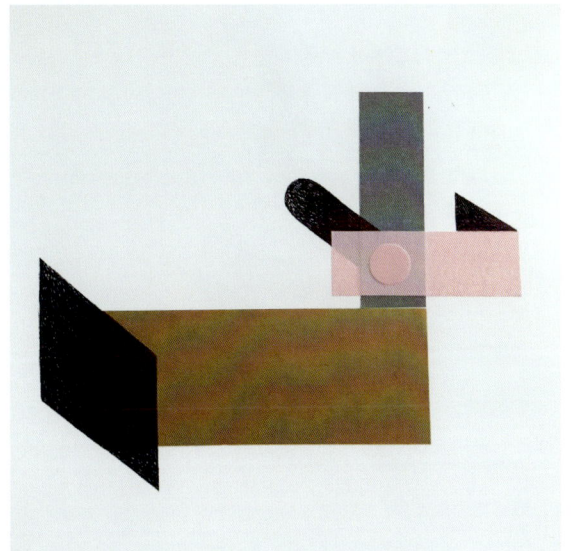

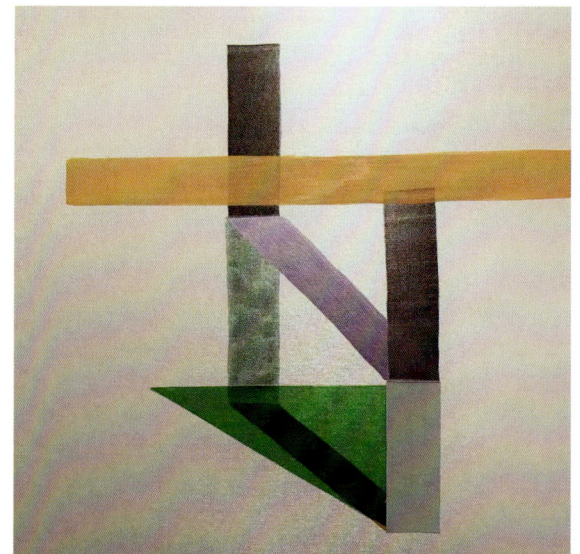
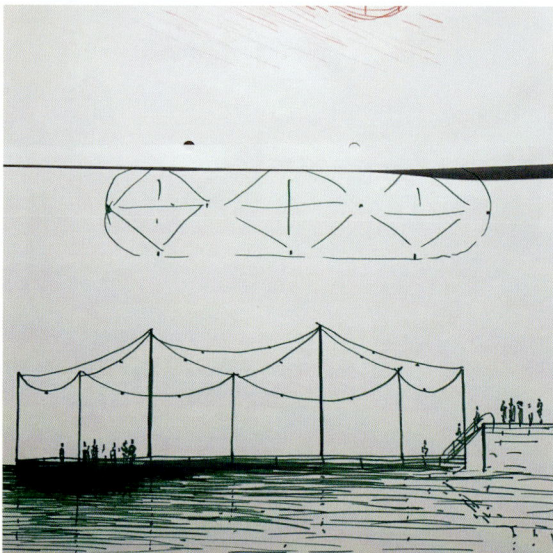
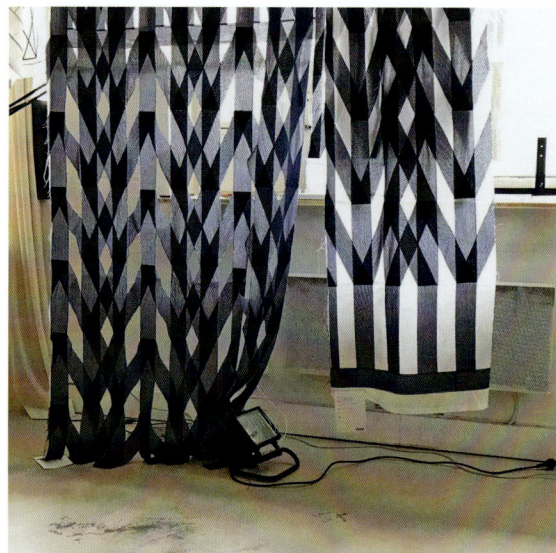

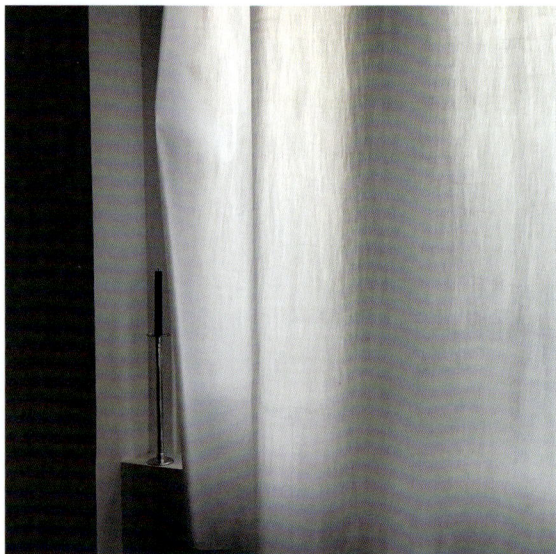
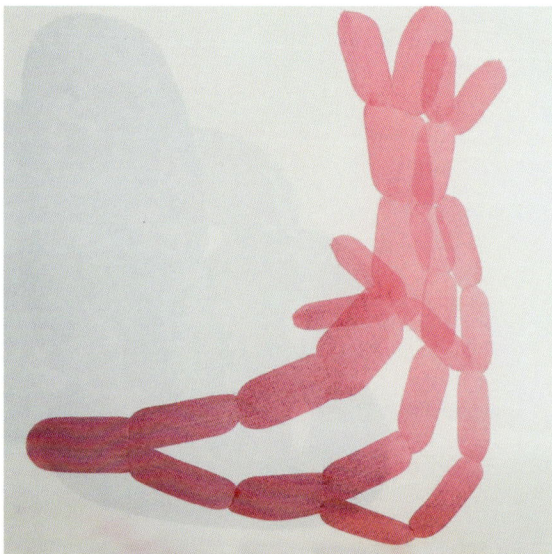

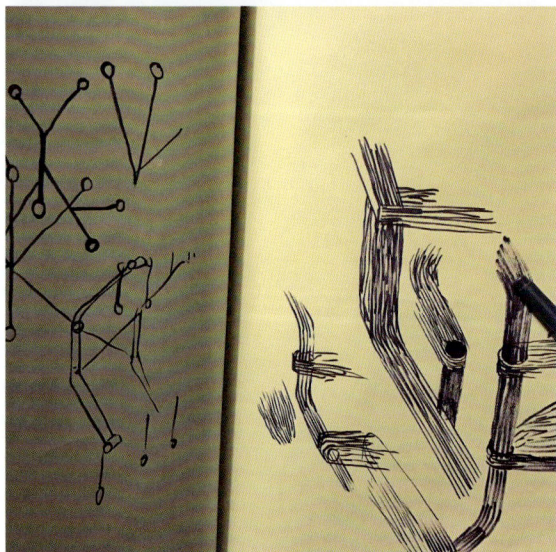

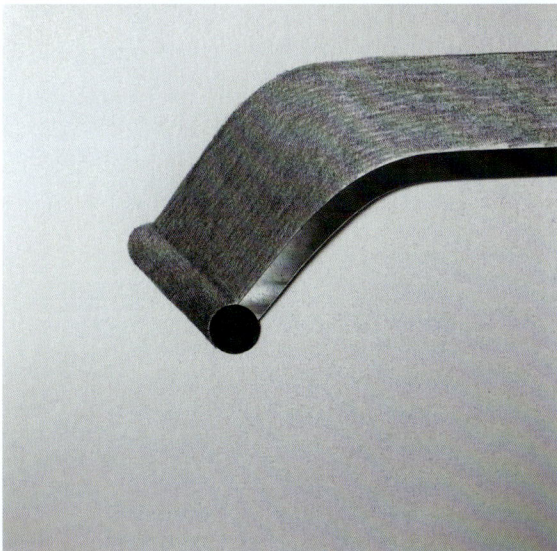

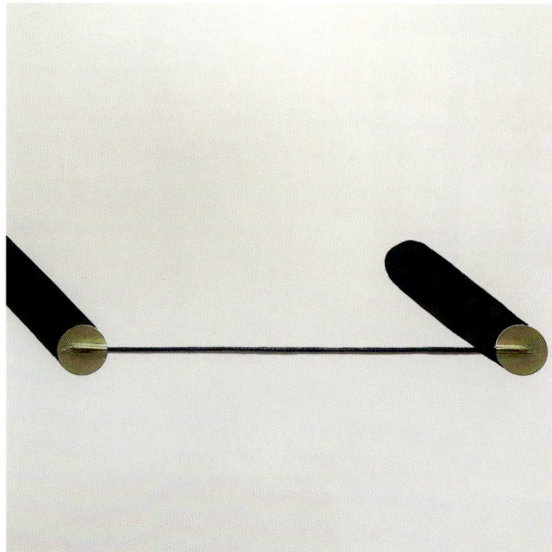

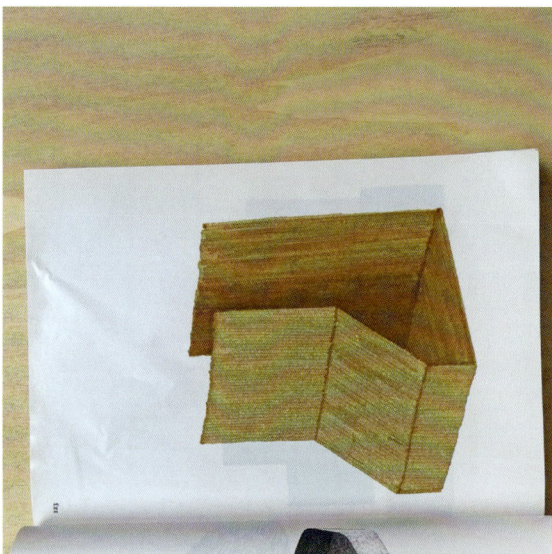
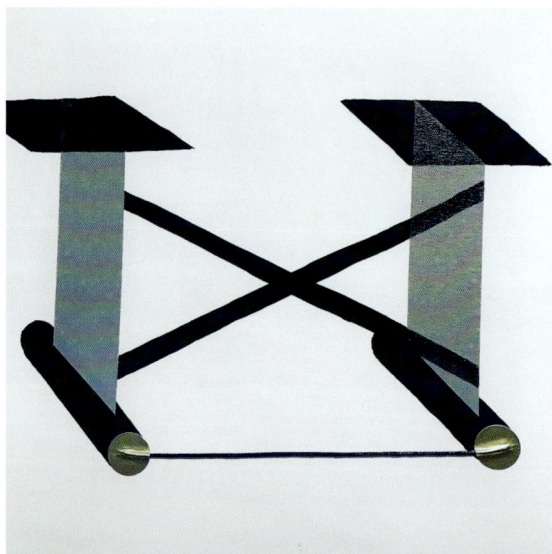
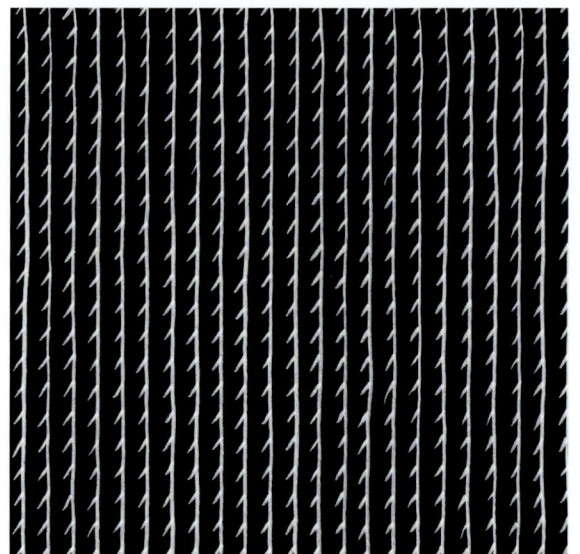

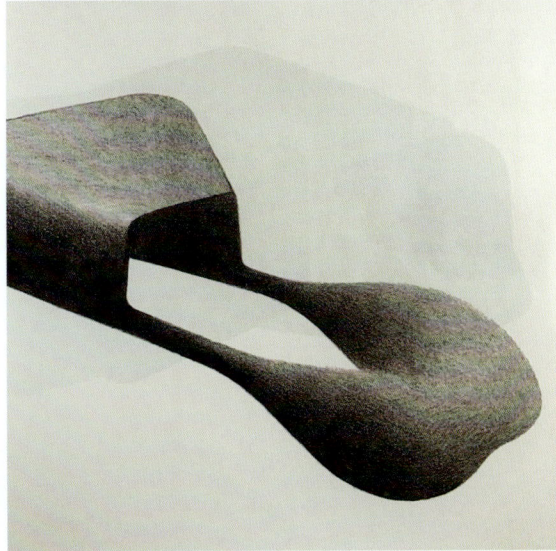
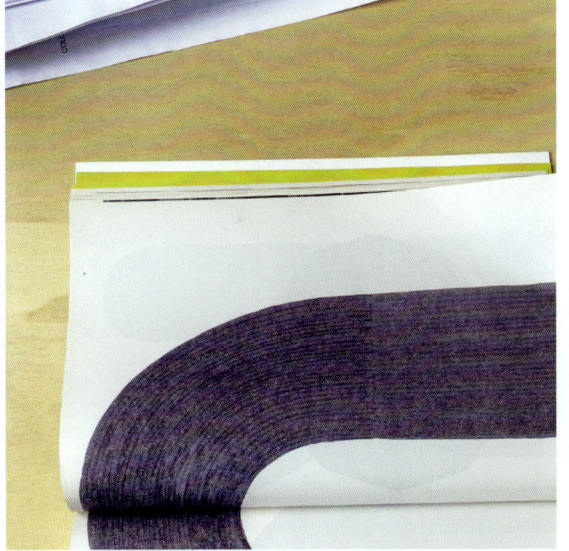
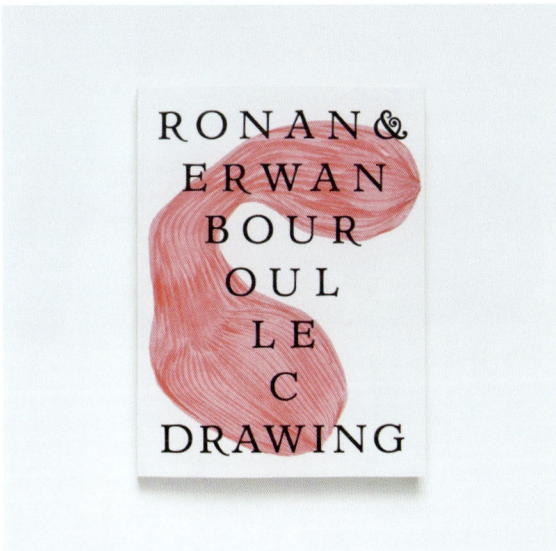
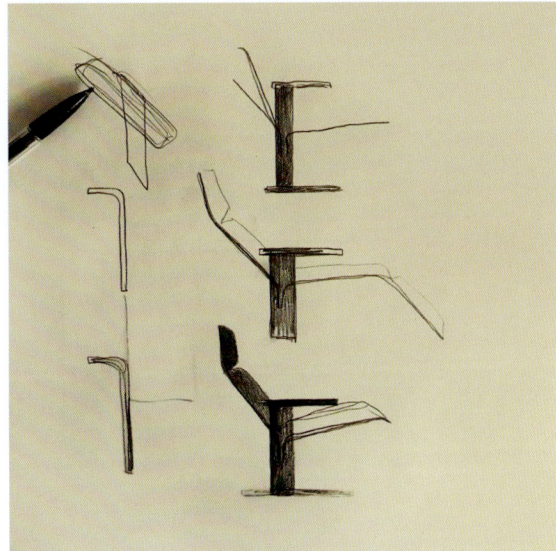
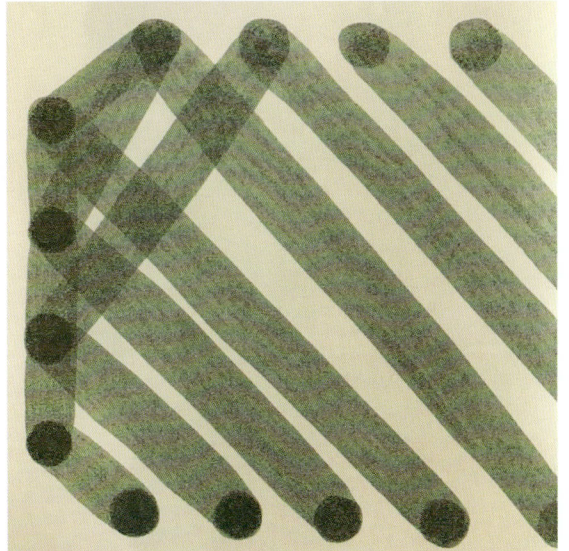

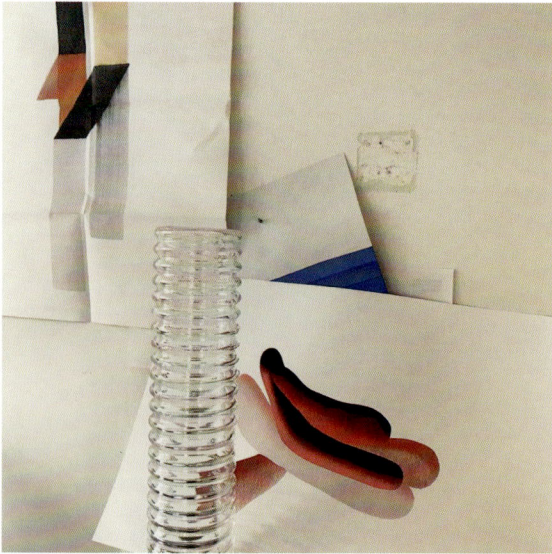

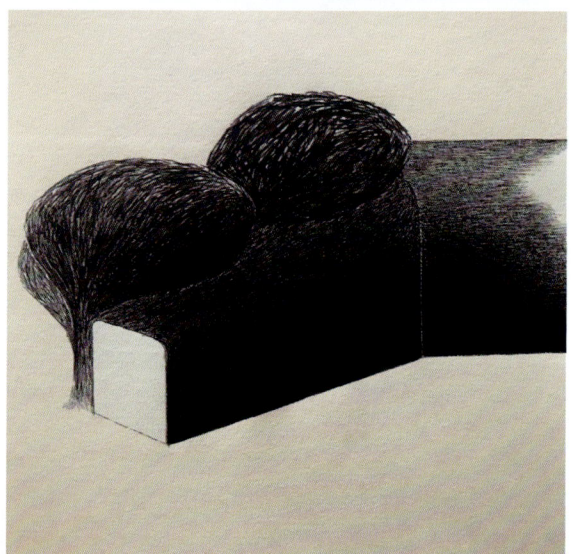

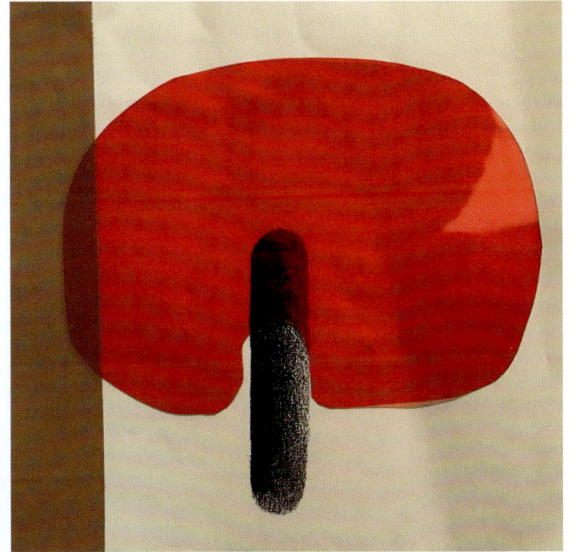

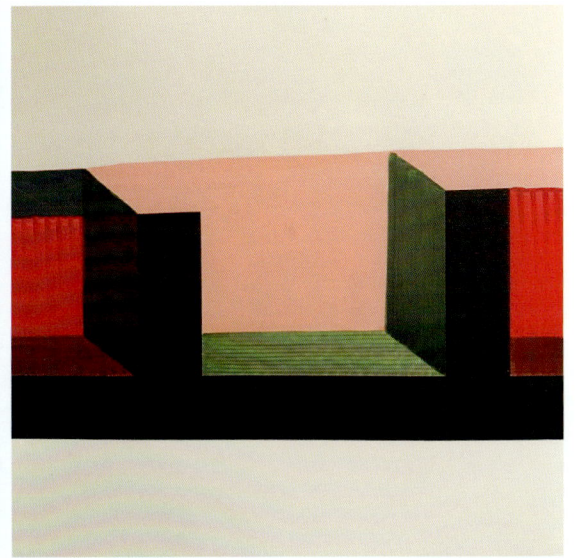

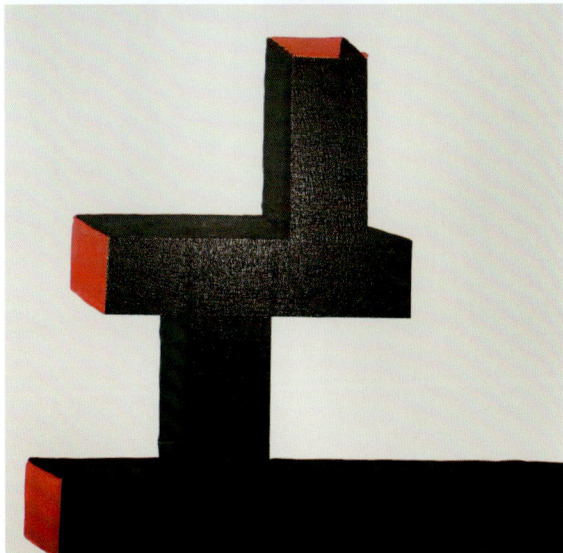

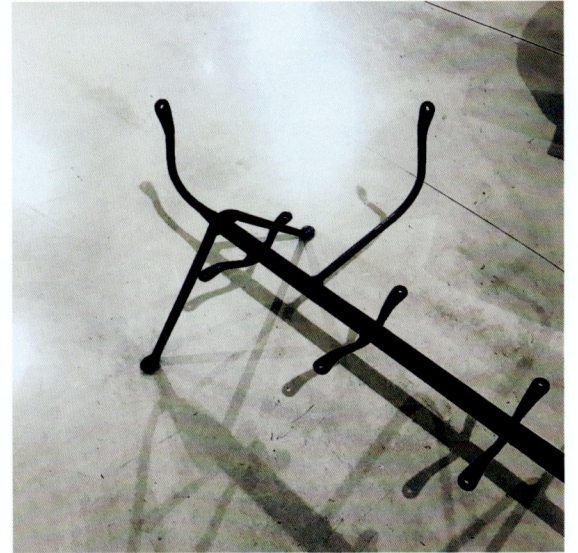

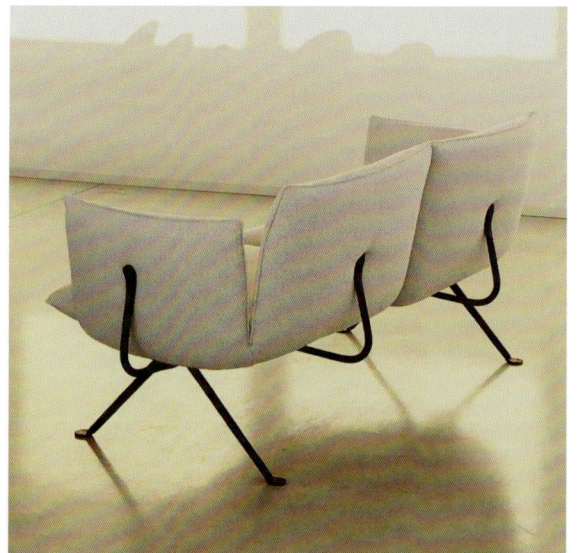
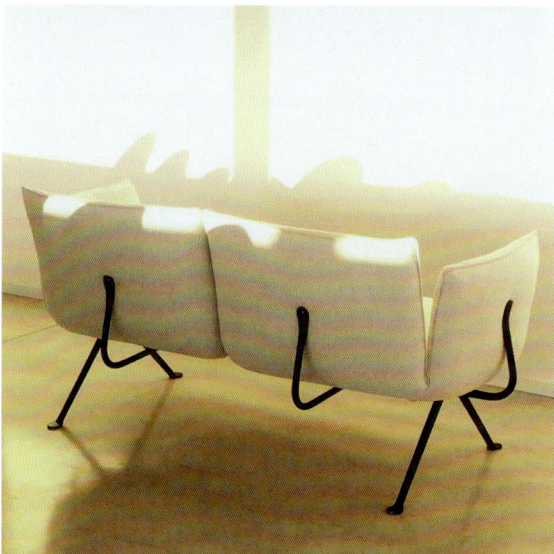

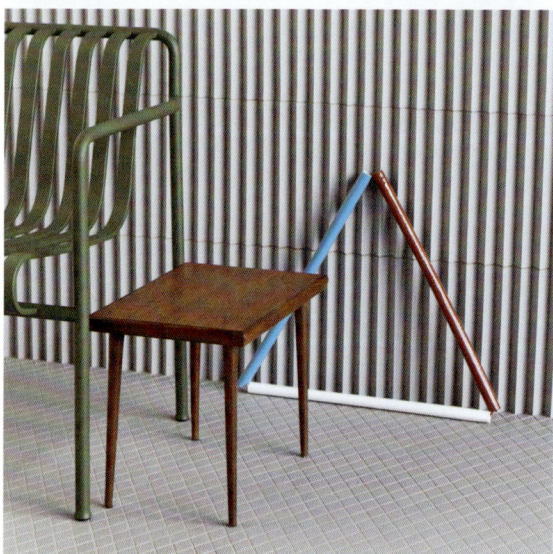

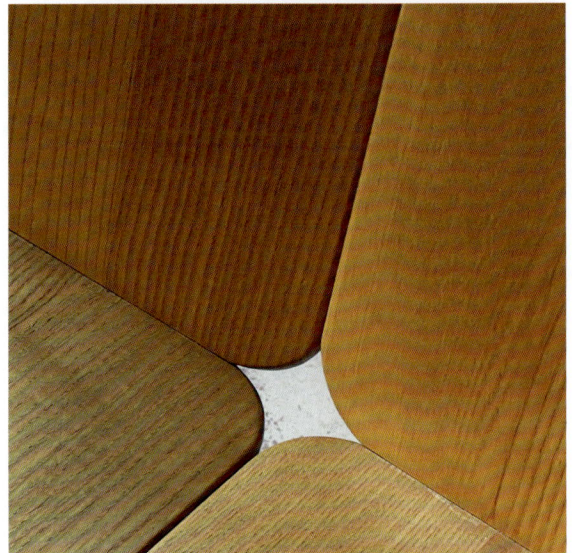
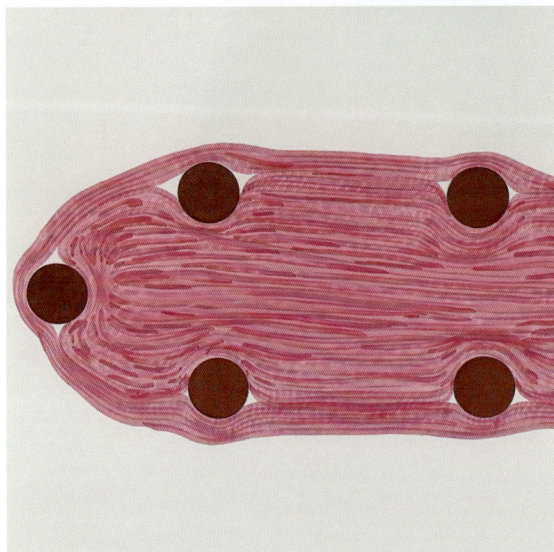

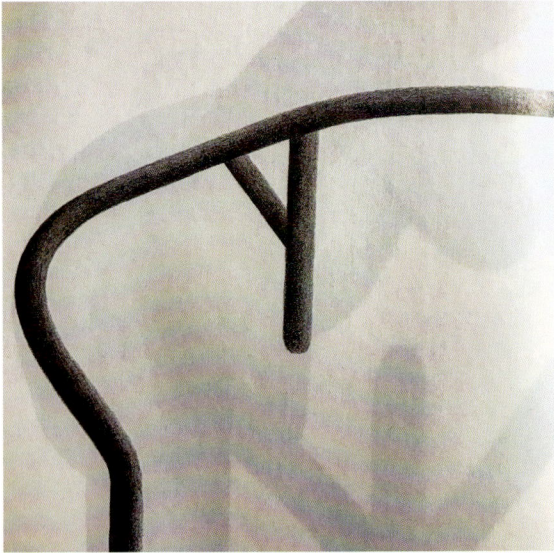

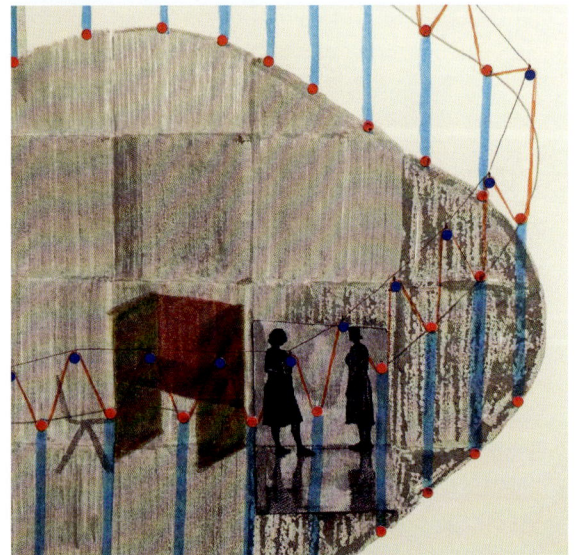

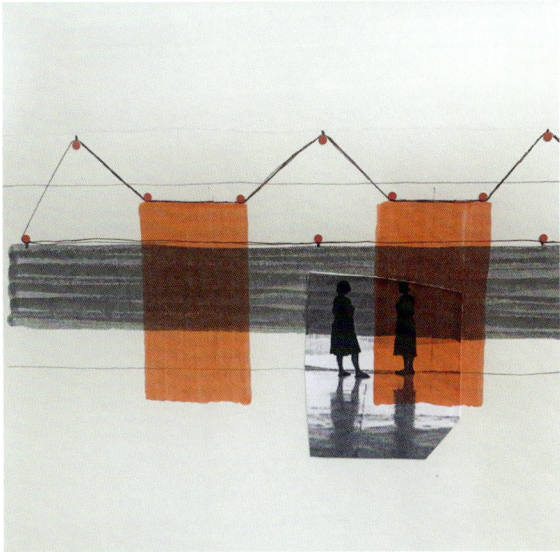

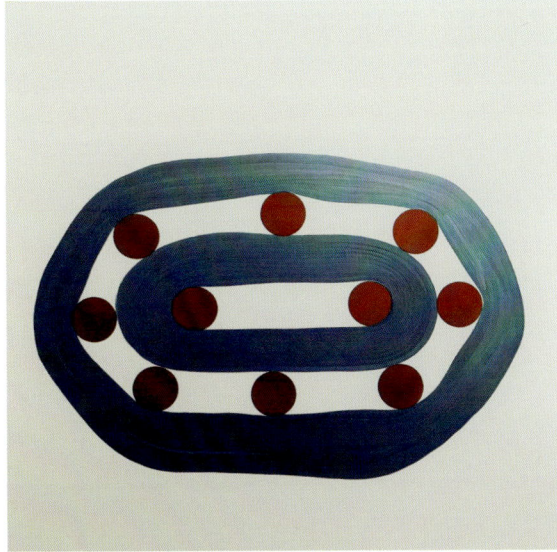

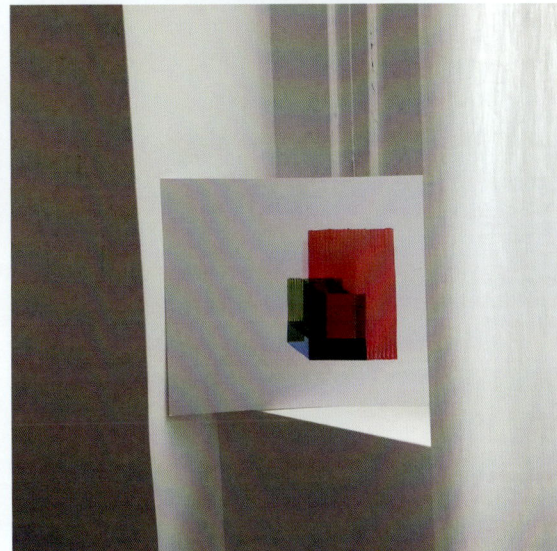

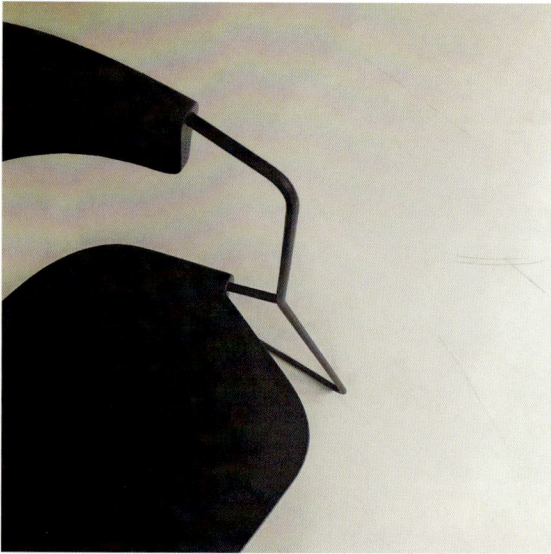

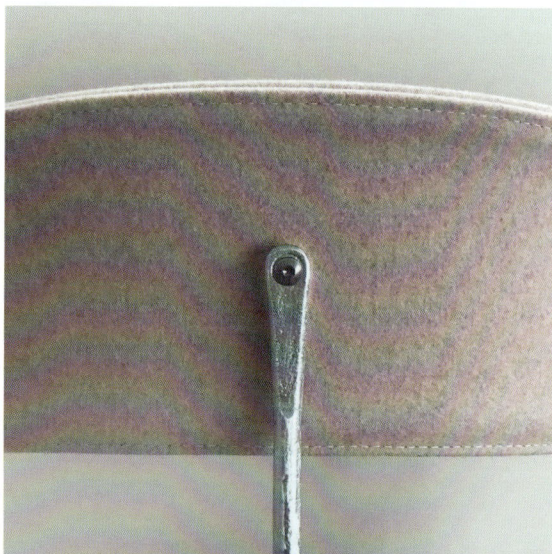

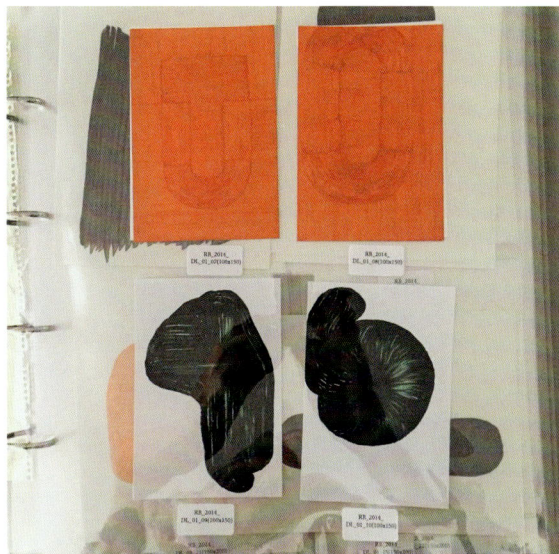

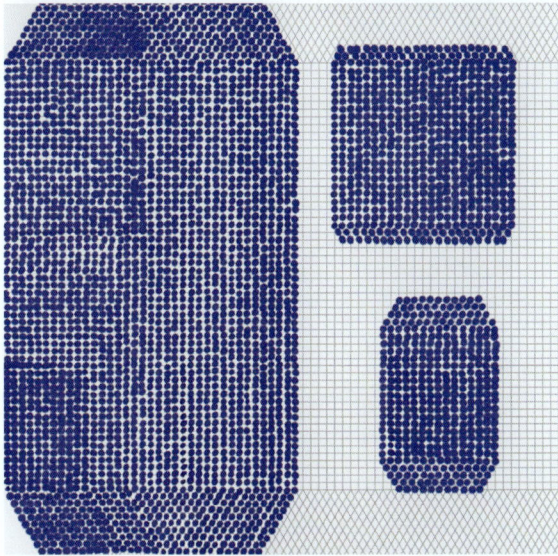

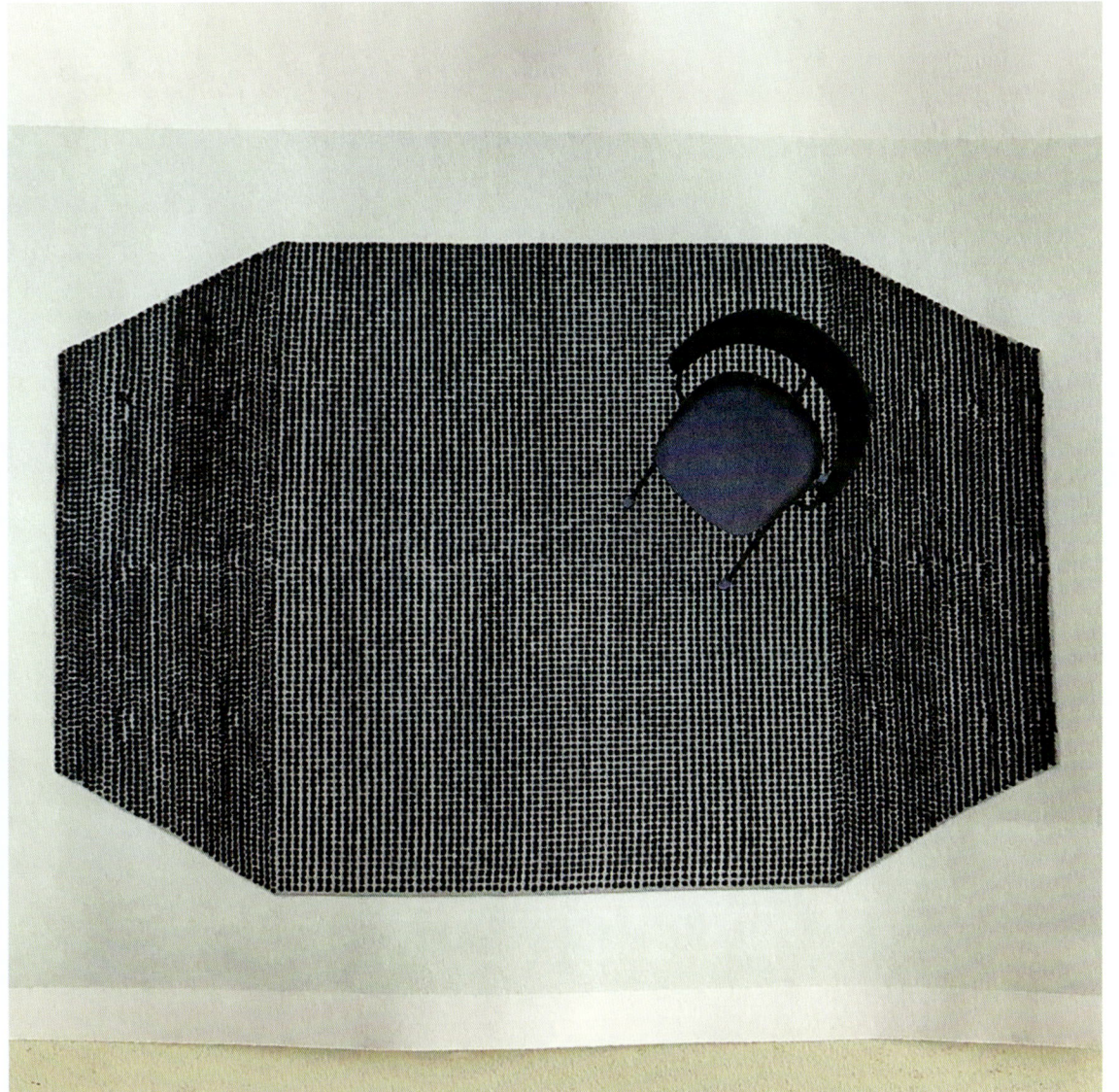

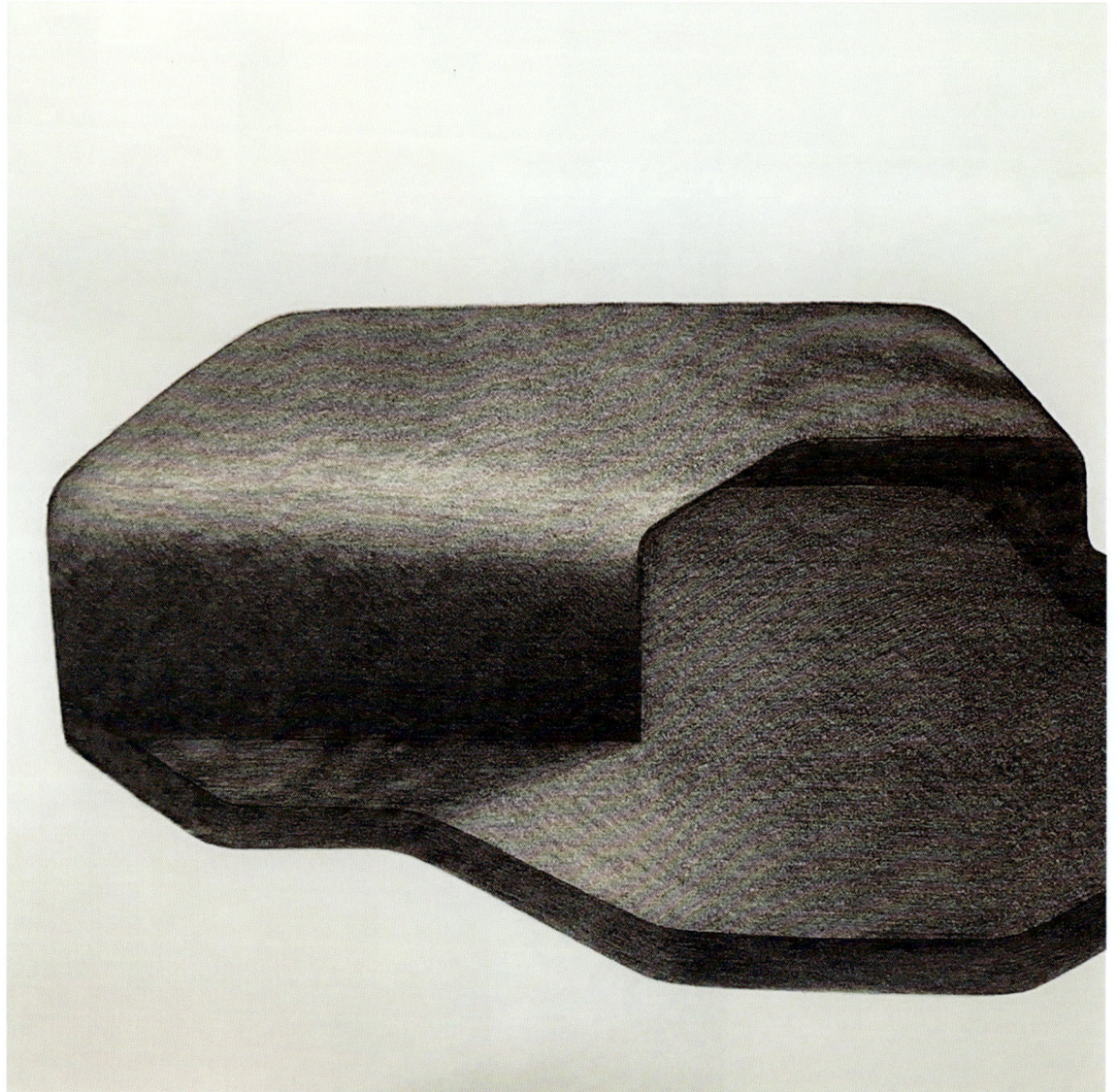

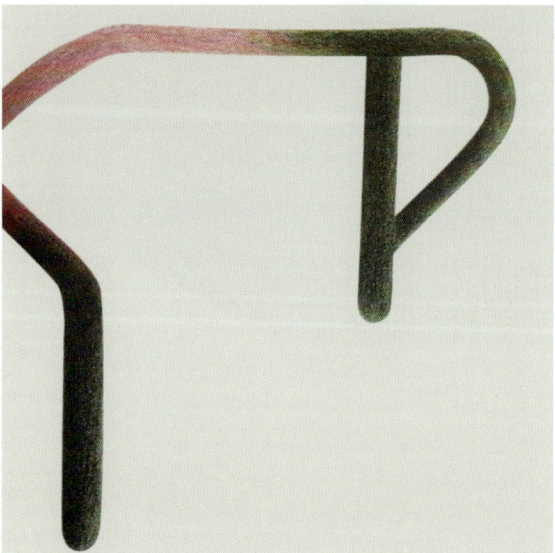

PROTOTYPE

Attention: sit with
caution, the joints are
not glued.

Cassina

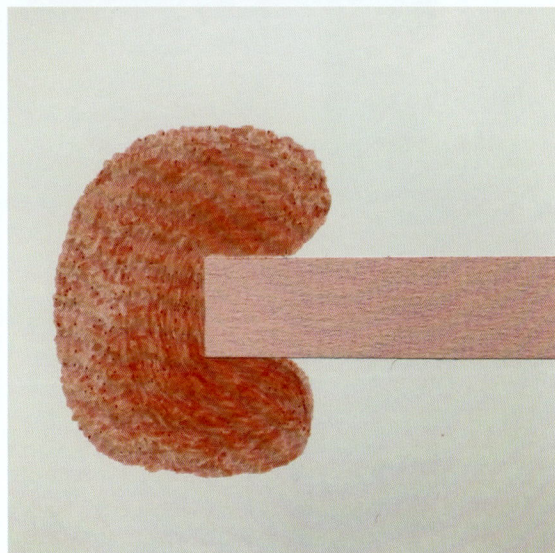

MILANO 2017

A DANSKINA
B CASSINA
C FLOS
D GLAS ITALIA
E MAGIS
F MATTIAZI
G WALLPAPER / LESAGE
H VITRA

MILANO 2017

A DANSKINA — HALL 20 STAND D09/E16
B CASSINA — VIA DURINI 16
C FLOS — HALL 13 COD D18
D GLAS ITALIA — H16 C23/D18
E MAGIS — HALL 20 C15/D12
F MATTIAZI — HALL 20 E08
G WALLPAPER / LESAGE — 28 VIA DELLA MOSCOVA
H VITRA — HALL 20 D09/E16

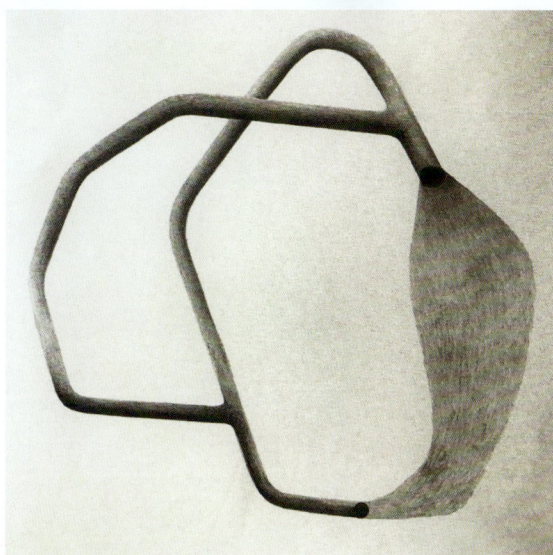

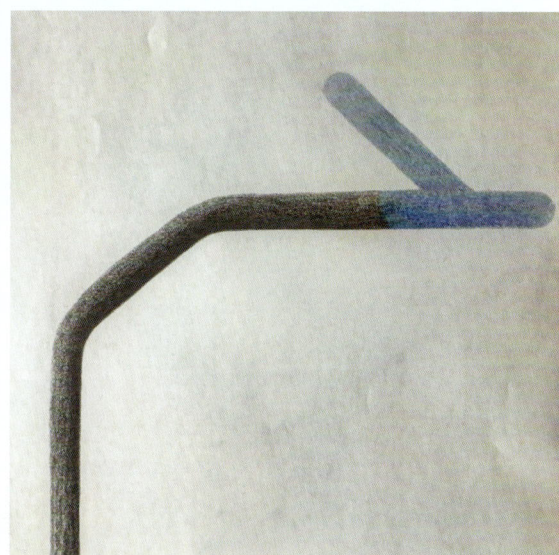

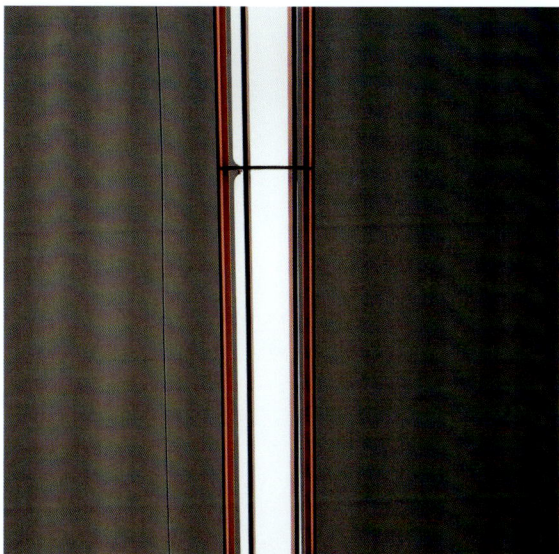

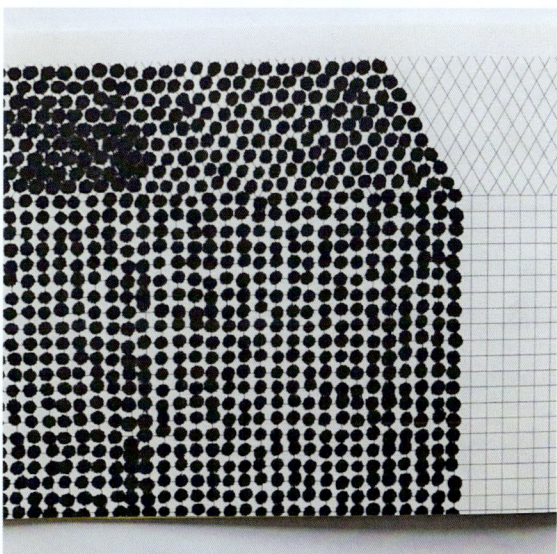

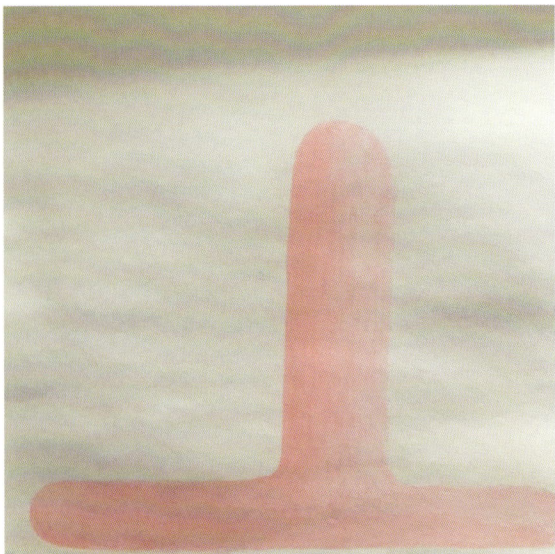
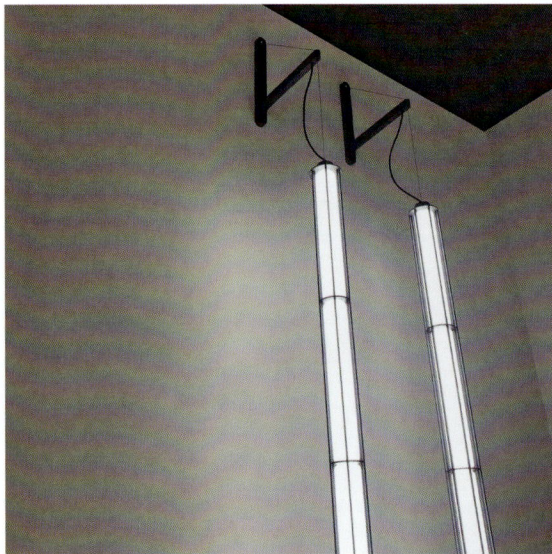
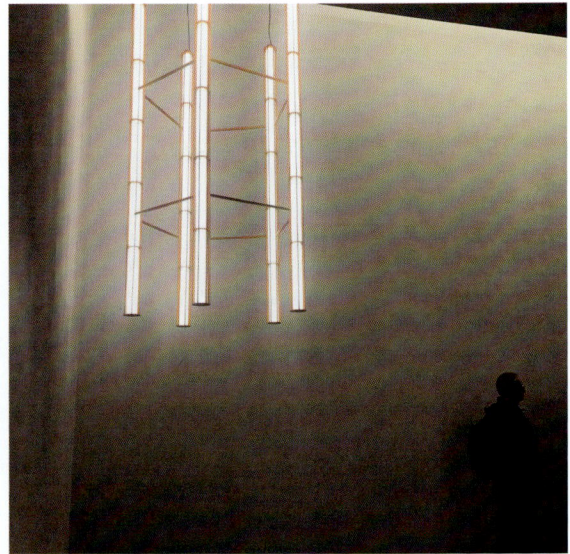
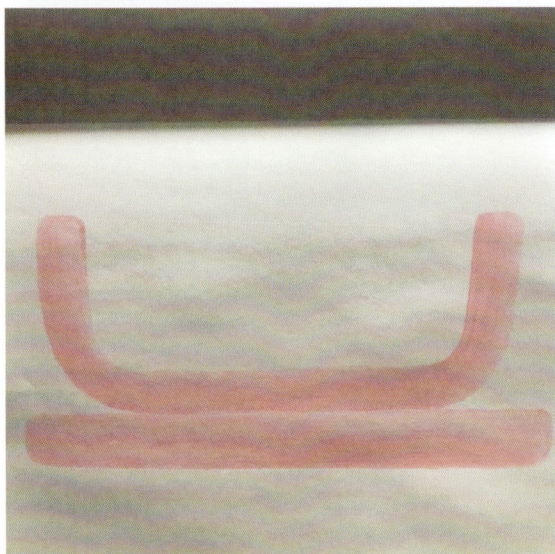

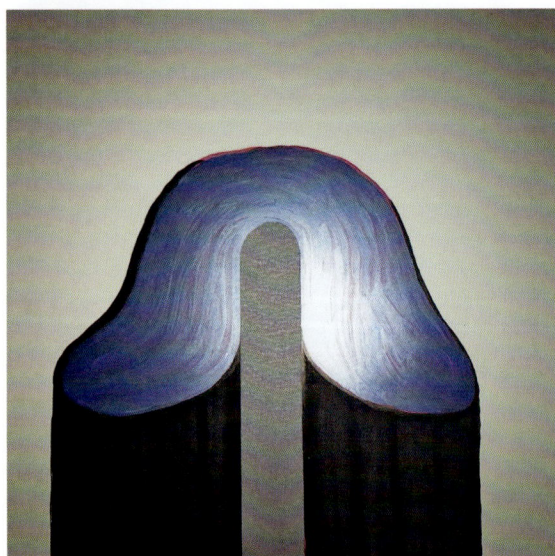
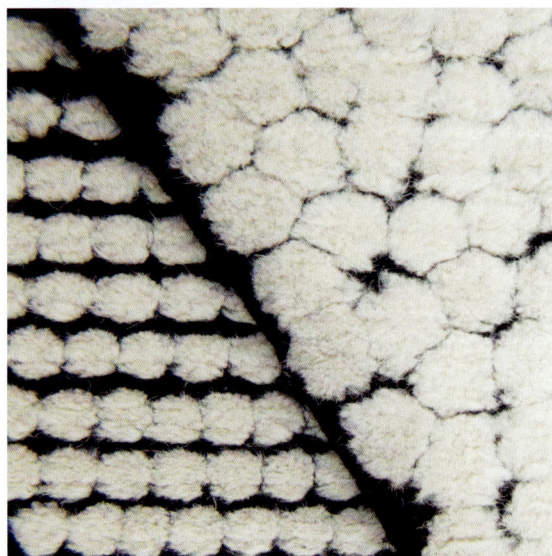
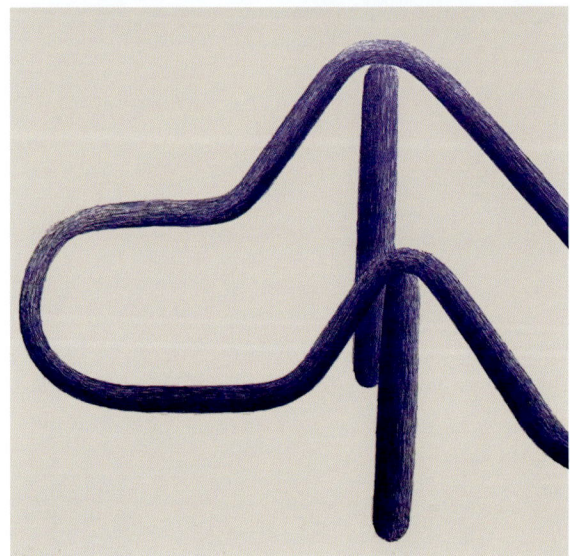

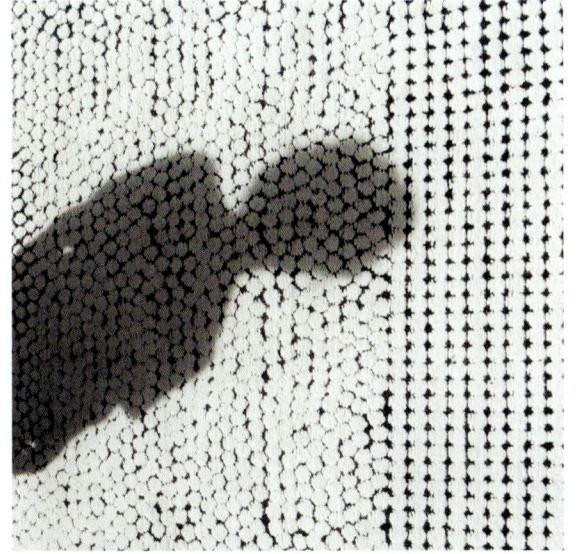

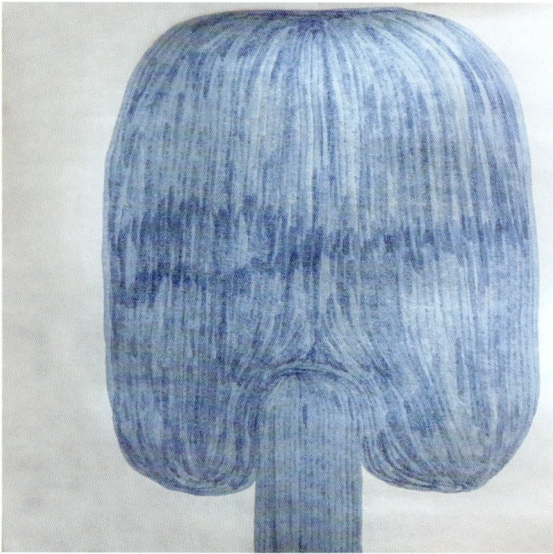
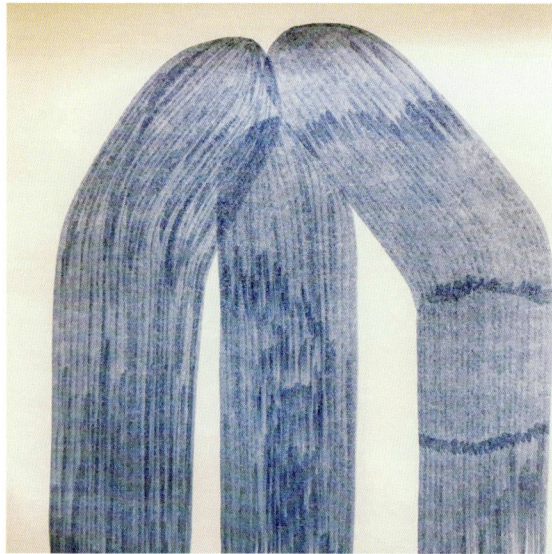

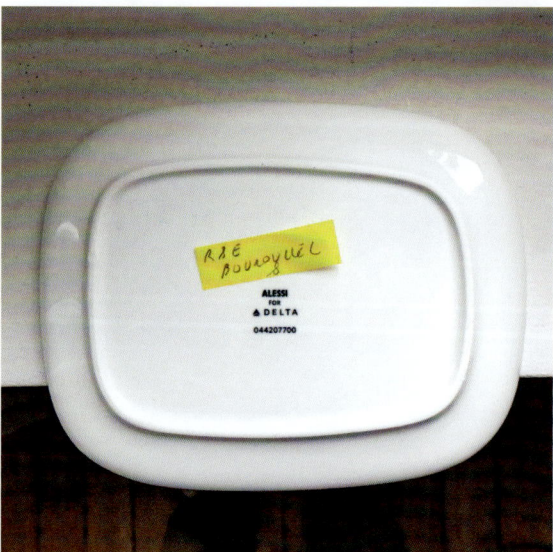

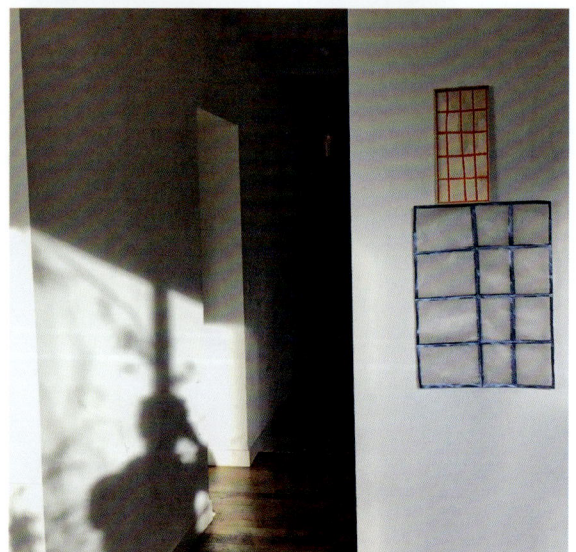

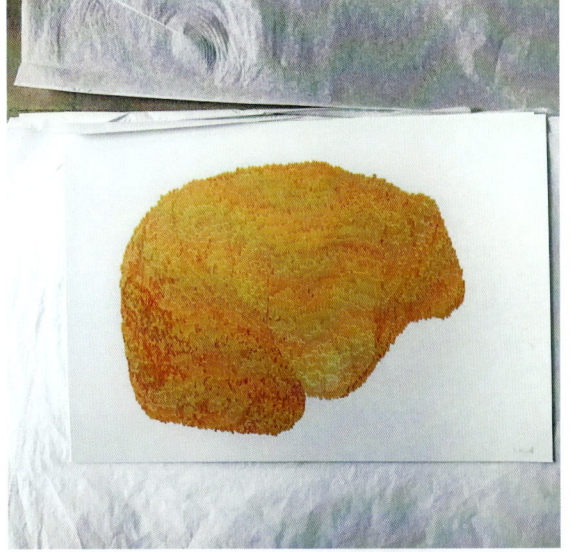

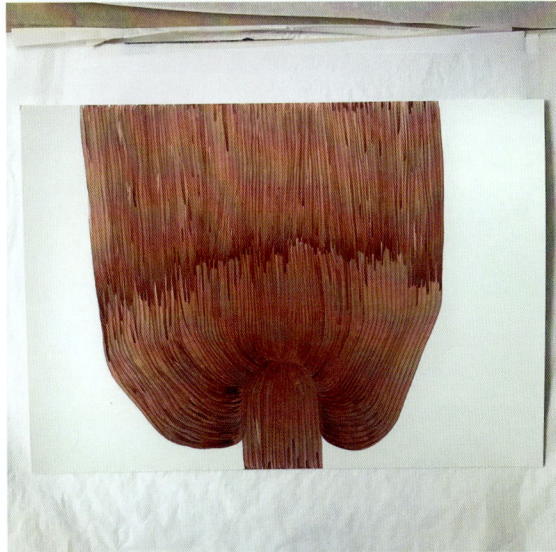
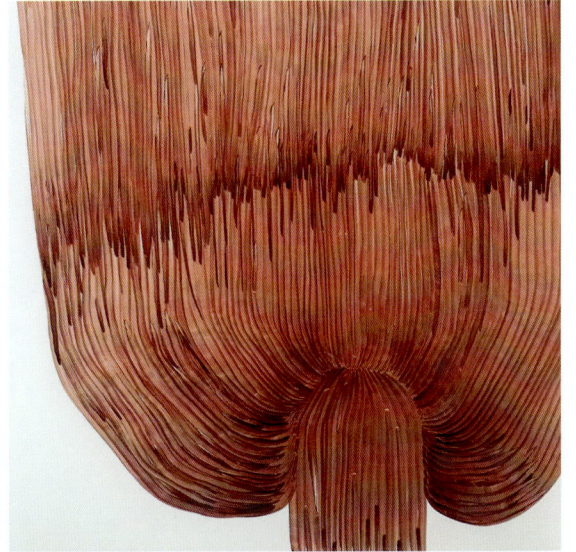

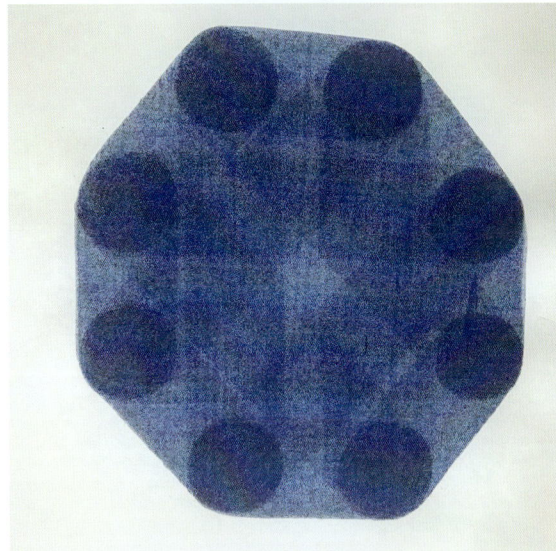
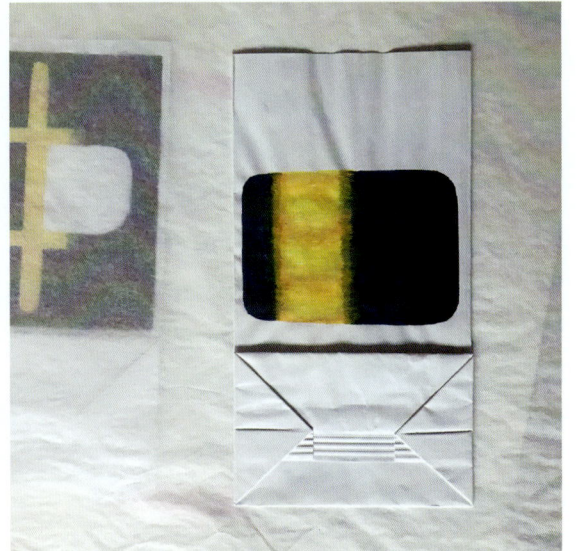

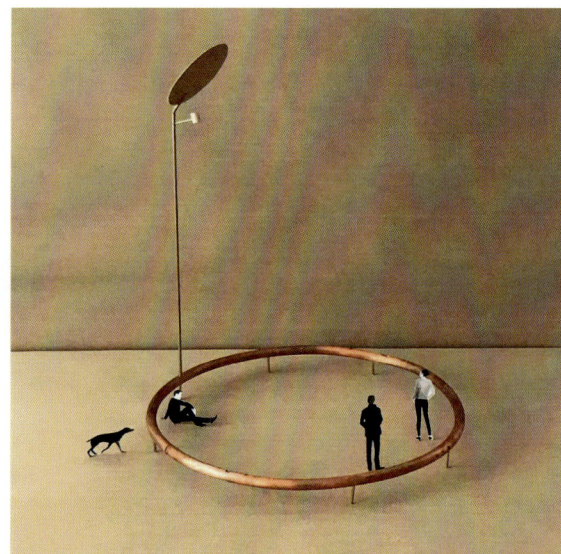

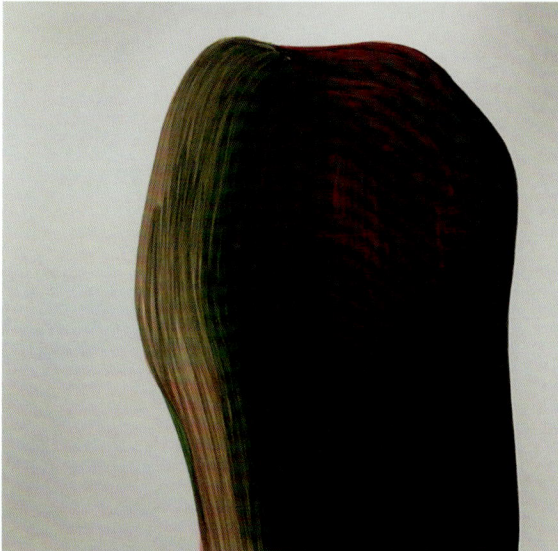  

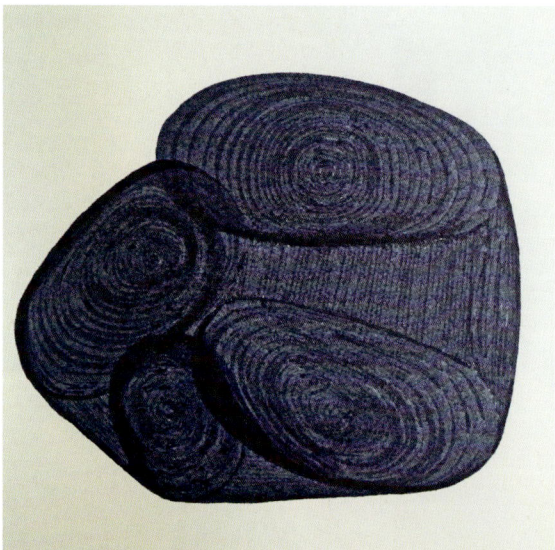
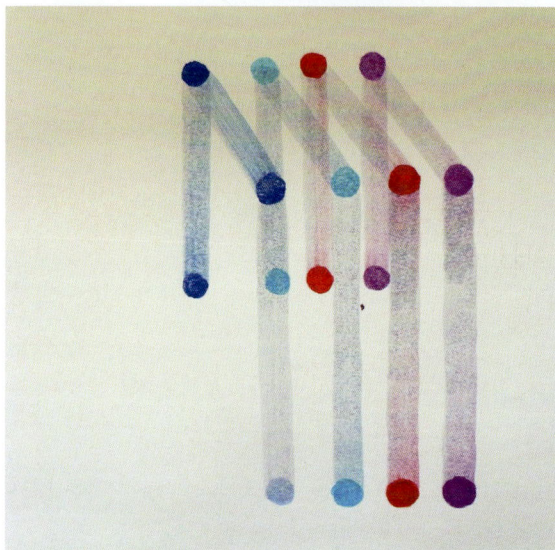

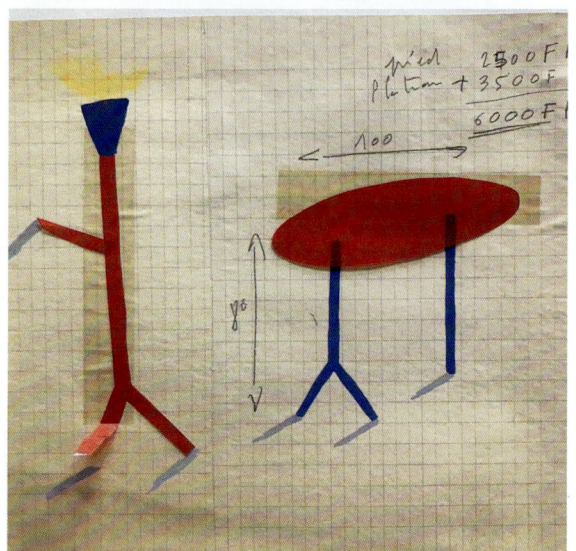

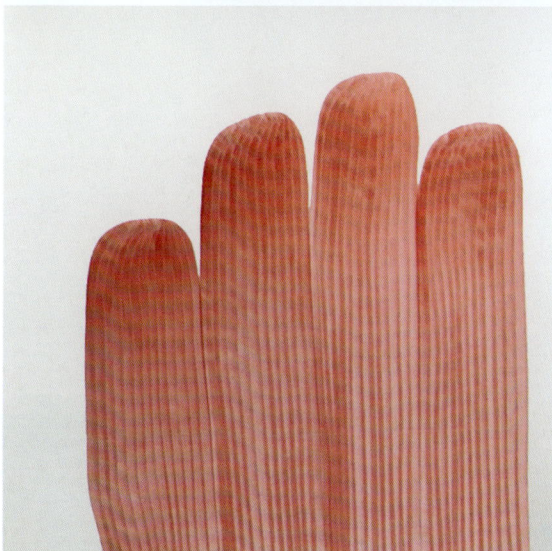

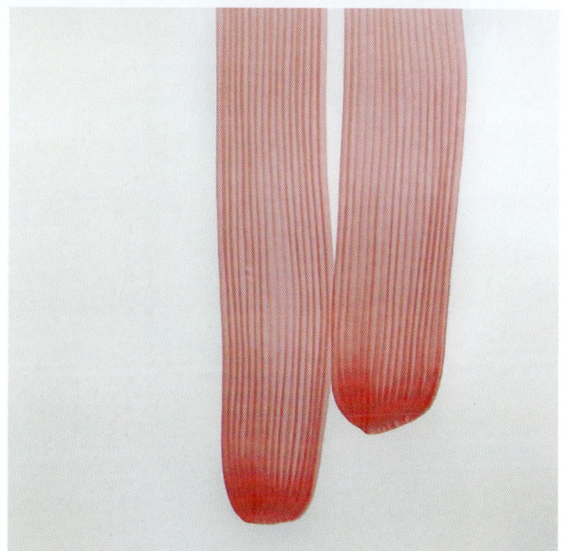

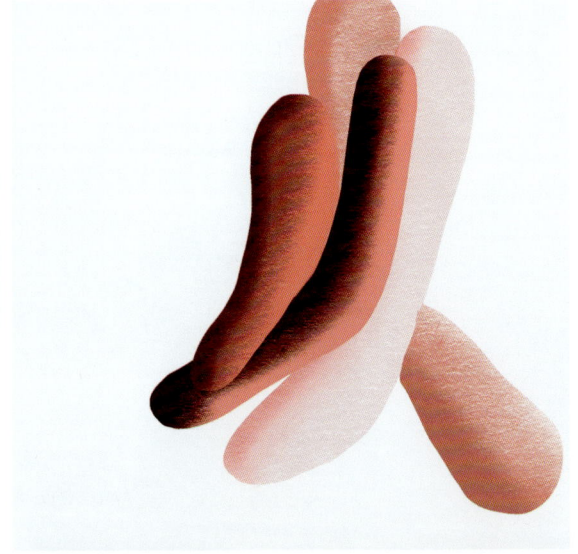

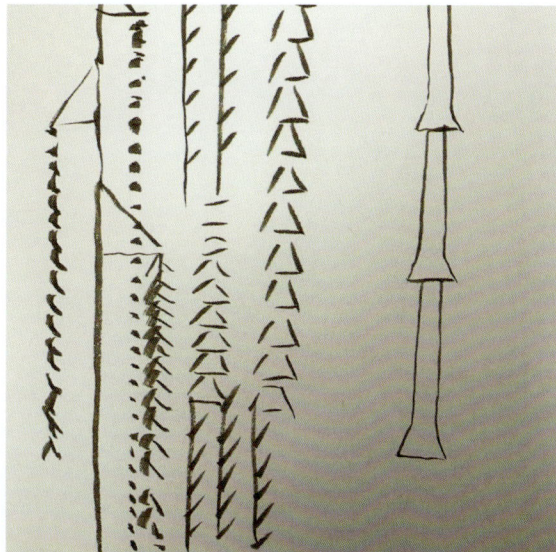

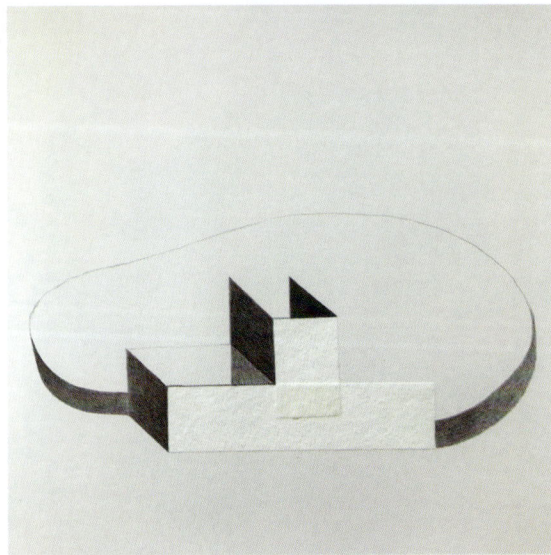

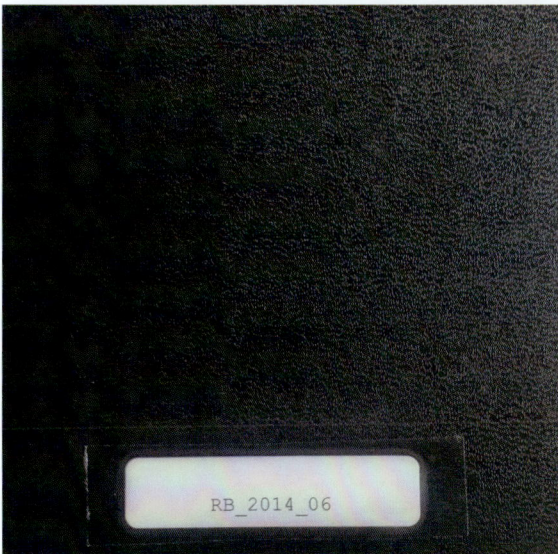

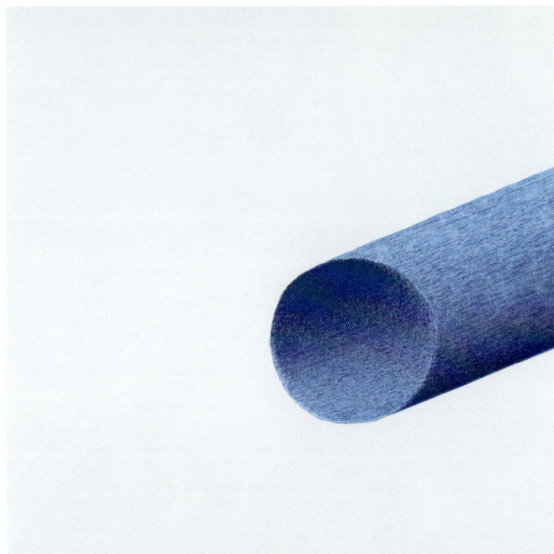

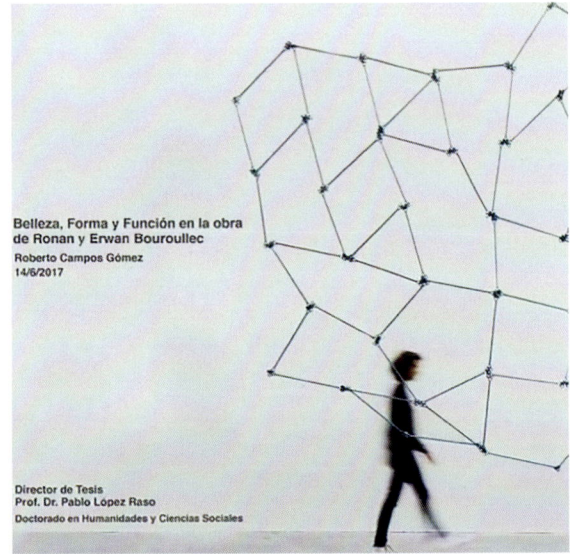

Belleza, Forma y Función en la obra
de Ronan y Erwan Bouroullec
Roberto Campos Gómez
14/6/2017

Director de Tesis
Prof. Dr. Pablo López Raso
Doctorado en Humanidades y Ciencias Sociales

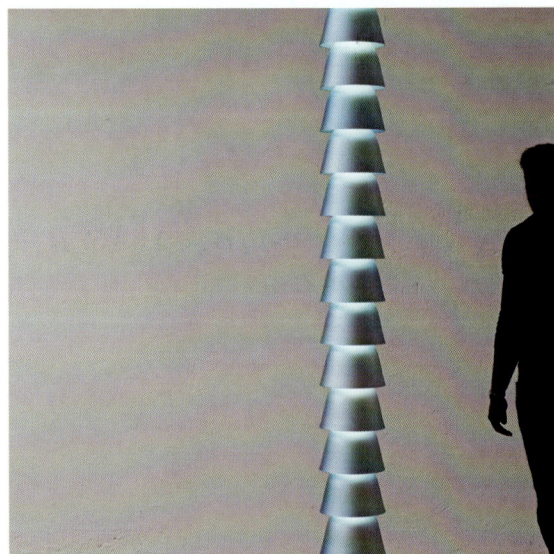

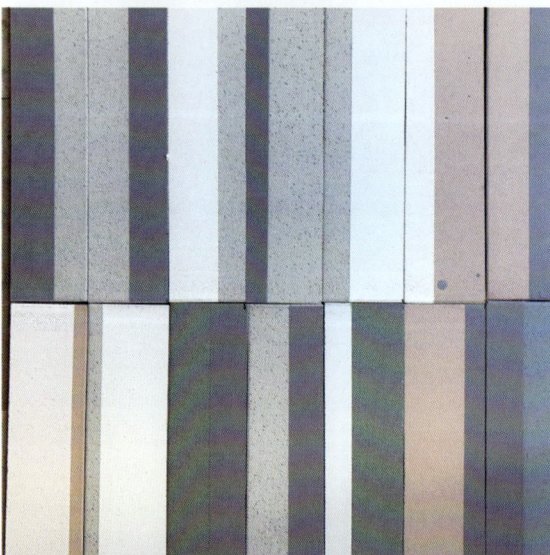

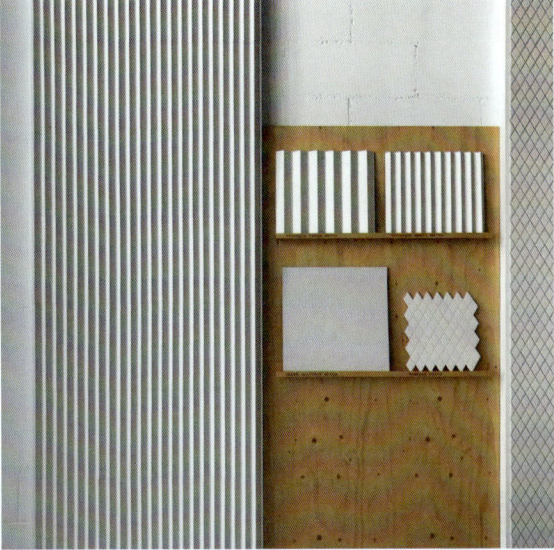

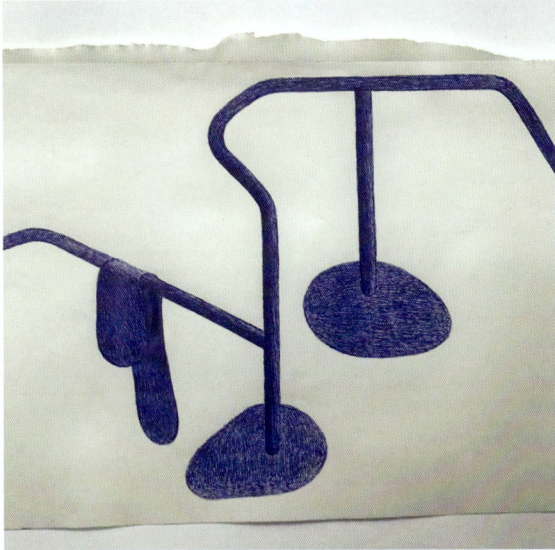

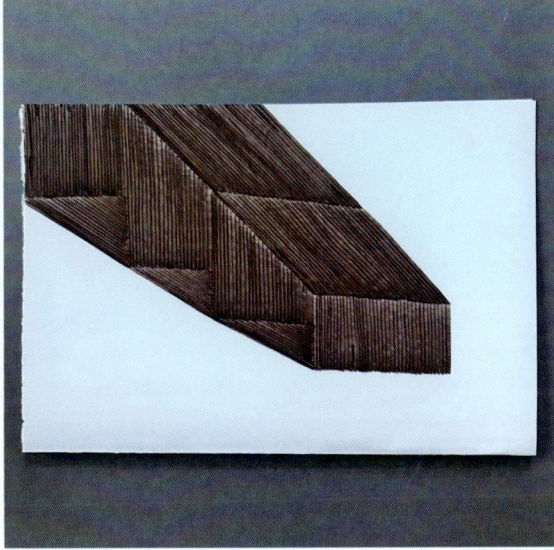

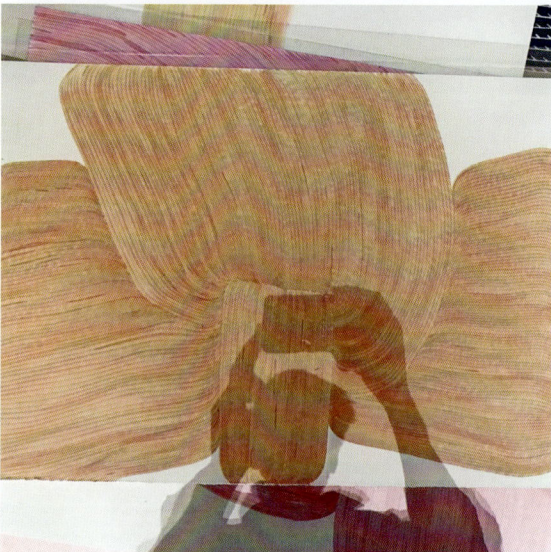

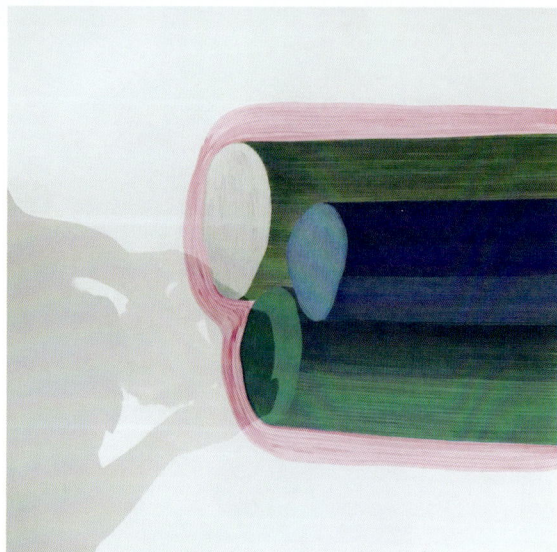

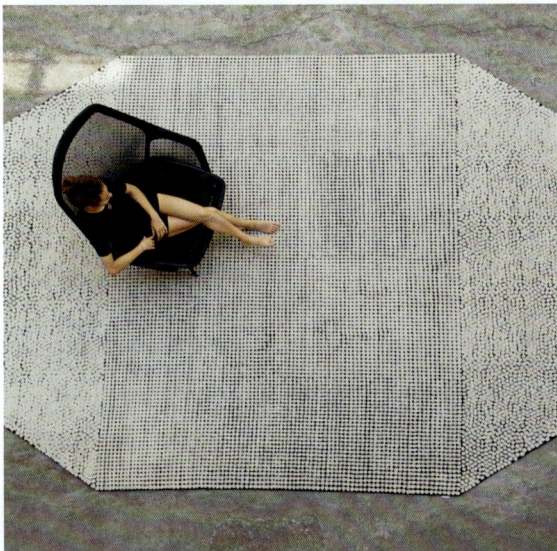

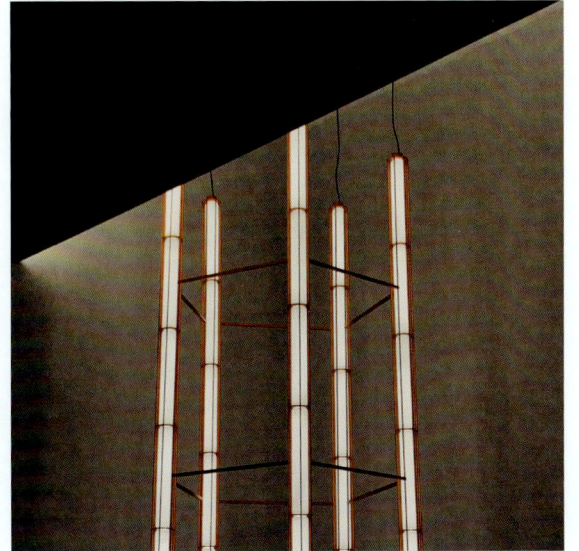
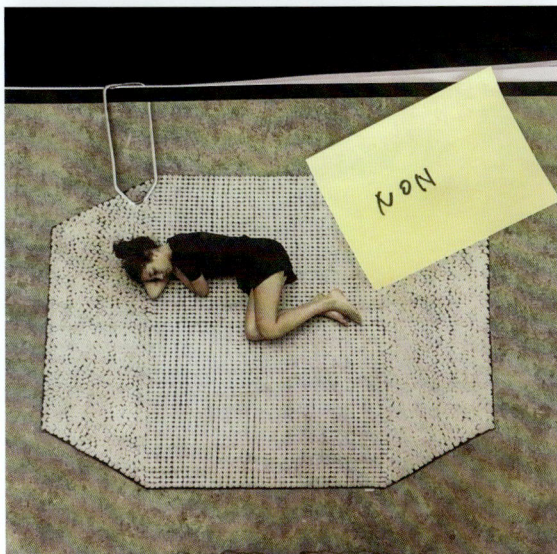

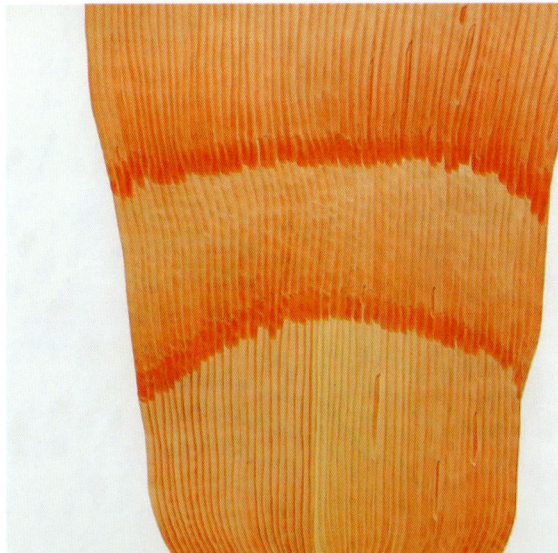

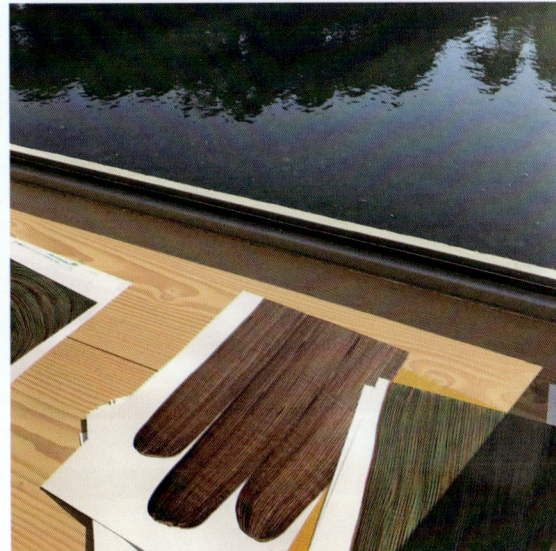

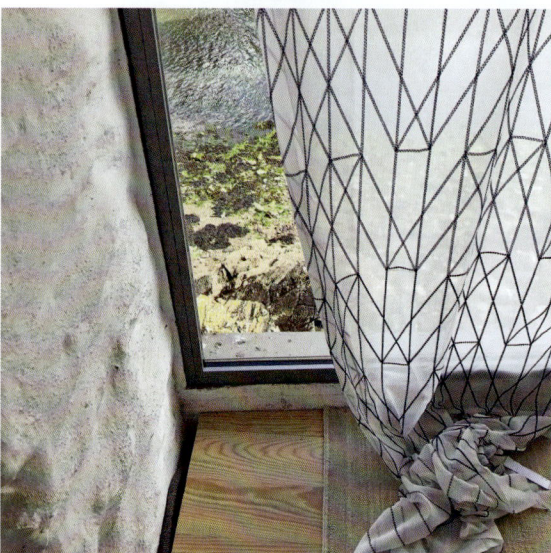
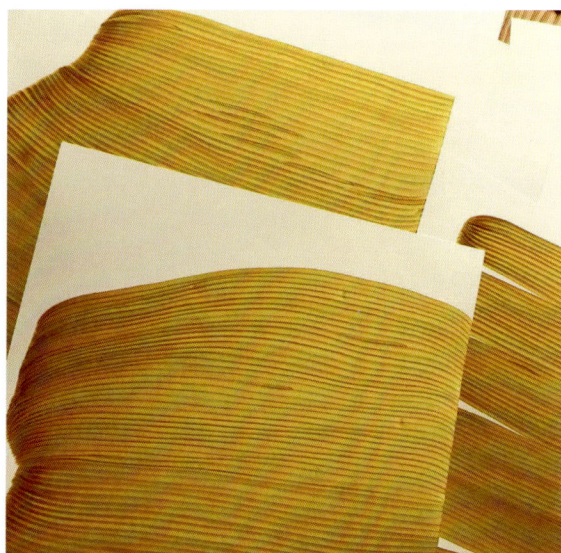

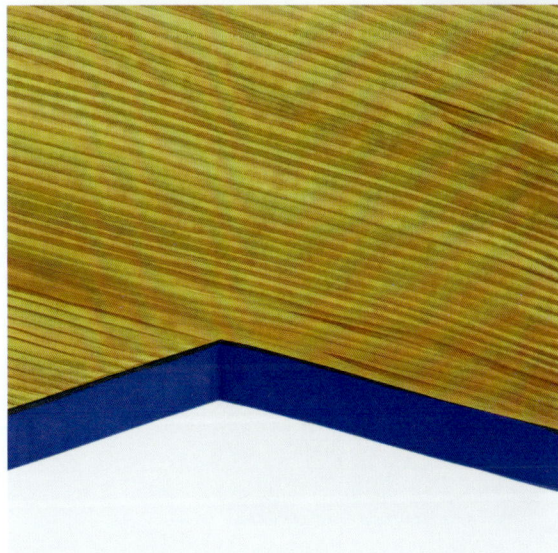

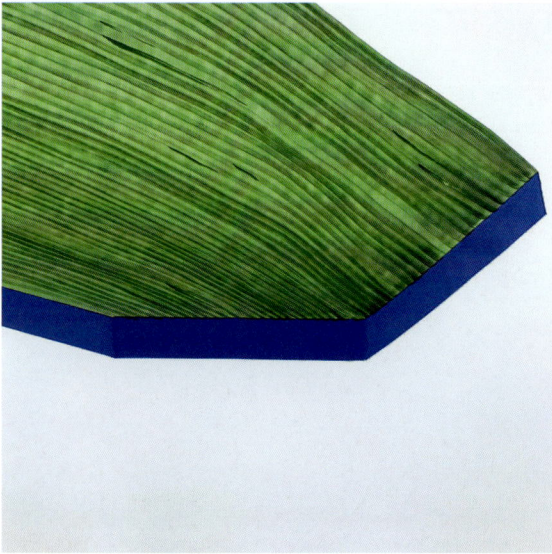
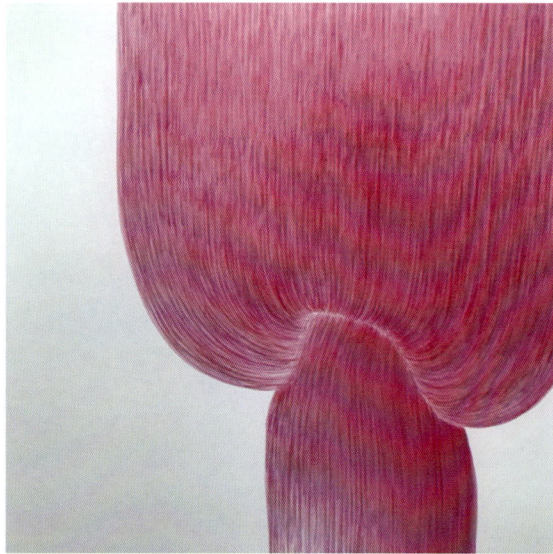

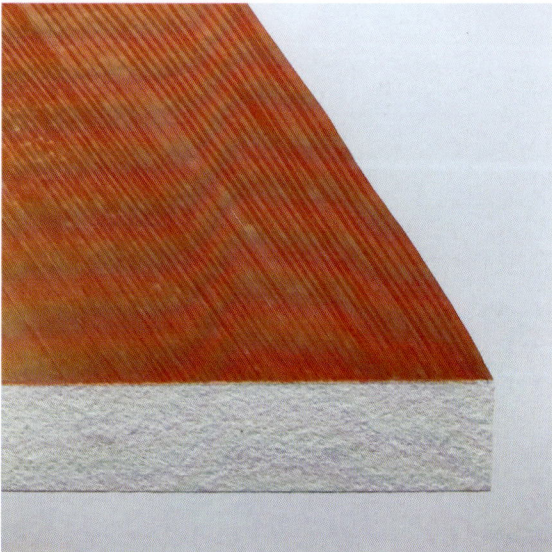

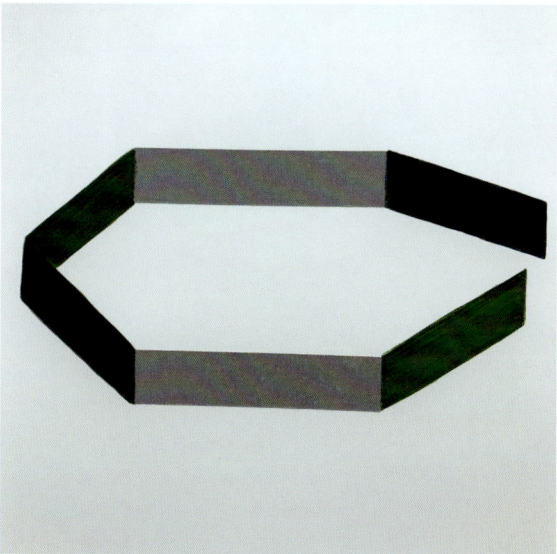
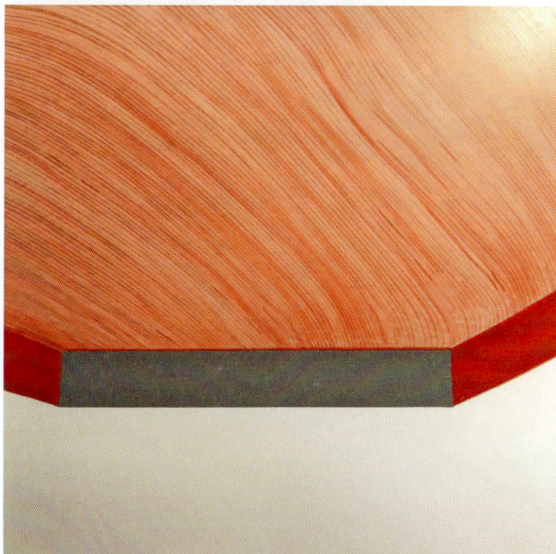

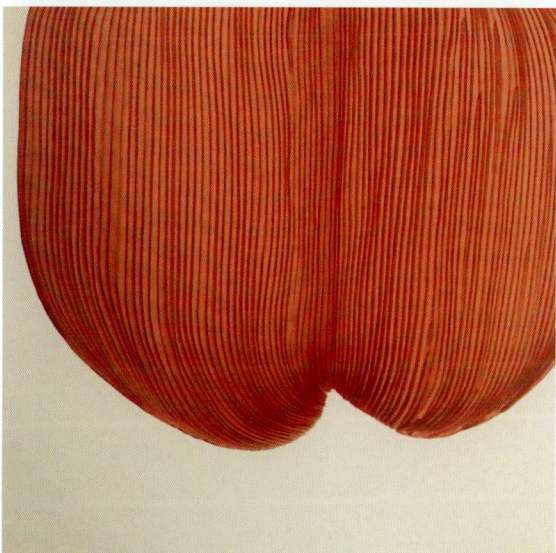

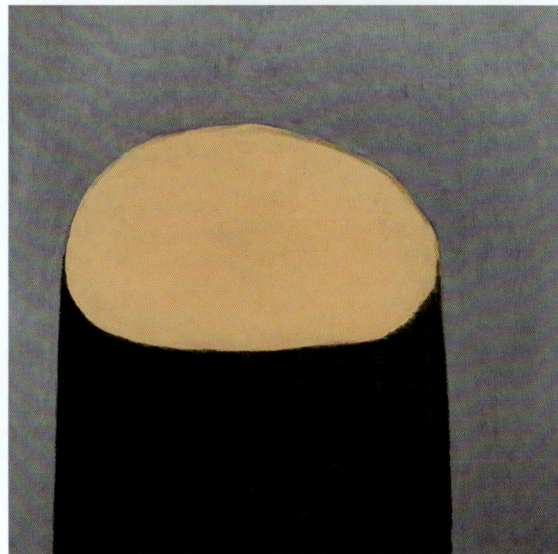

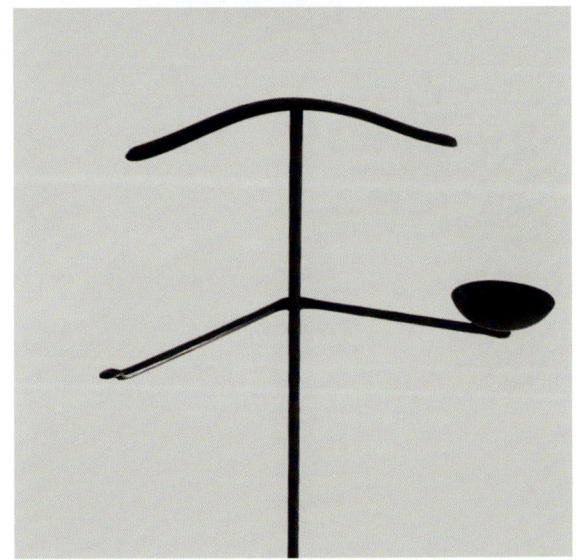

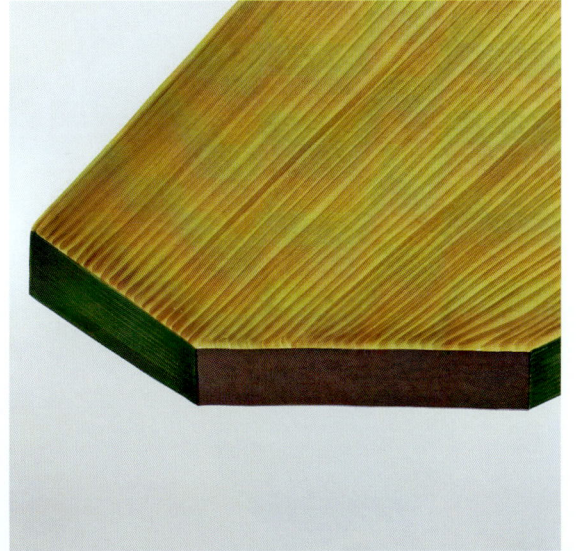
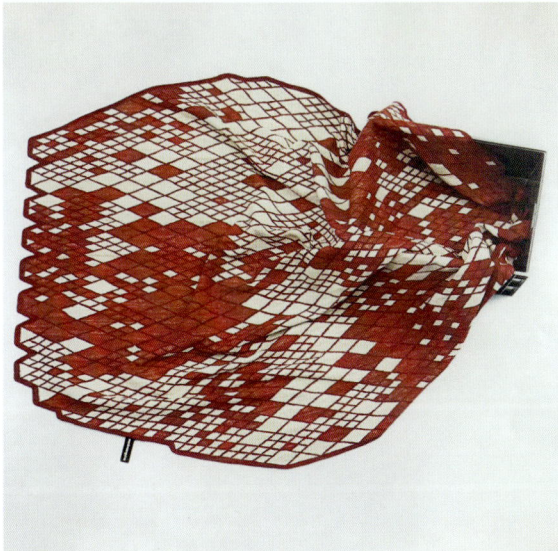

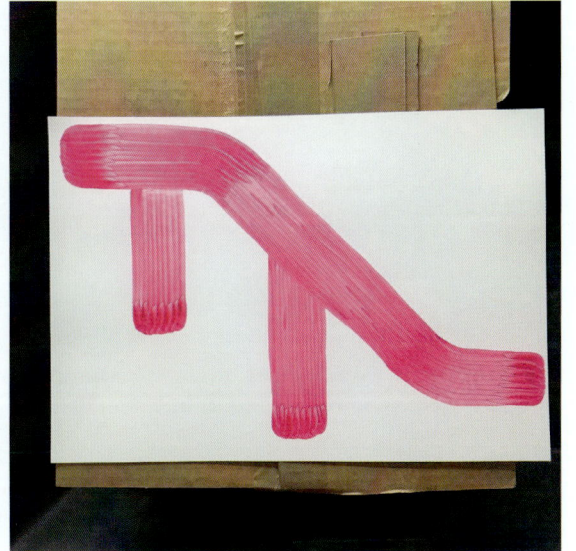

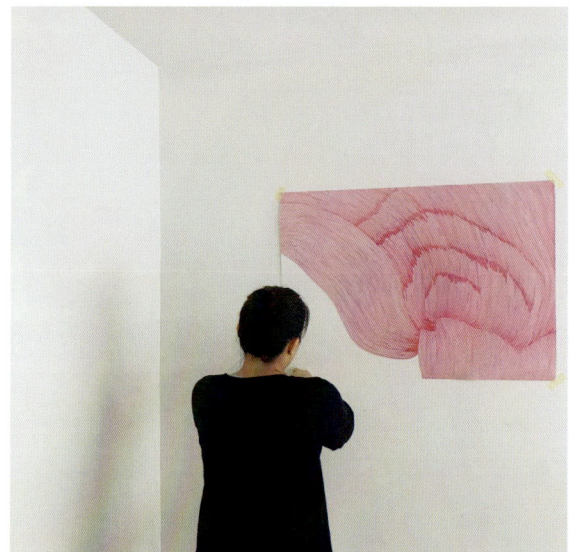

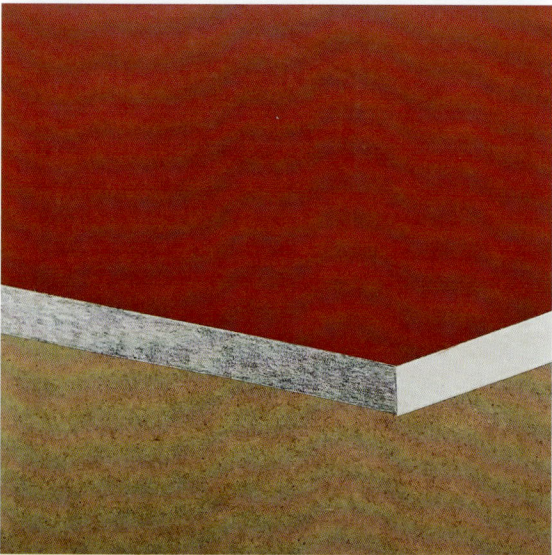
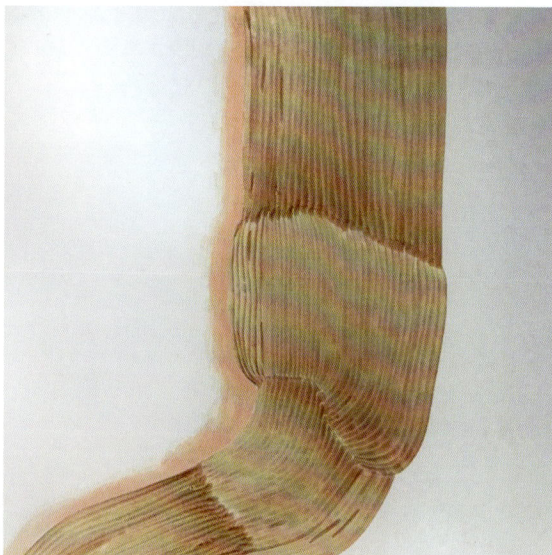

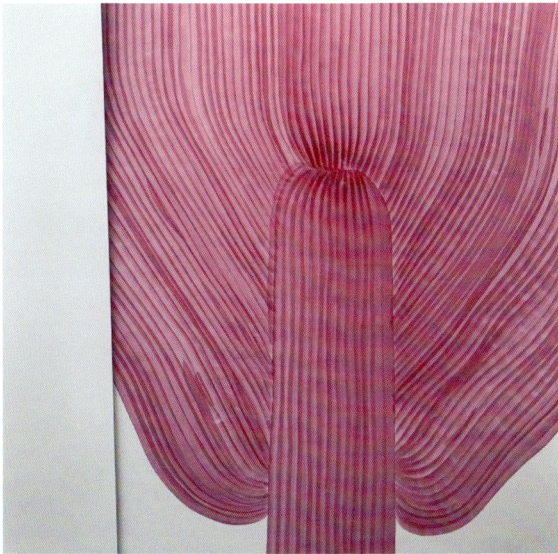

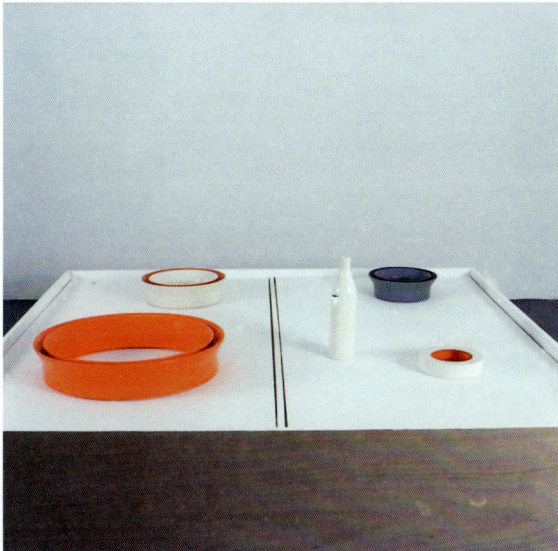

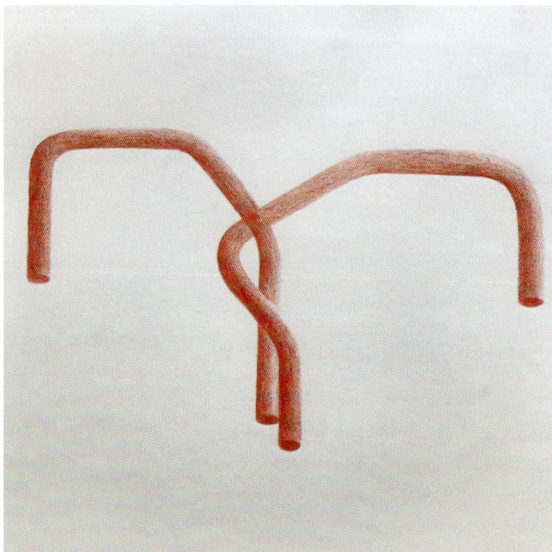

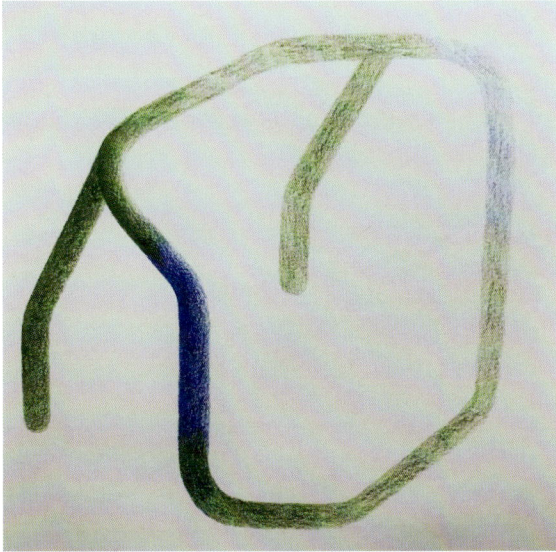
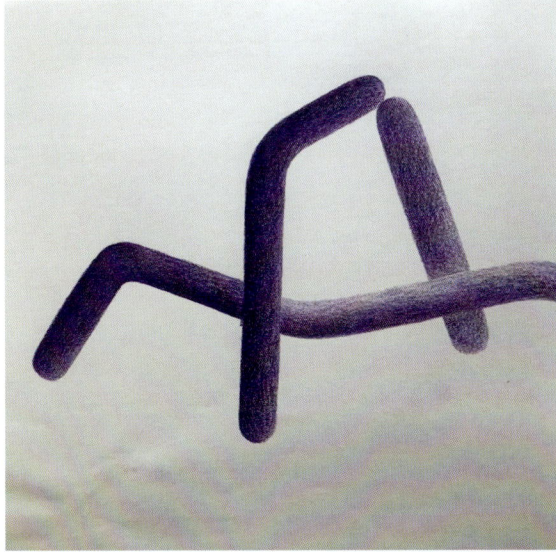
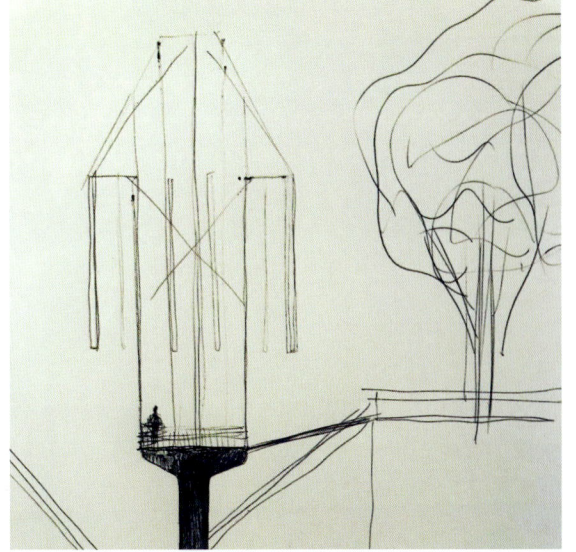

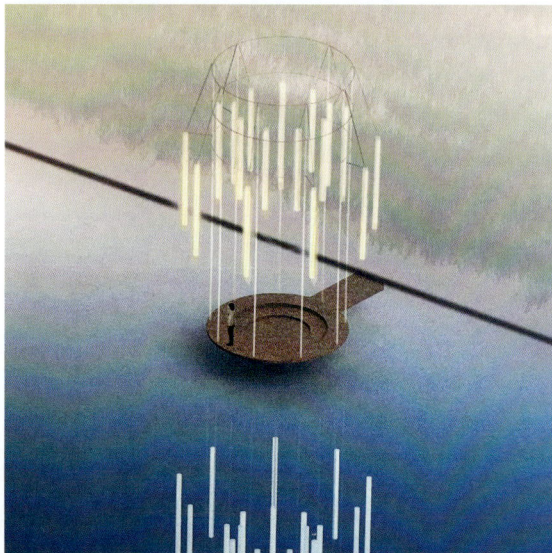

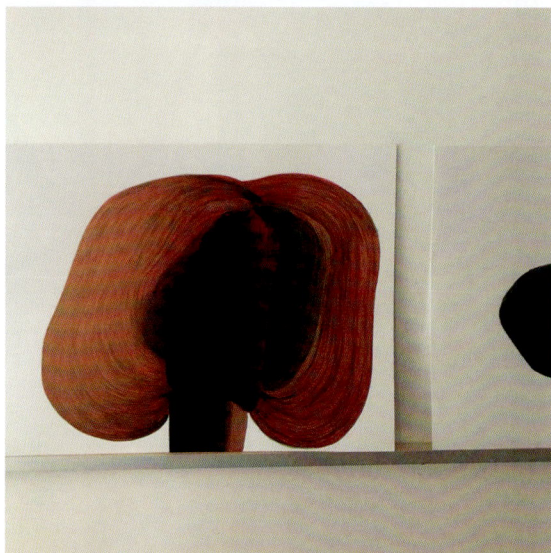

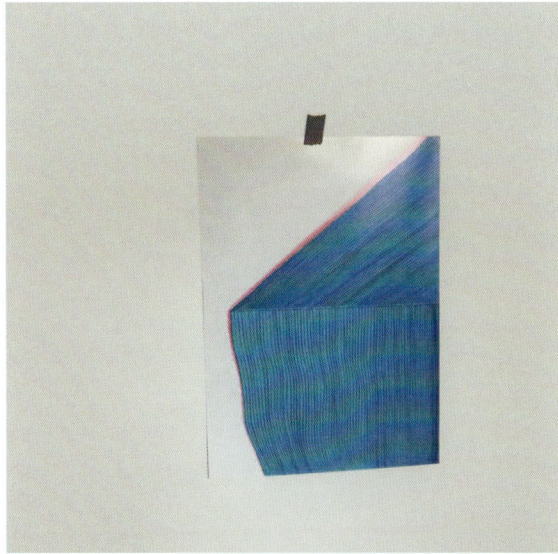

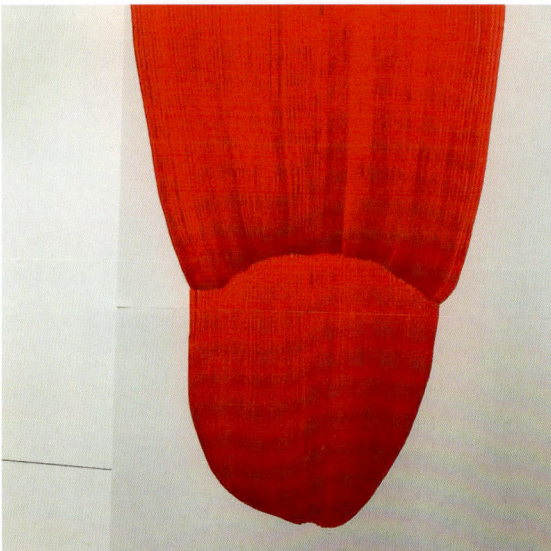

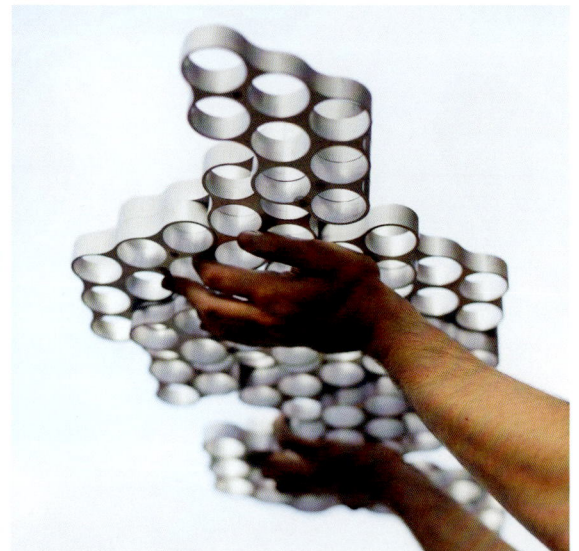
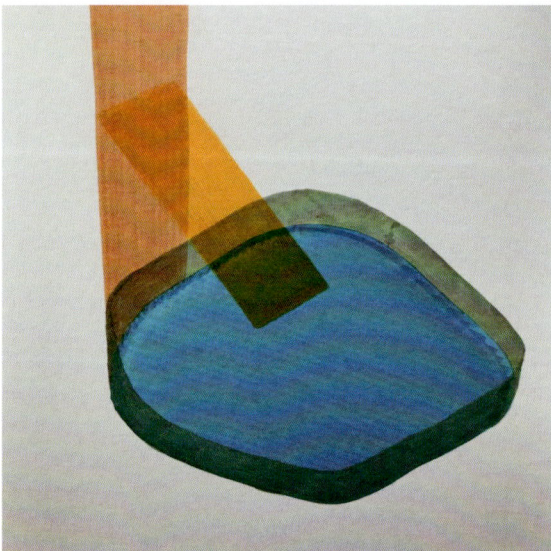

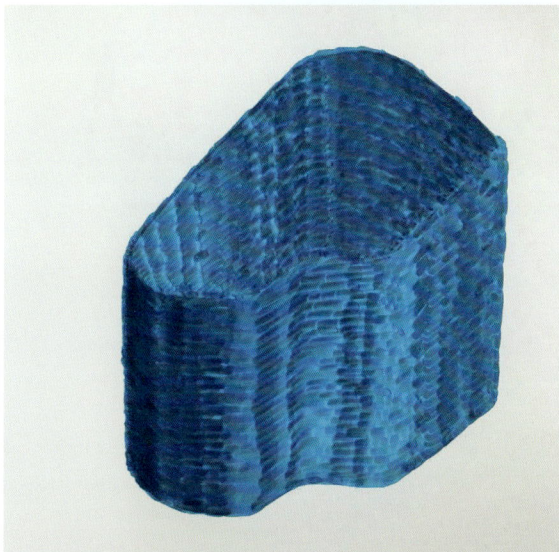

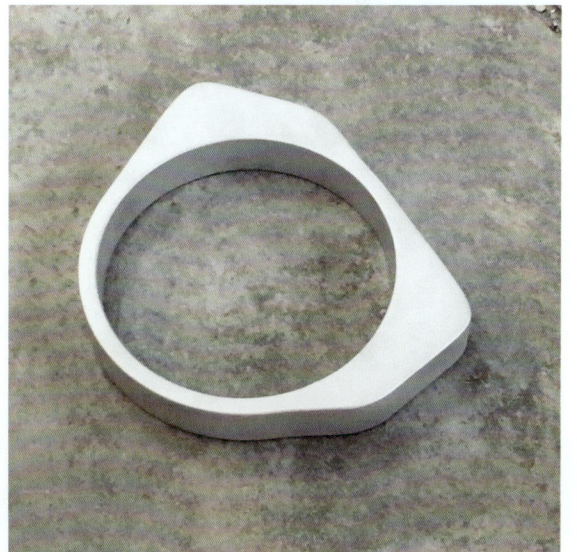

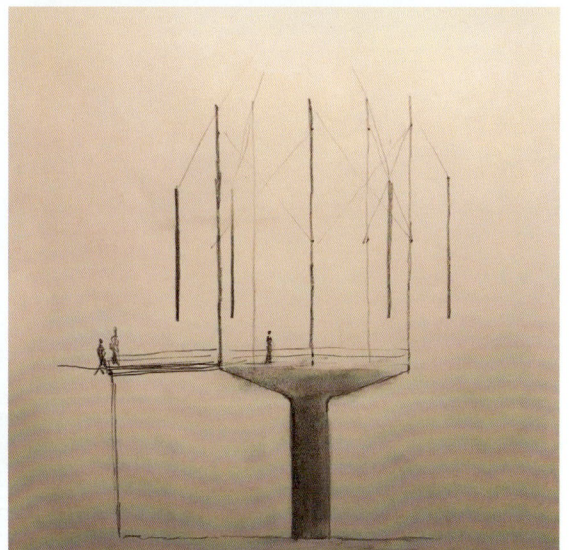

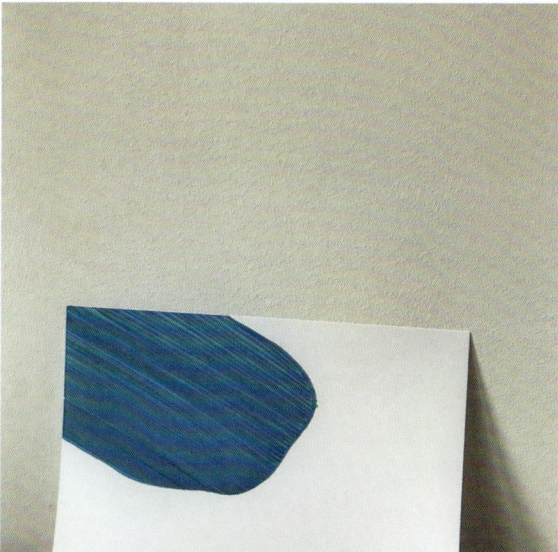

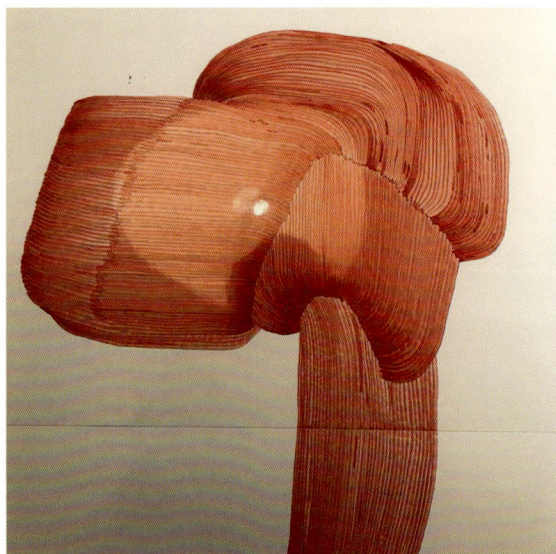

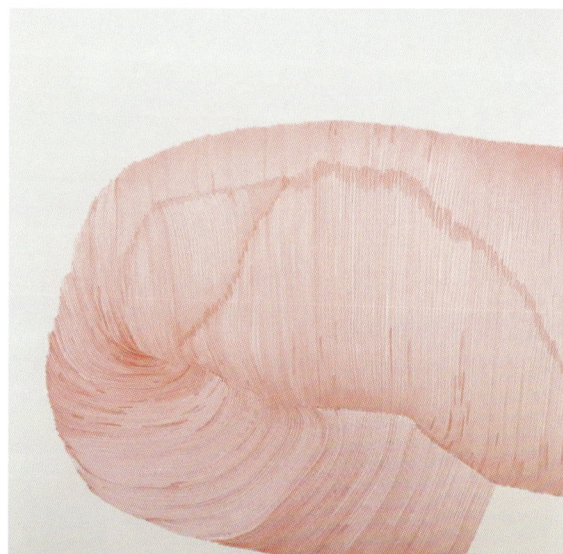

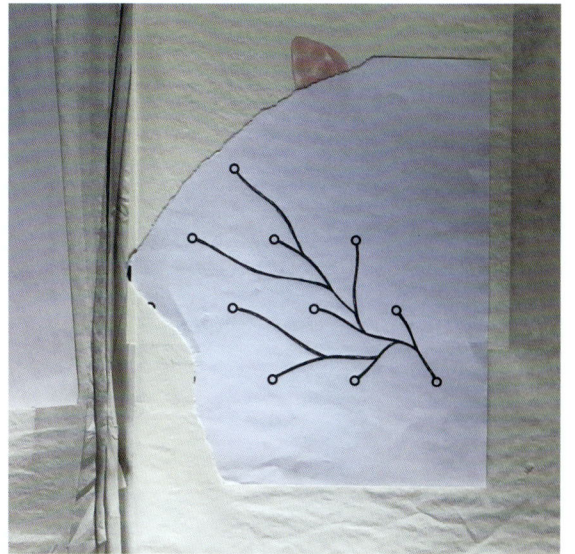
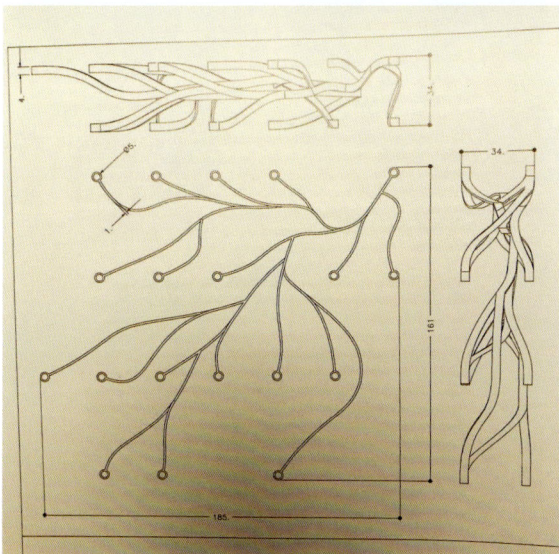
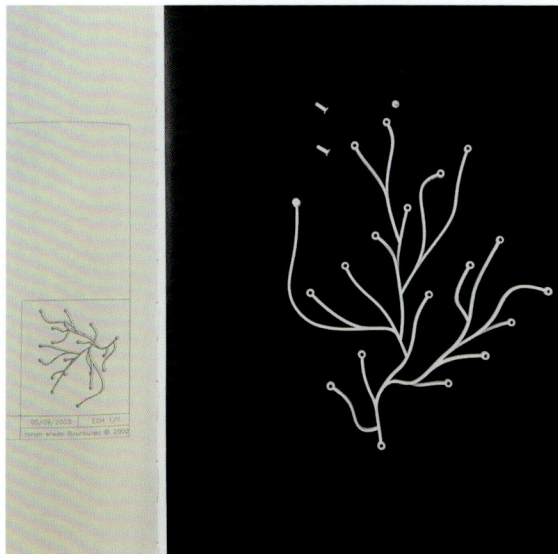

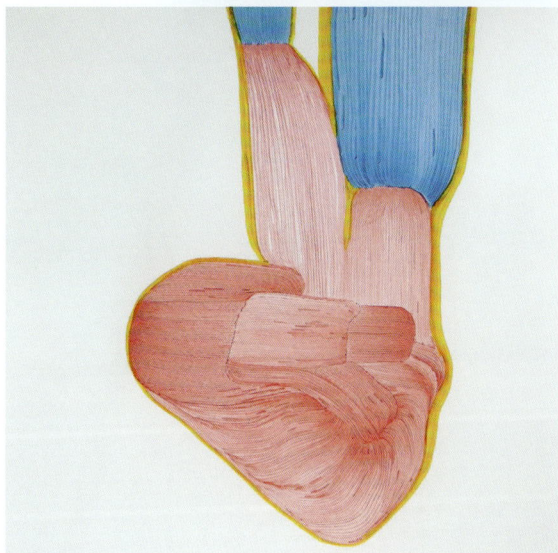
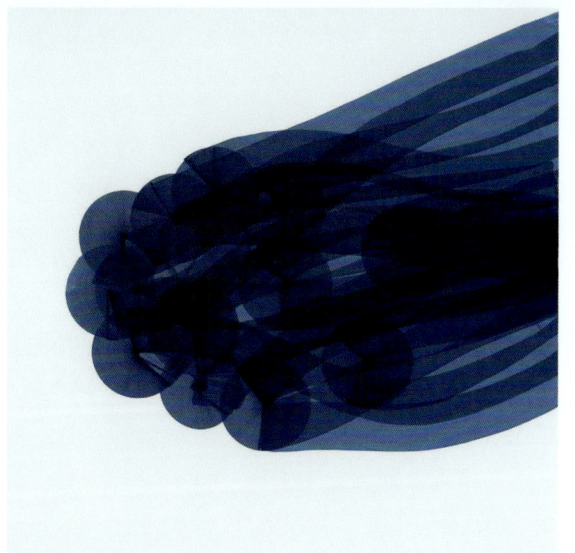

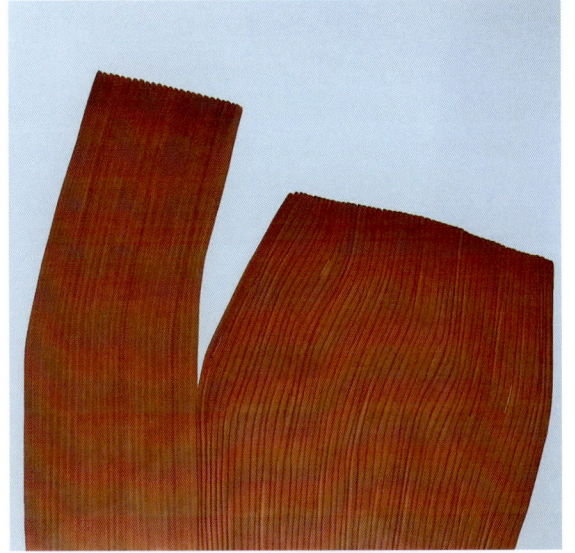
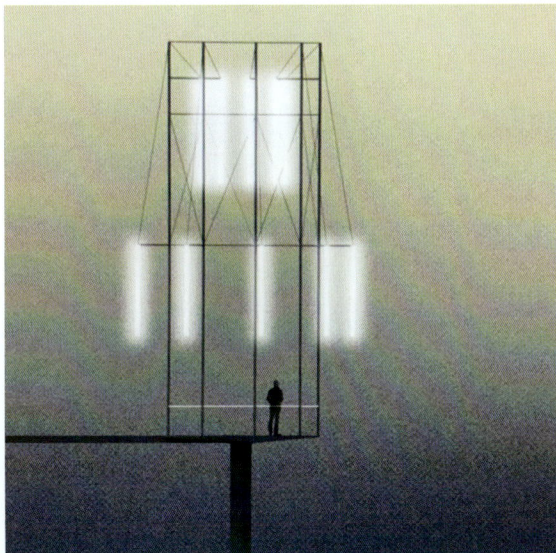

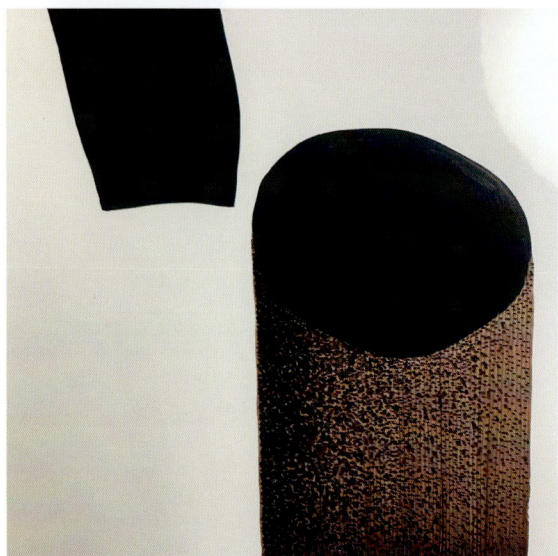
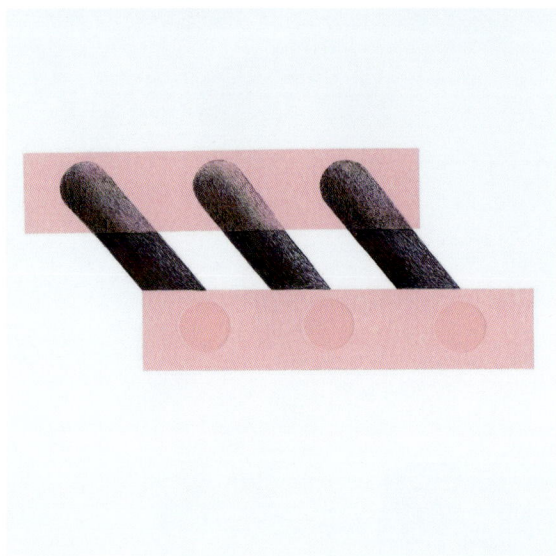

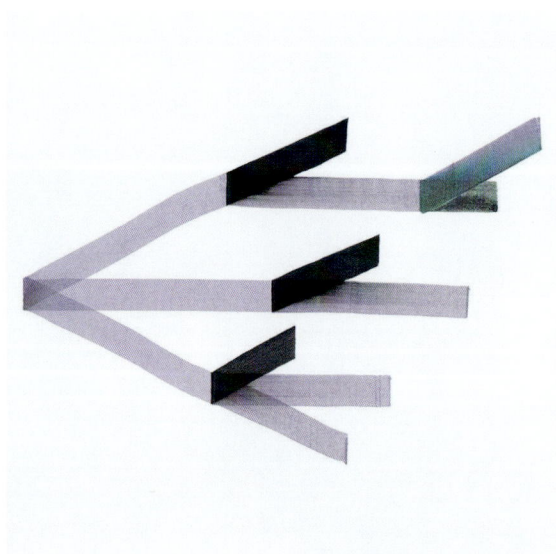

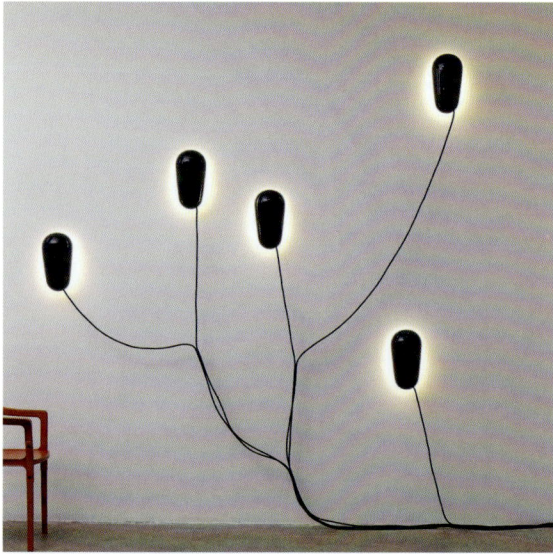

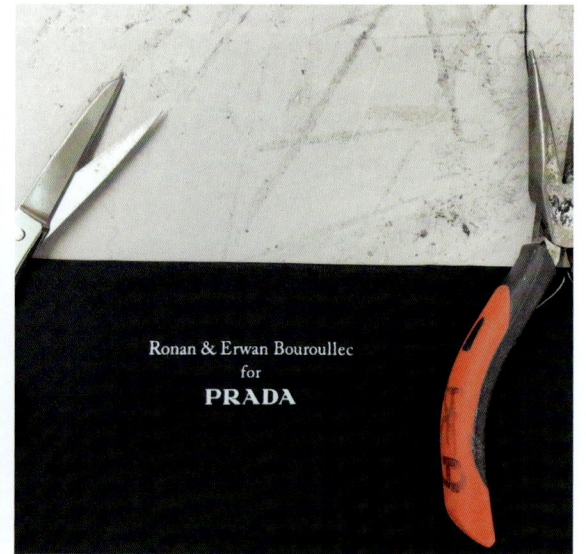

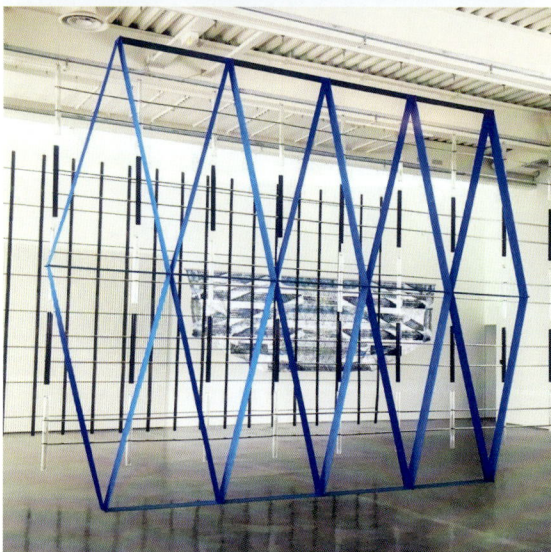

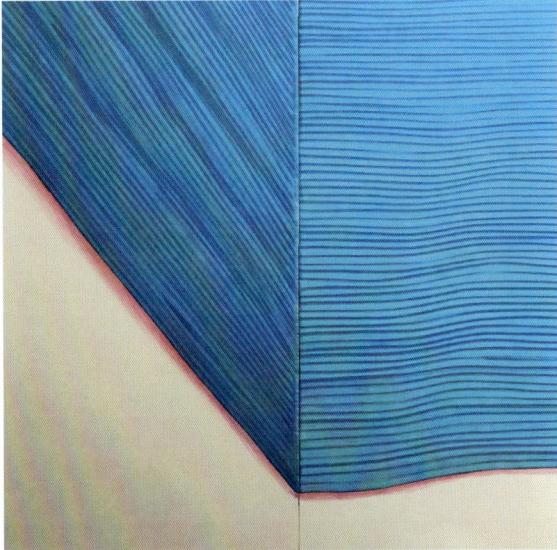
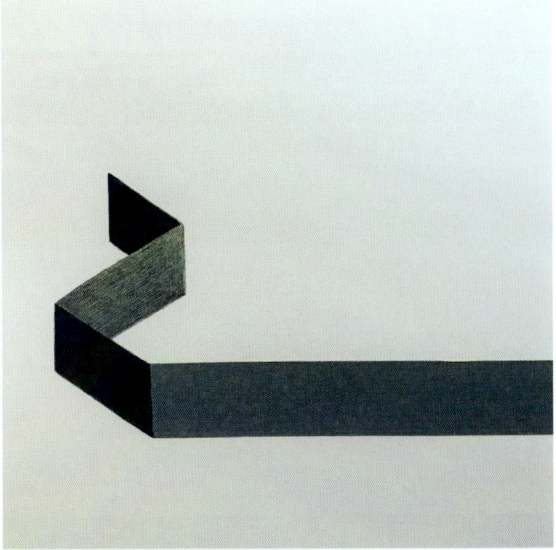

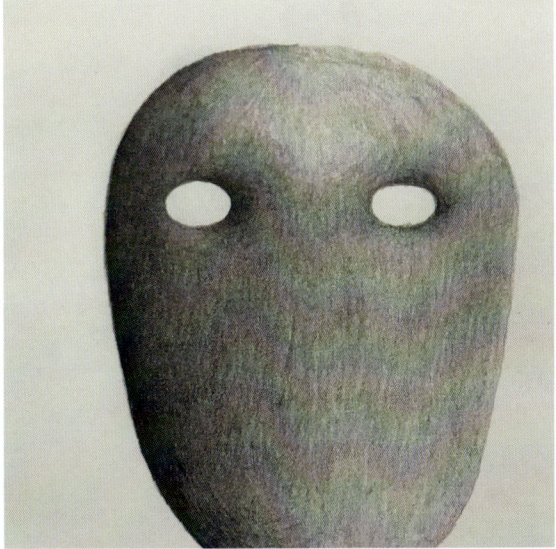

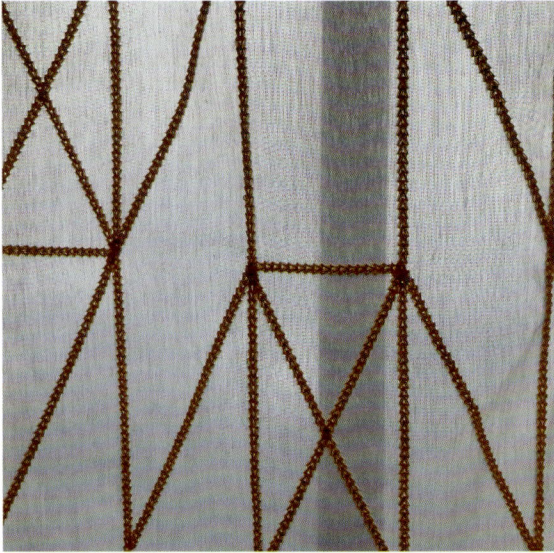

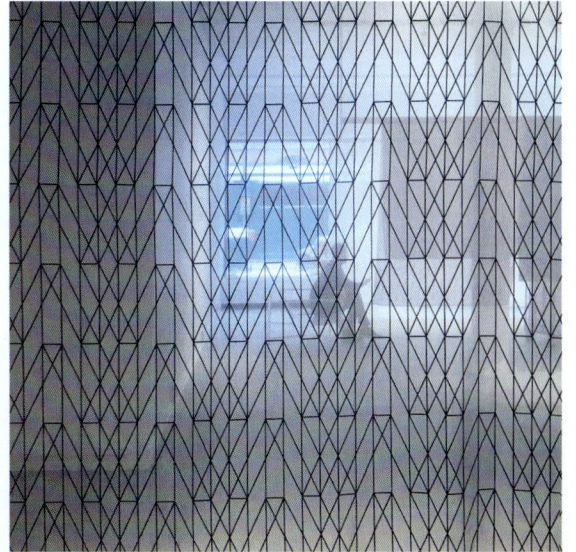

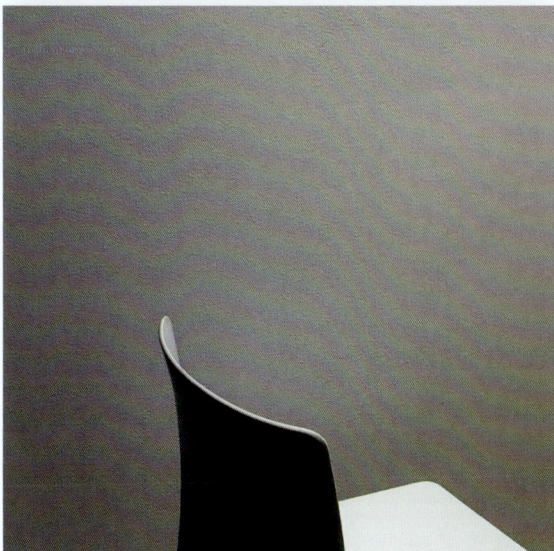
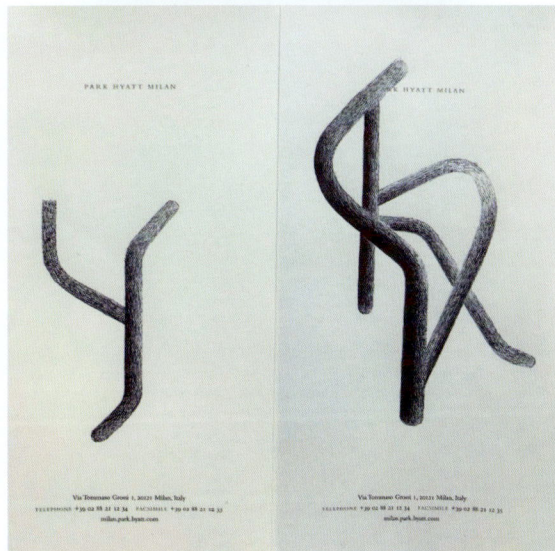
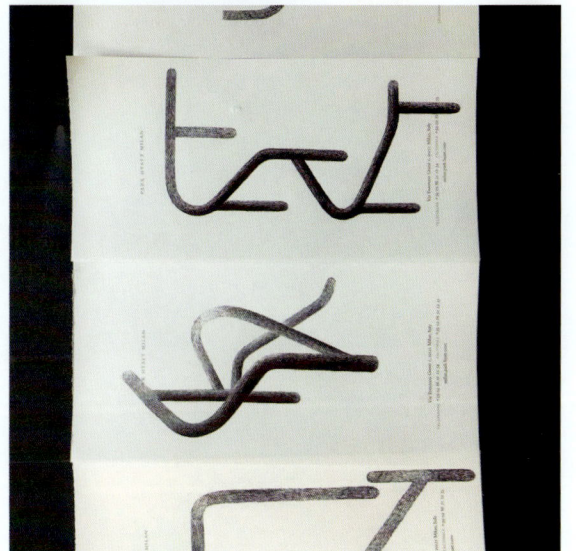

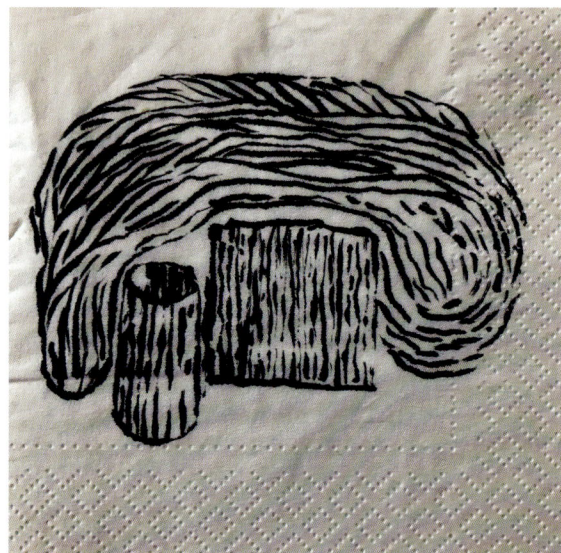

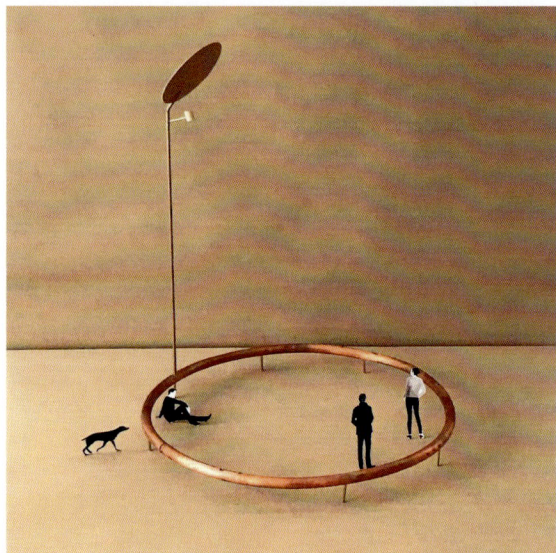

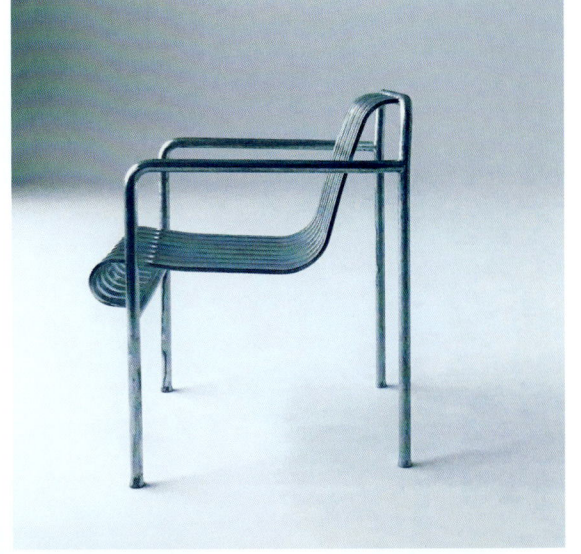

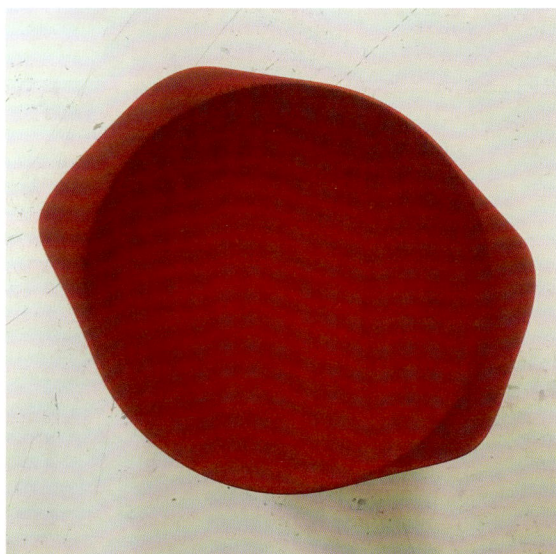
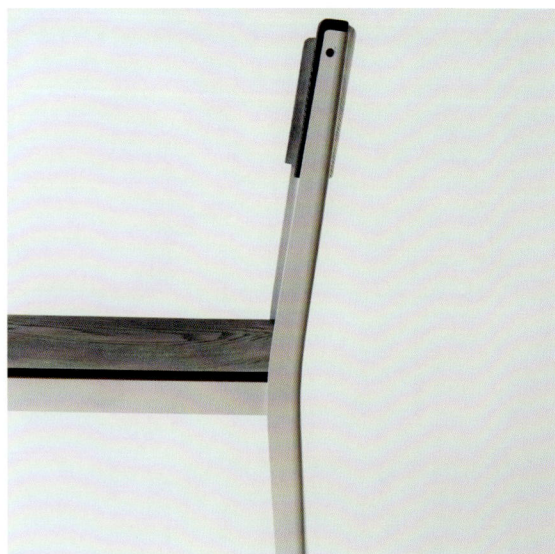
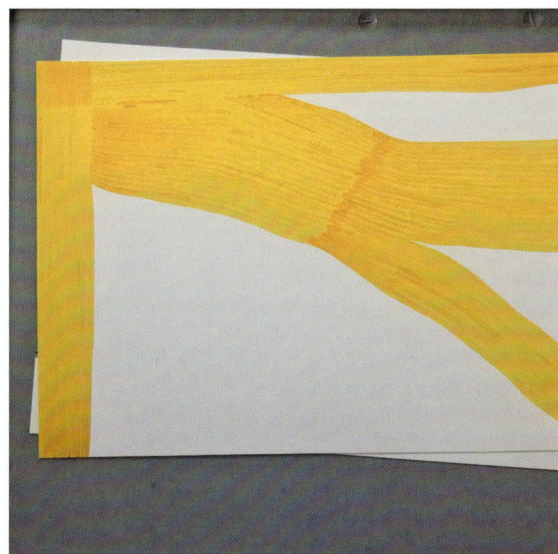
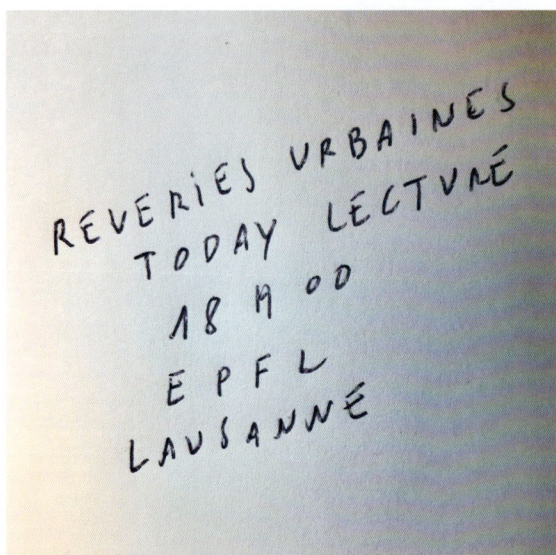

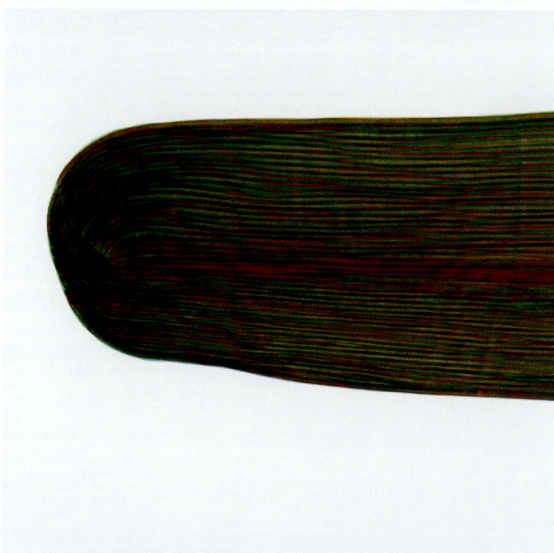
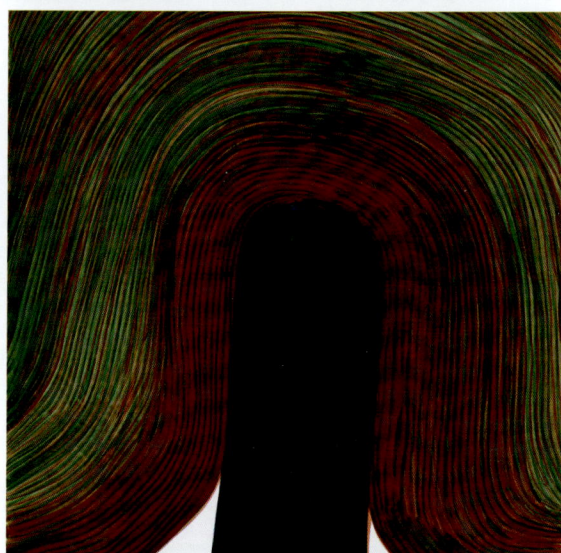

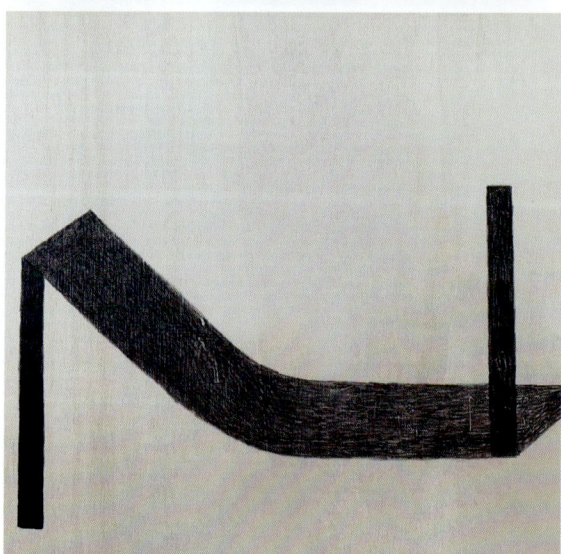

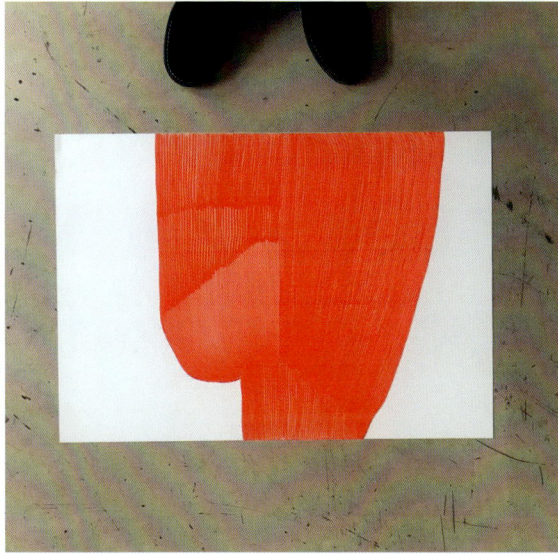
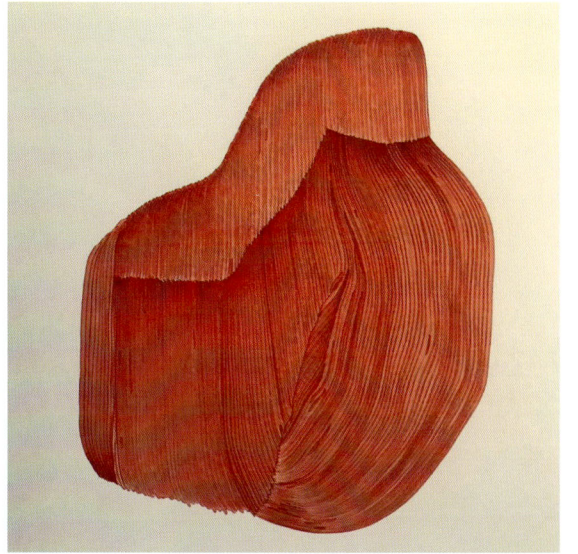

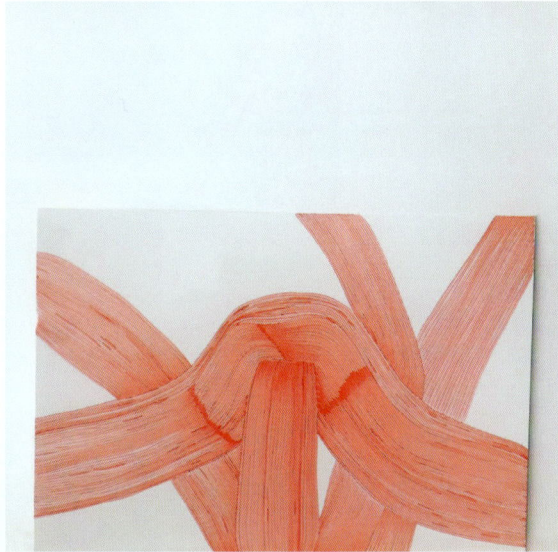

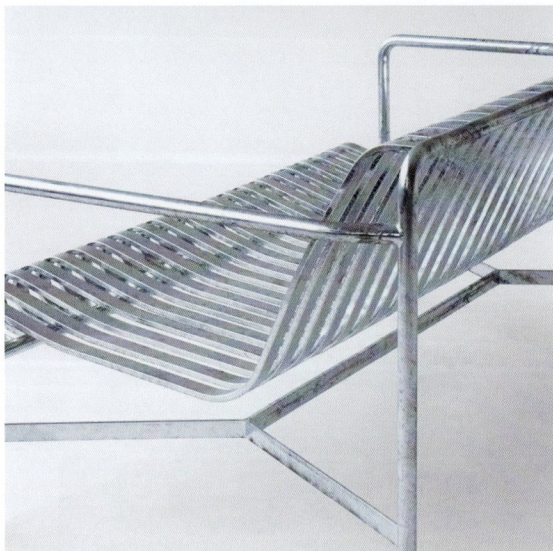

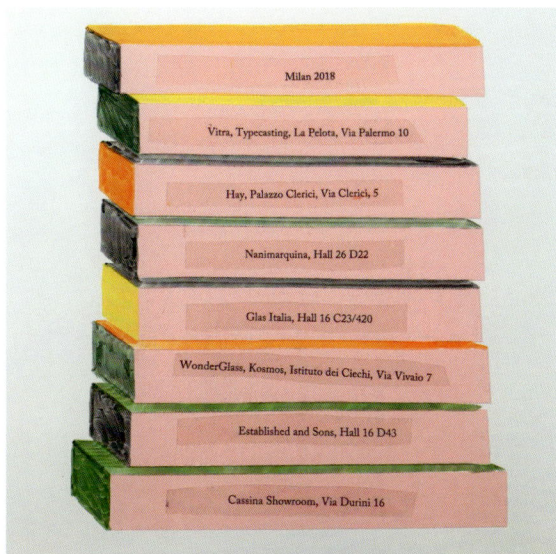

Milan 2018

Vitra, Typecasting, La Pelota, Via Palermo 10

Hay, Palazzo Clerici, Via Clerici, 5

Nanimarquina, Hall 26 D22

Glas Italia, Hall 16 C23/420

WonderGlass, Kosmos, Istituto dei Ciechi, Via Vivaio 7

Established and Sons, Hall 16 D43

Cassina Showroom, Via Durini 16

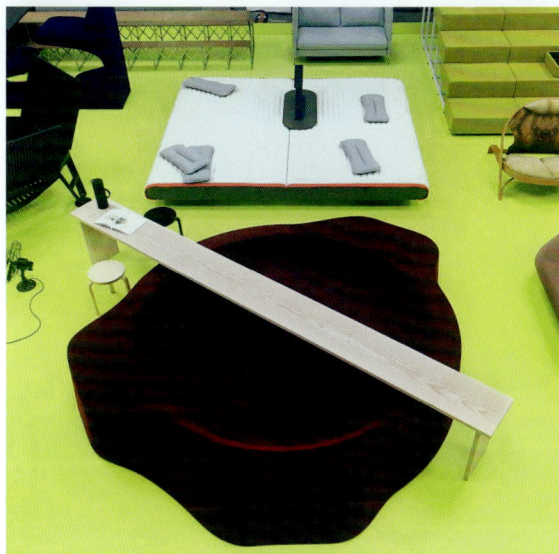

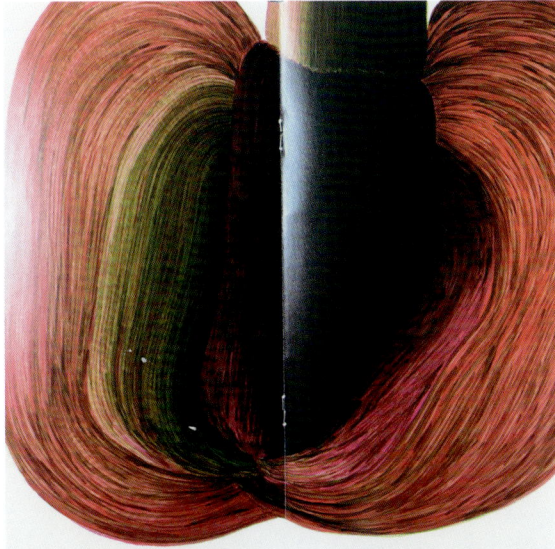

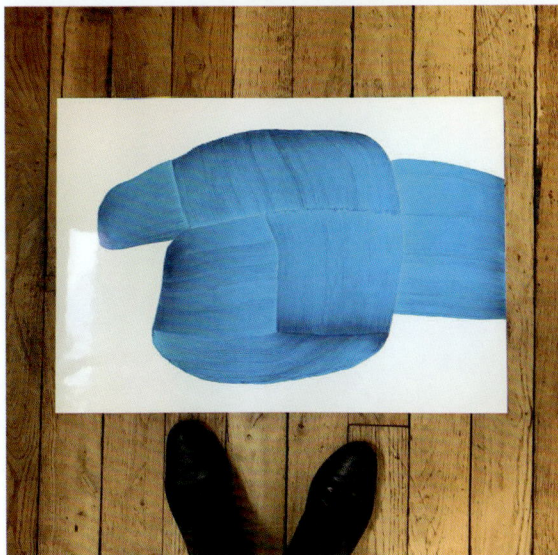

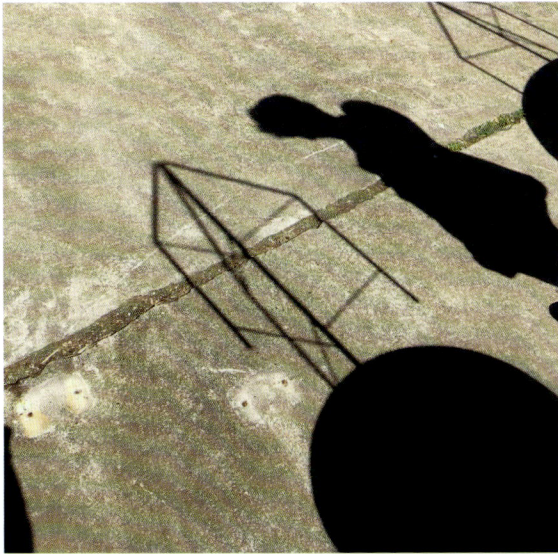

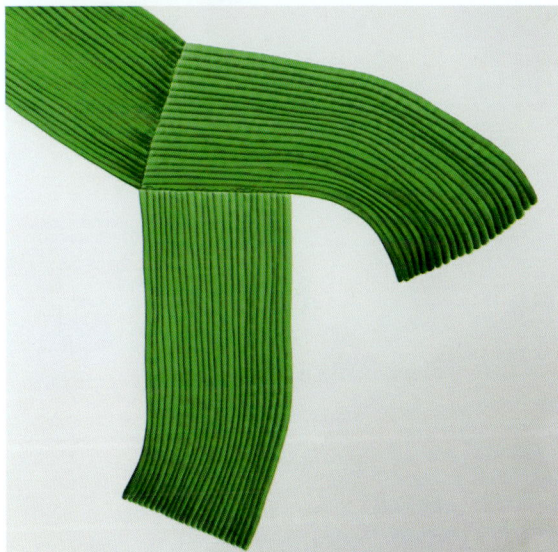

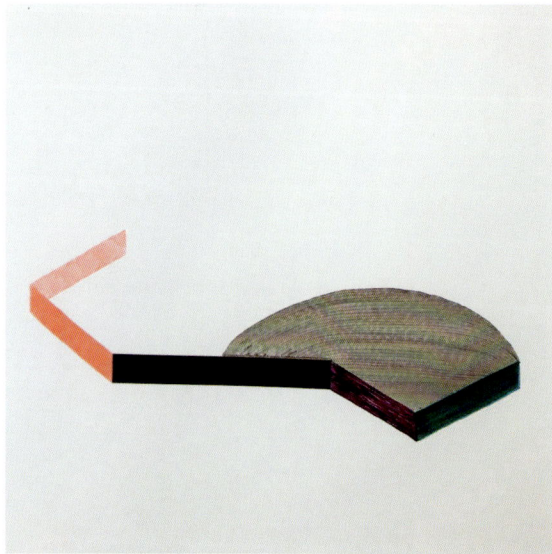

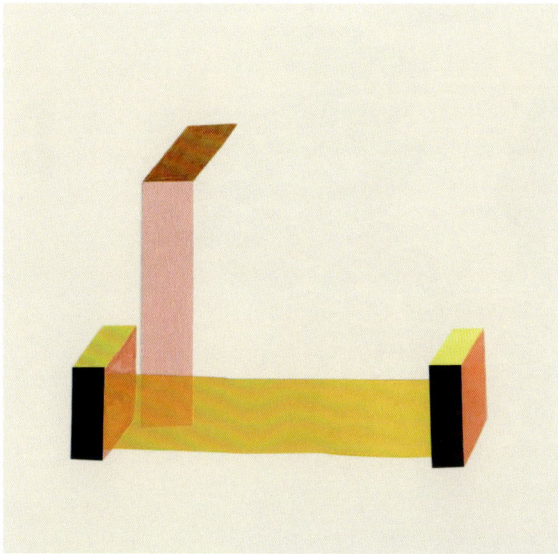
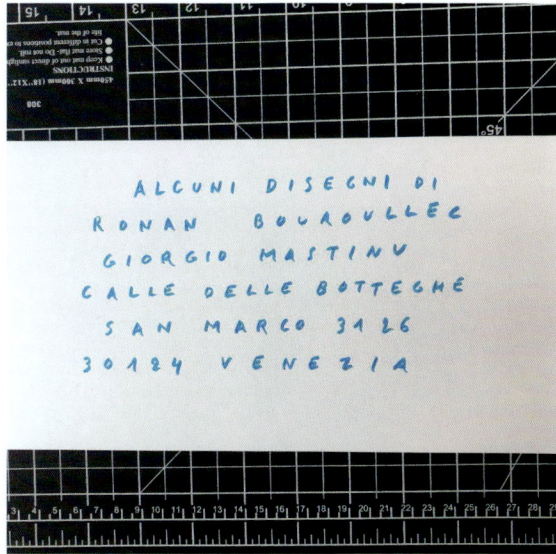

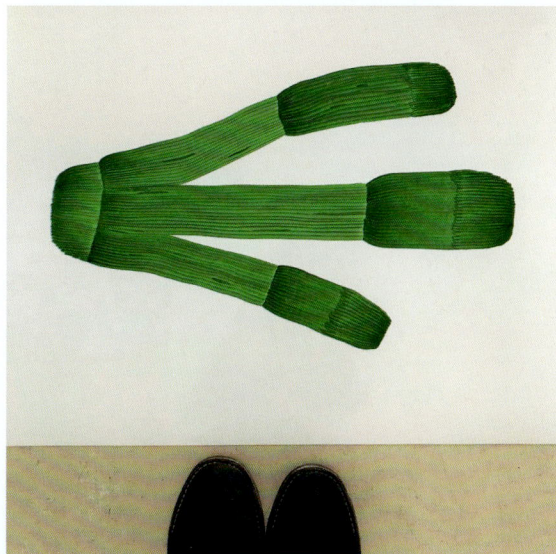
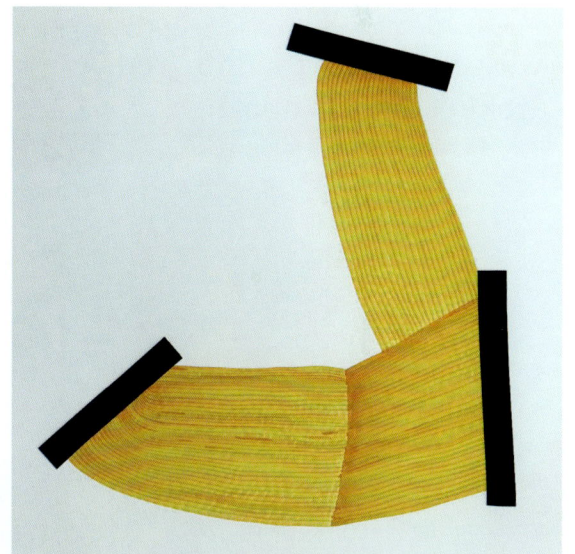

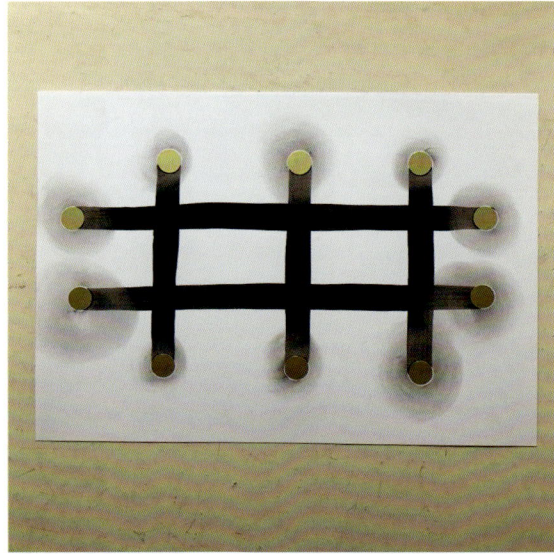

ART FAIR INSIDER

Must-See Art at the 16th Venice Architecture Biennale

BY SOTHEBY'S | 24 MAY 2018

Alongside a myriad of thought-provoking pavilions at the 16th Venice Architecture Biennale, a notable lineup of art exhibitions will also debut.

Ronan & Erwan Bouroullec   *Objets Dessins Maquettes*

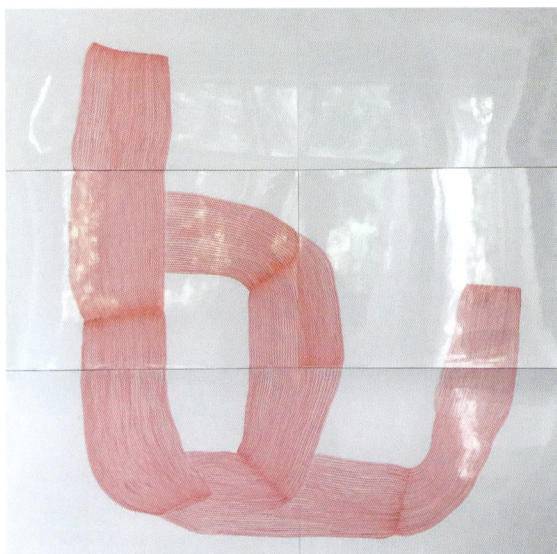

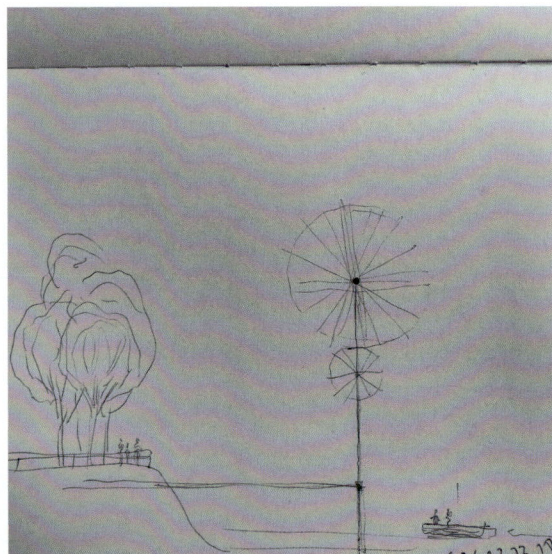
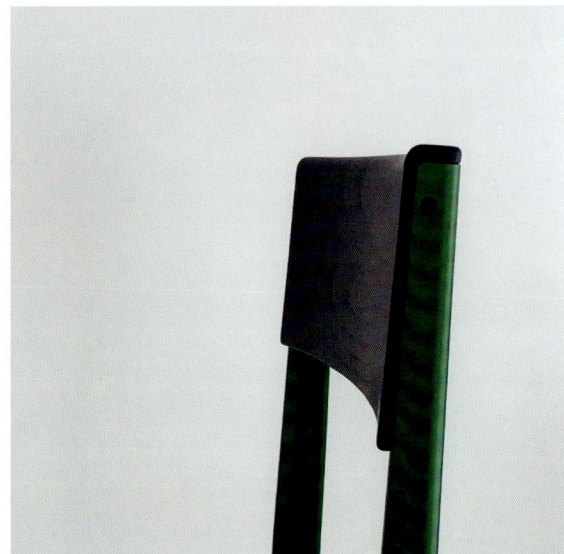

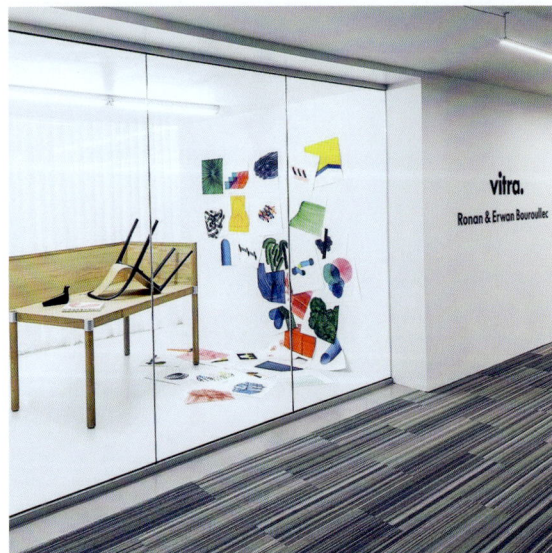

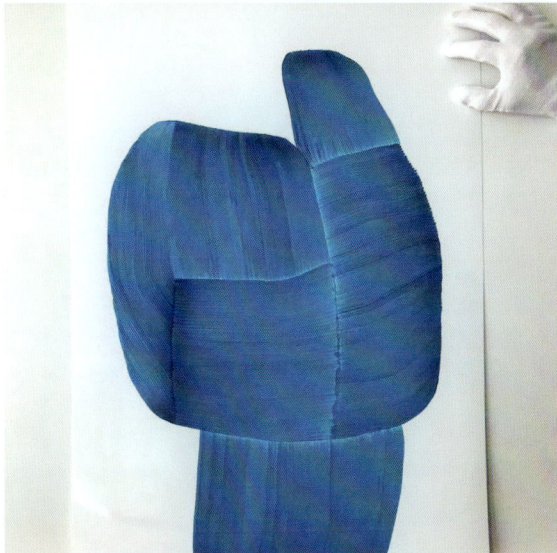

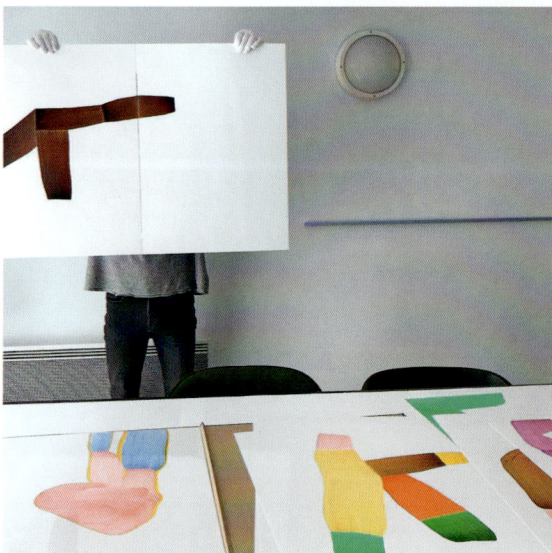

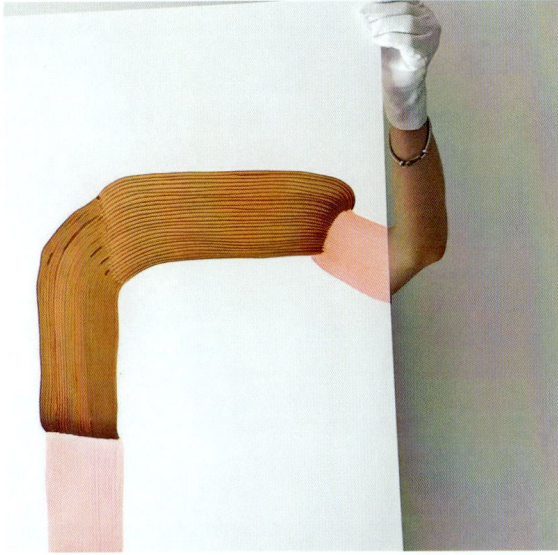

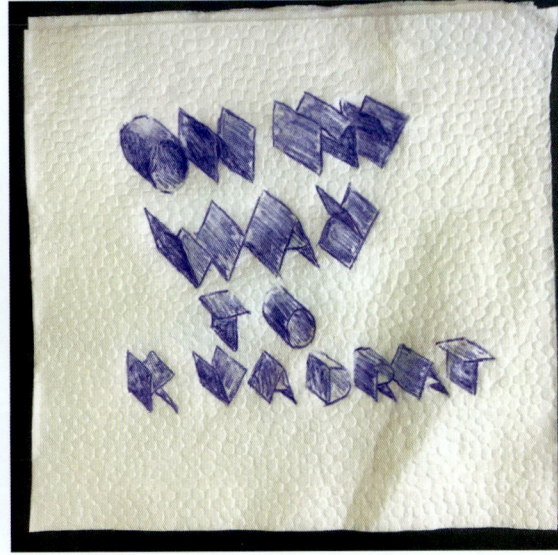

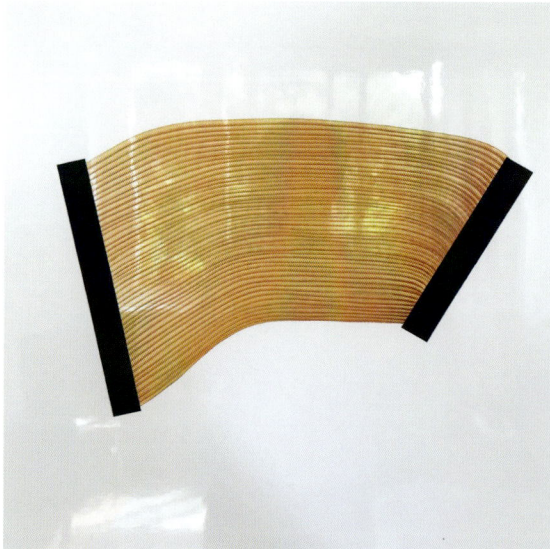

Design   : Chaînette
Designer   : Ronan & Erwan Bouroullec
Composition   : 100% Polyester FR
Width   : 290 cm (Embroidery : 274 cm)
Type   : CUR

Noon 102 / V-107

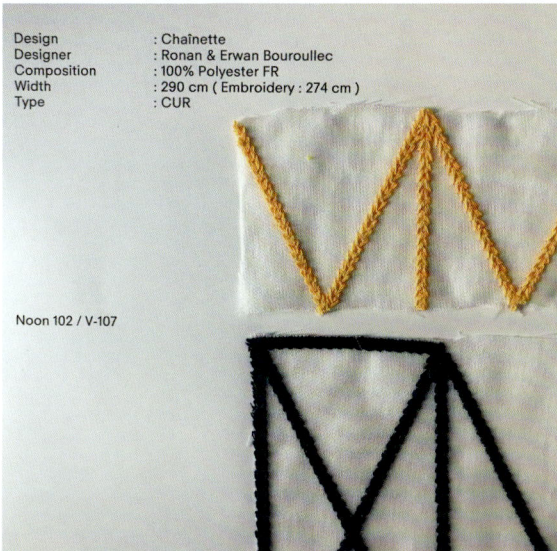

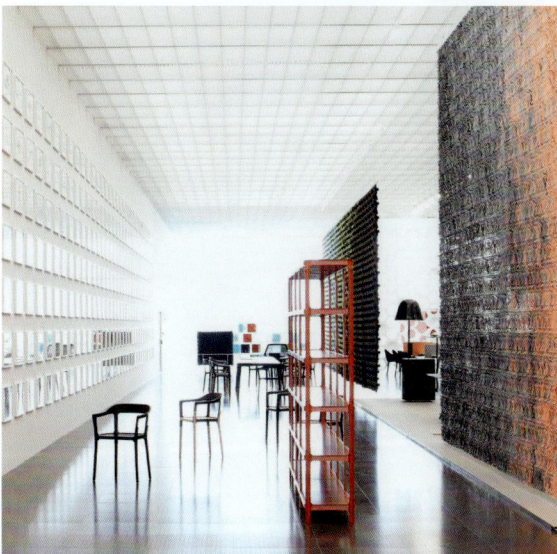

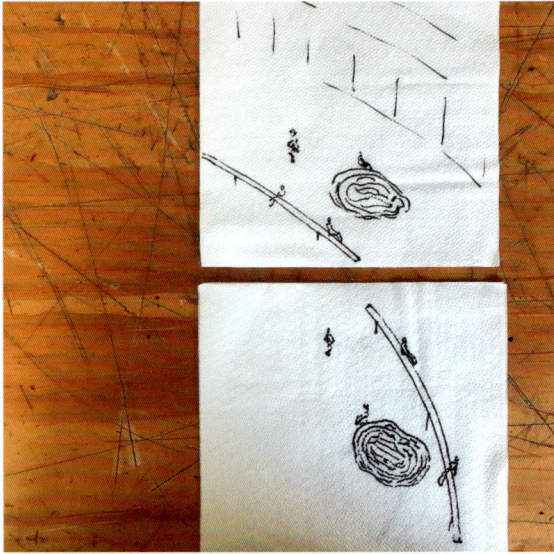

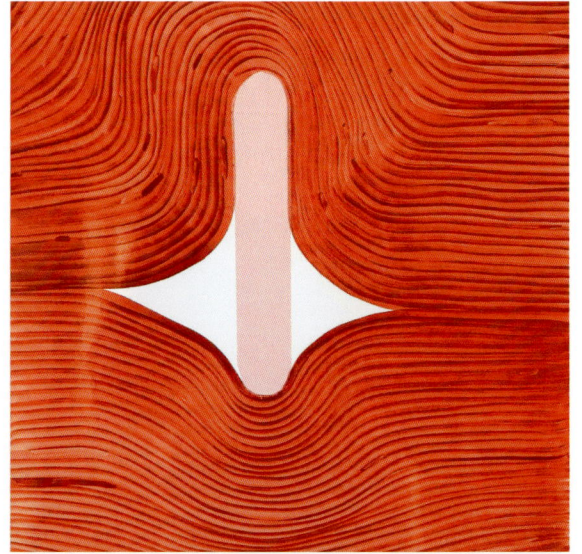

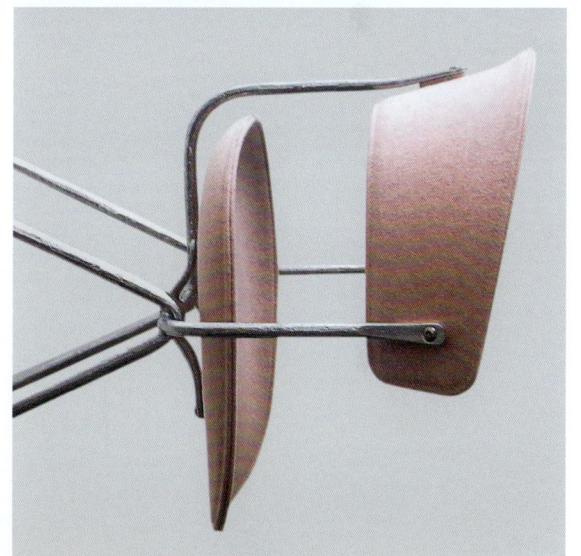

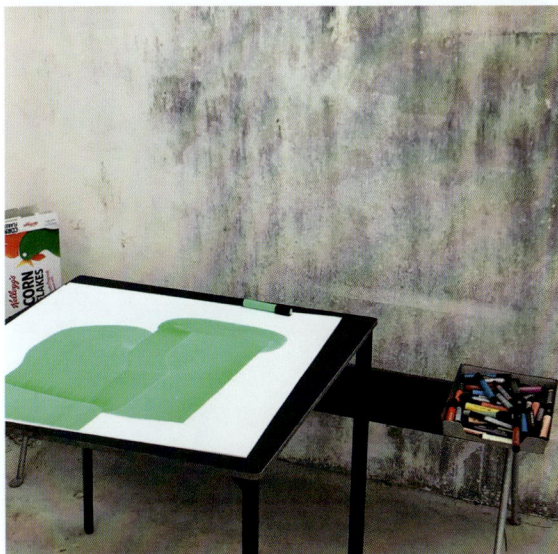

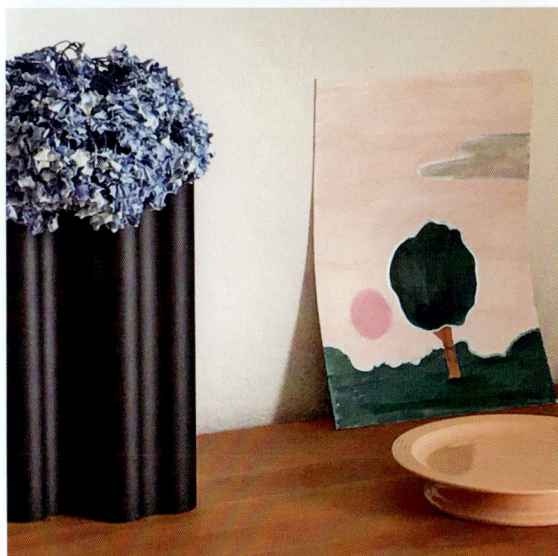

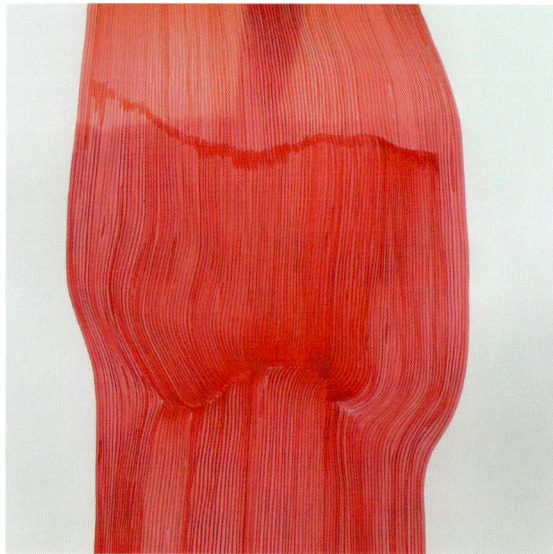

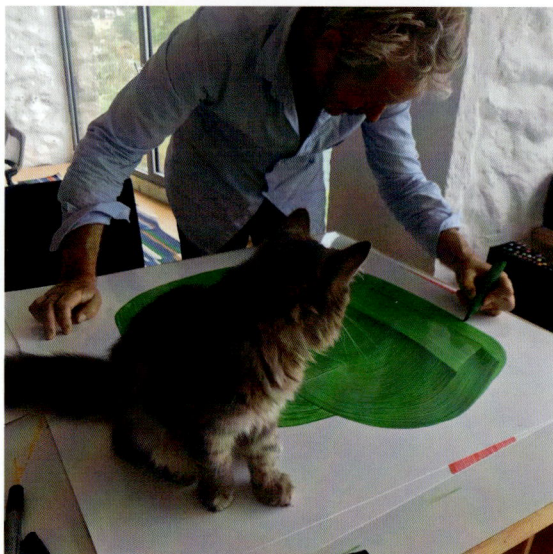

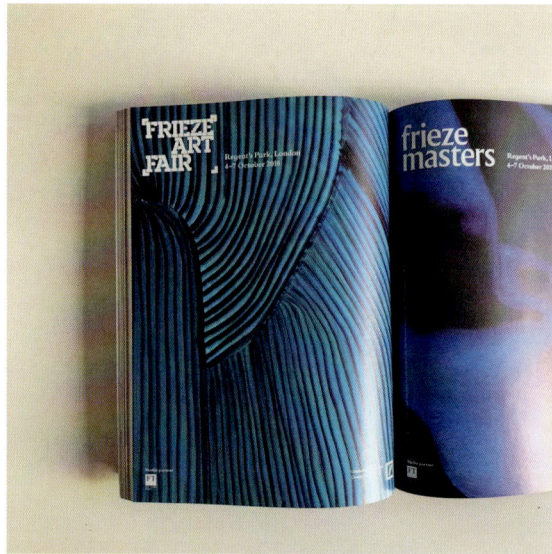
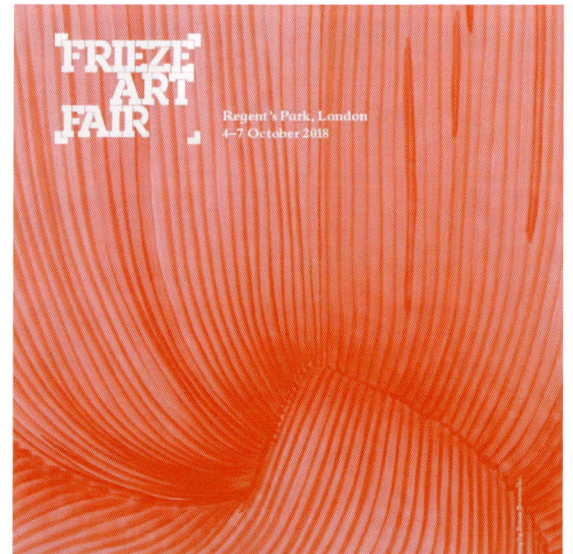

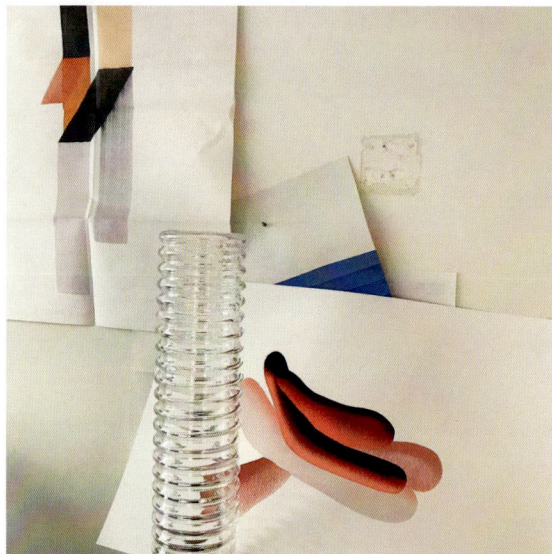
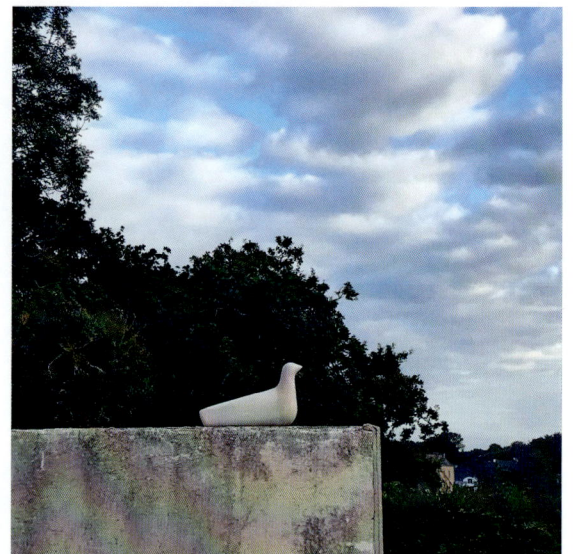

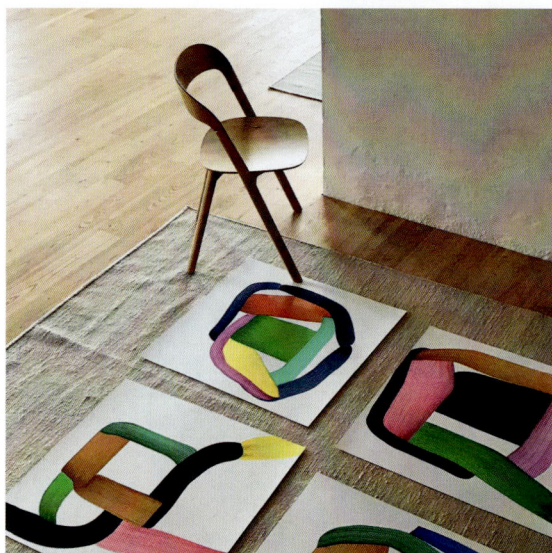

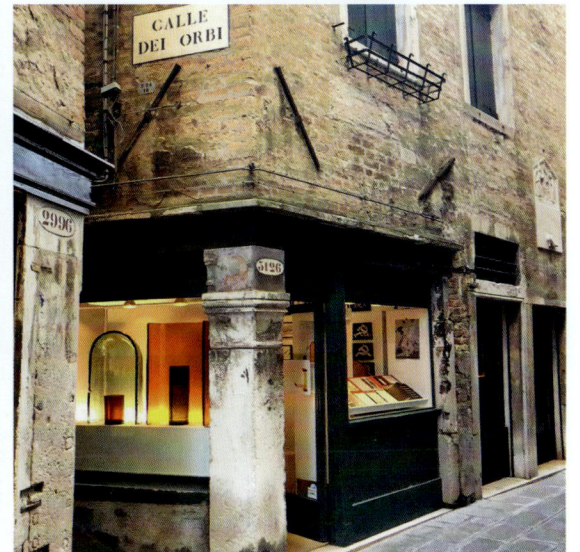

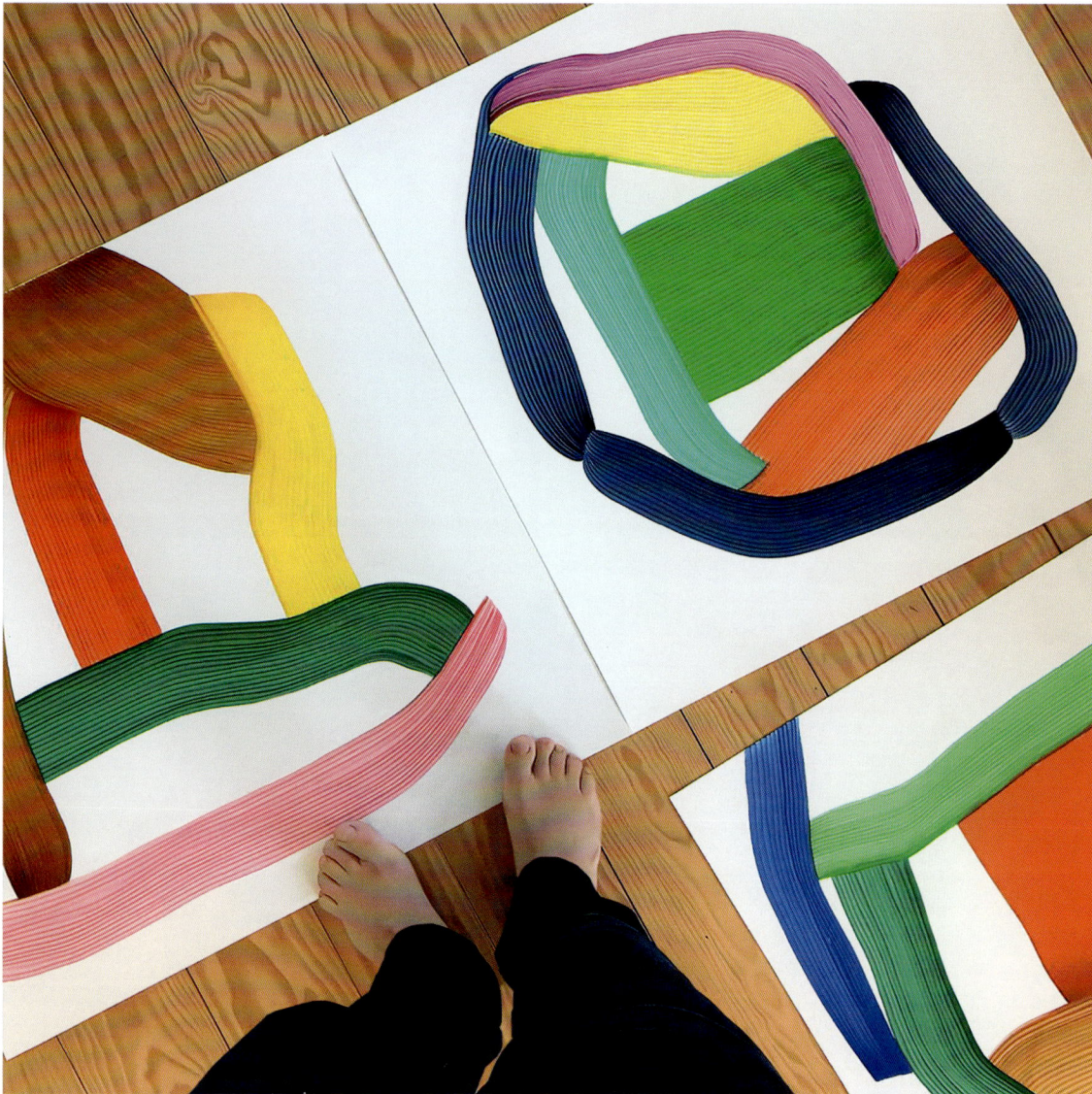

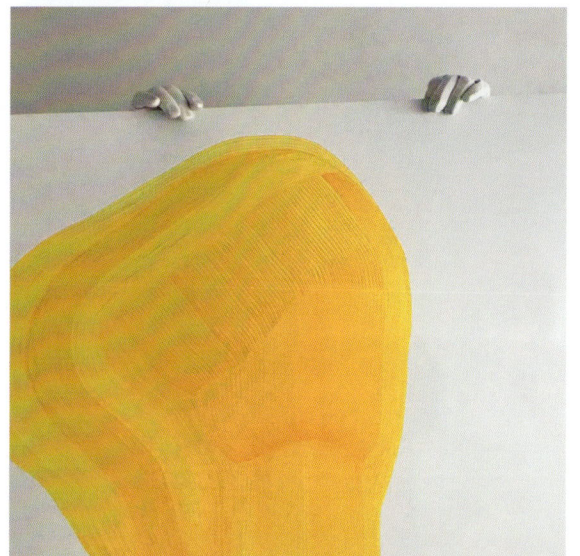
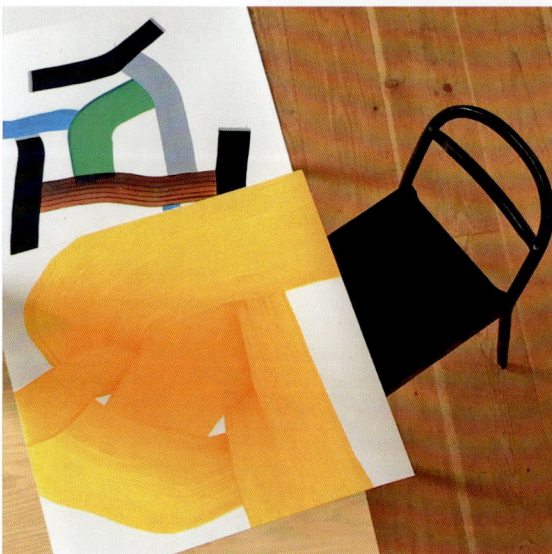
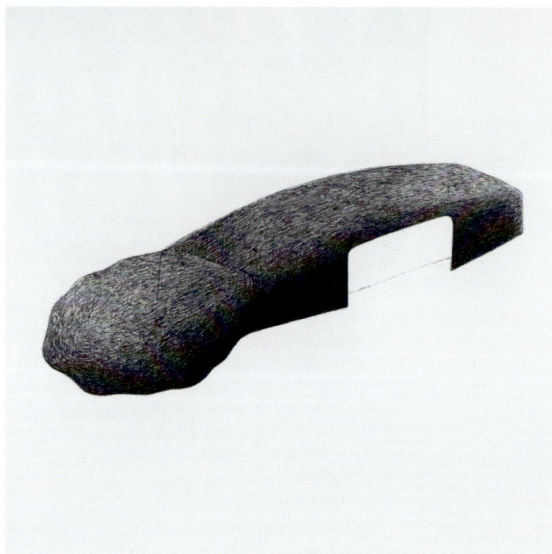

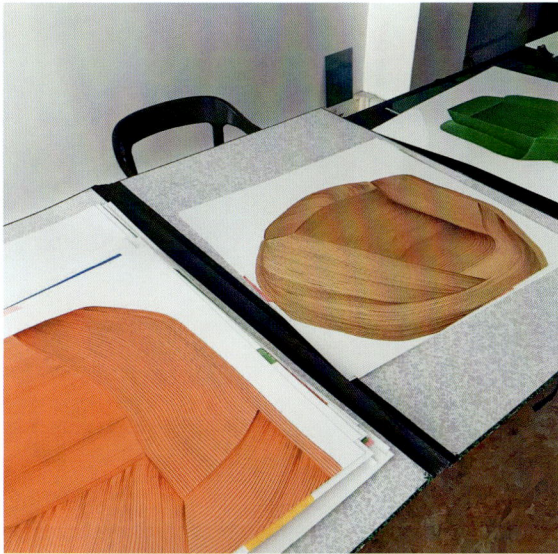
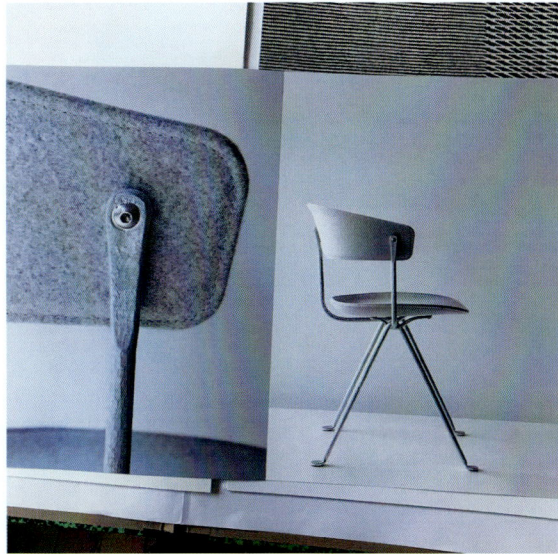

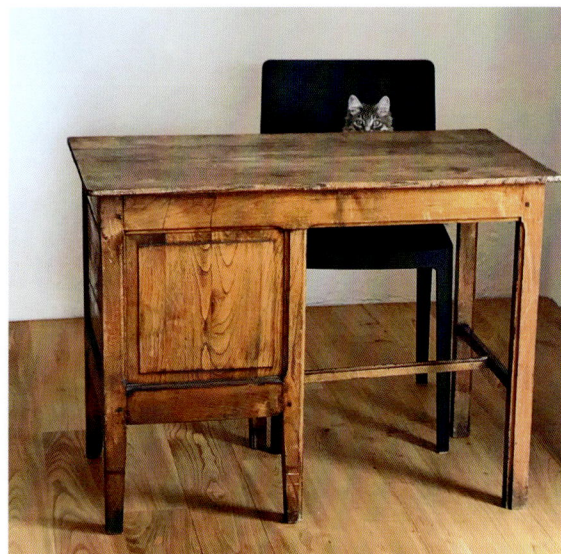

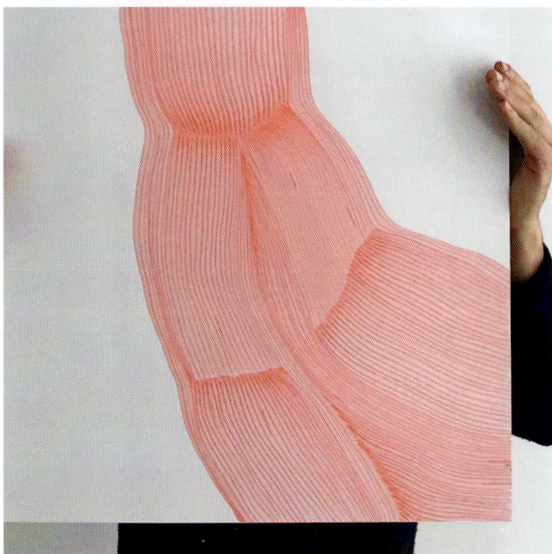
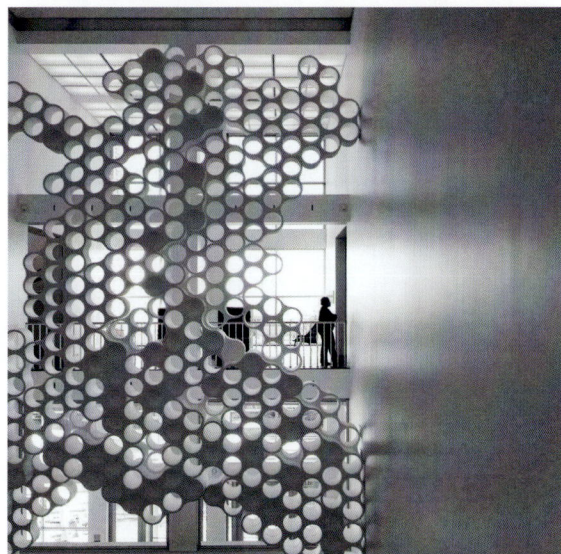

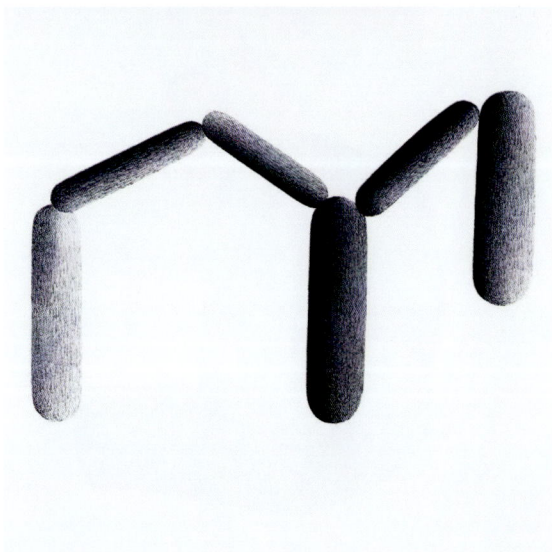

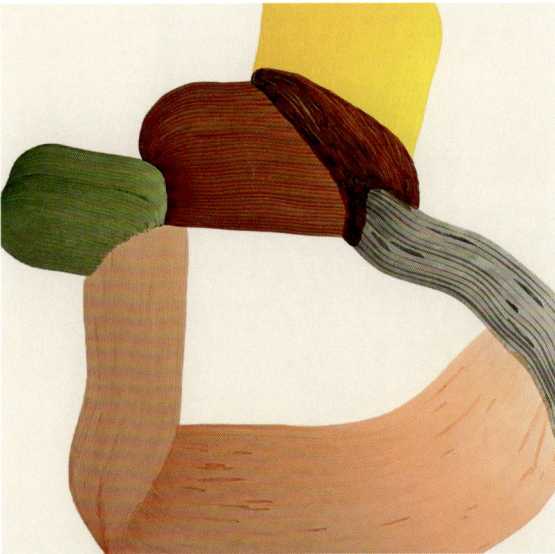
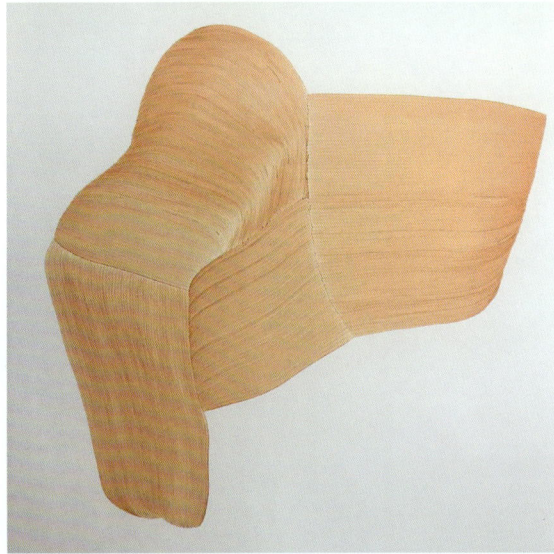

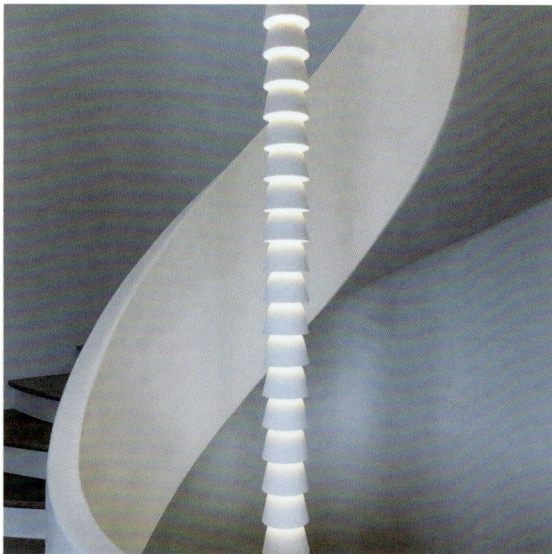

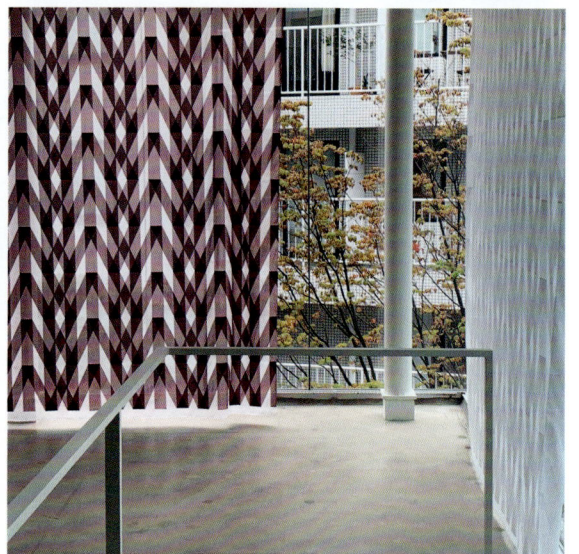

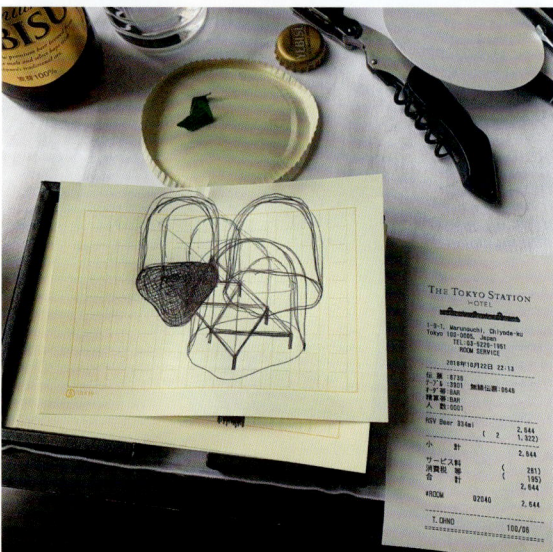

Ronan & Erwan Bouroullec
Urban Daydreaming
夢建城市
27.10 2018 – 17.02.2019

Master
Lecture
Series

Ronan
Bouroullec
Works

26 October 2018
5:00pm – 6:00pm
A004

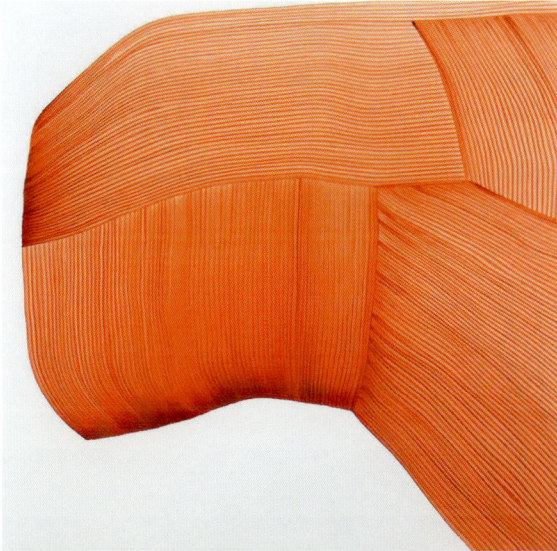

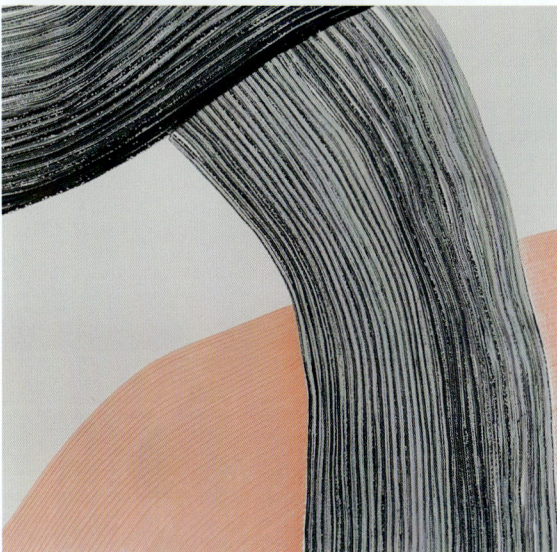
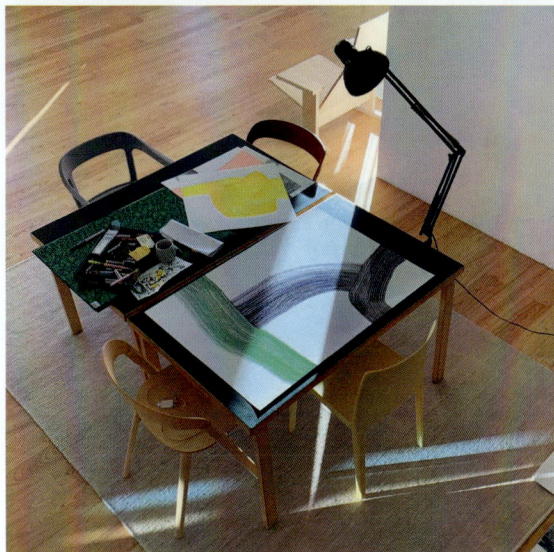
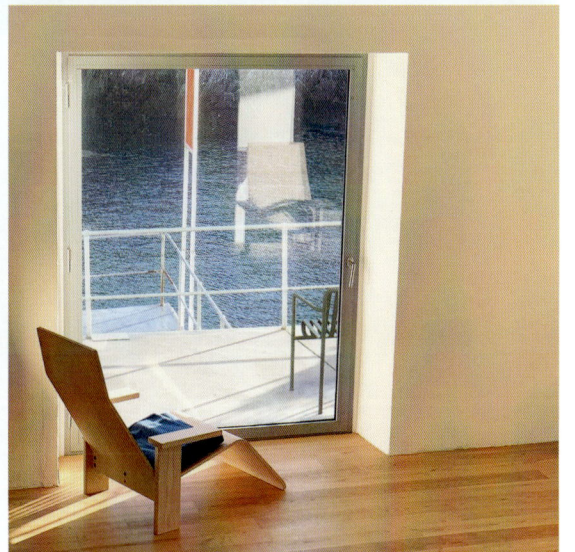

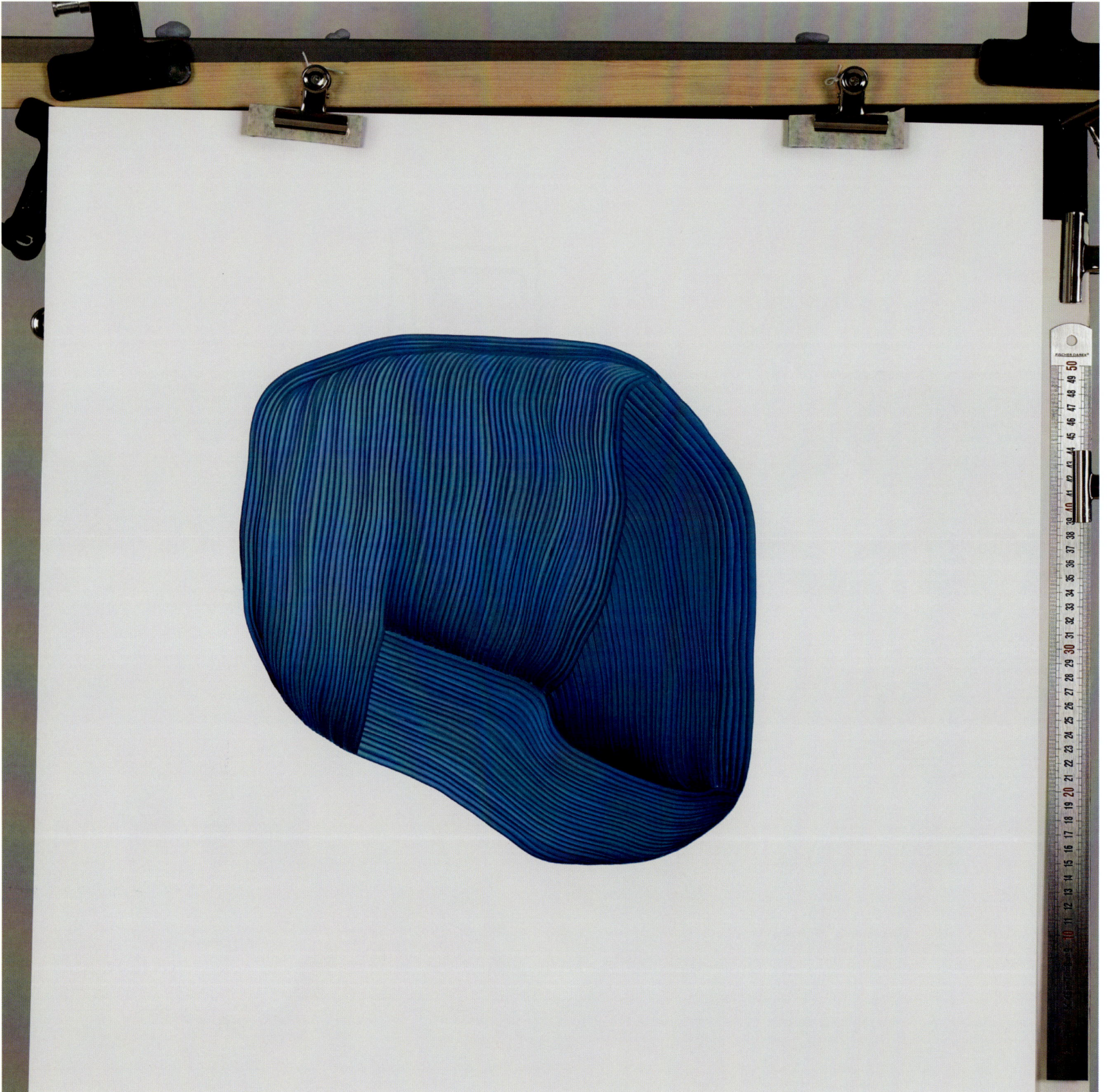

CONFÉRENCE
RONAN BOUROULLEC
THÉÂTRE DE LIÈGE
SALLE DE LA GRANDE MAIN
15 / 11   20 : 00
AVEC
- FACULTÉ D'ARCHITECTURE
  V LIÈGE
- SAINT LUC ÉCOLE SUPÉRIEURE
  DES ARTS
- VITRA

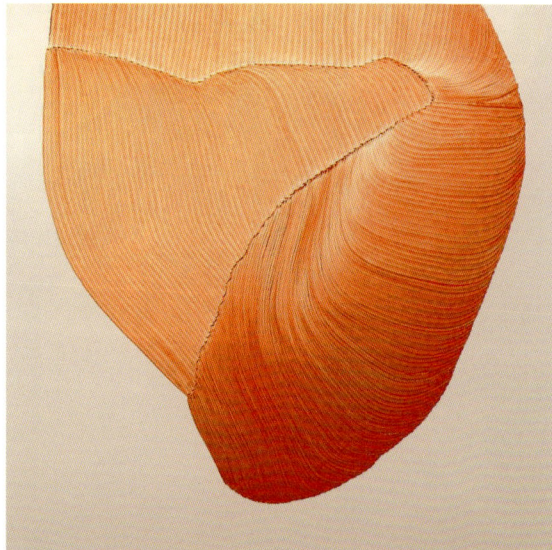

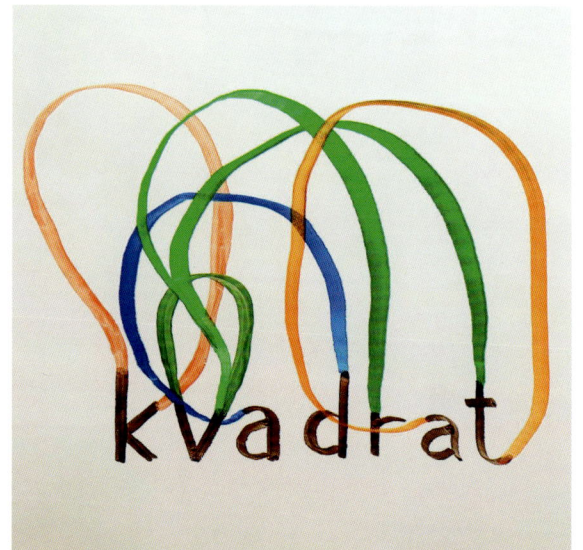

kvadrat

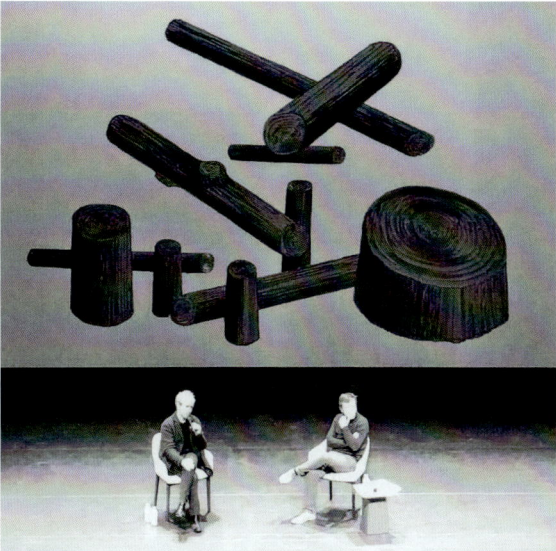
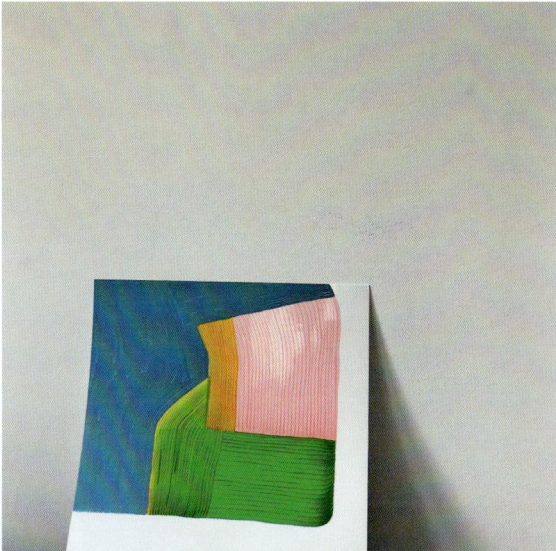

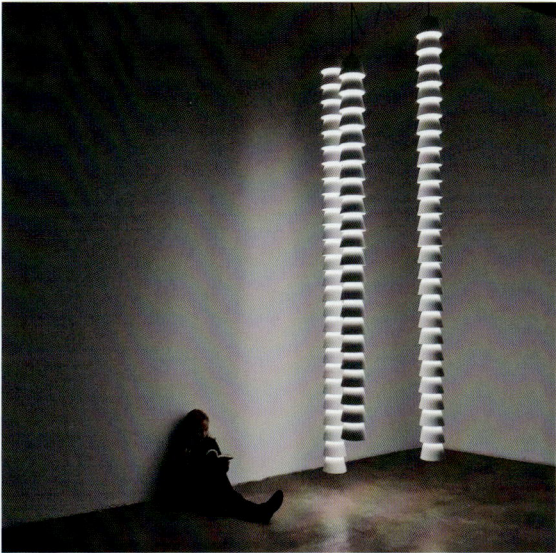

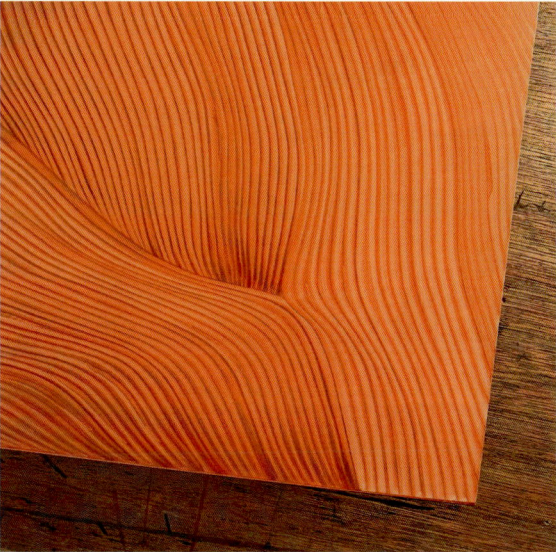

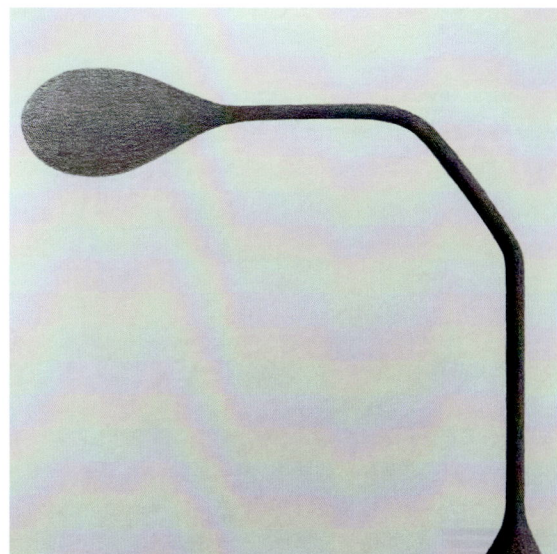

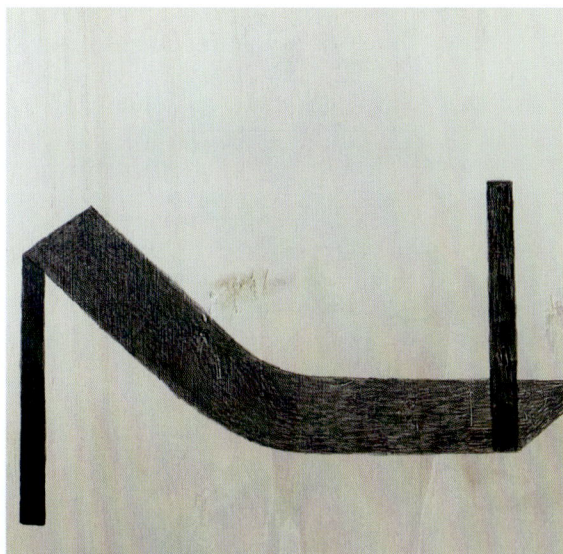

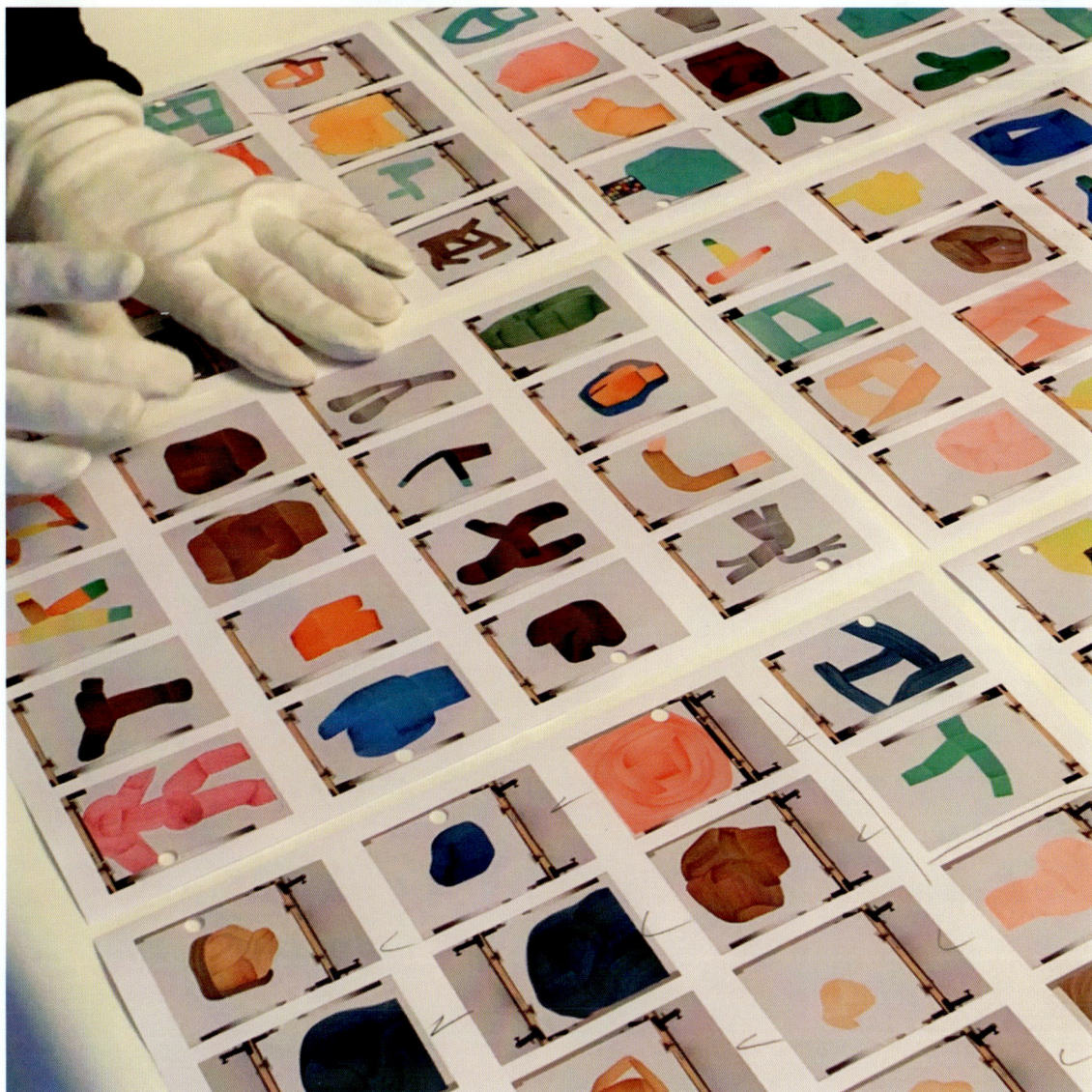

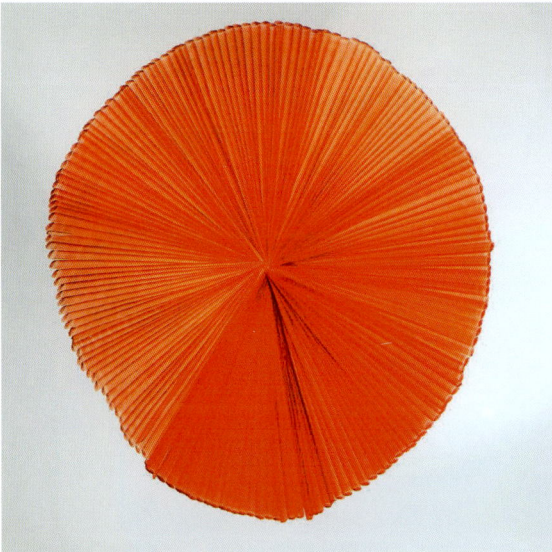
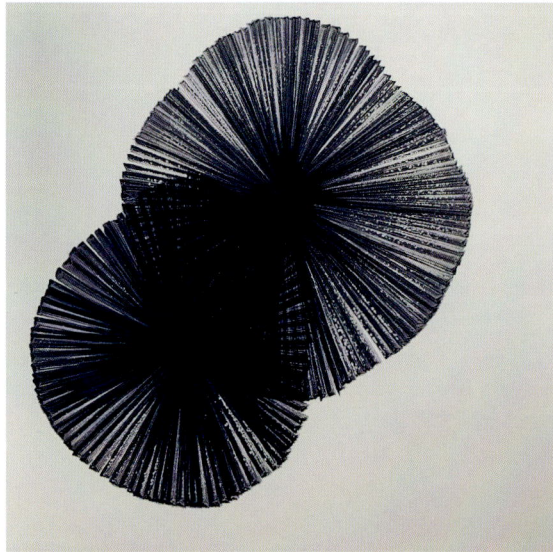

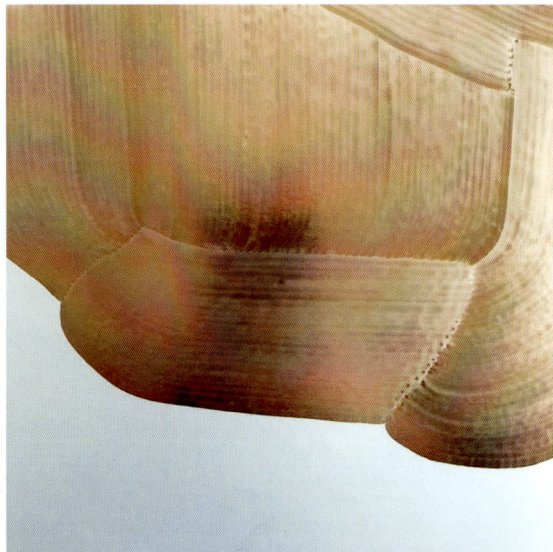

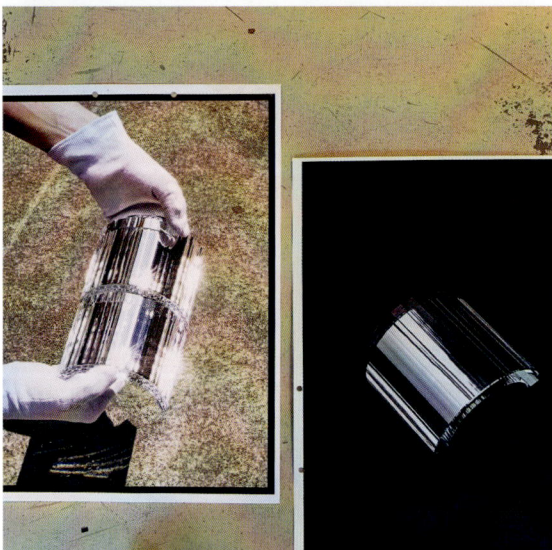

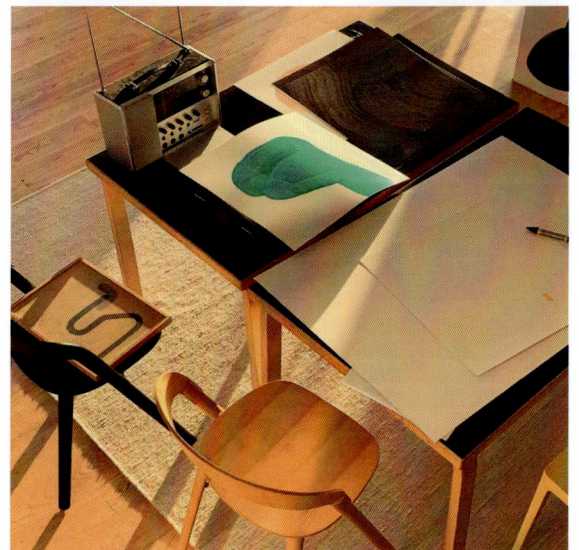

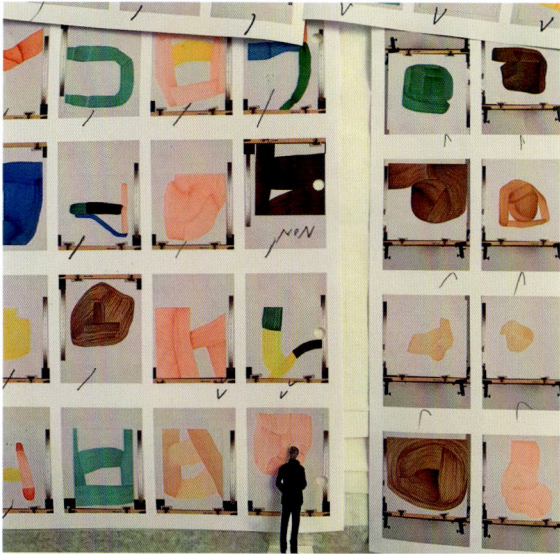

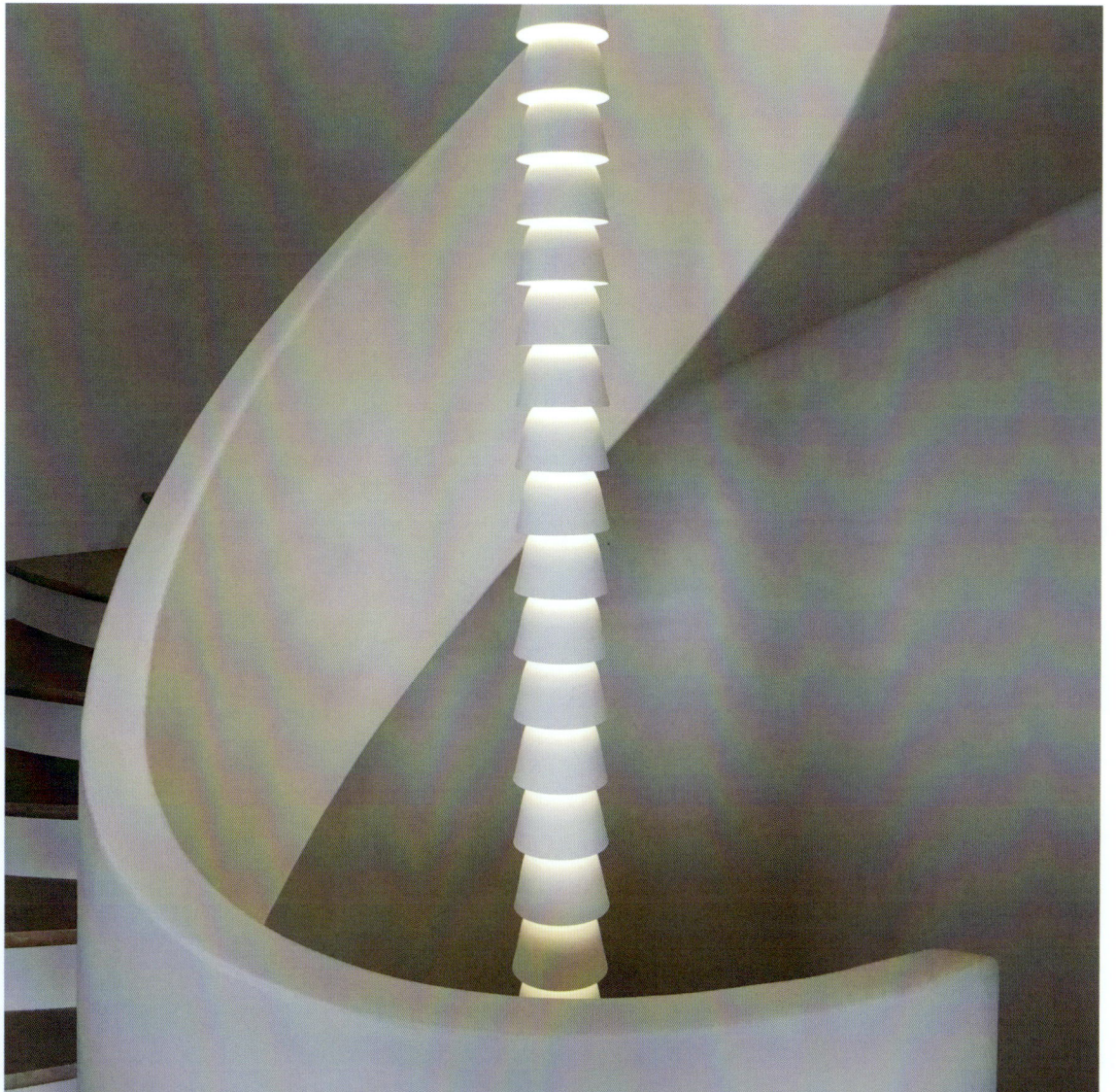

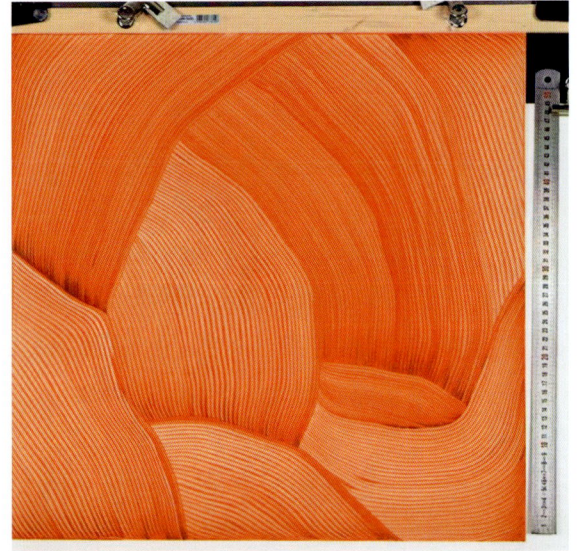

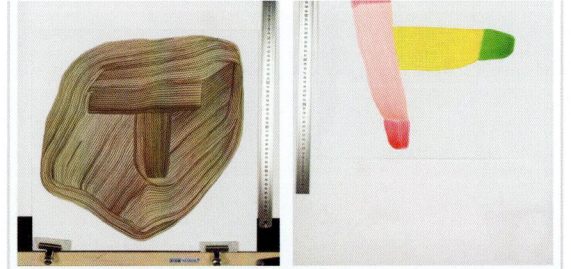
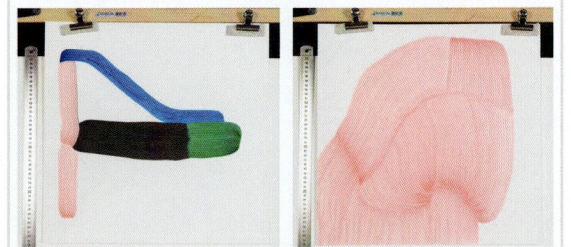

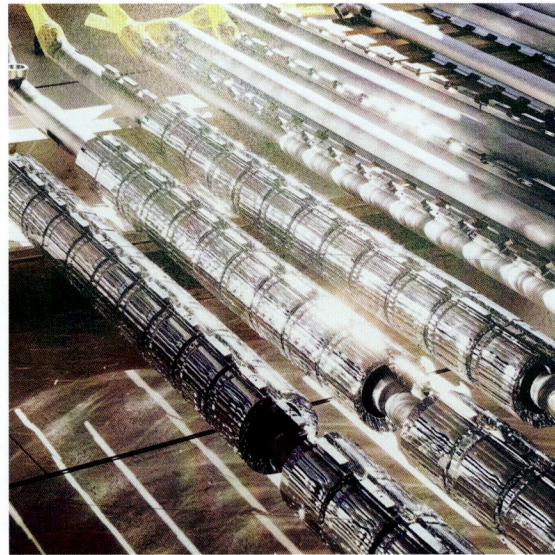
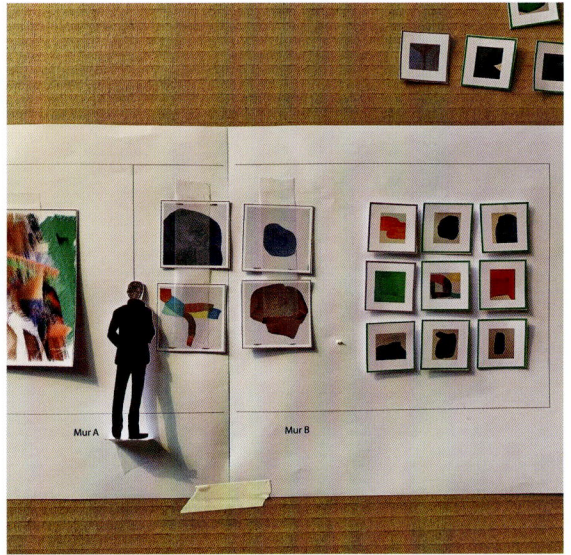
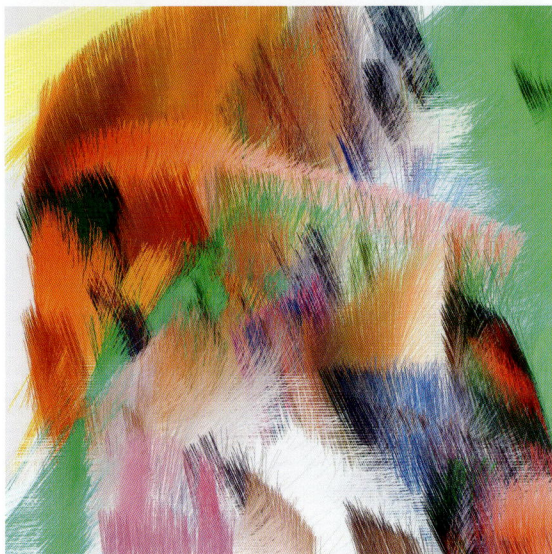

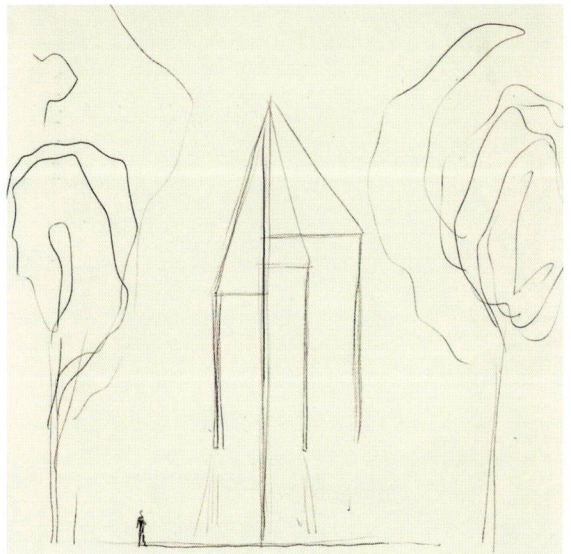

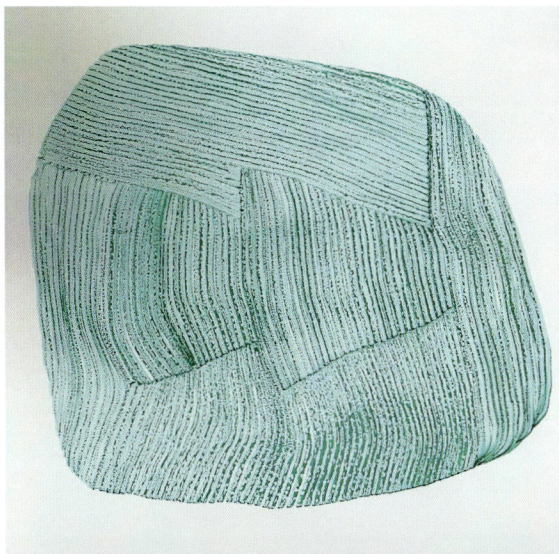
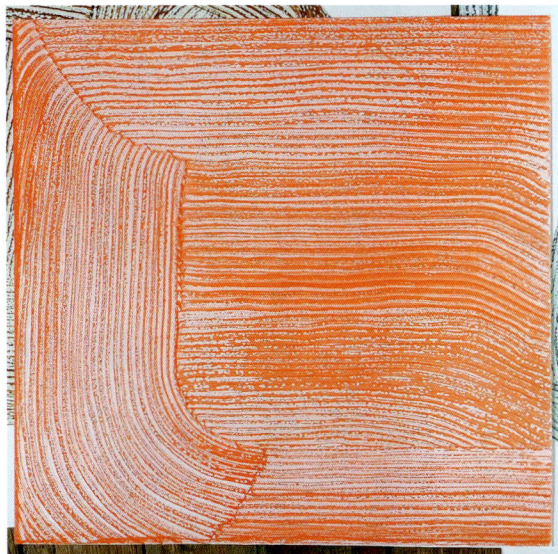
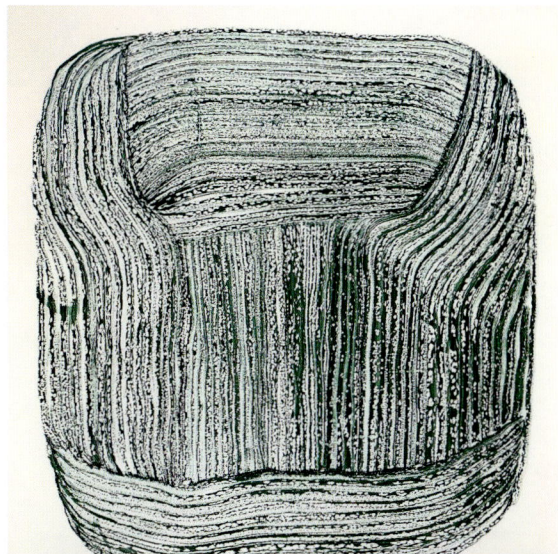

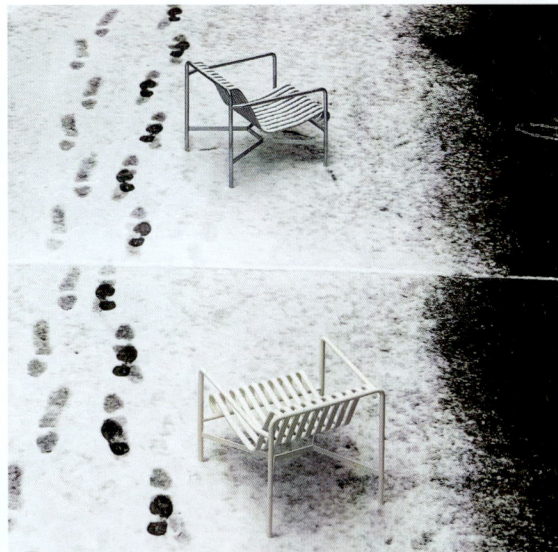

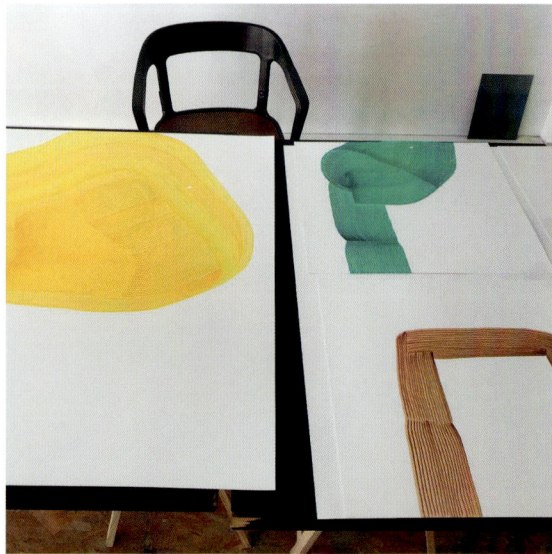

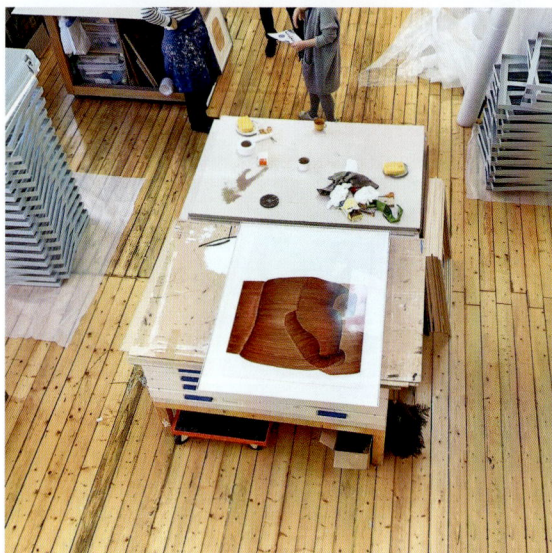
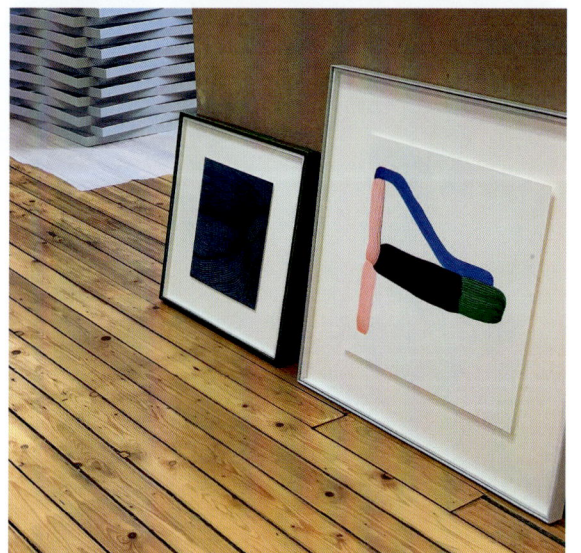

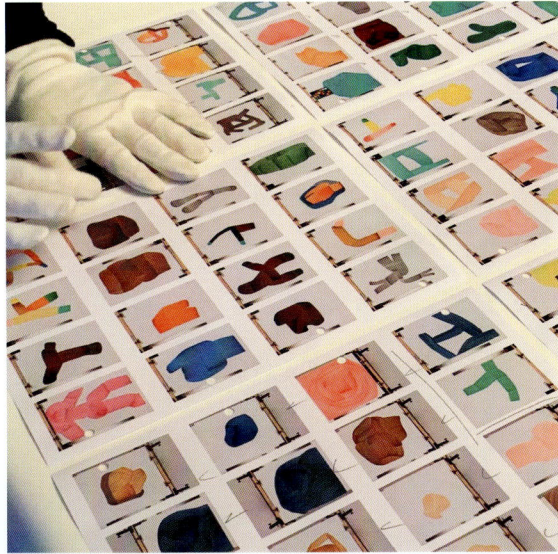

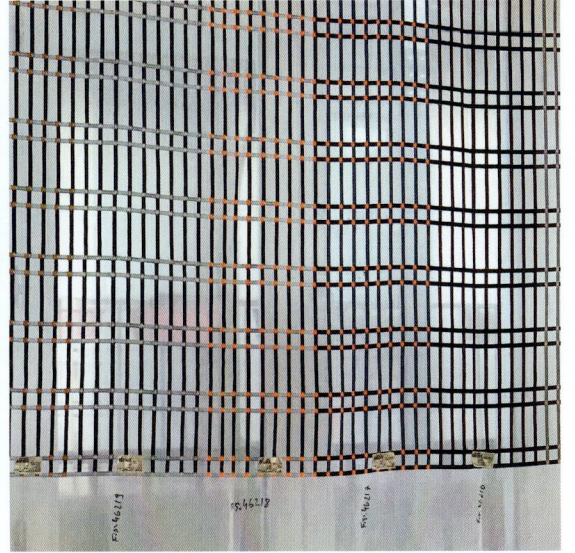

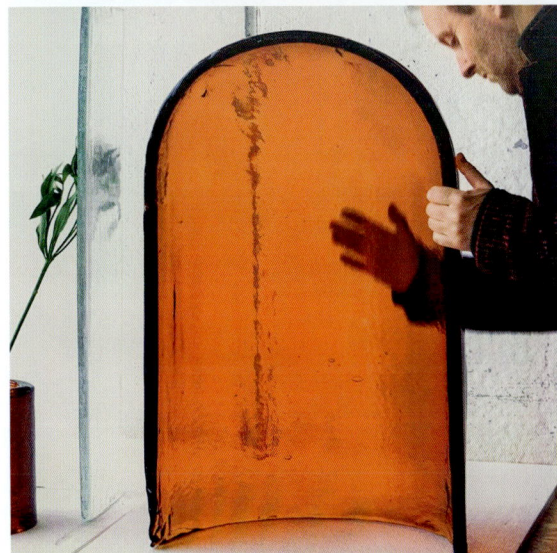
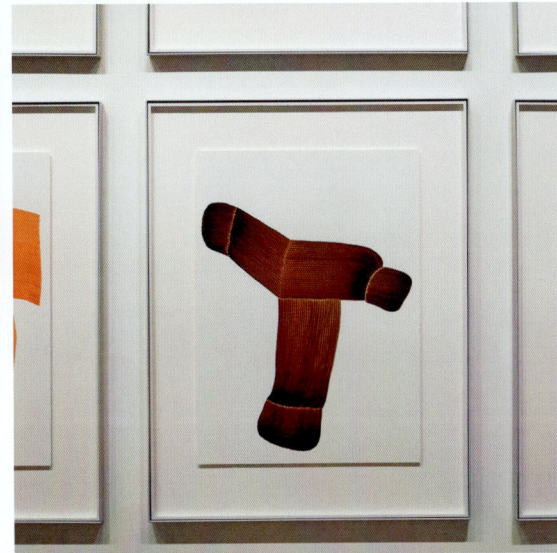
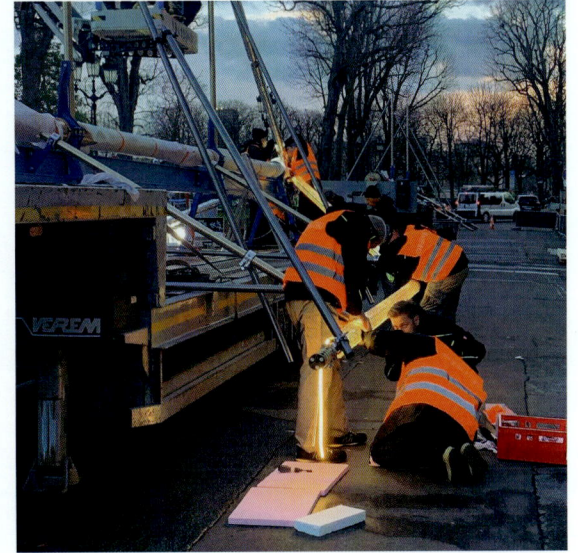

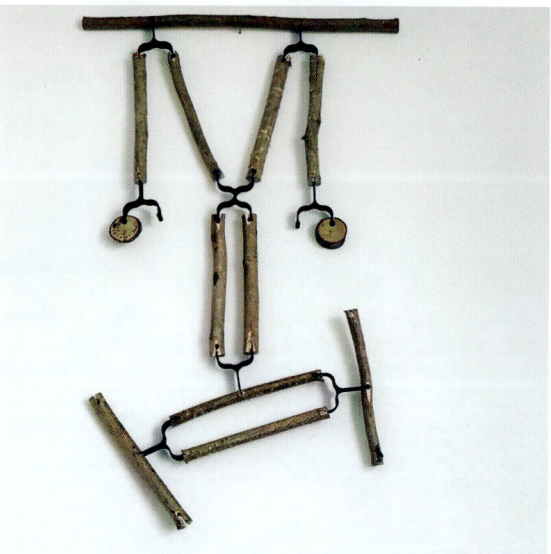
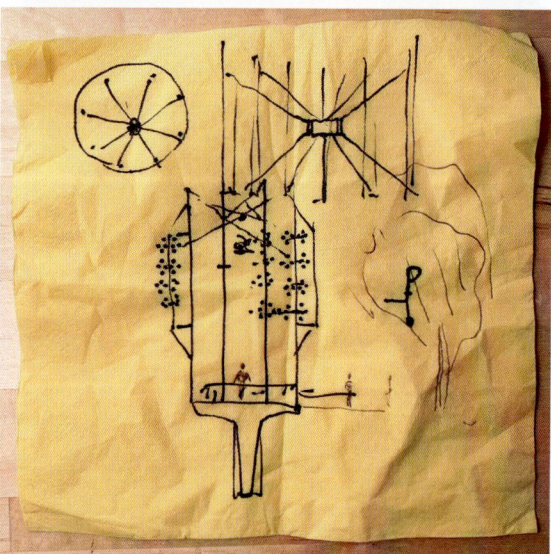

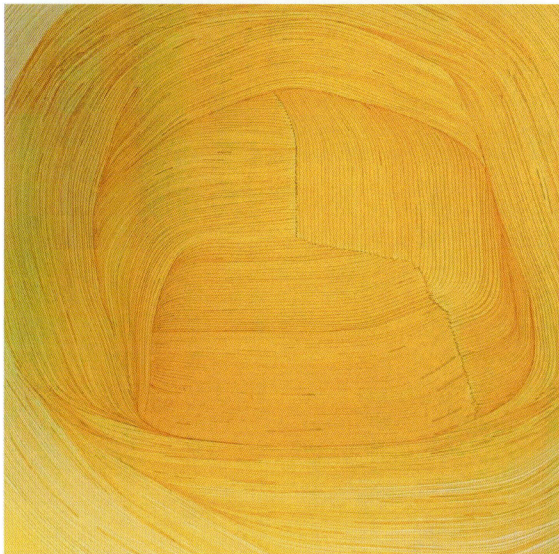

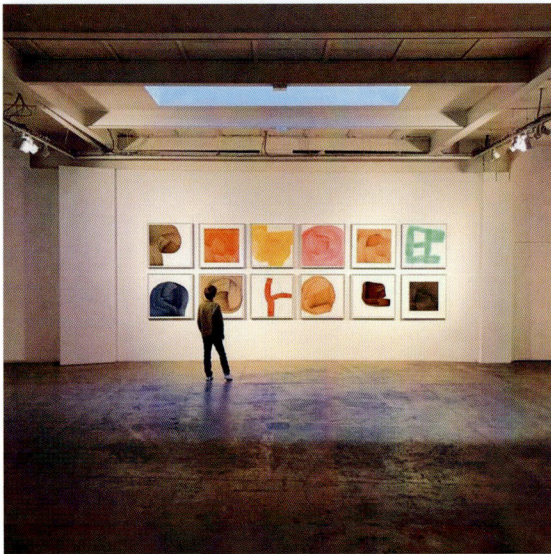

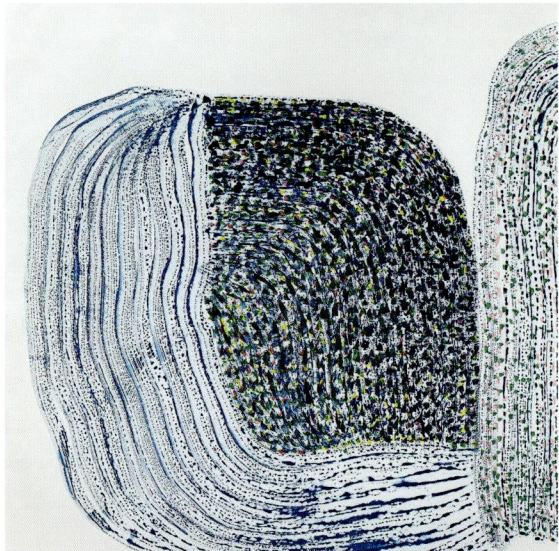
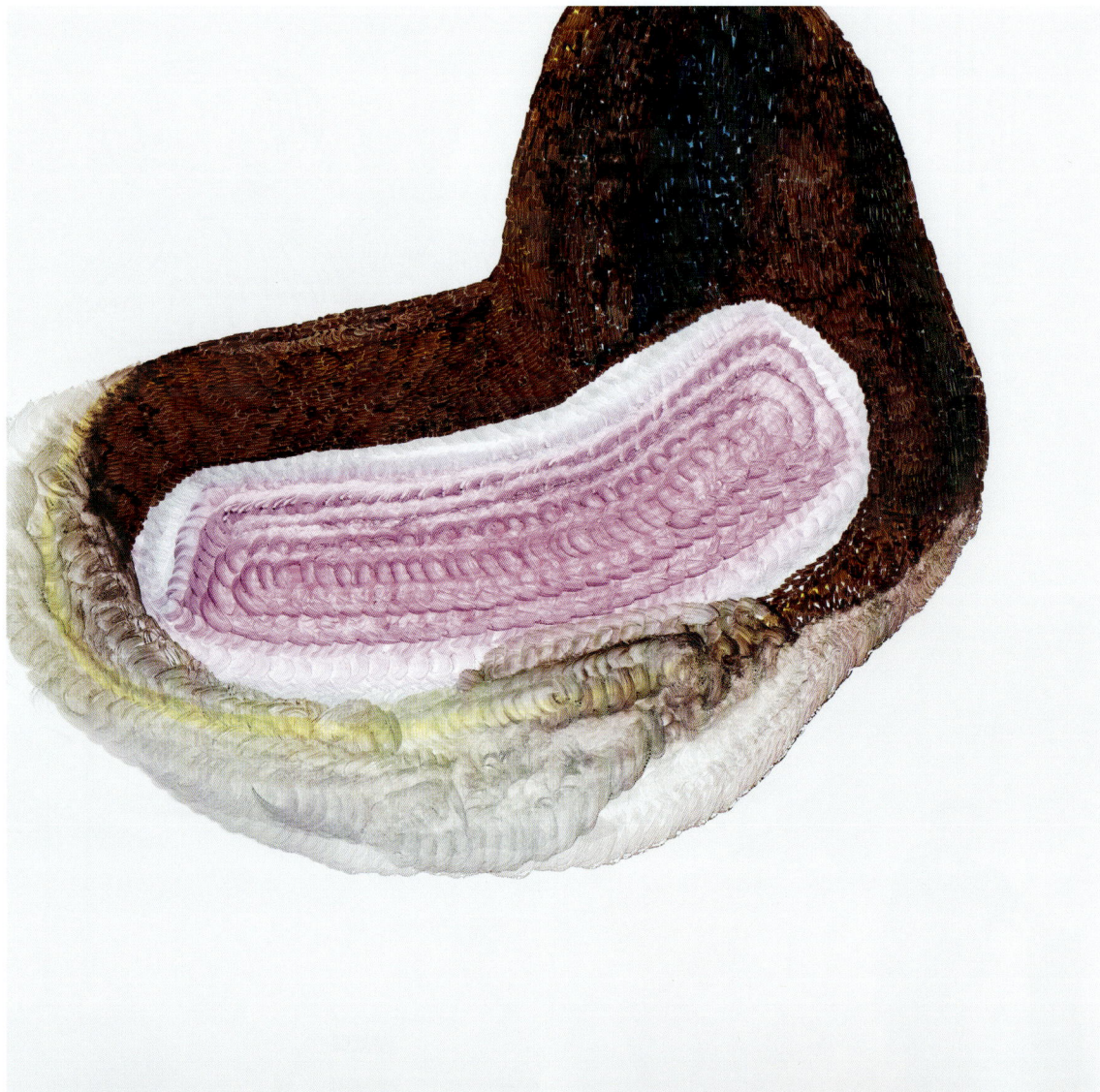
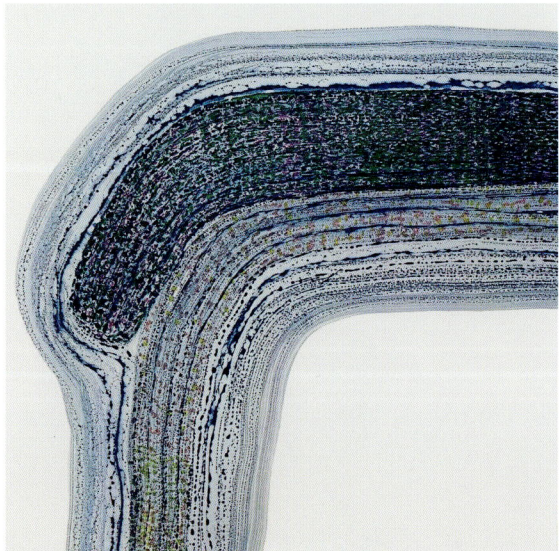

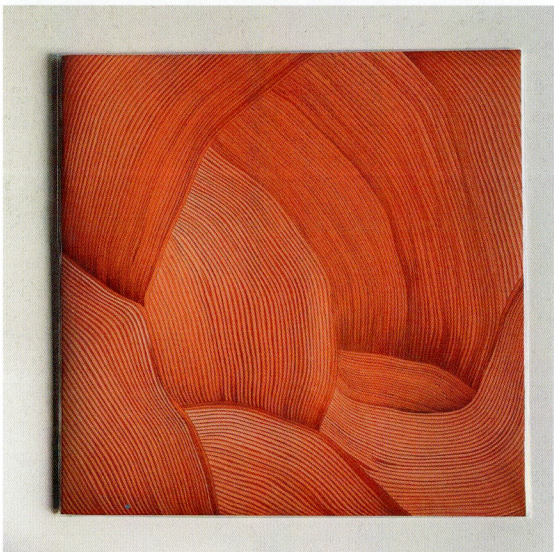
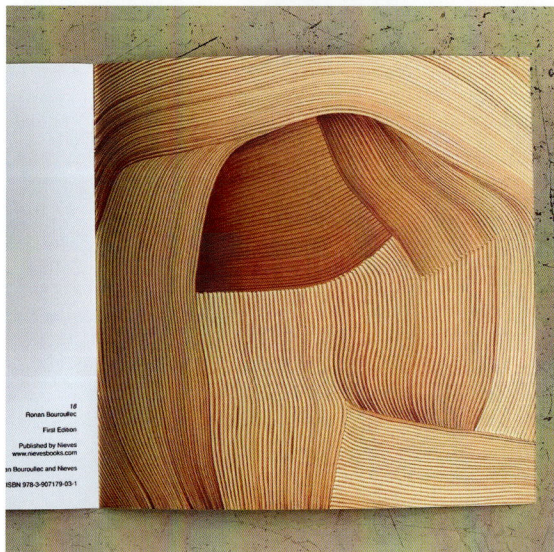

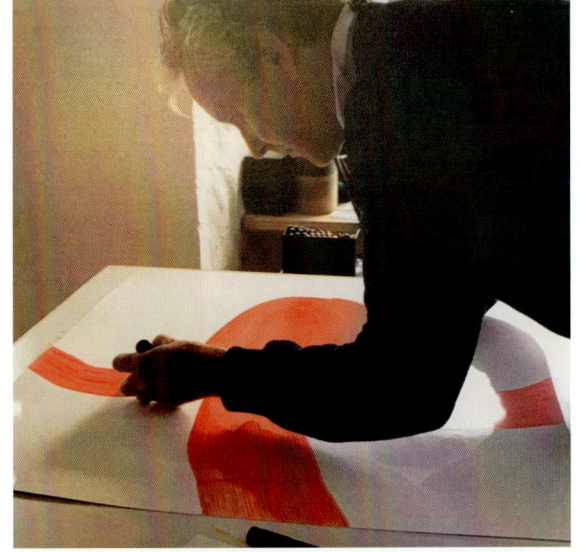

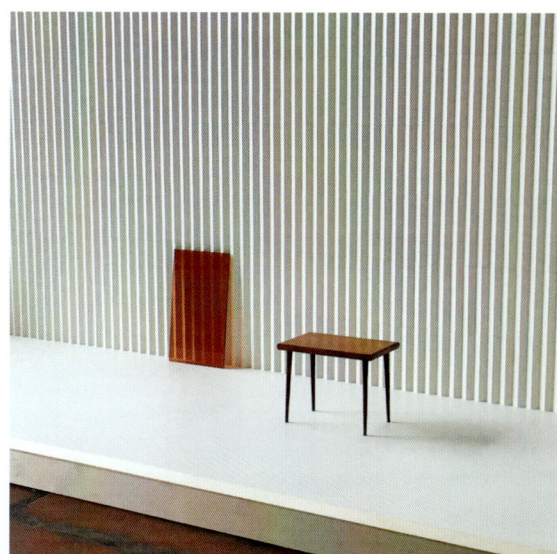
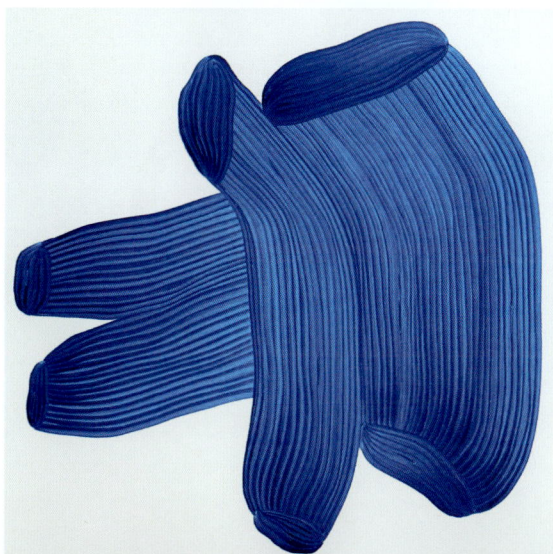

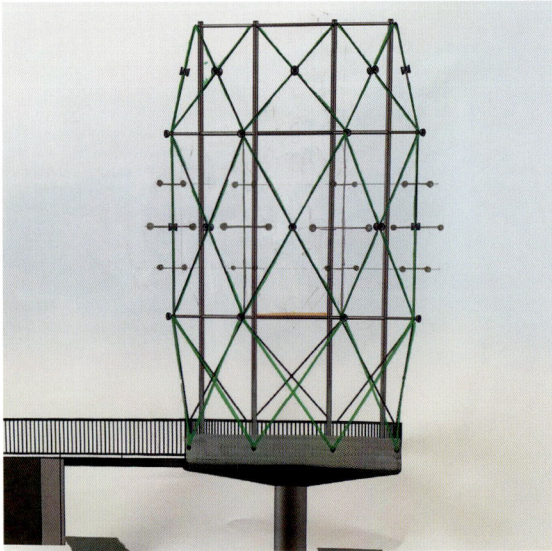

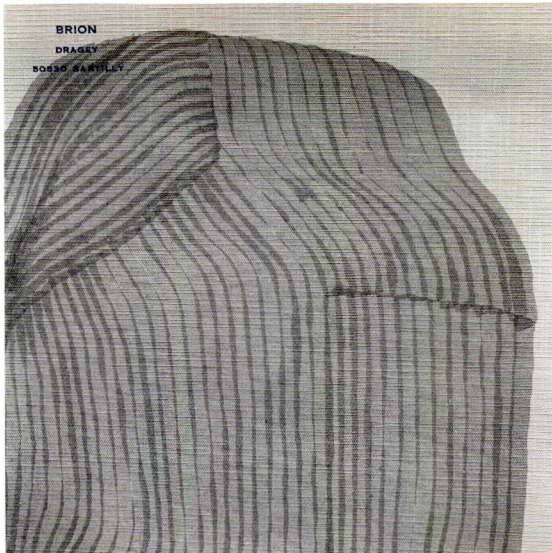
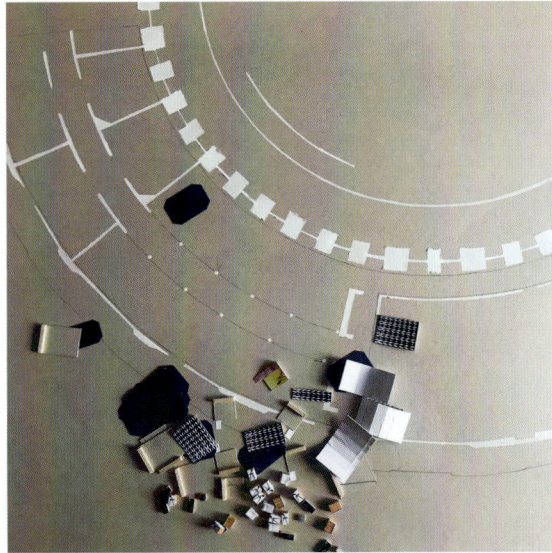
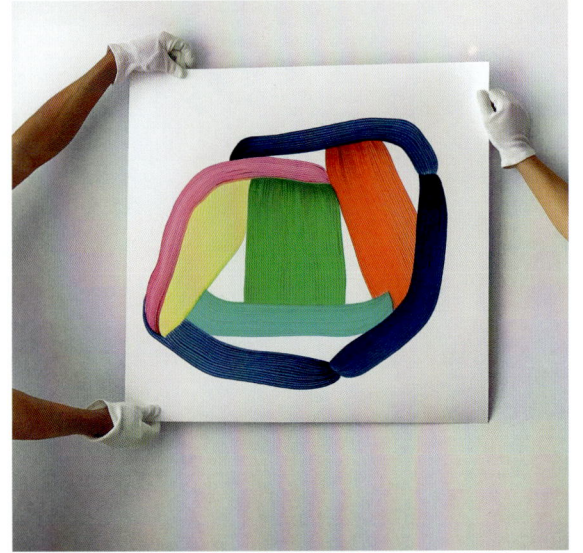

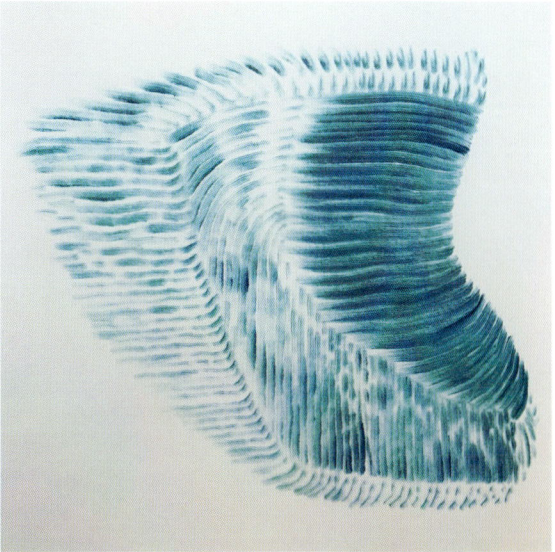

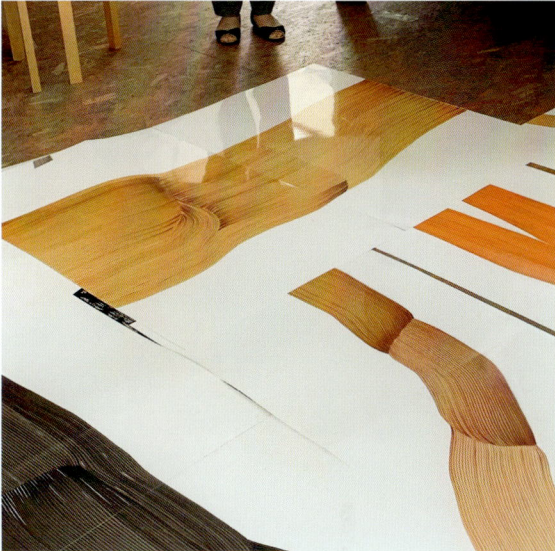

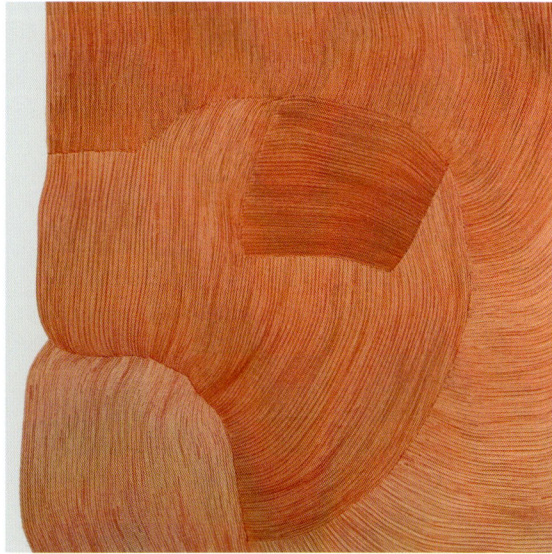

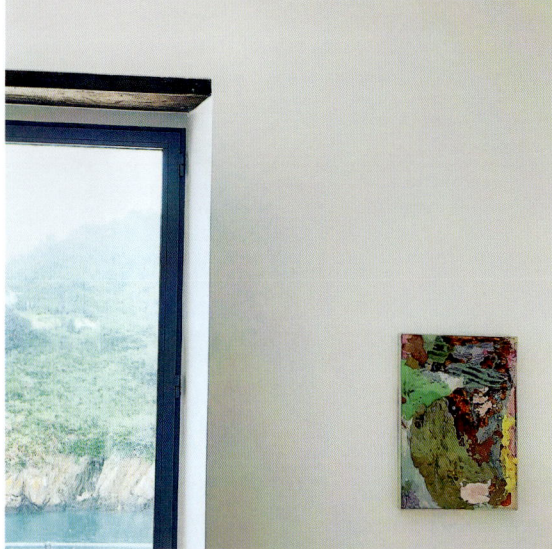
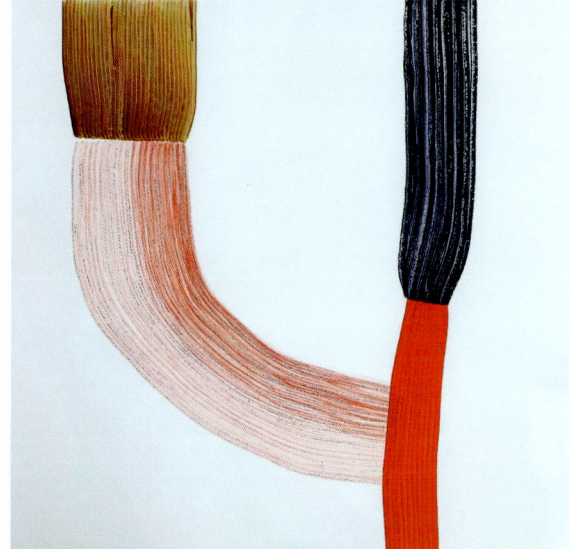

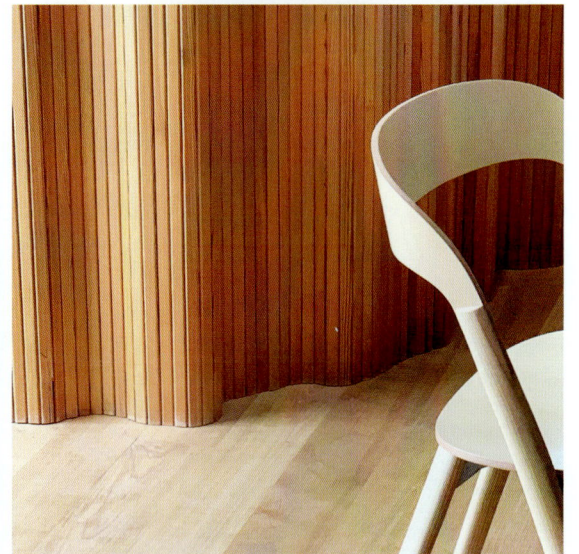

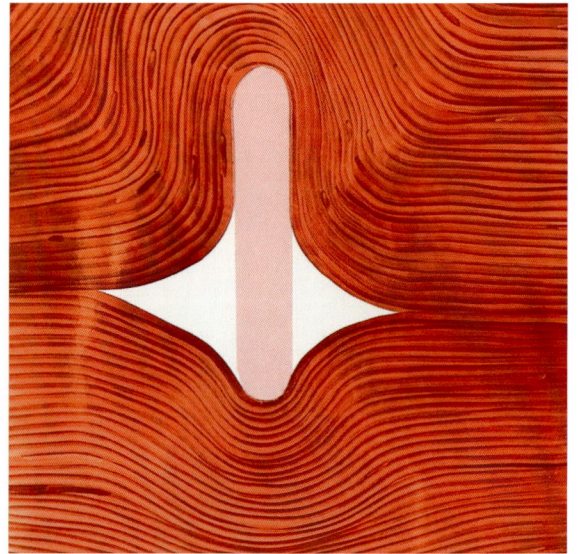

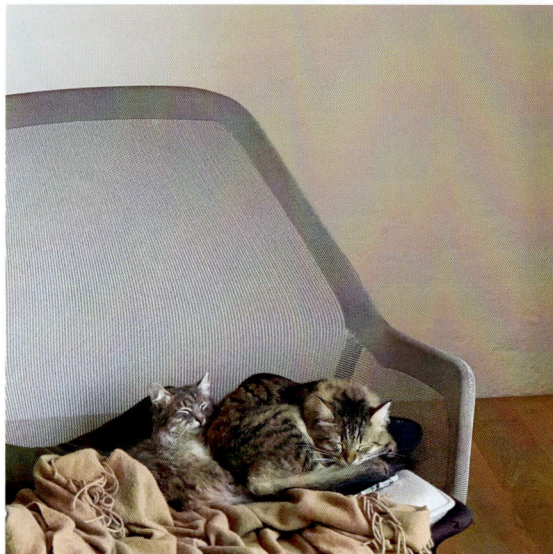

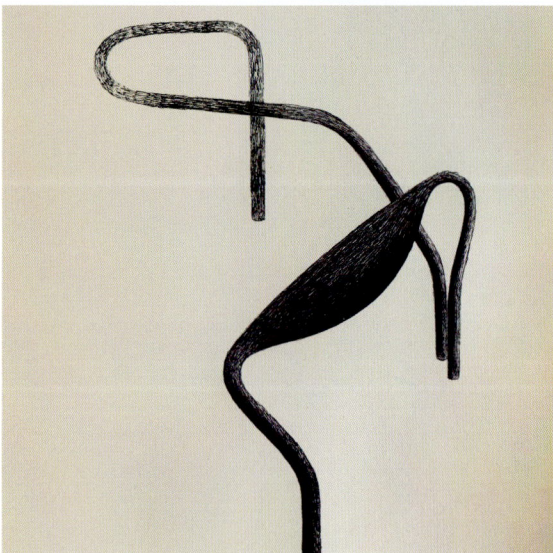

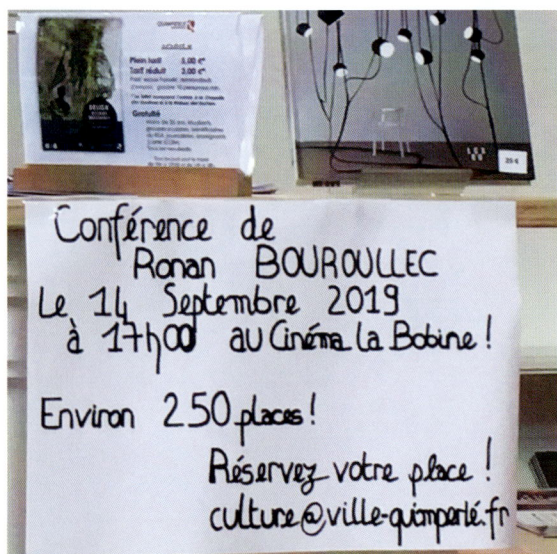

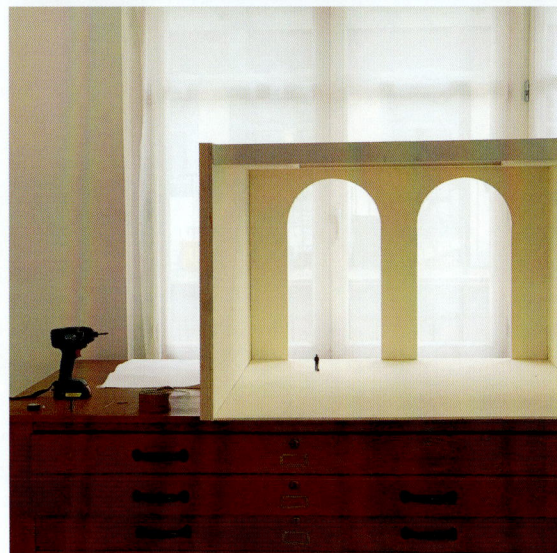

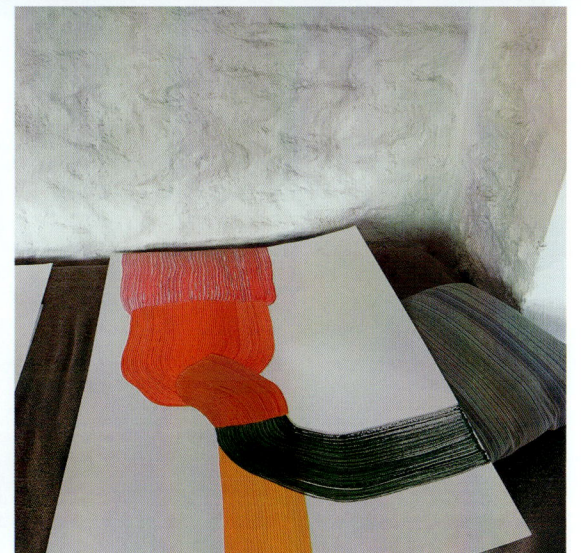

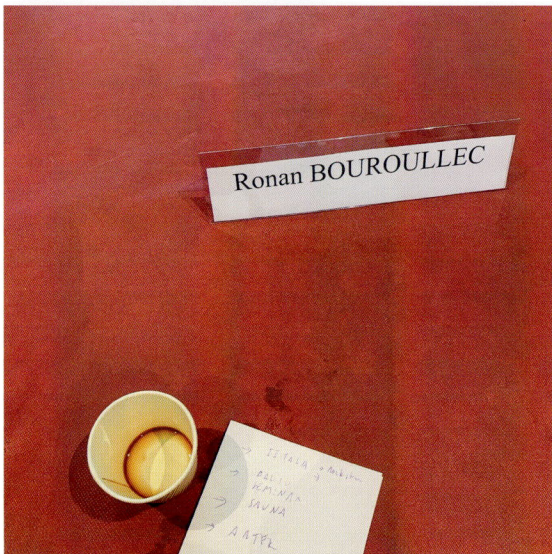

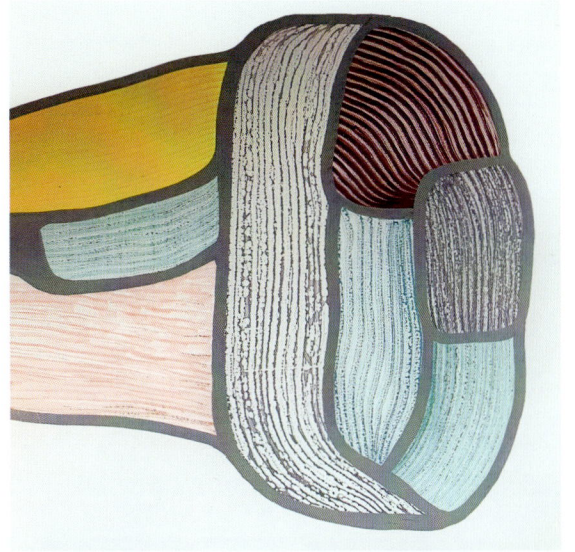

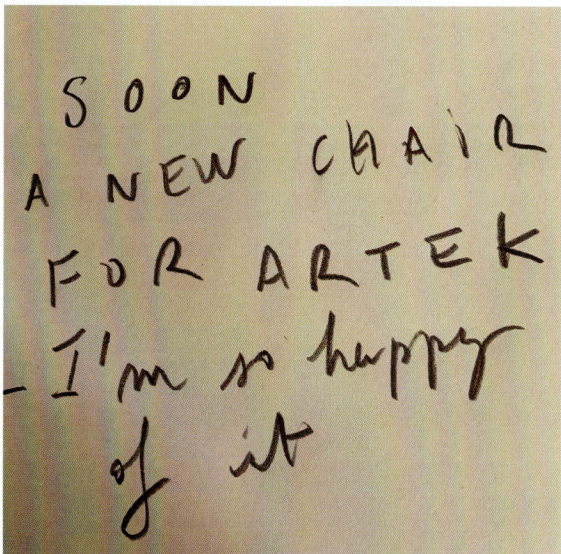

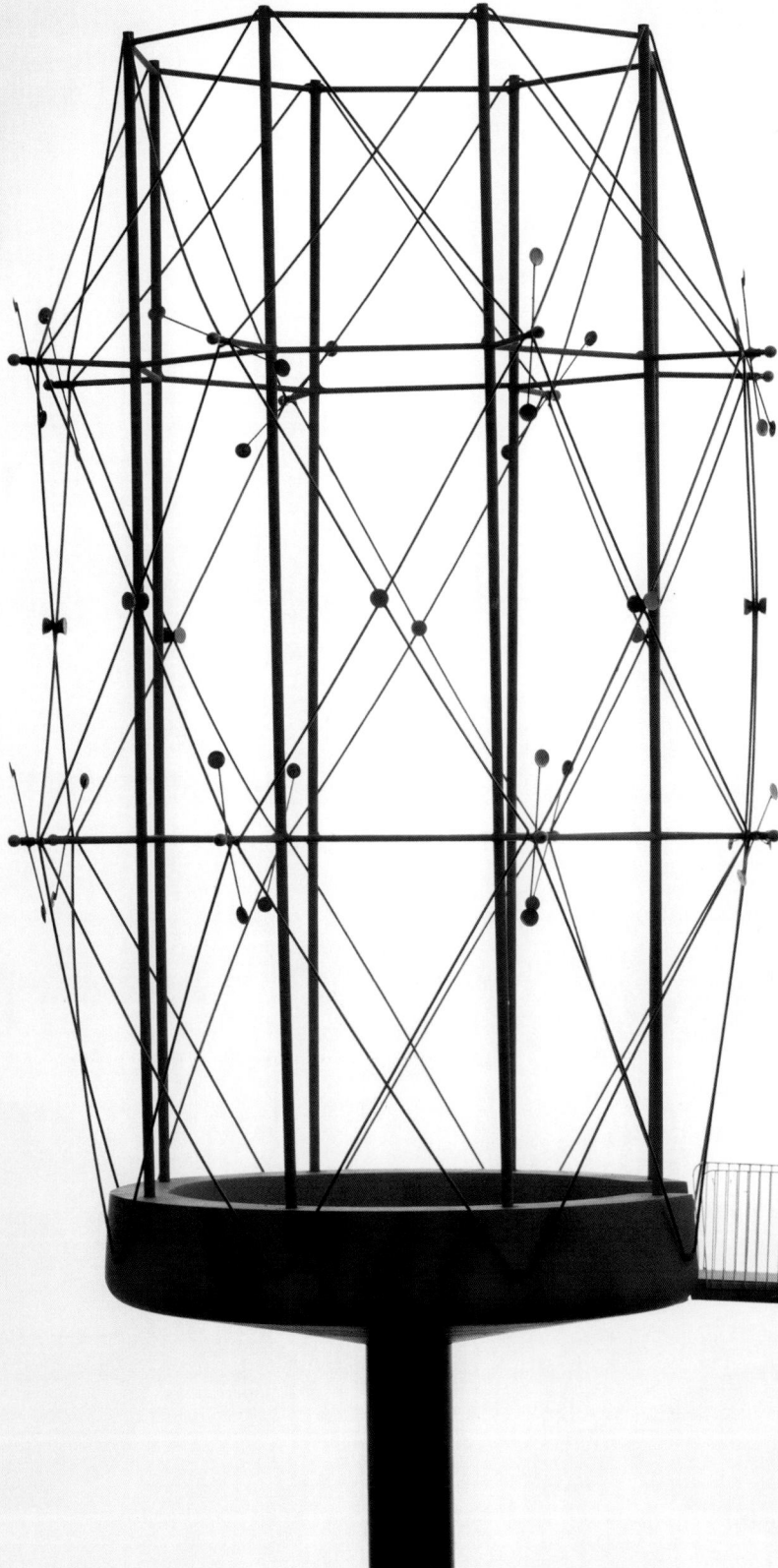

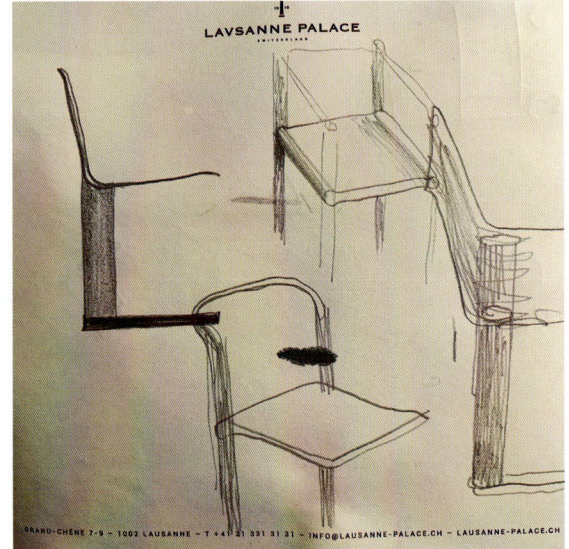

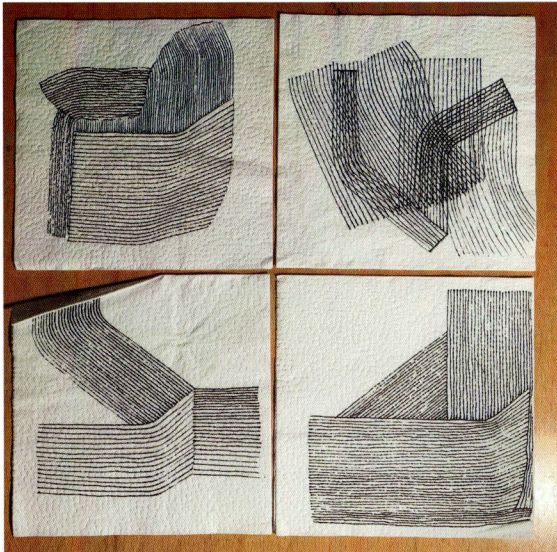

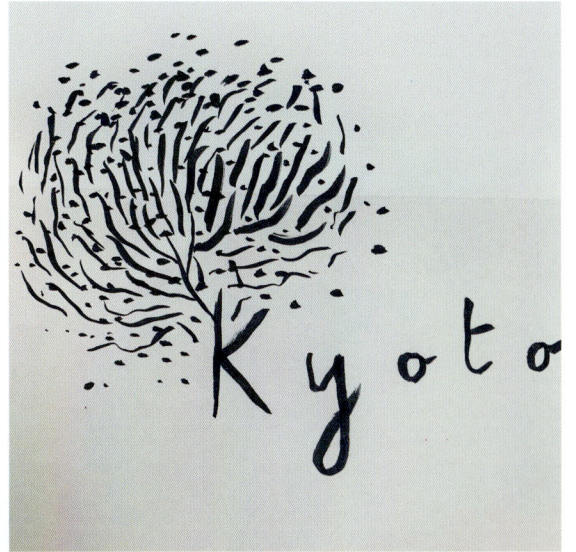

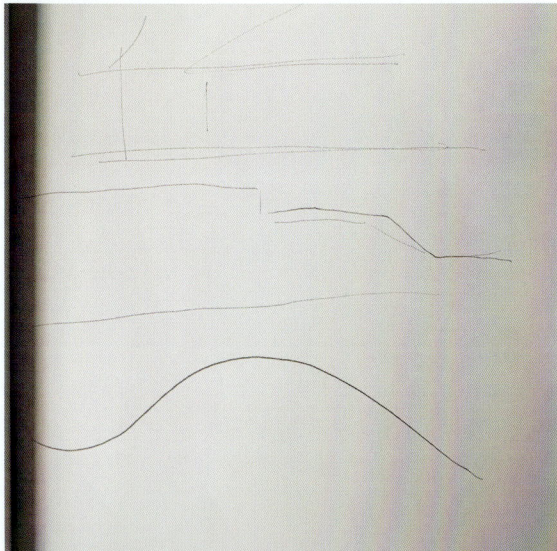

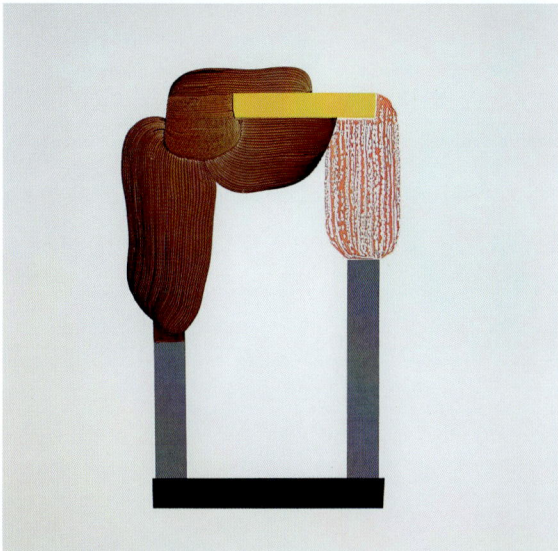

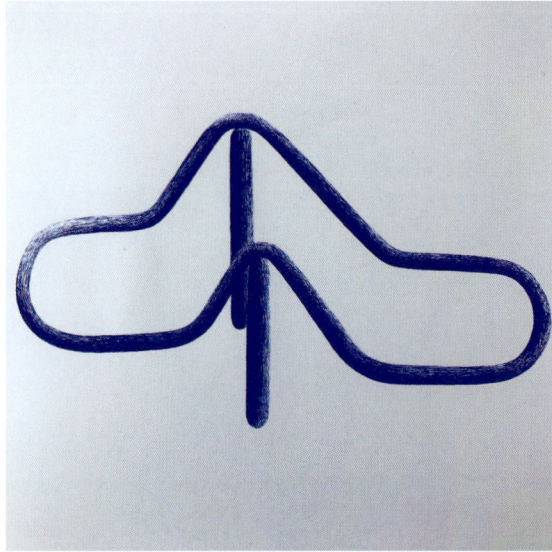

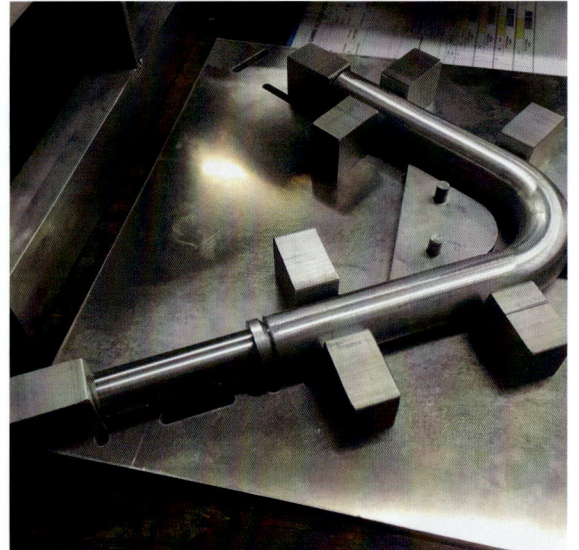
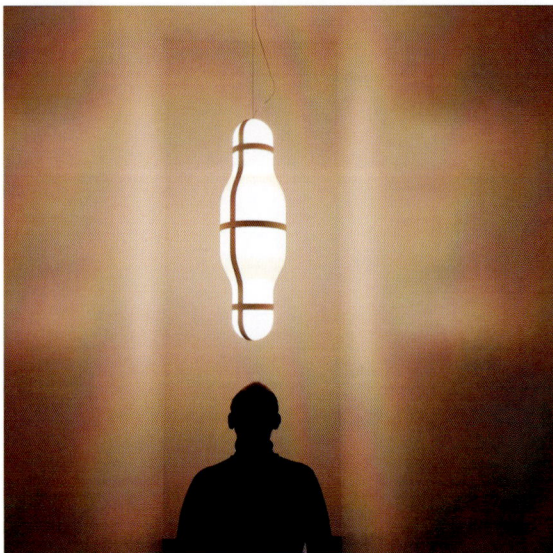

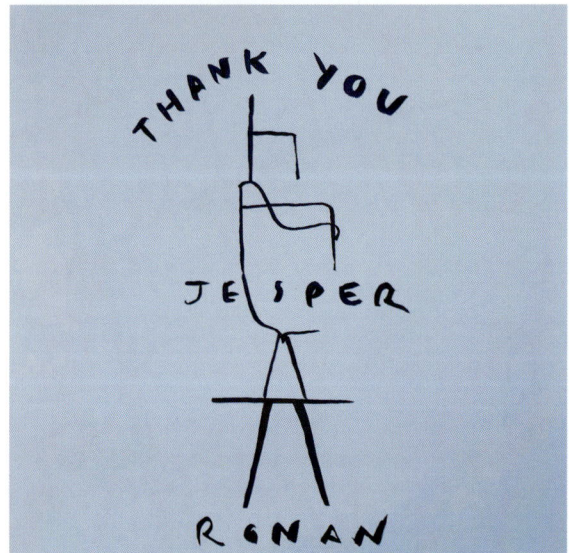

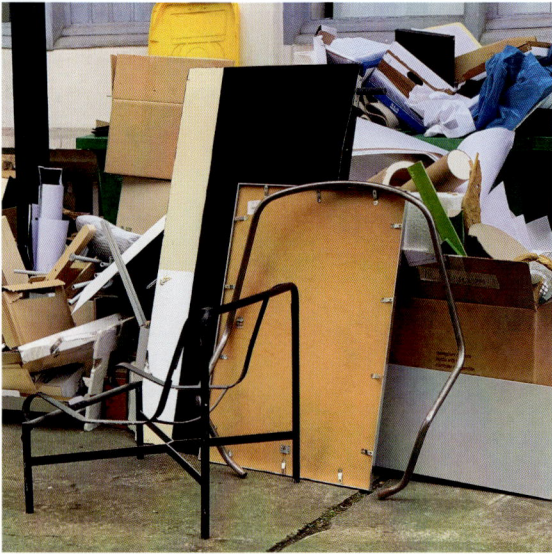

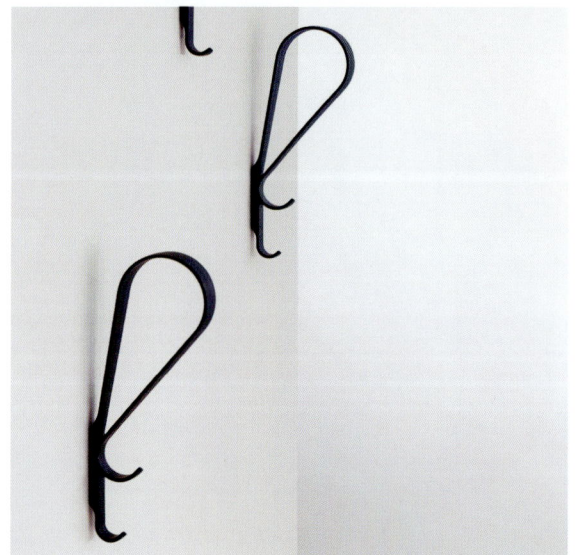

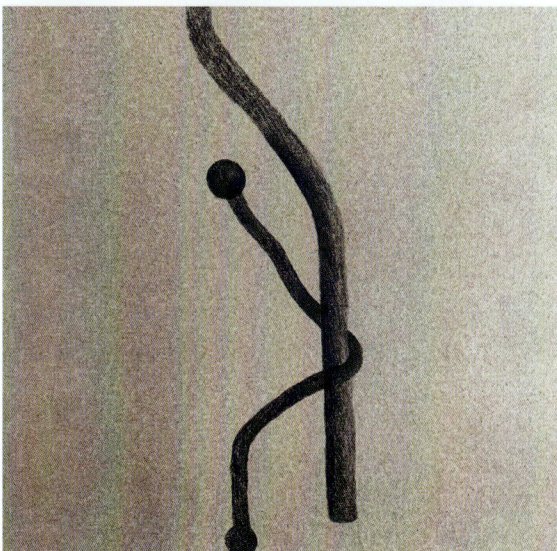

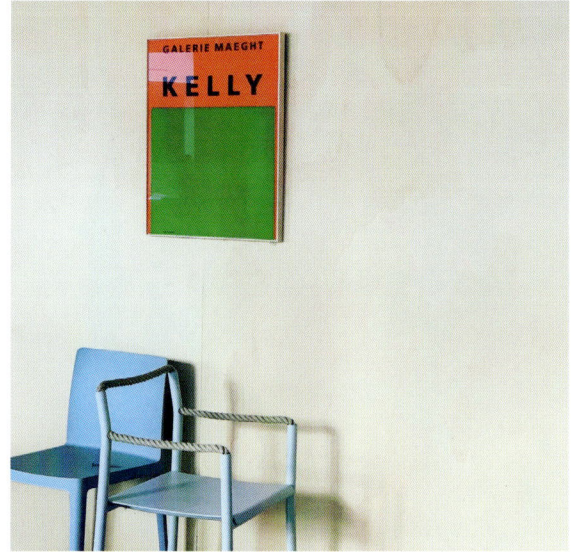

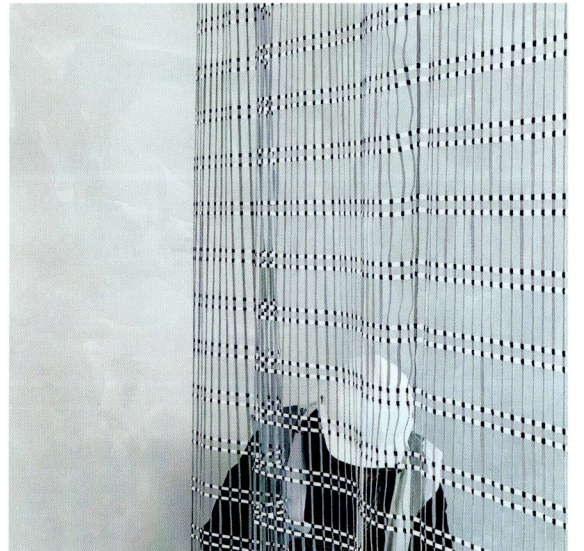

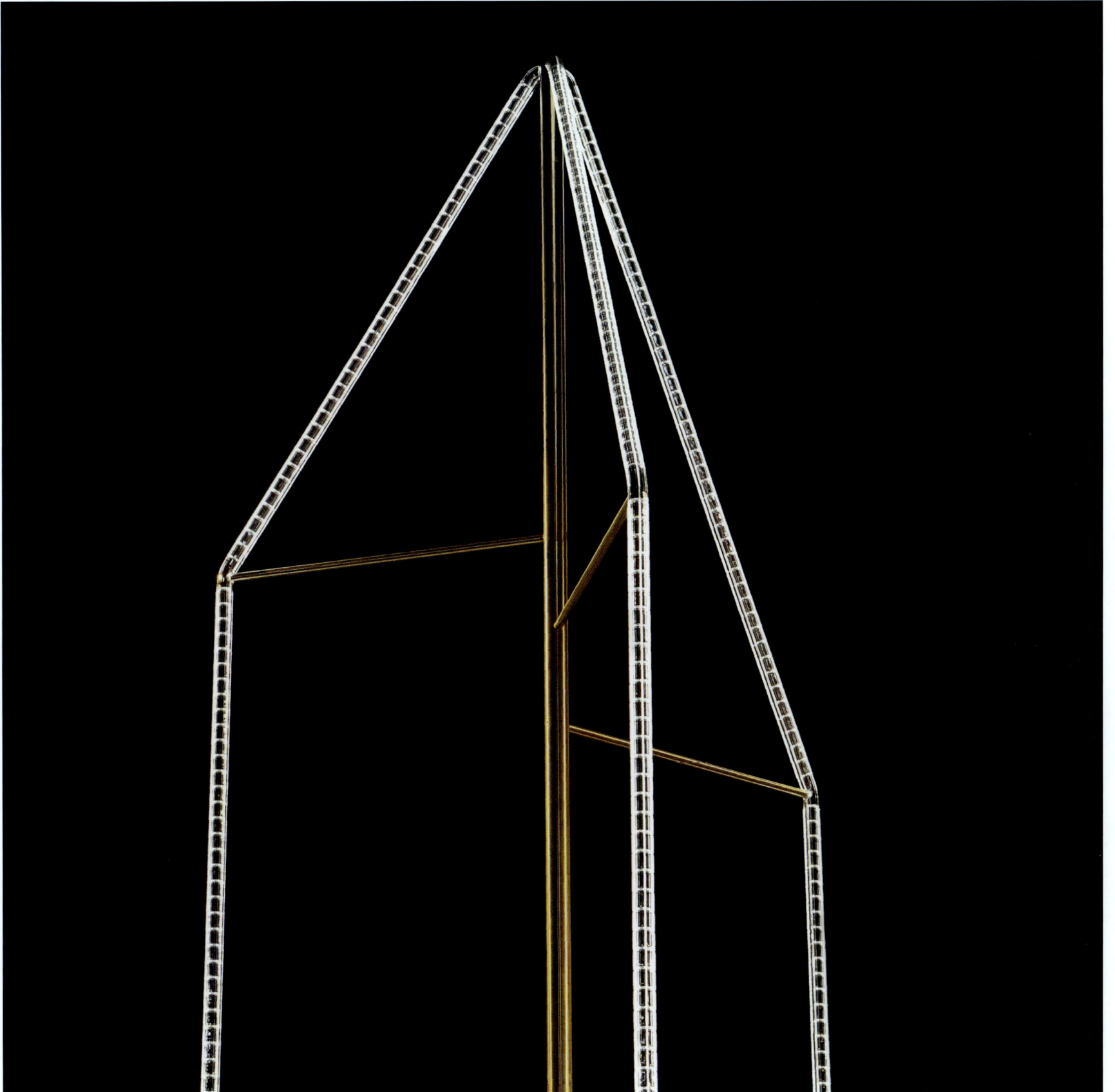

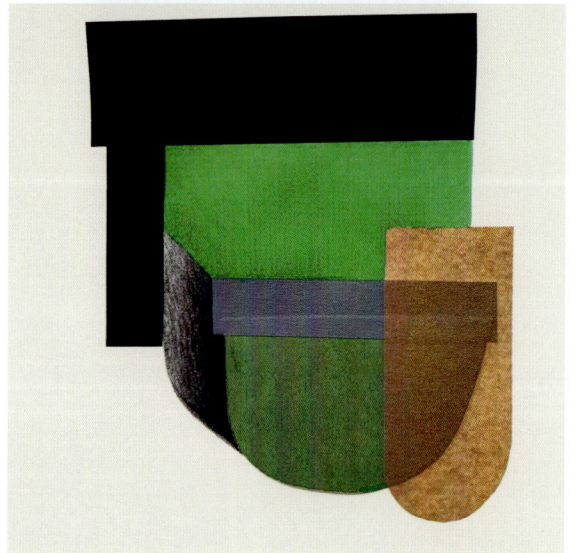

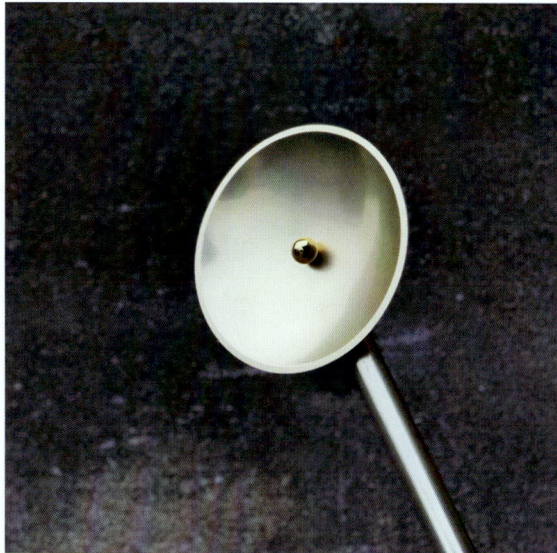
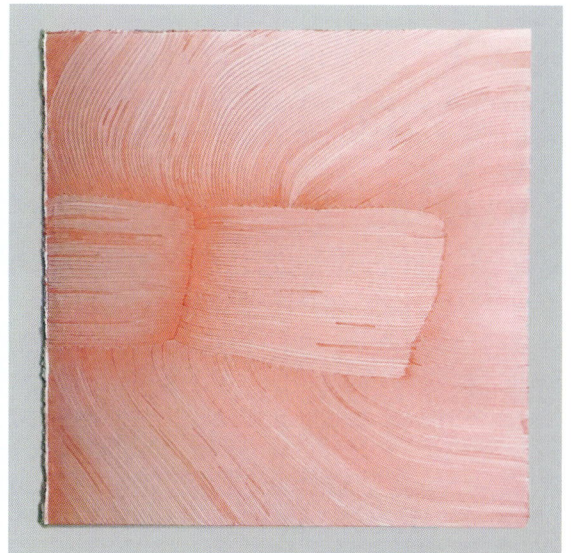

In front of the appartement, the school is open for children of the doctors, nurses, medical staff all those courageous people

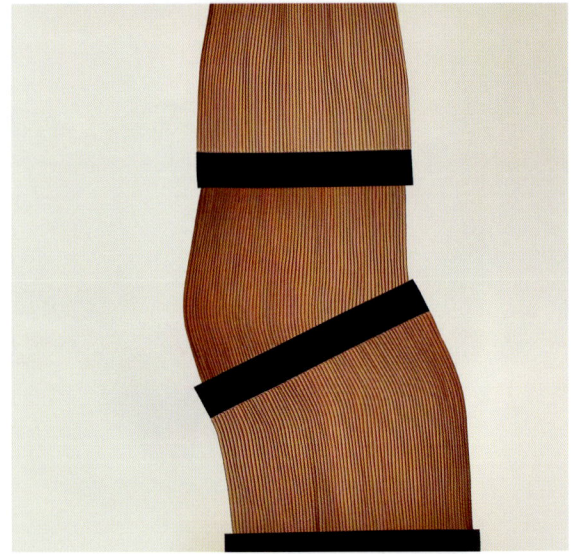

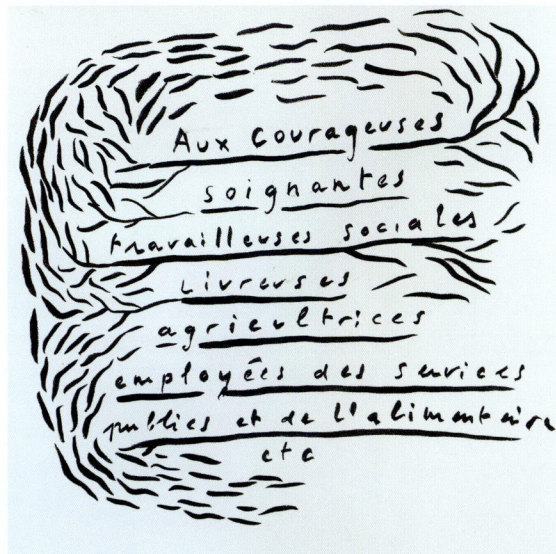

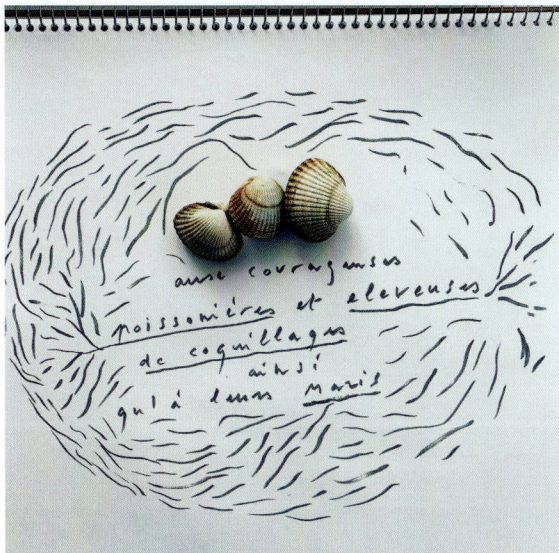

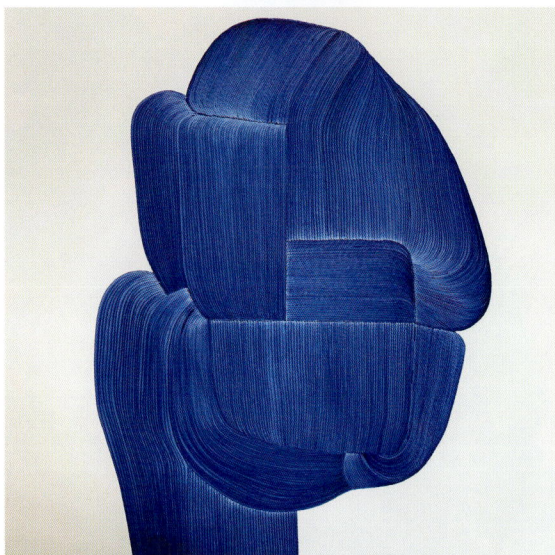

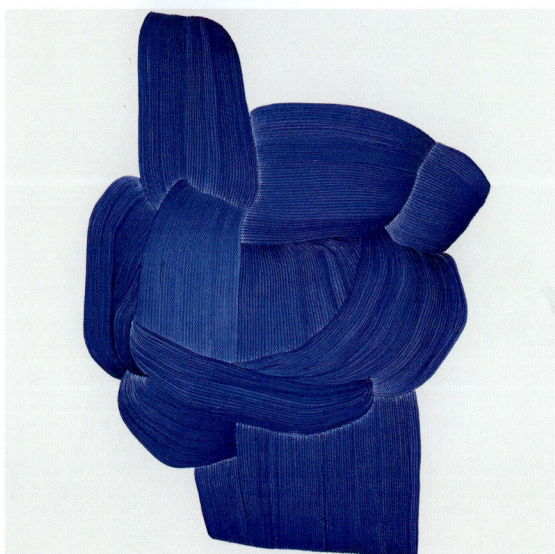

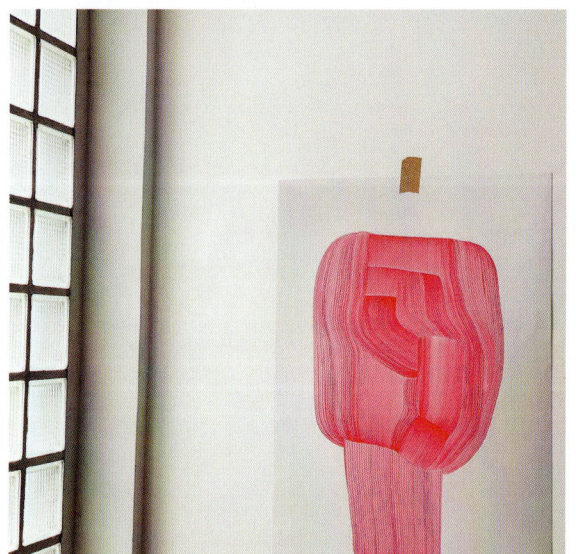

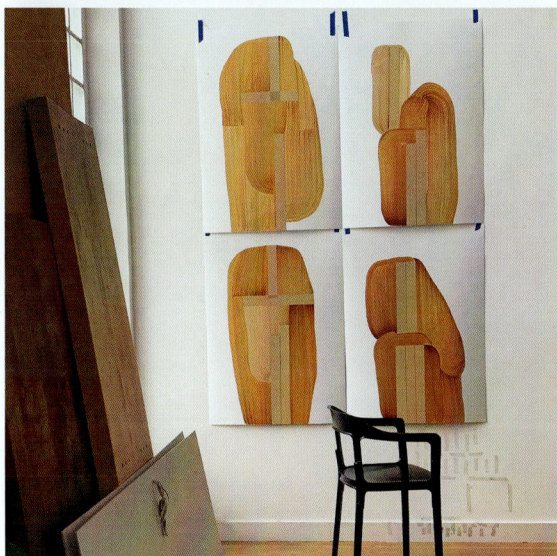

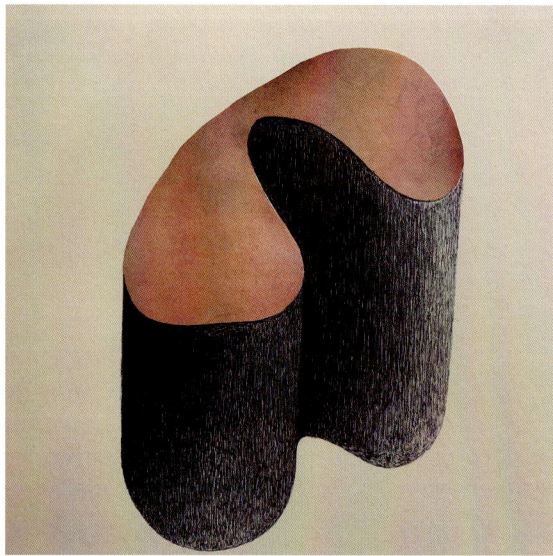
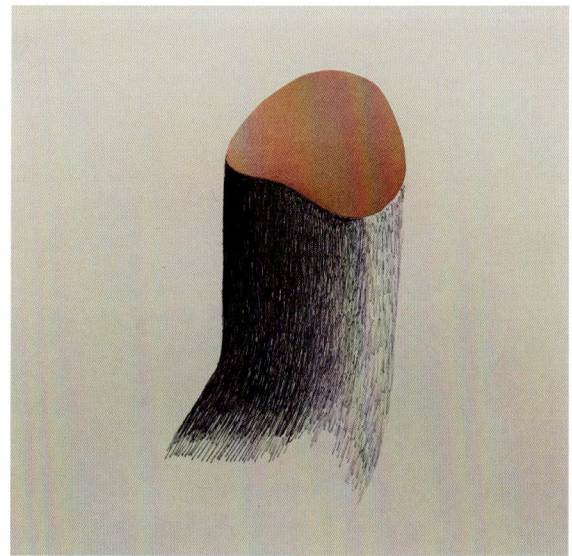

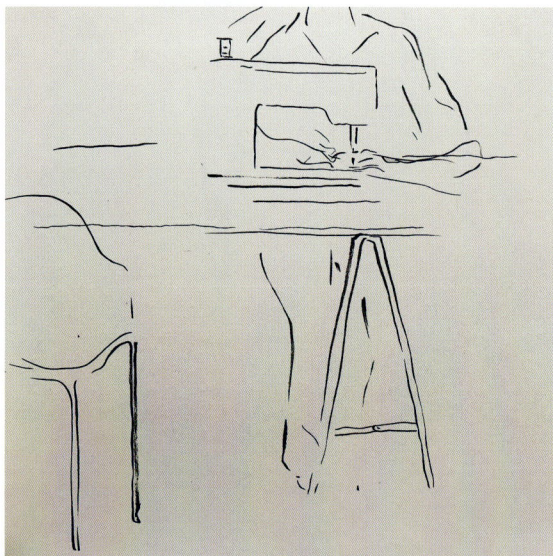

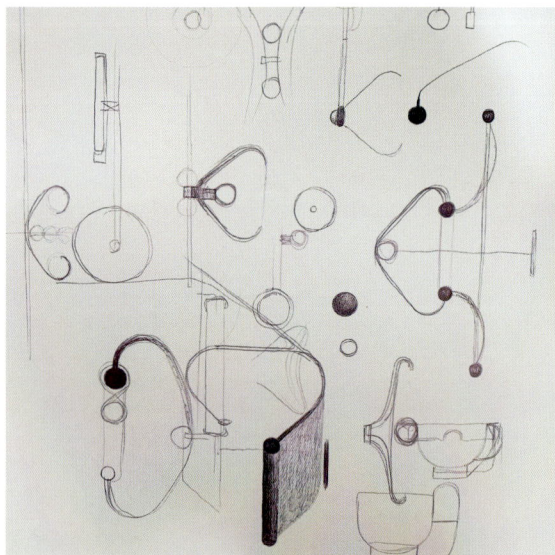
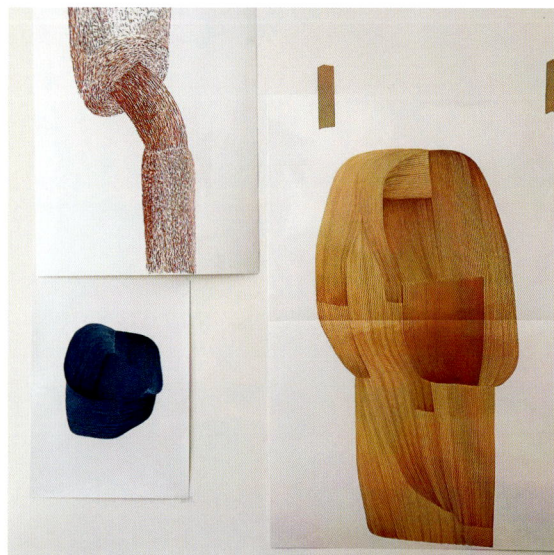

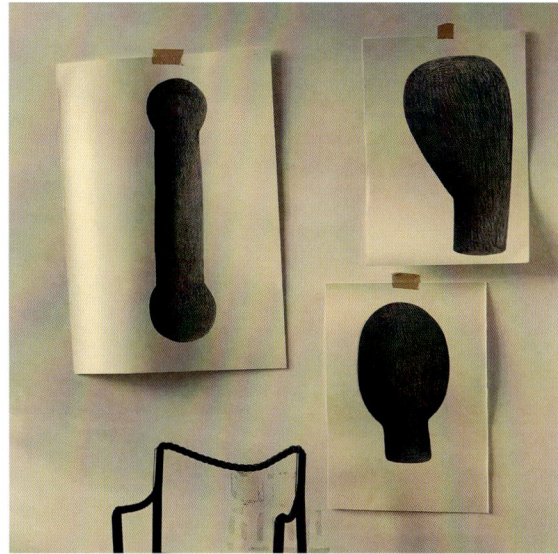

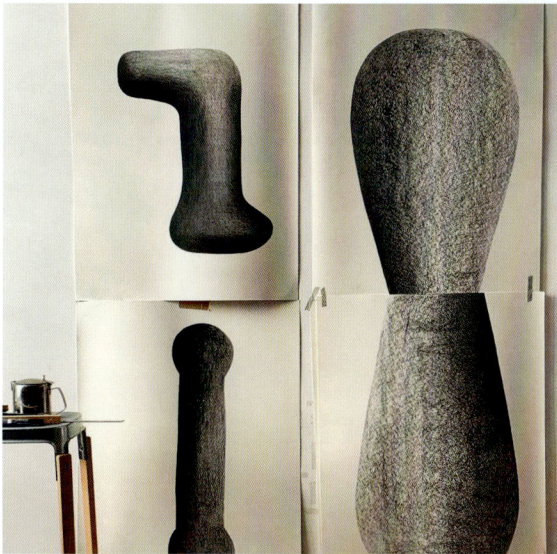
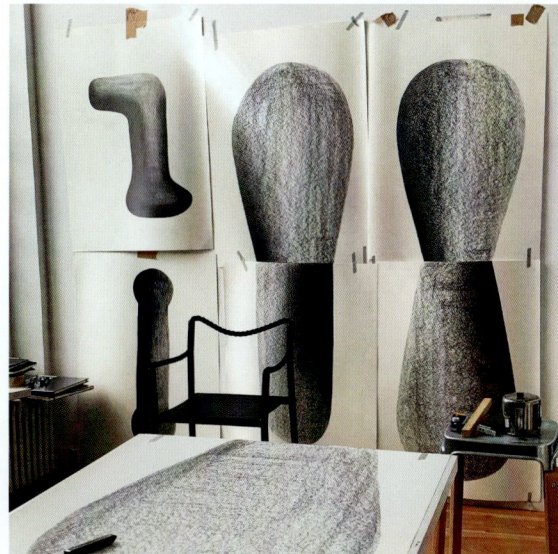

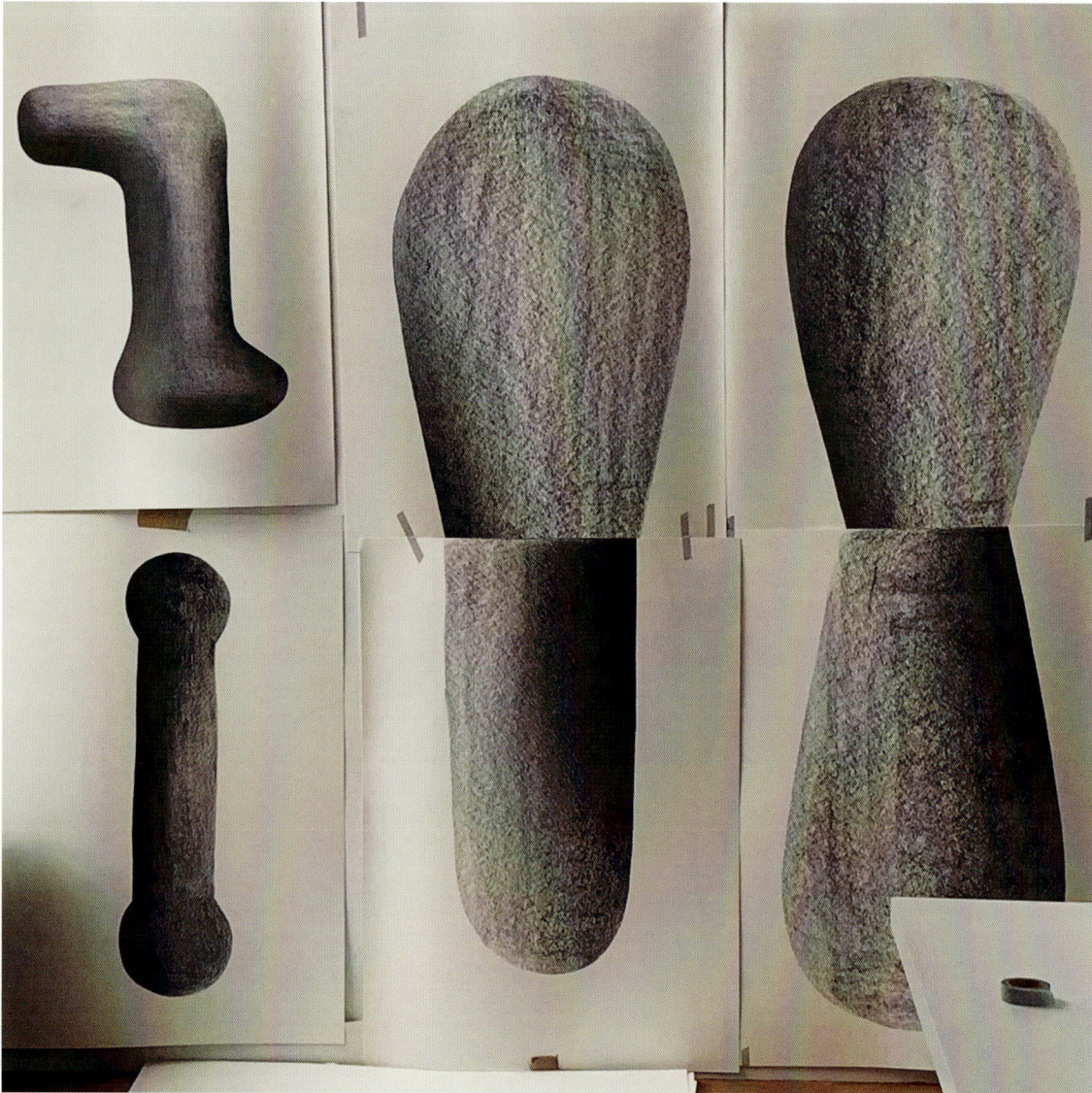

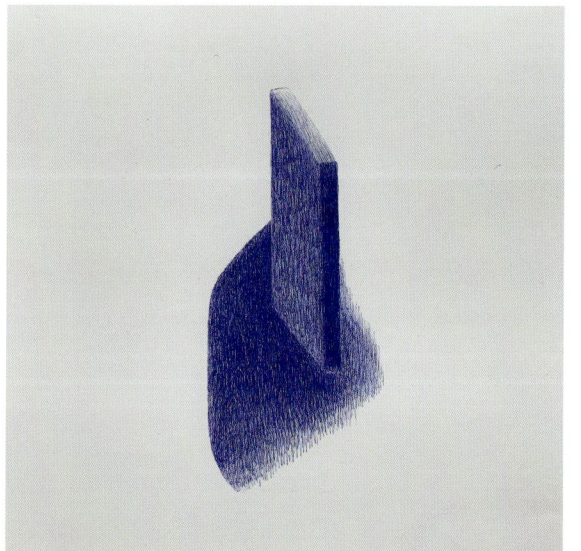

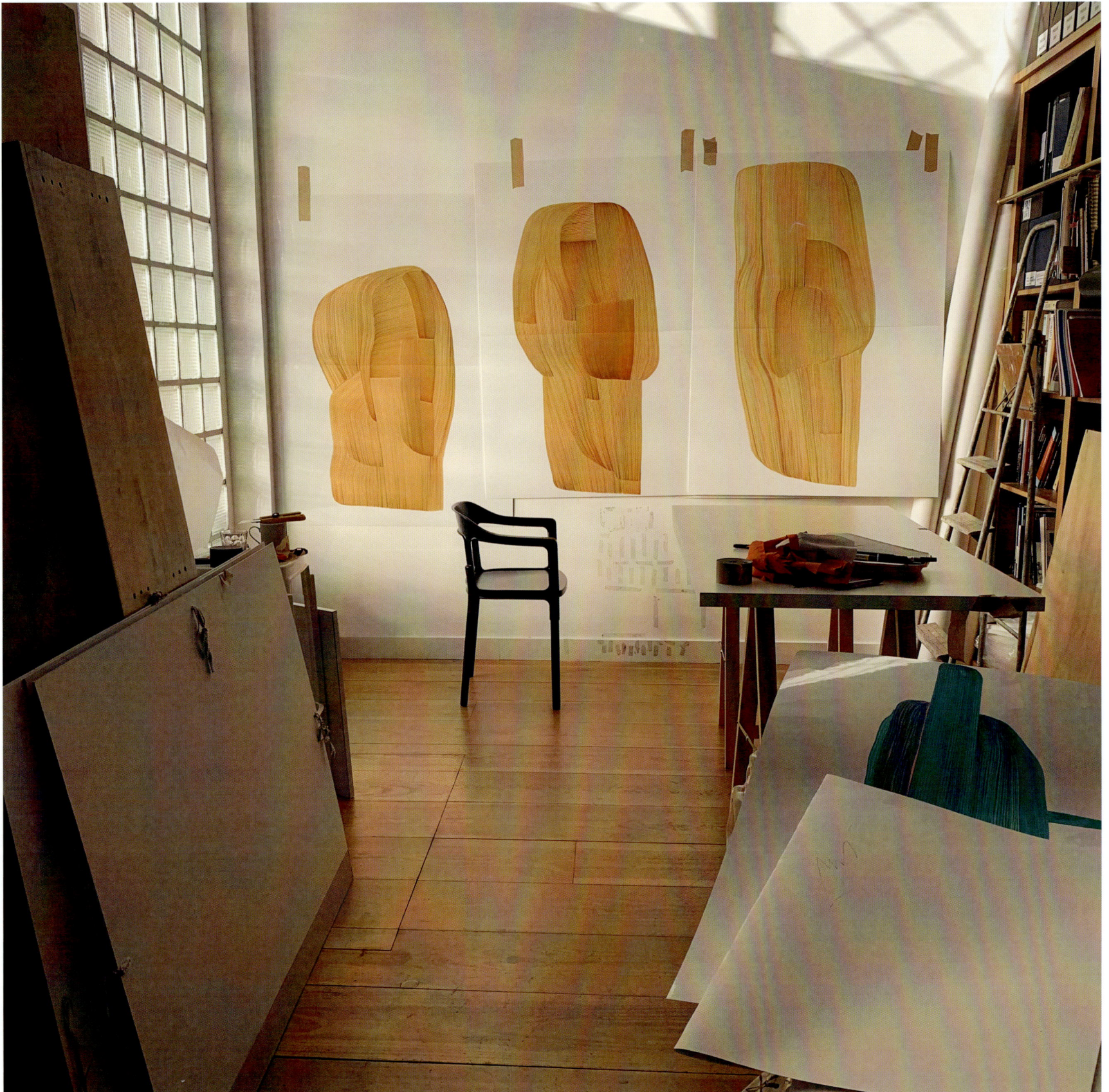

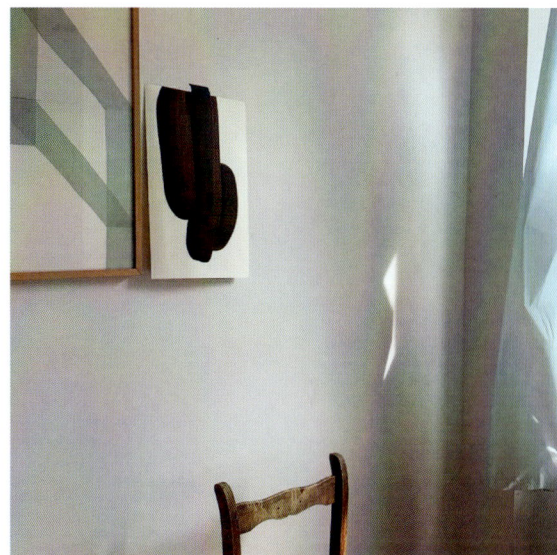
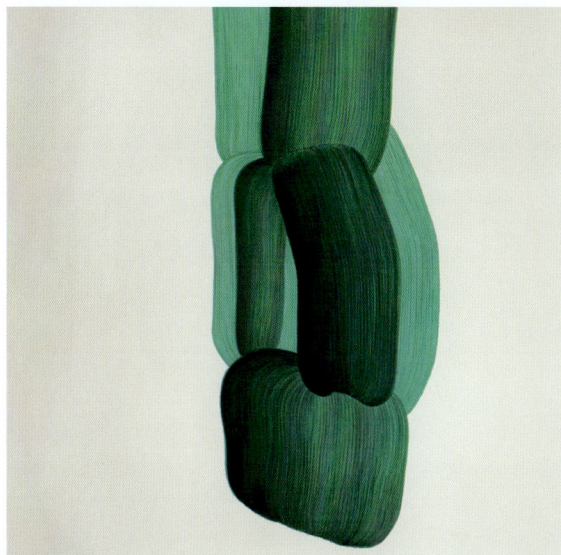

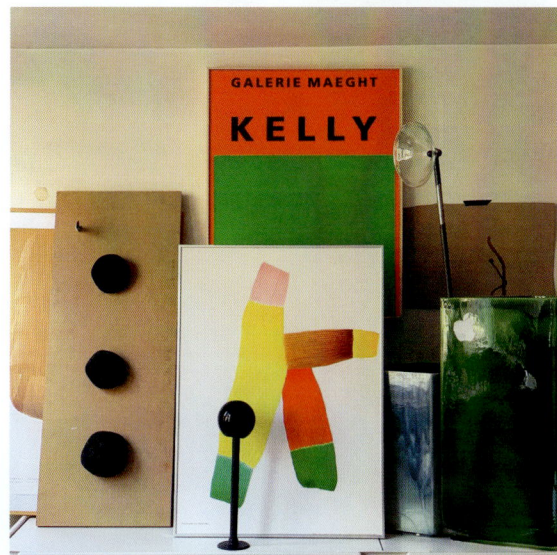

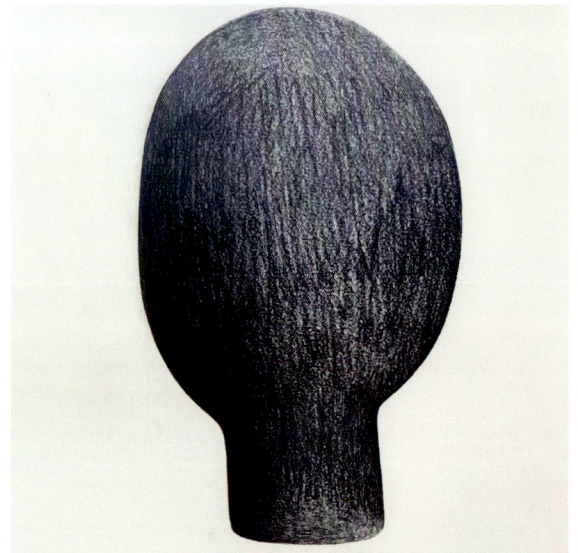

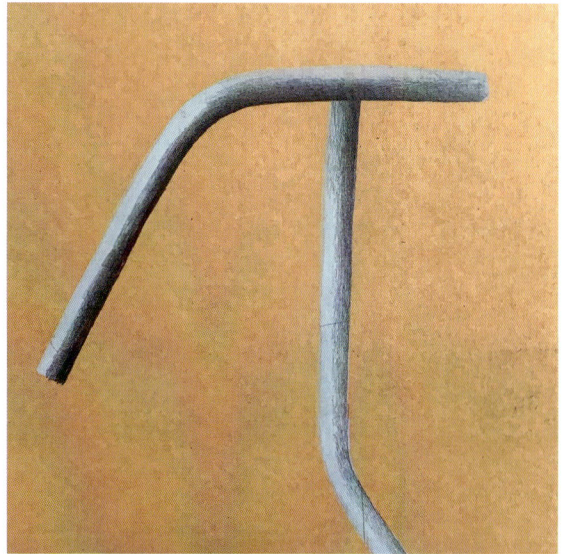

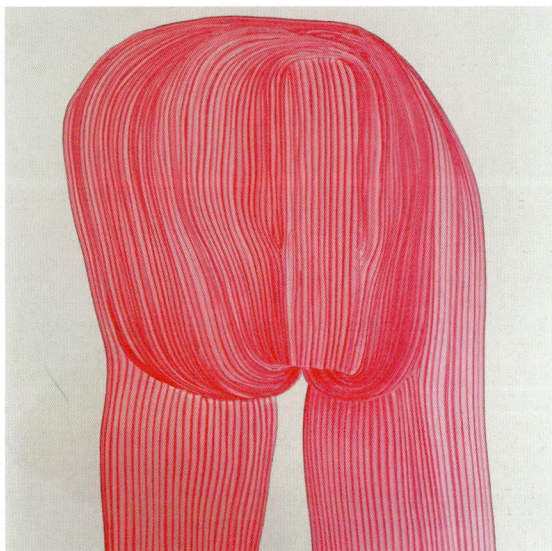

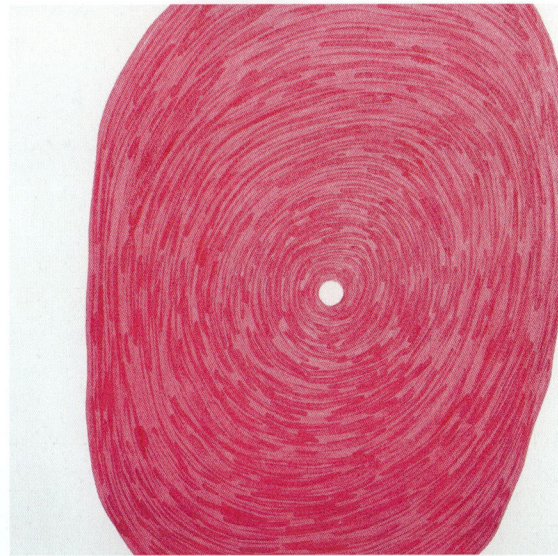

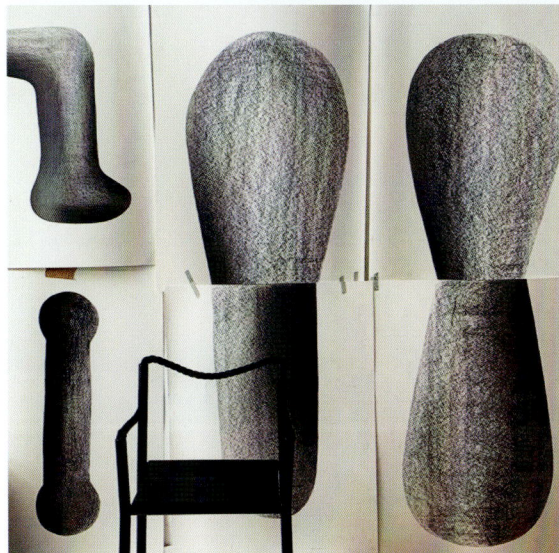

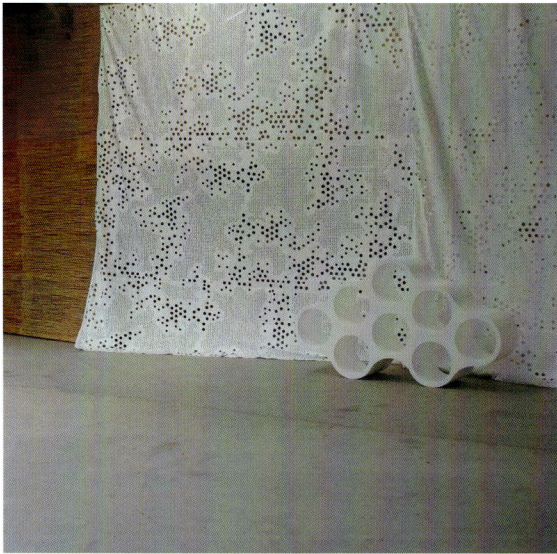

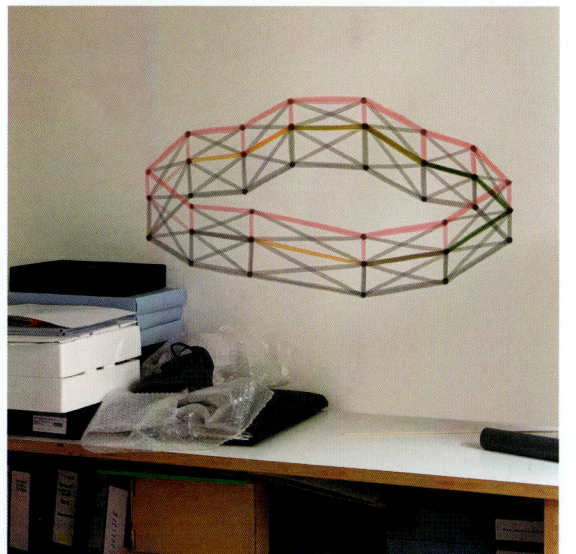

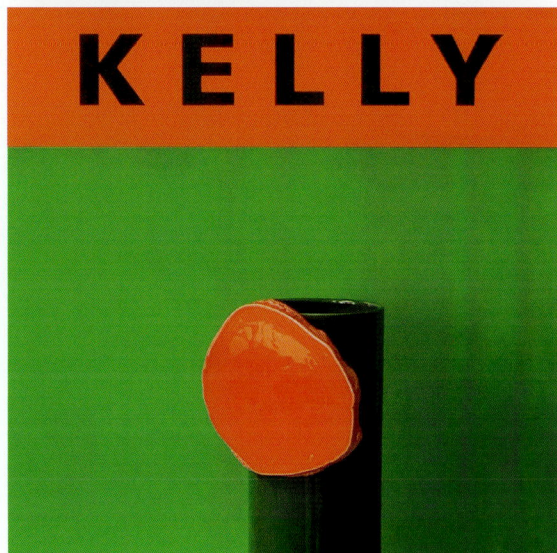

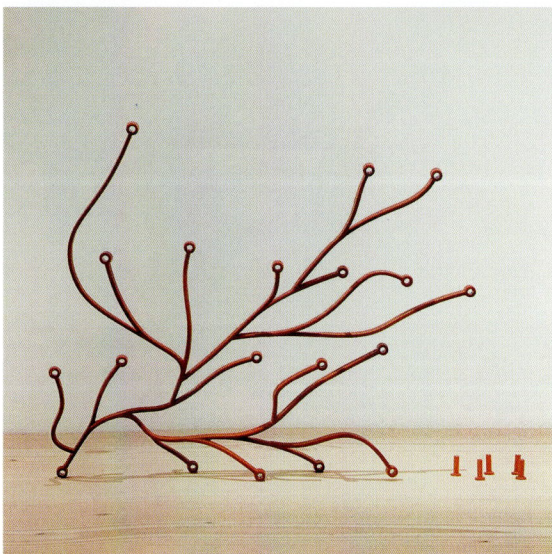

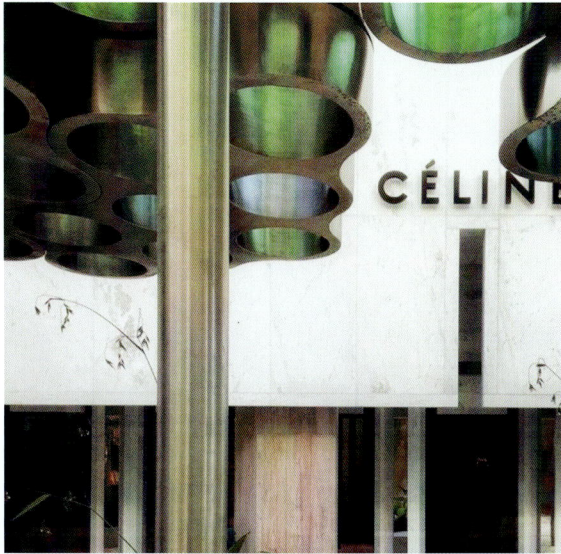

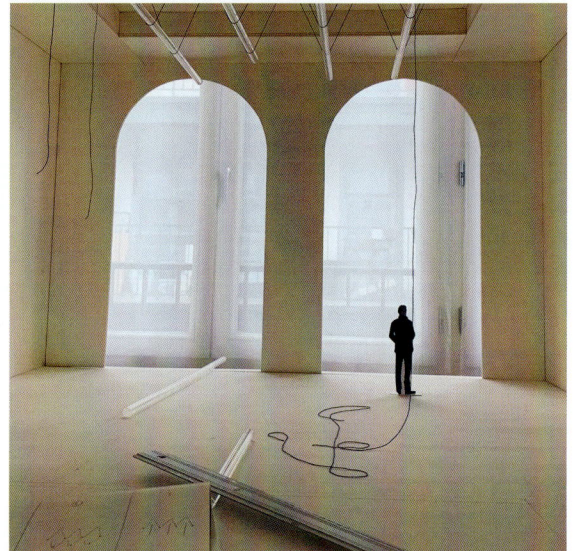
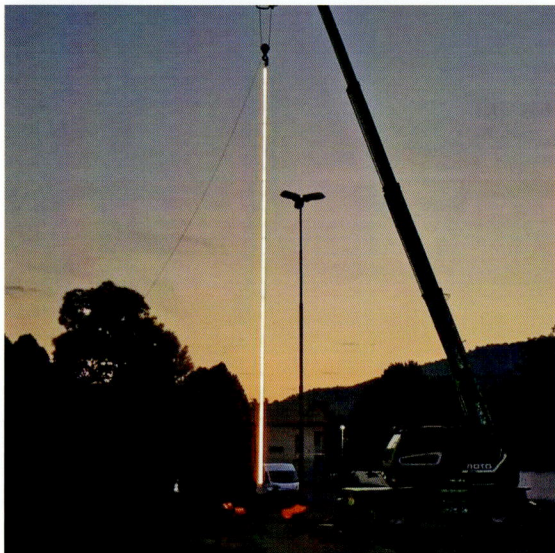

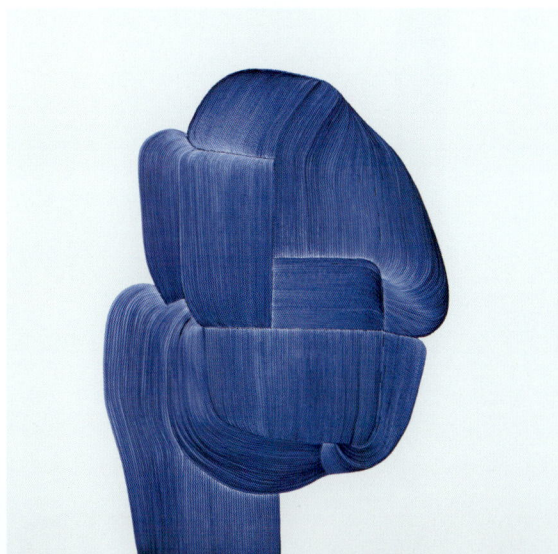

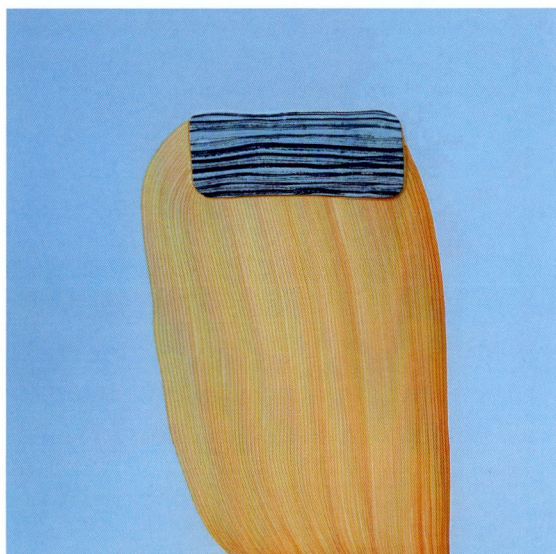
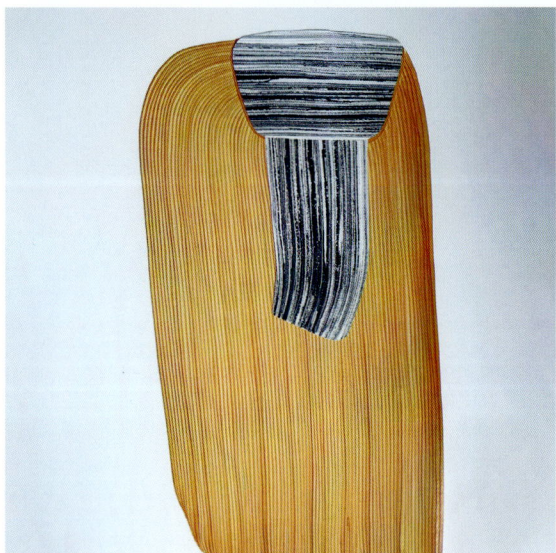

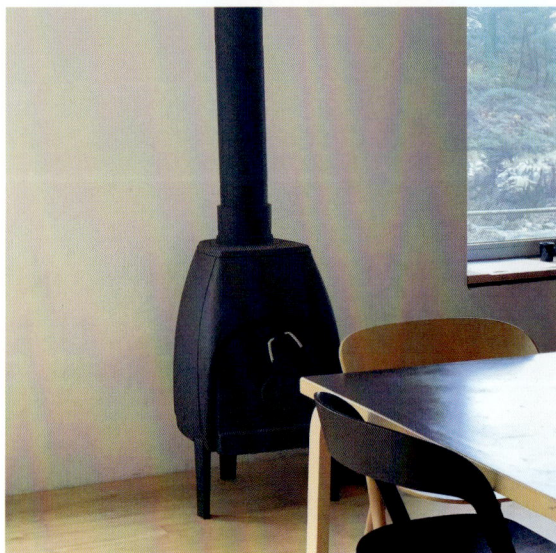

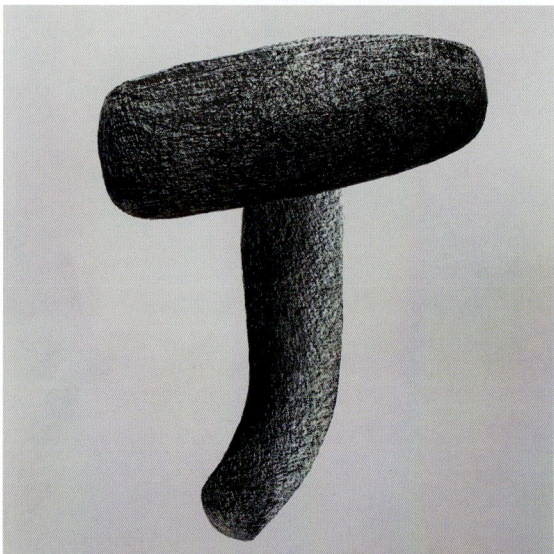

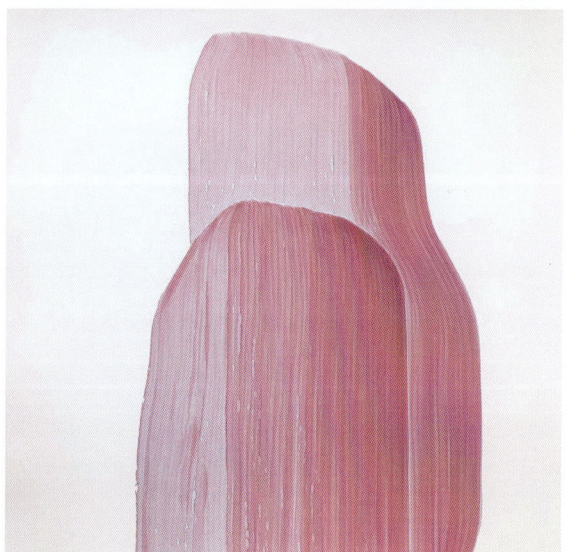

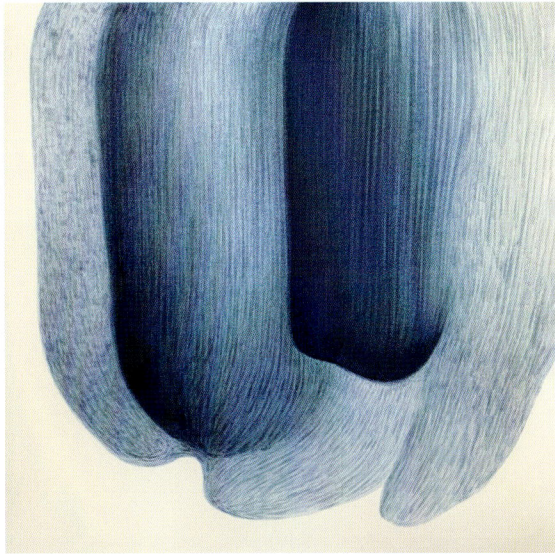
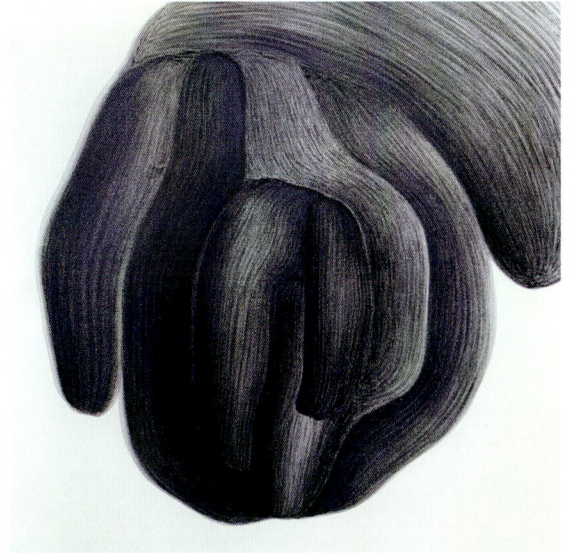
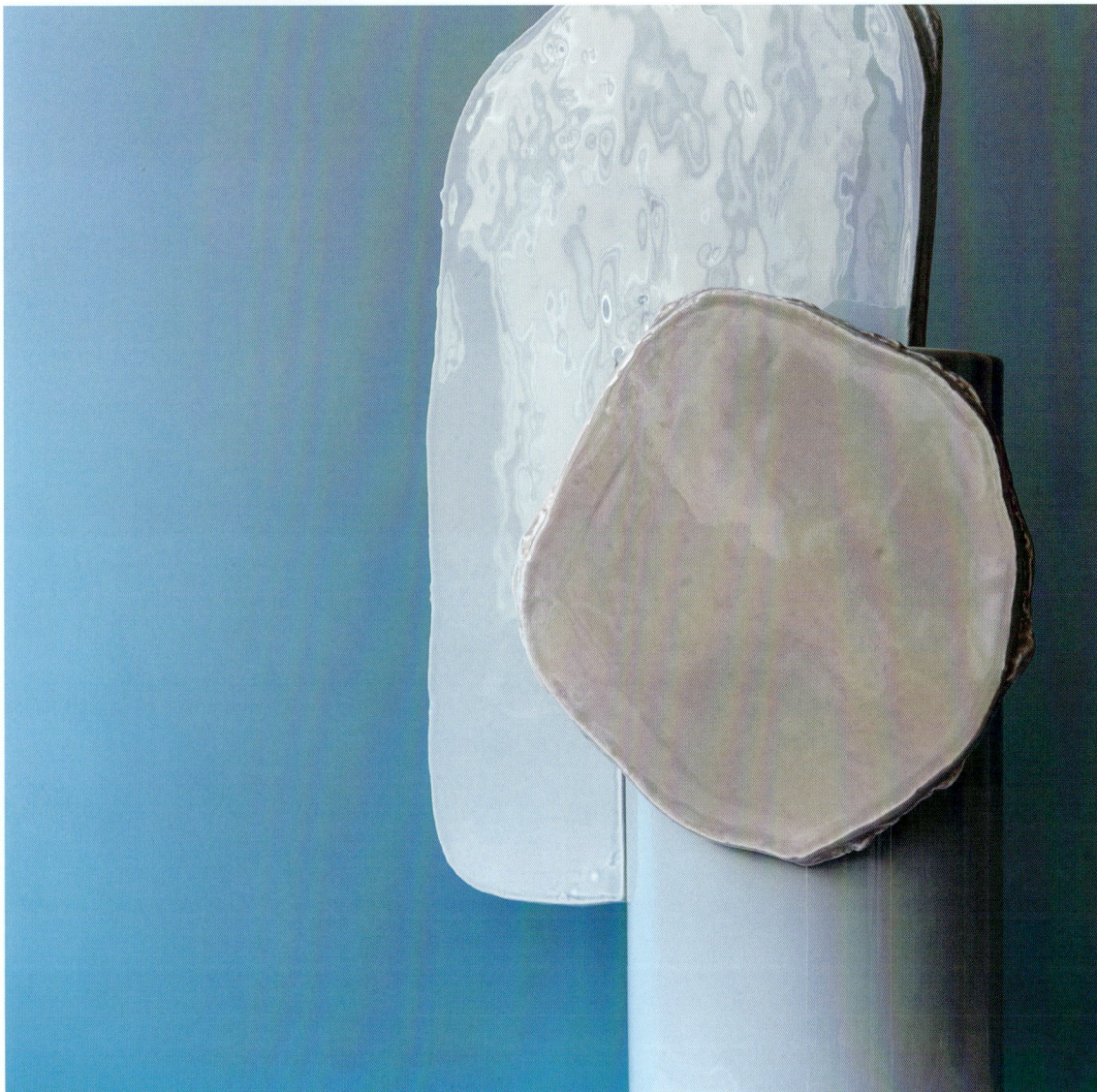

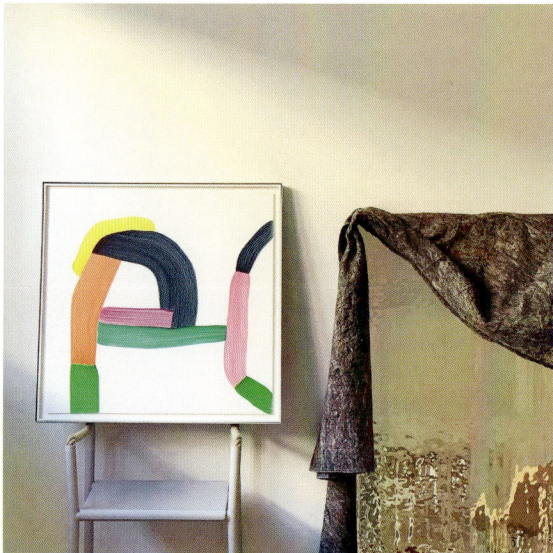

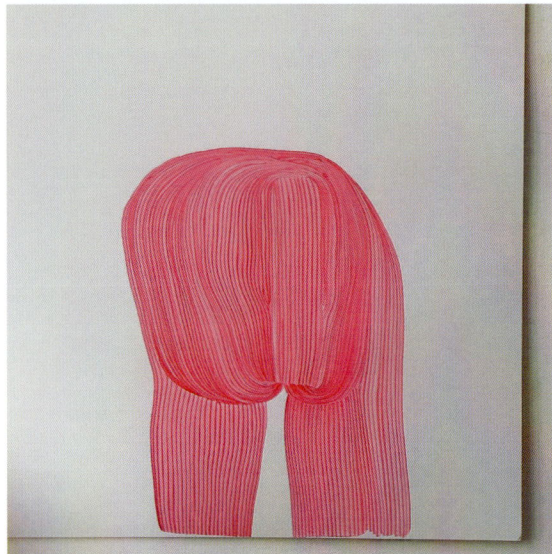

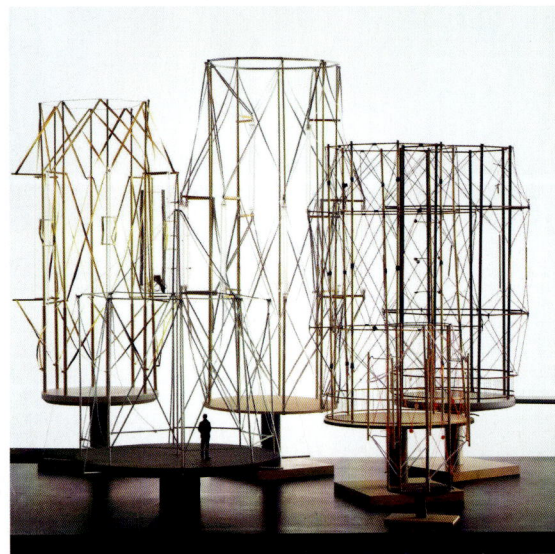

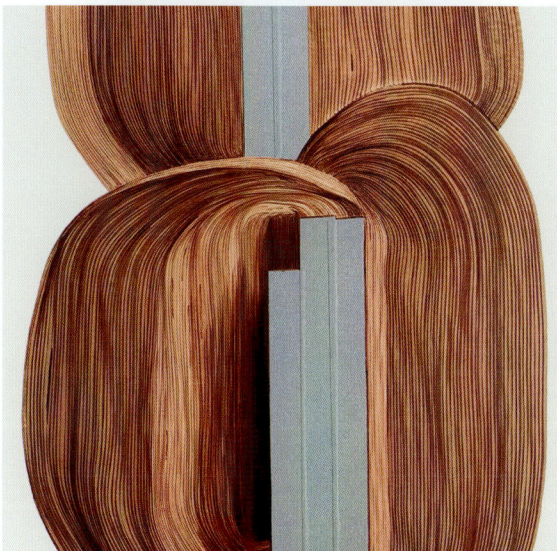

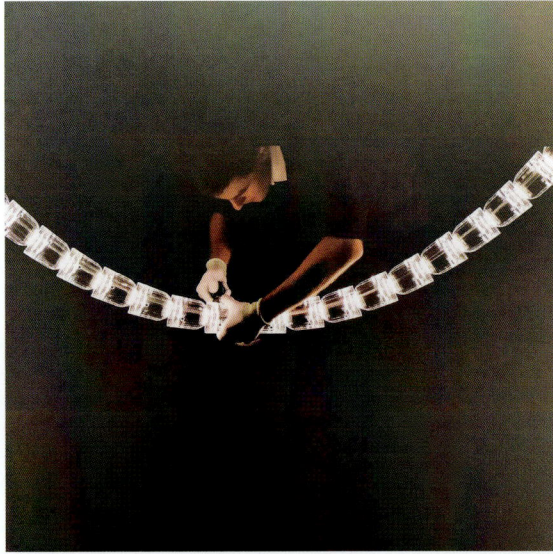

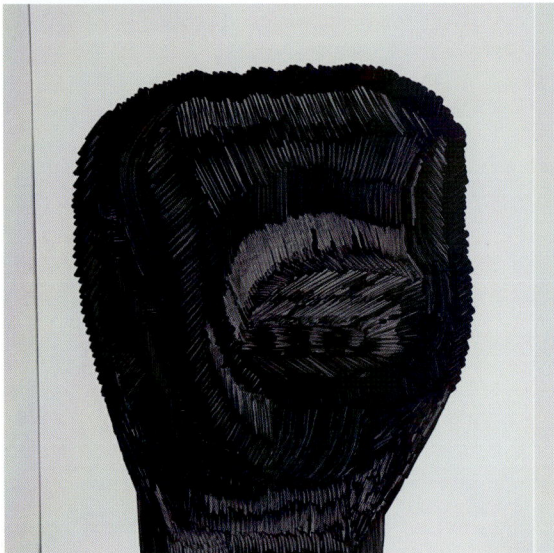

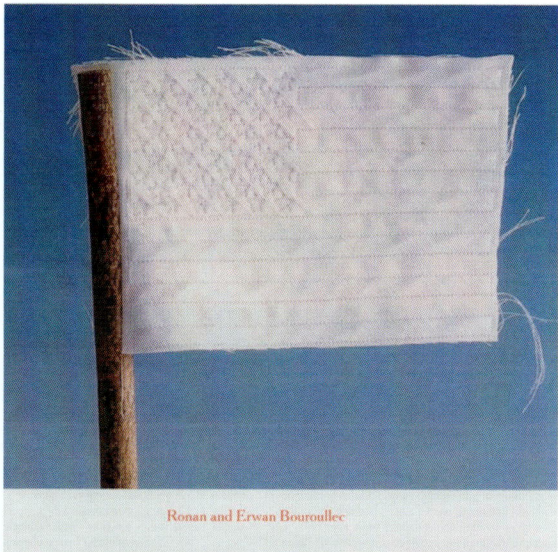

Ronan and Erwan Bouroullec

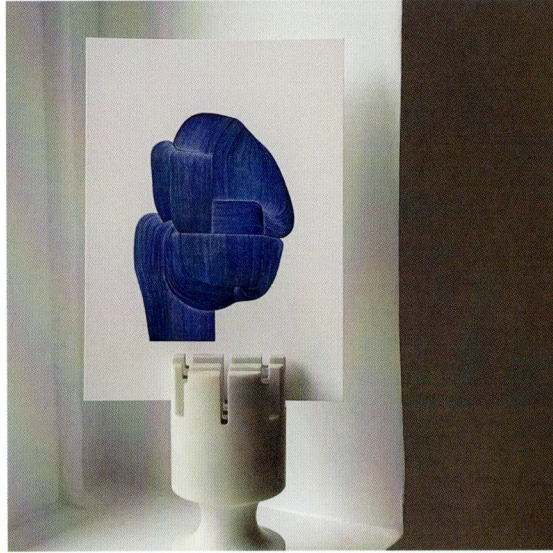

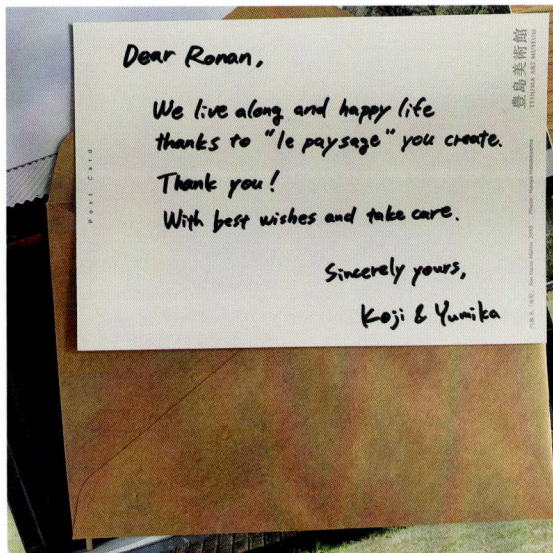

Dear Ronan,

We live a long and happy life
thanks to "le paysage" you create.

Thank you!
With best wishes and take care.

Sincerely yours,

Koji & Yumika

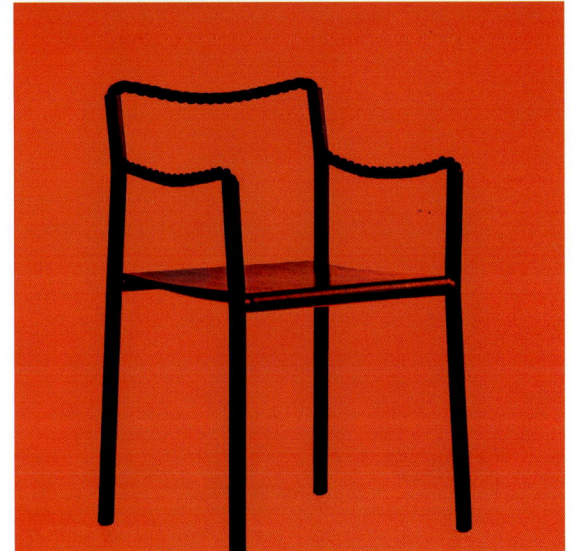

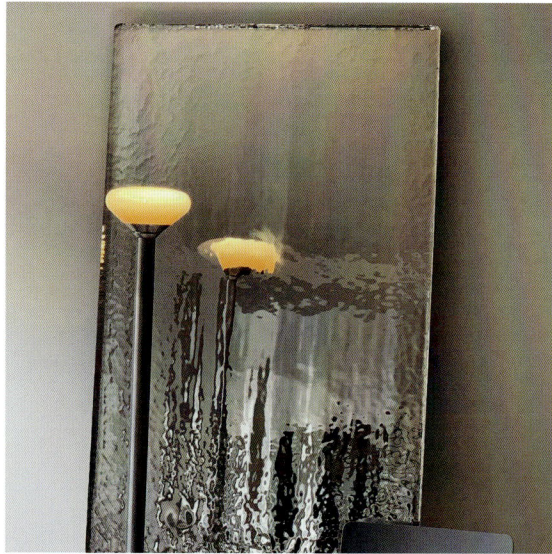
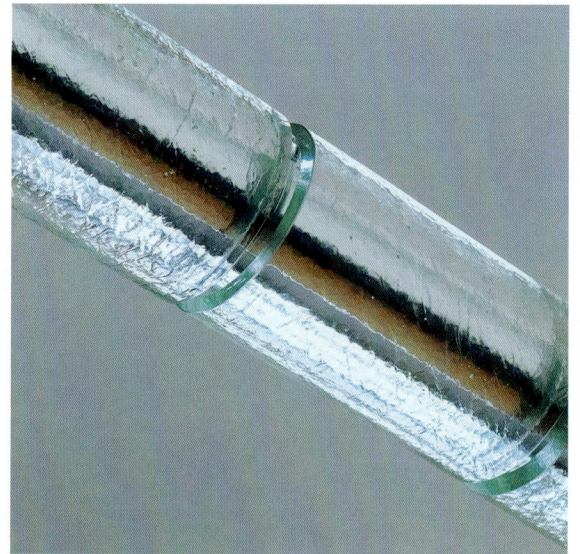

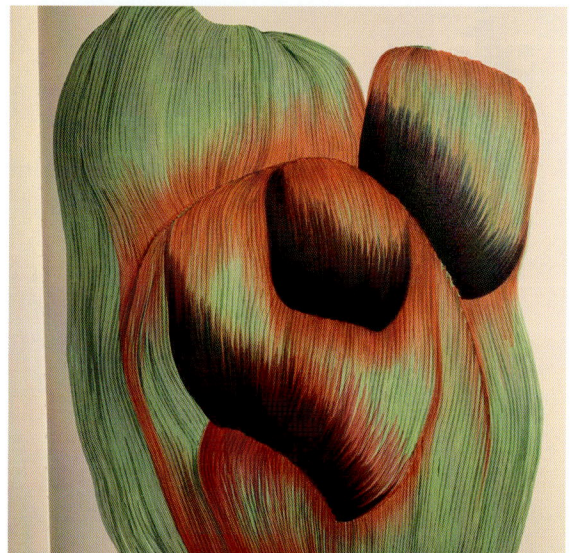
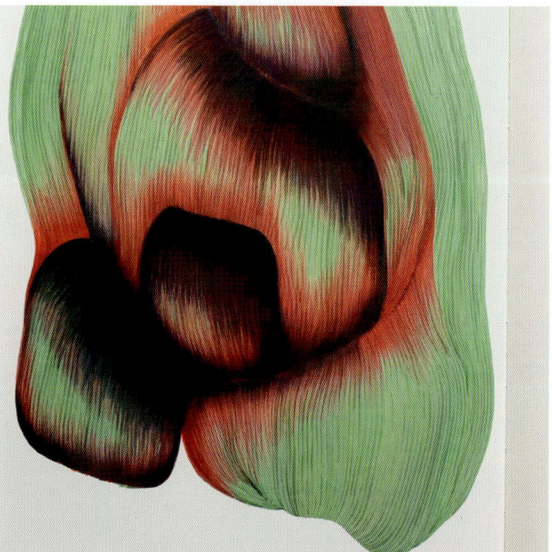

December / Décembre

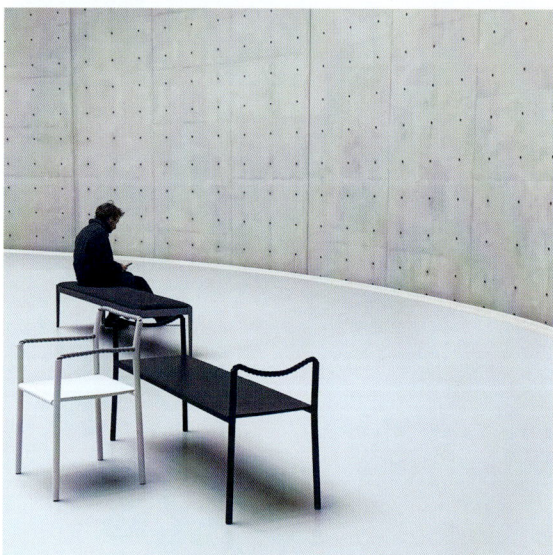

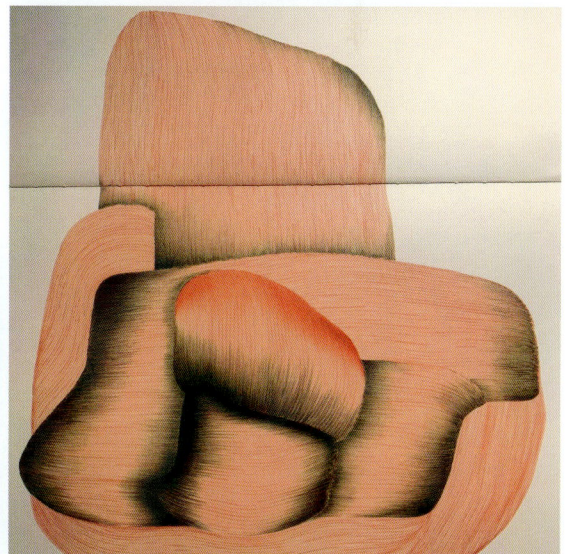

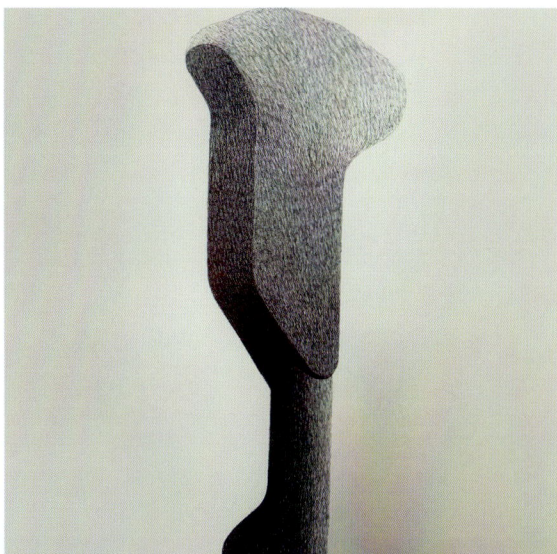
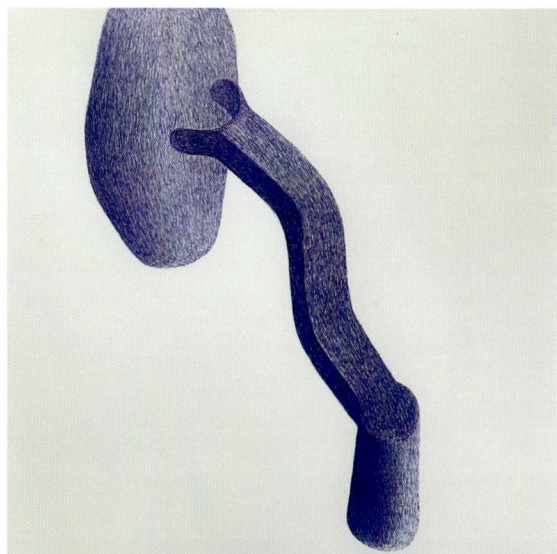
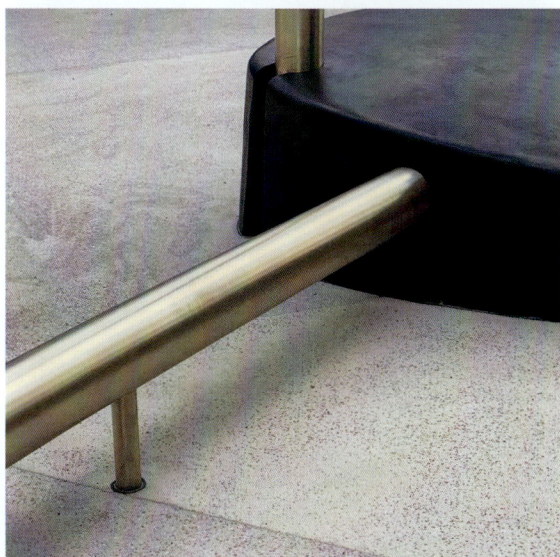

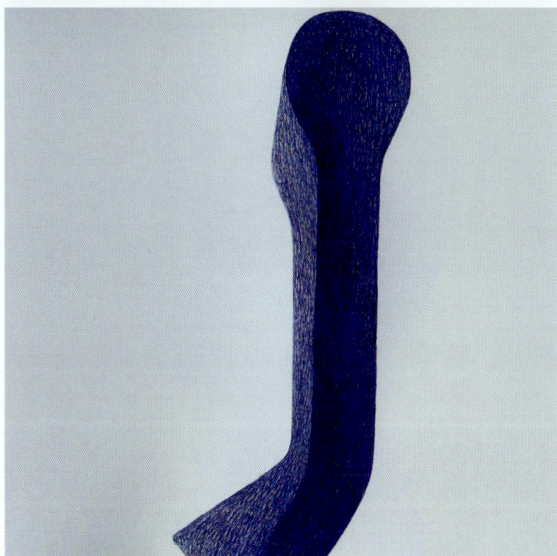
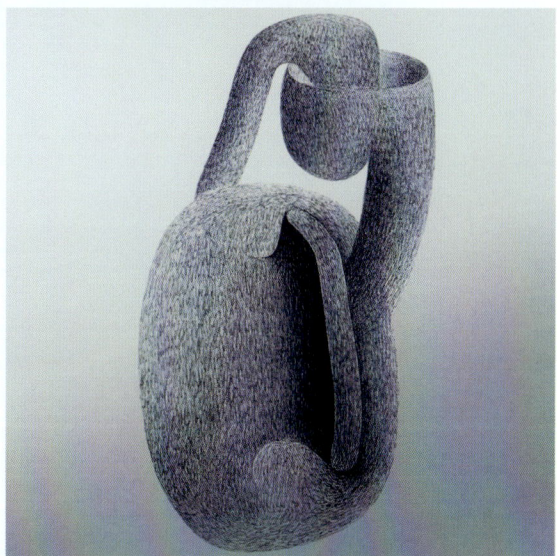

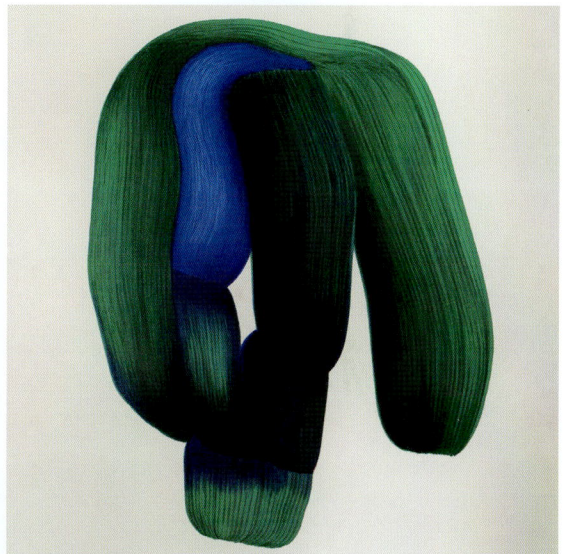

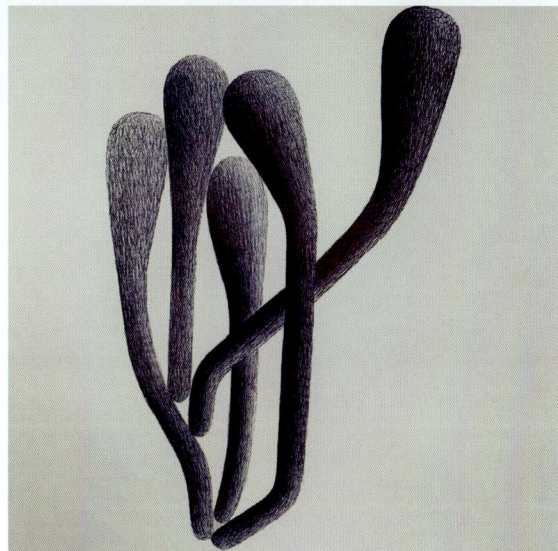

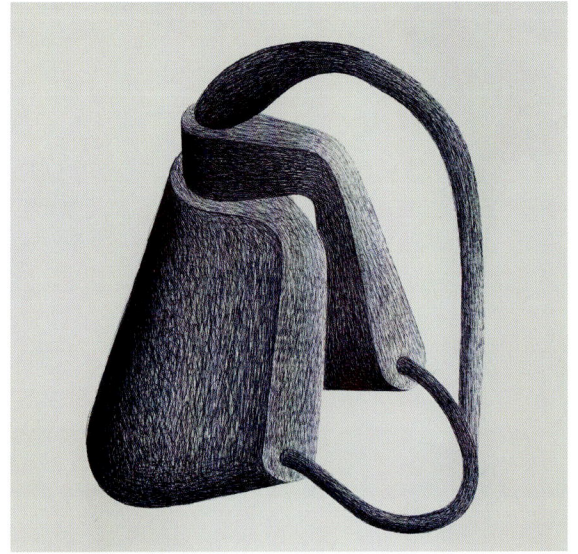

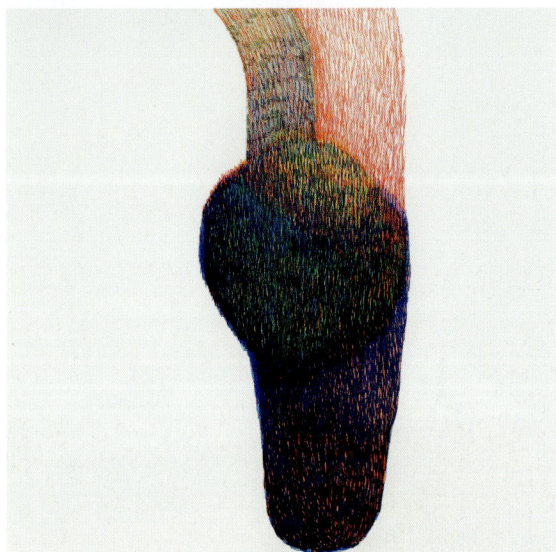

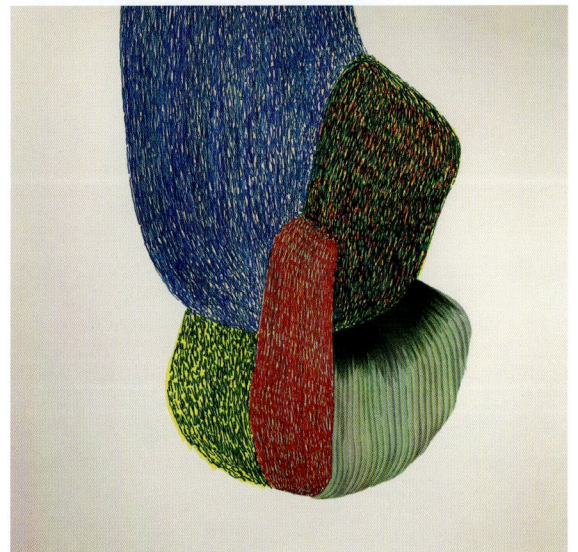

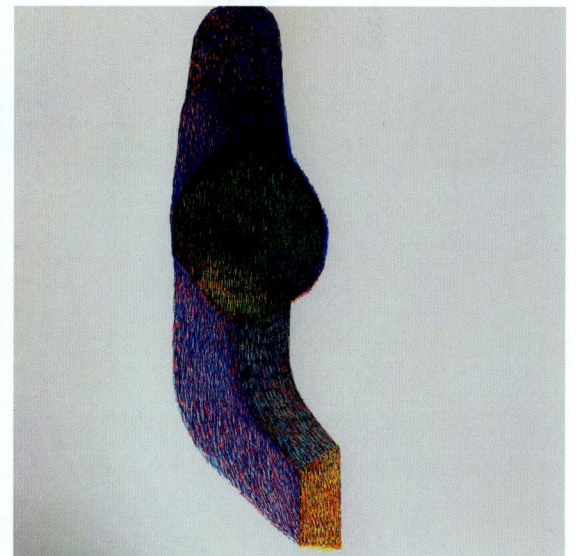

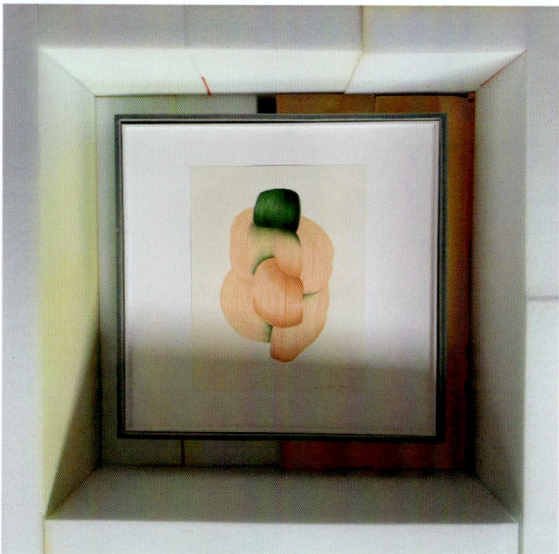

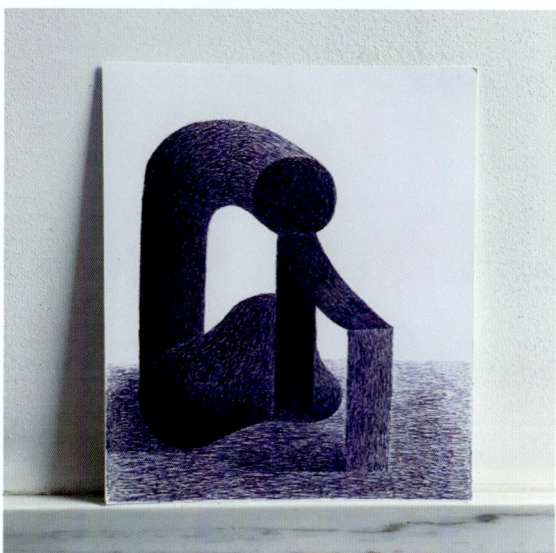
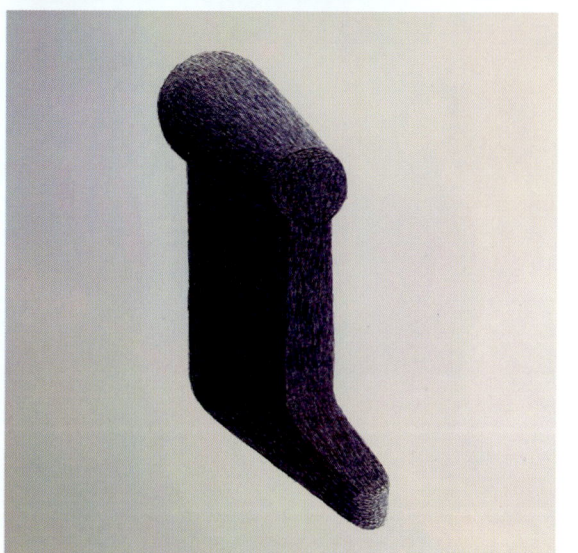

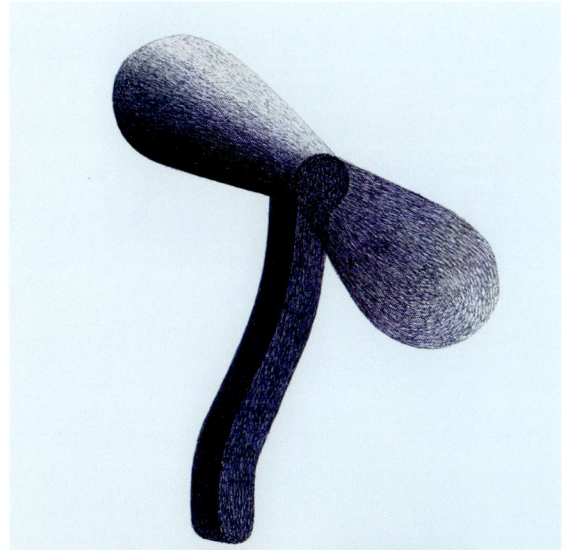

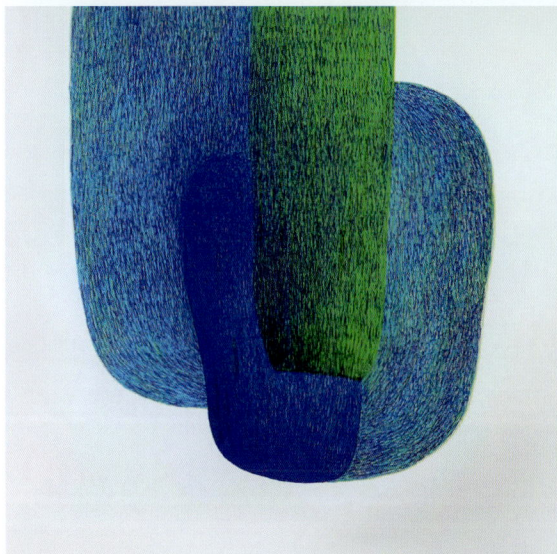

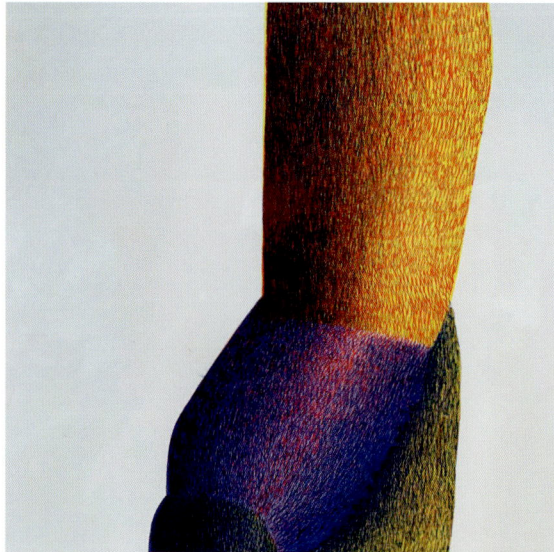

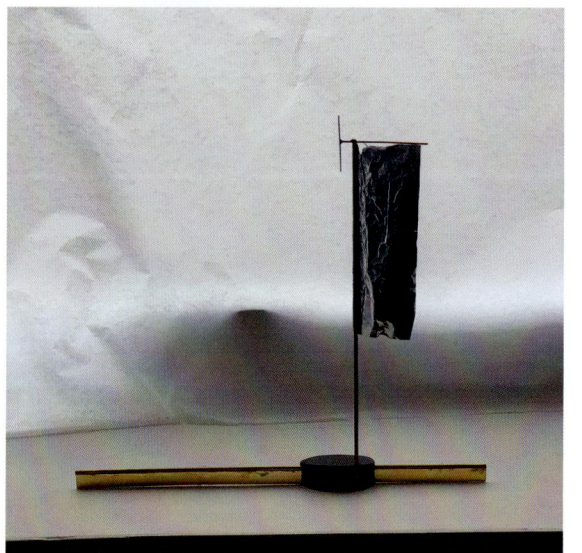

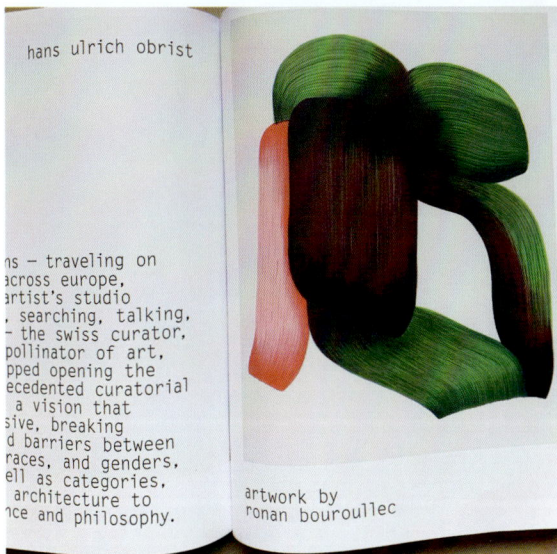

hans ulrich obrist

ns – traveling on
across europe,
artist's studio
, searching, talking,
– the swiss curator,
pollinator of art,
pped opening the
ecedented curatorial
a vision that
sive, breaking
d barriers between
races, and genders,
ell as categories,
architecture to
ce and philosophy.

artwork by
ronan bouroullec

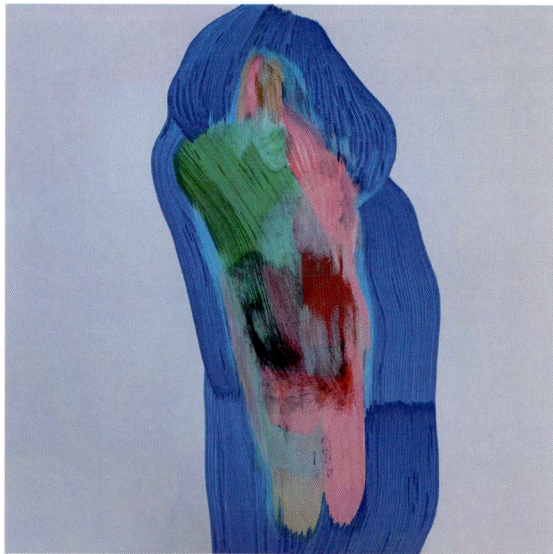
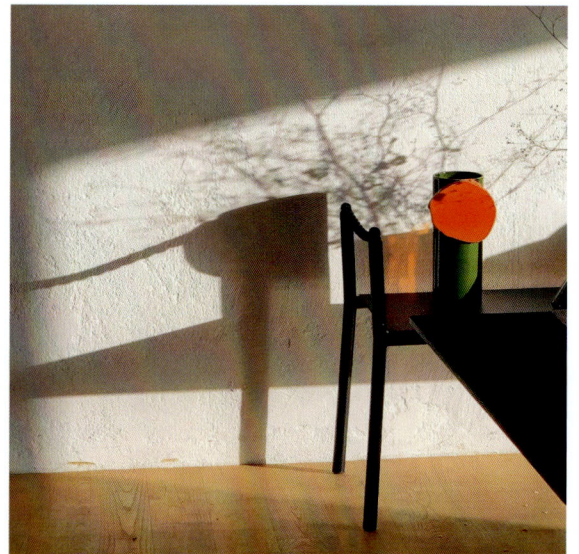

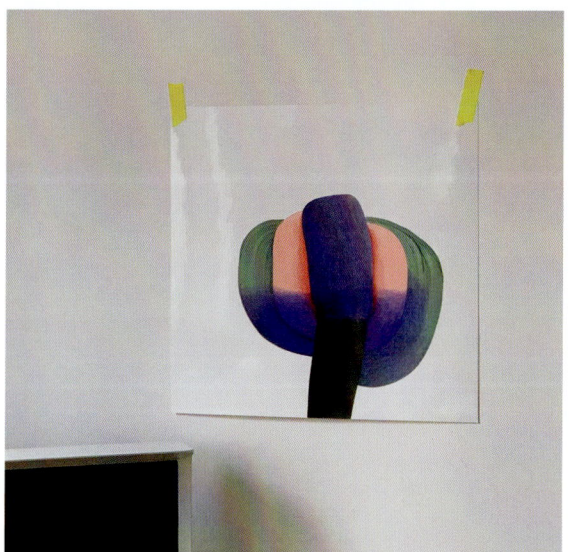

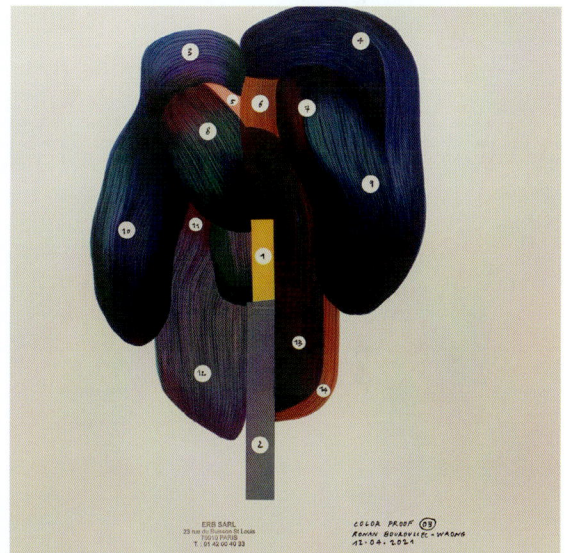
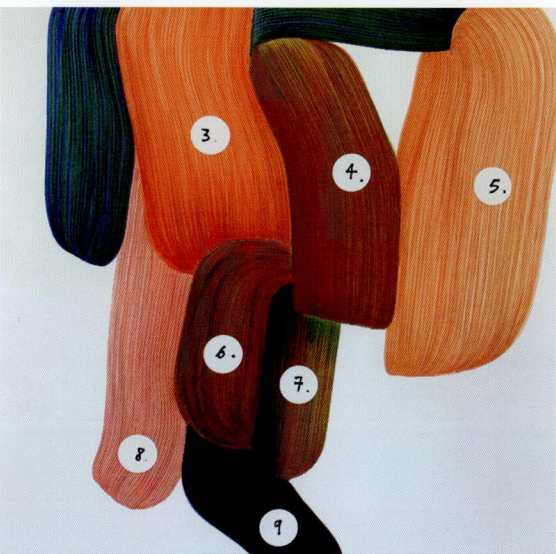

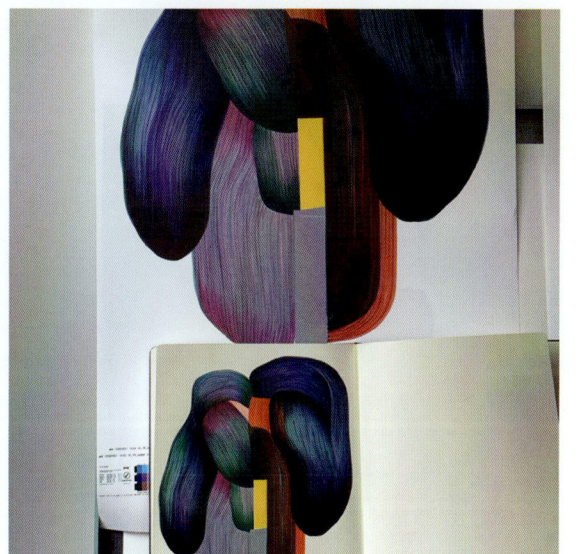

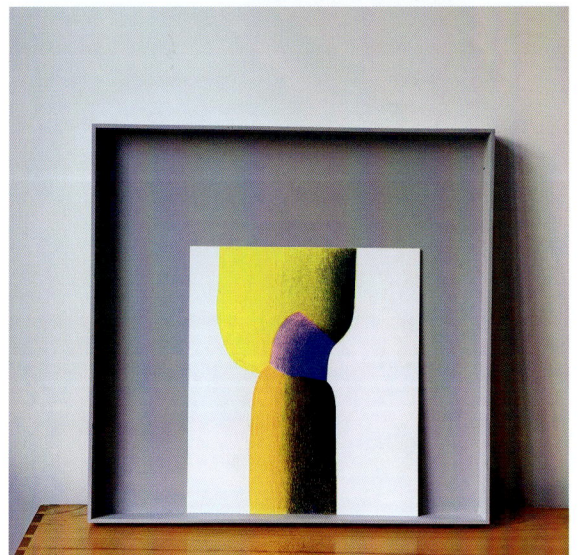

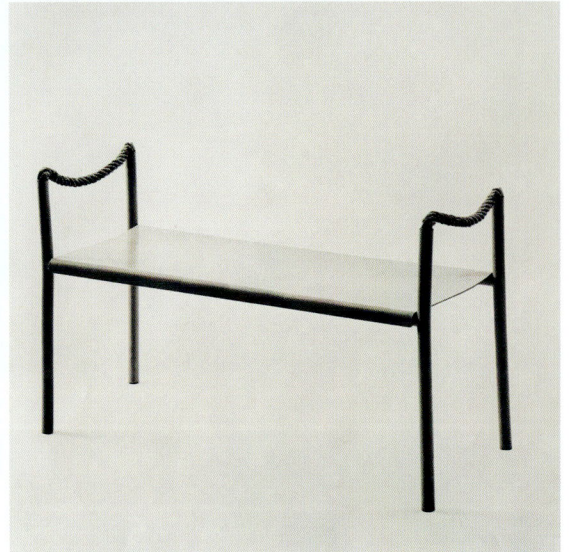

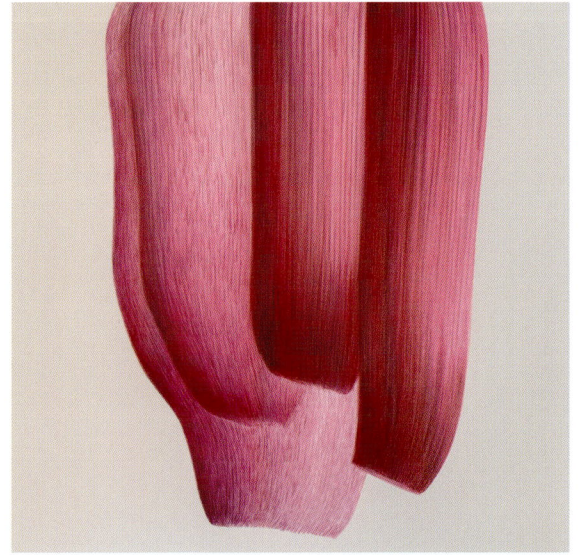

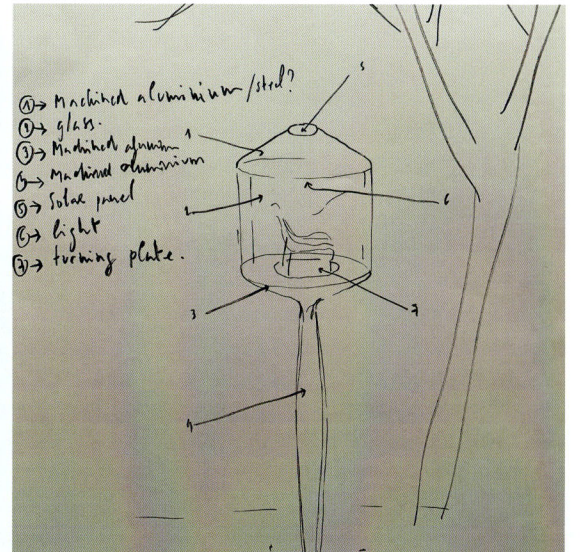

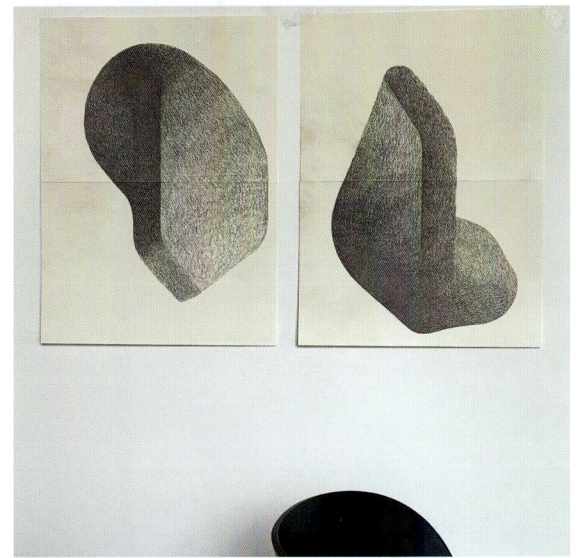

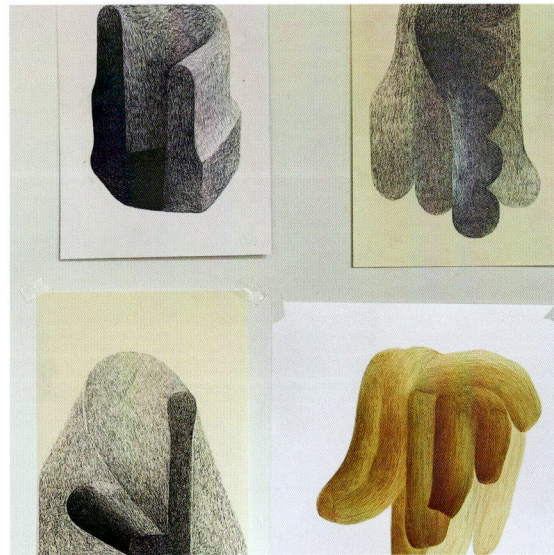

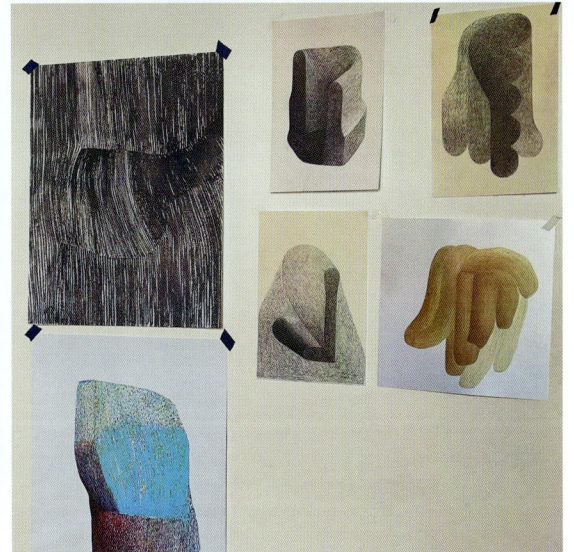

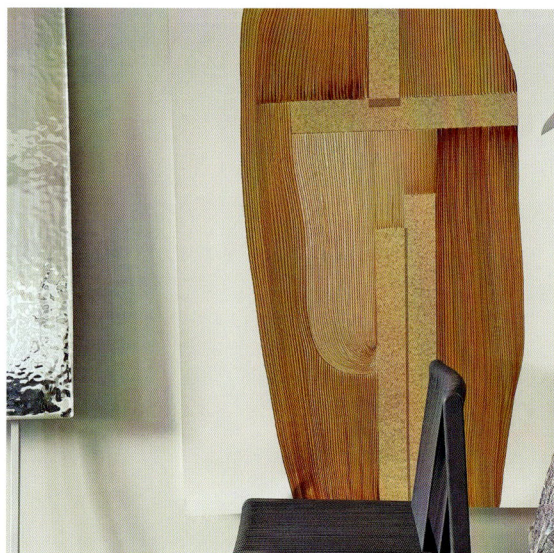

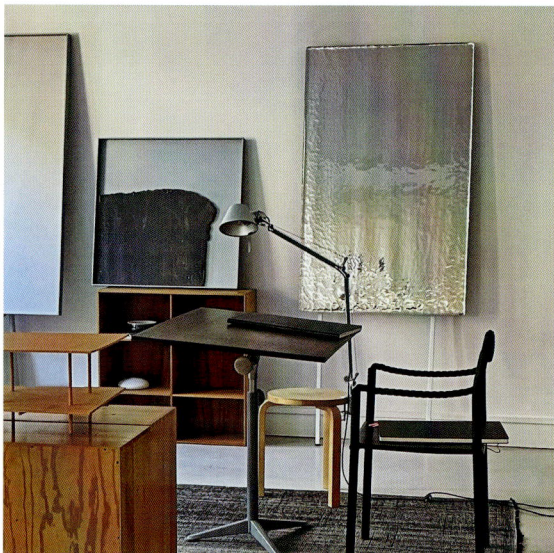

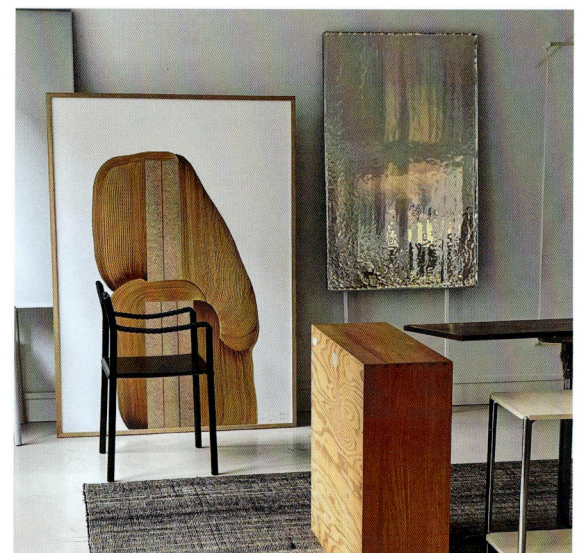

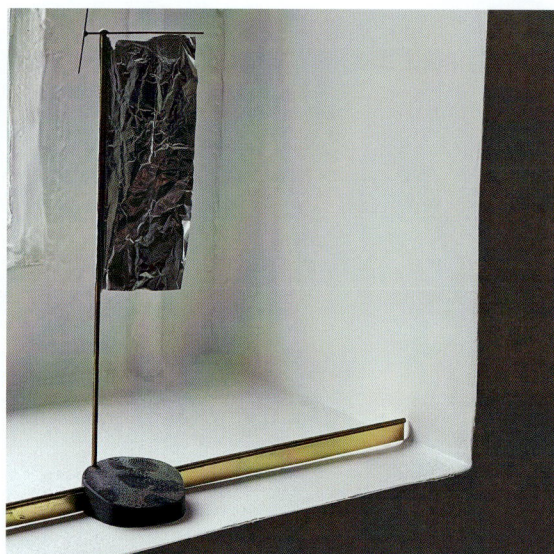

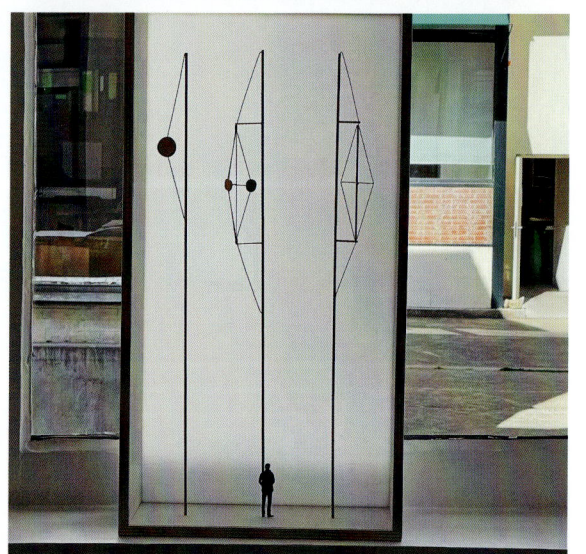

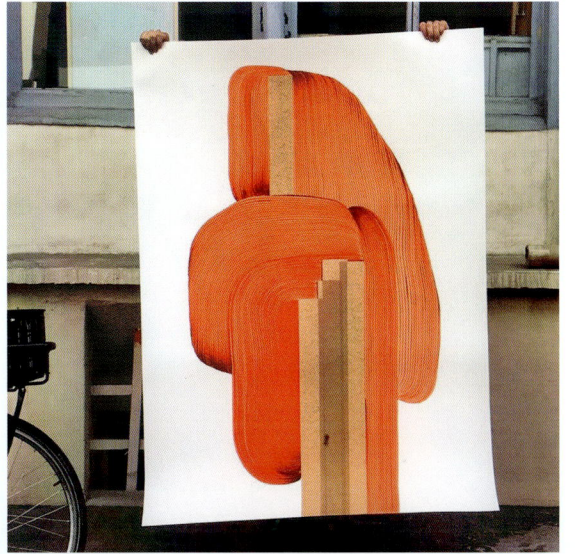
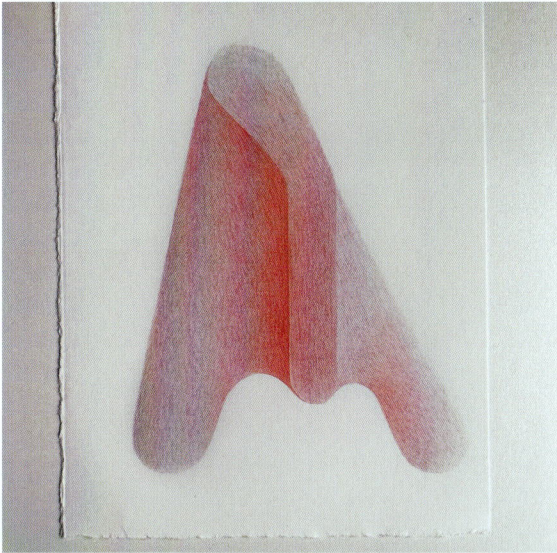

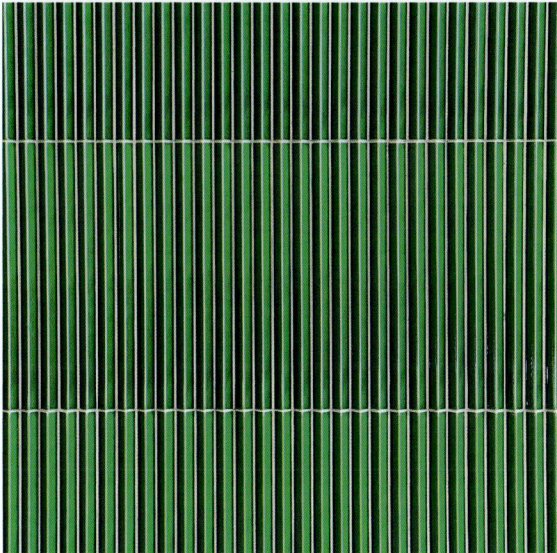

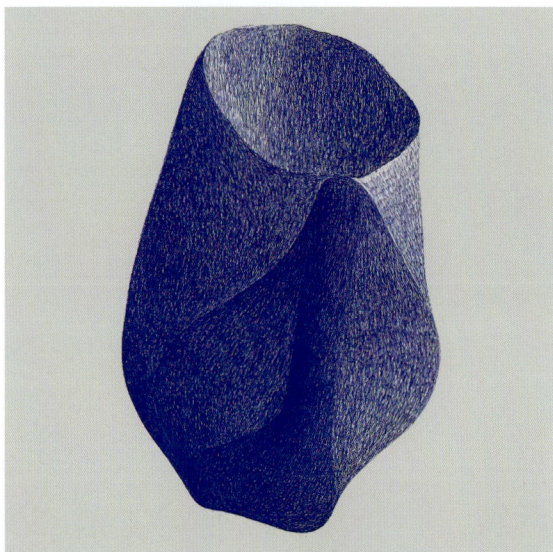

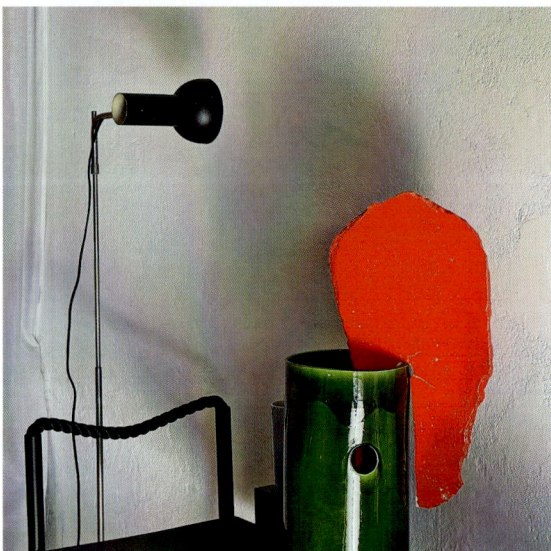
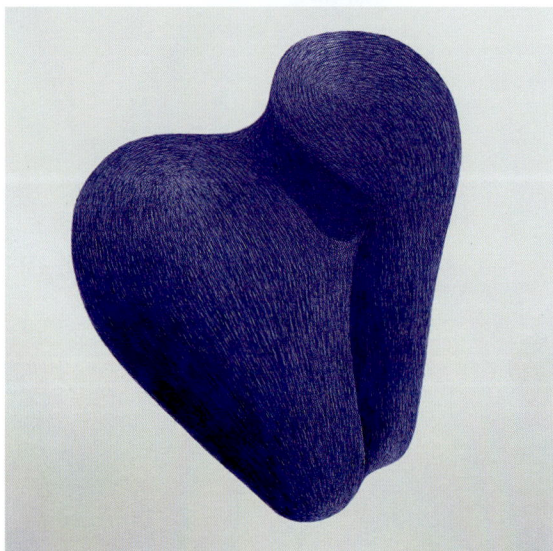
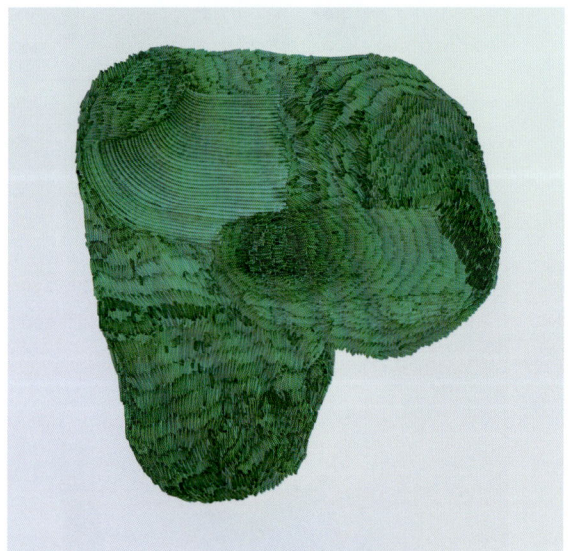

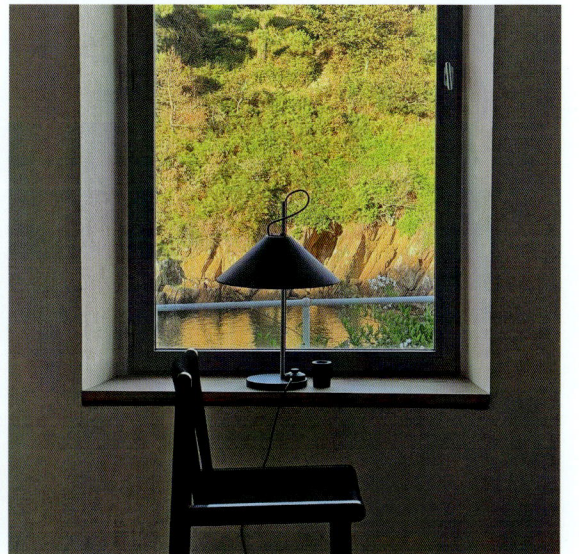

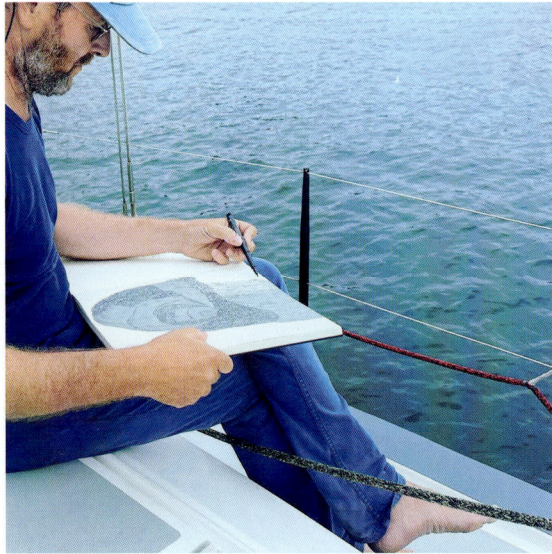

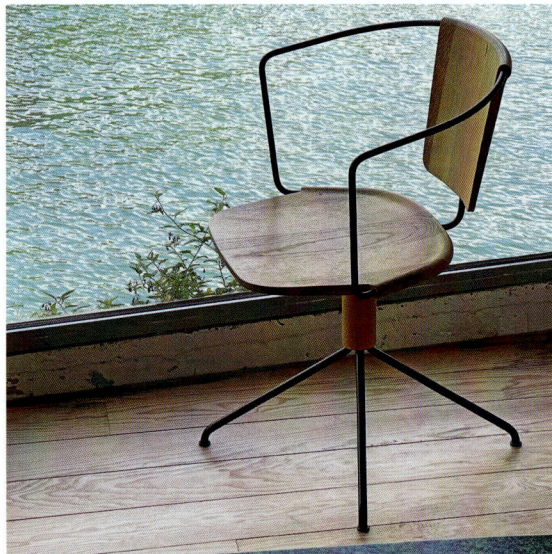
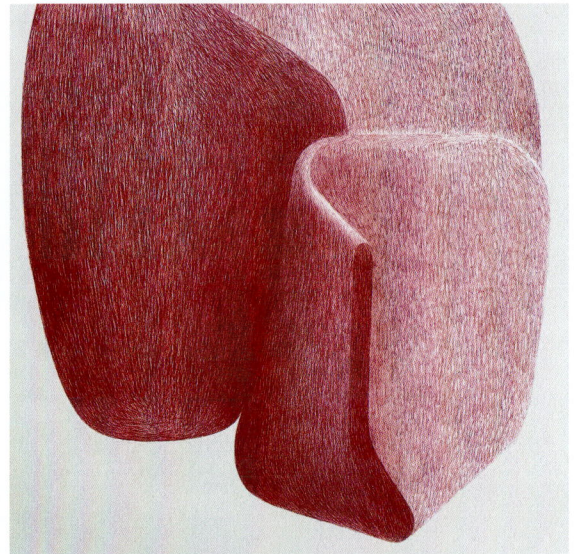

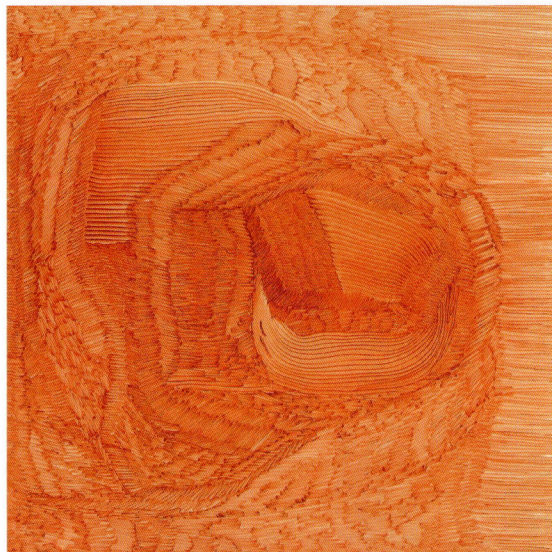

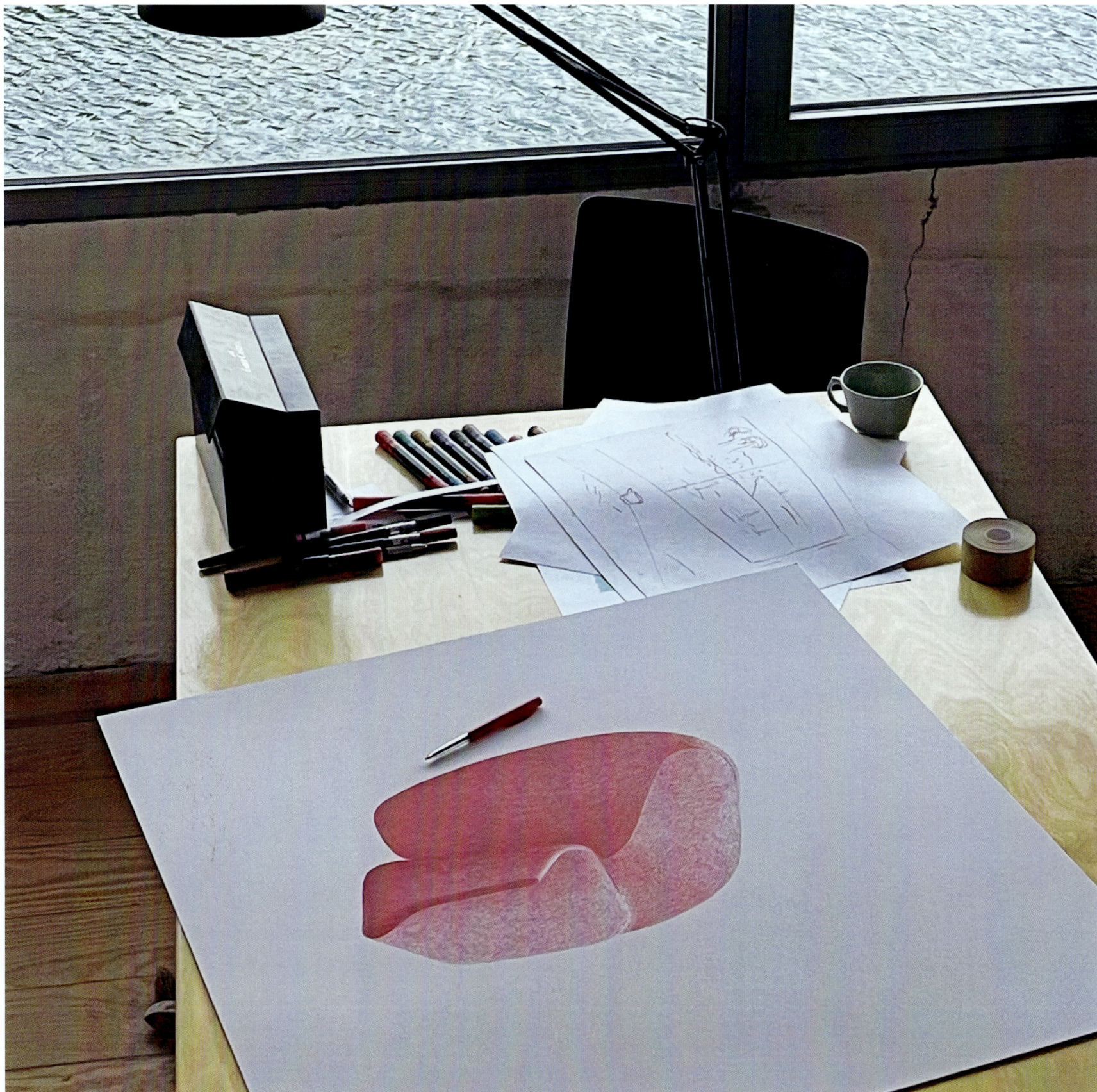

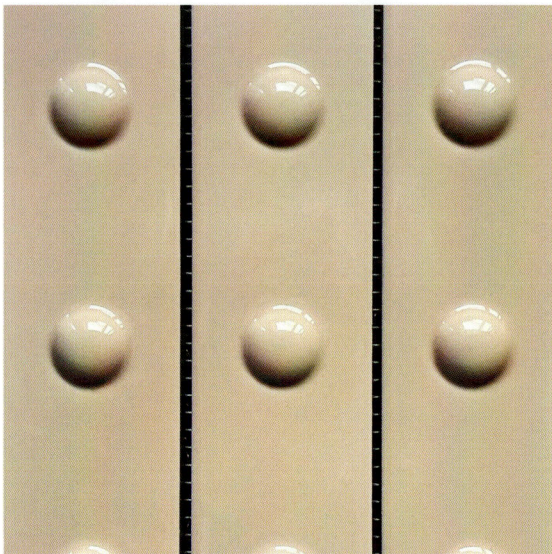

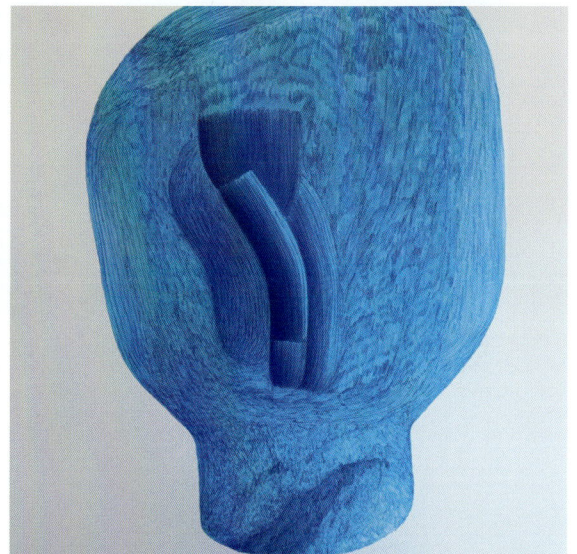

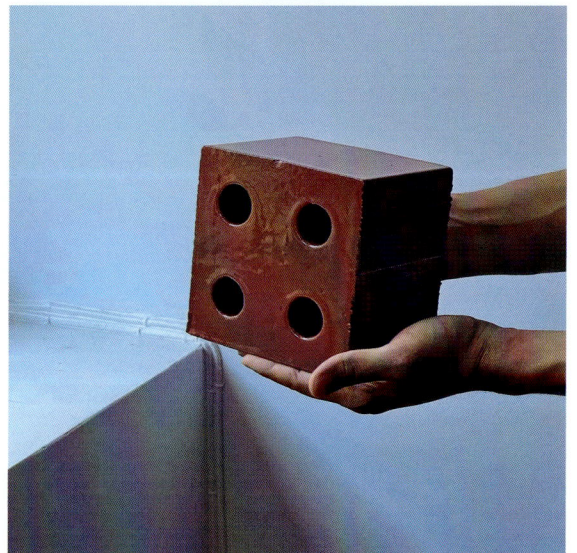

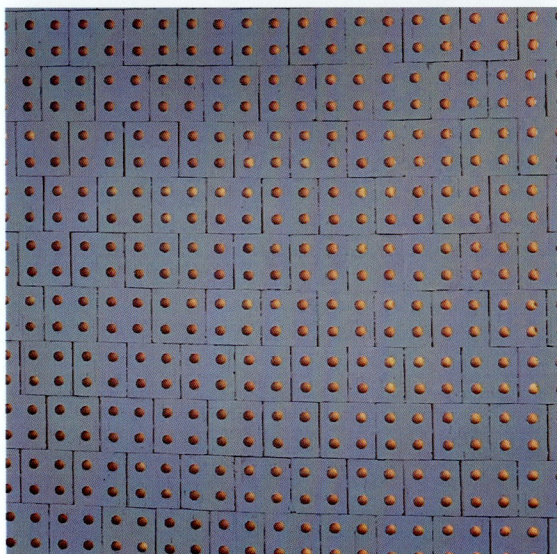

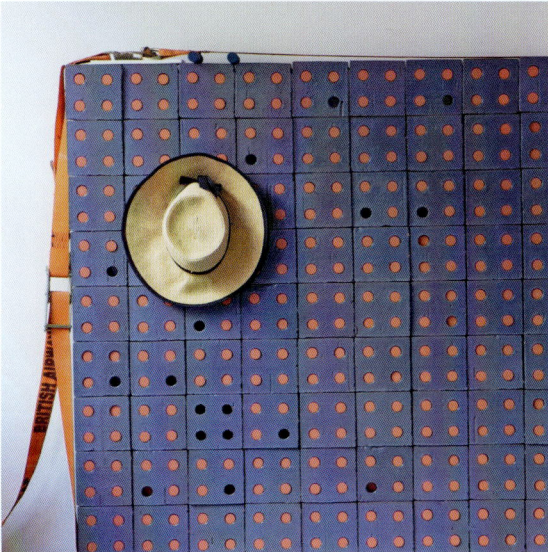

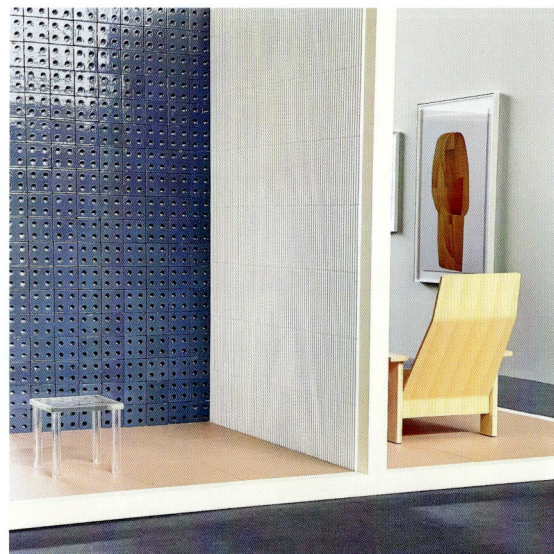

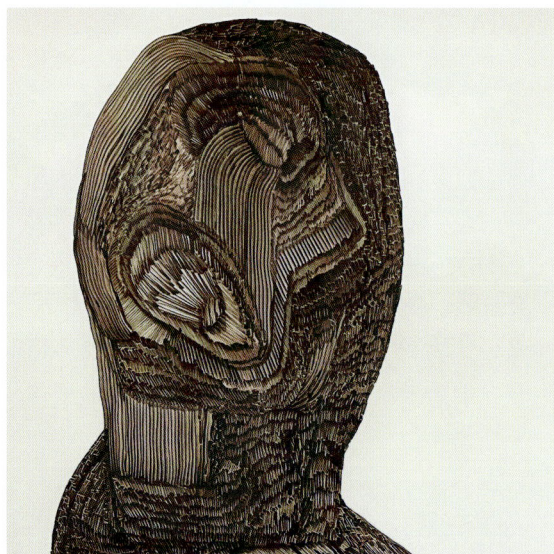
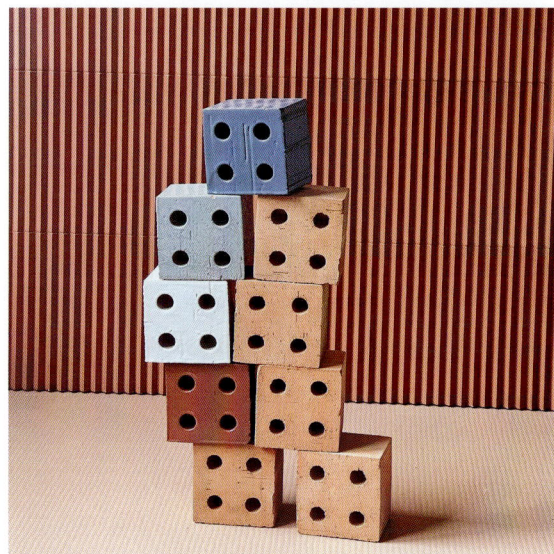
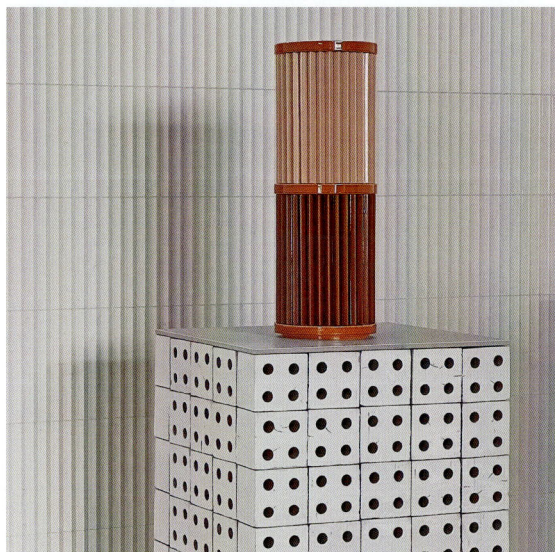

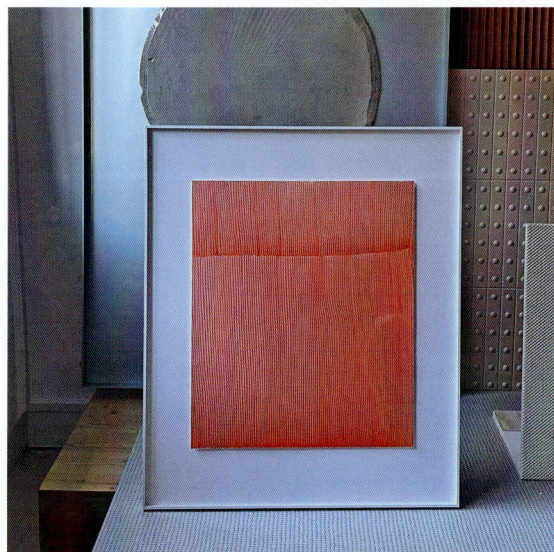

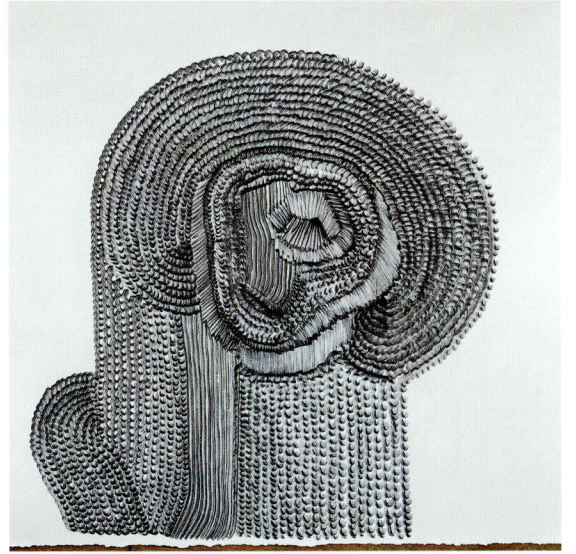

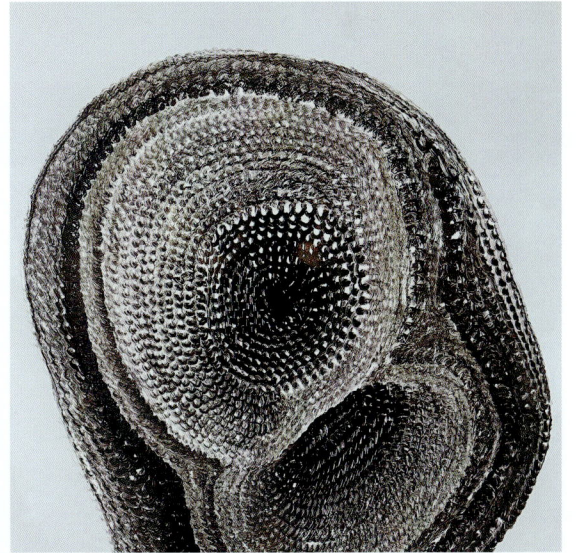

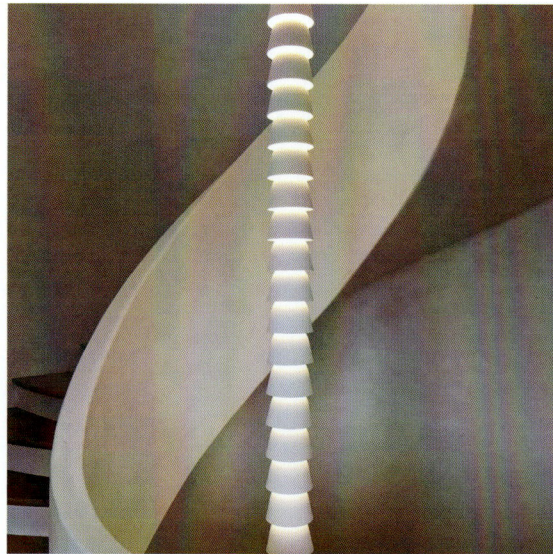

Ronan Bouroullec
Drawing Poster Exhibition
23rd Oct - 7th Nov, at LICHT gallery

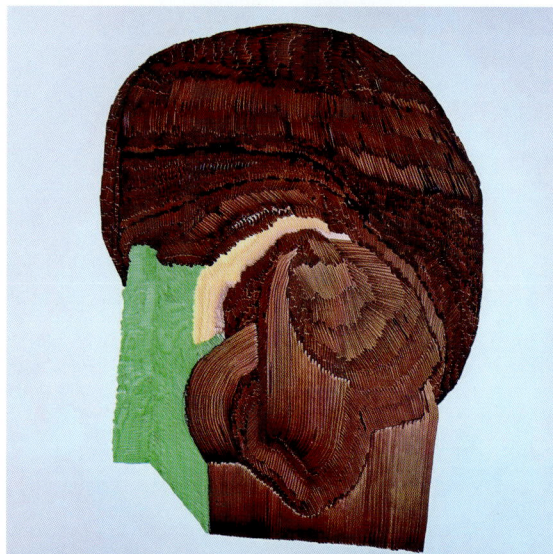
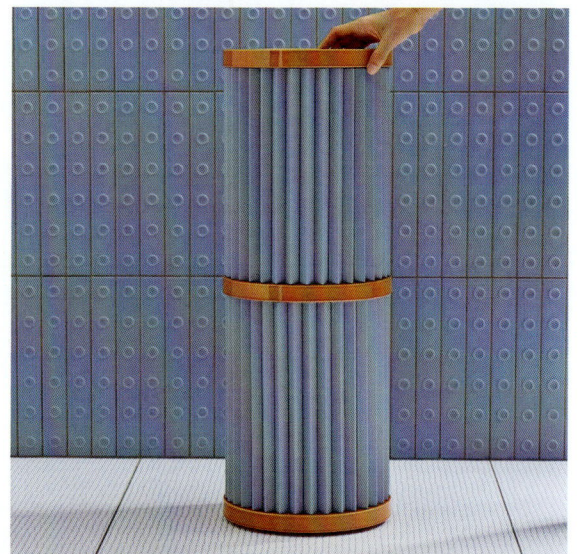

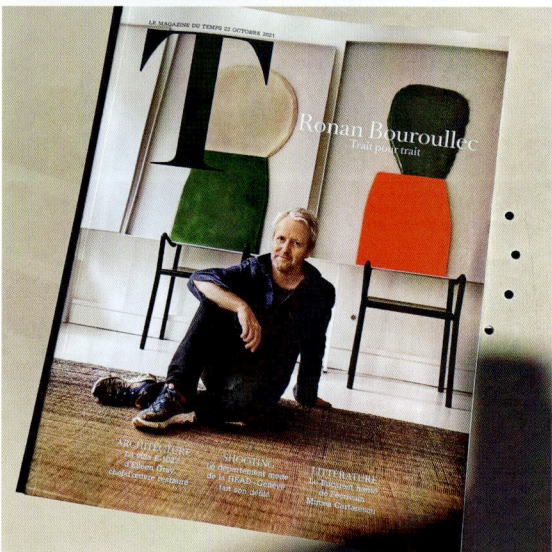
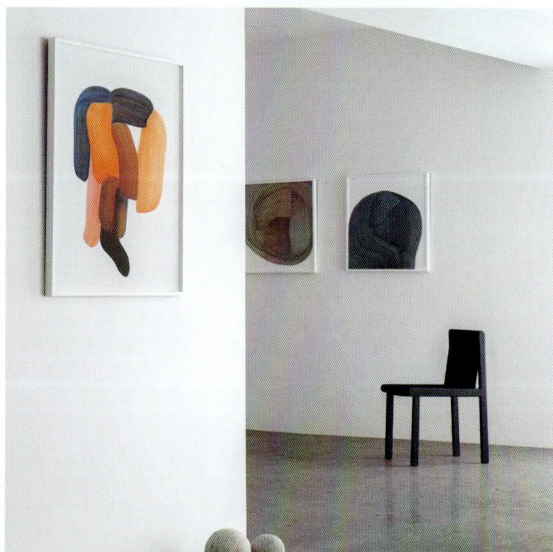

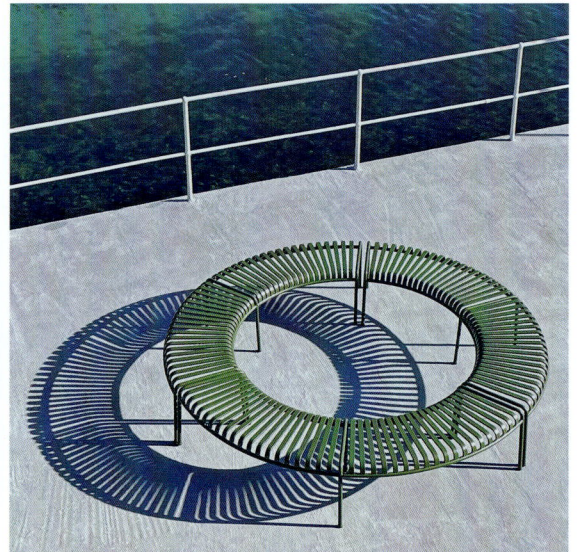

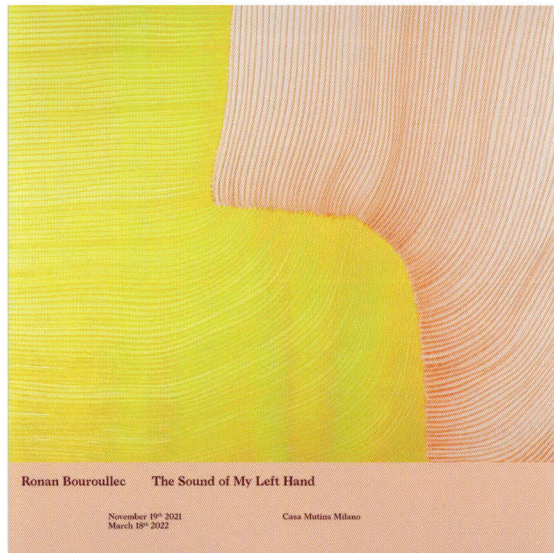
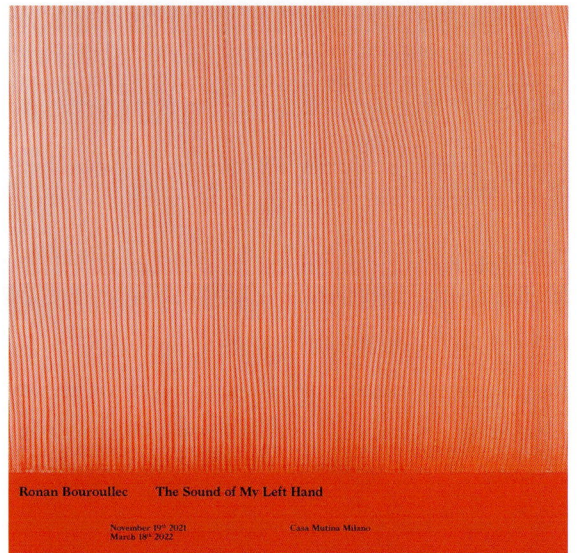

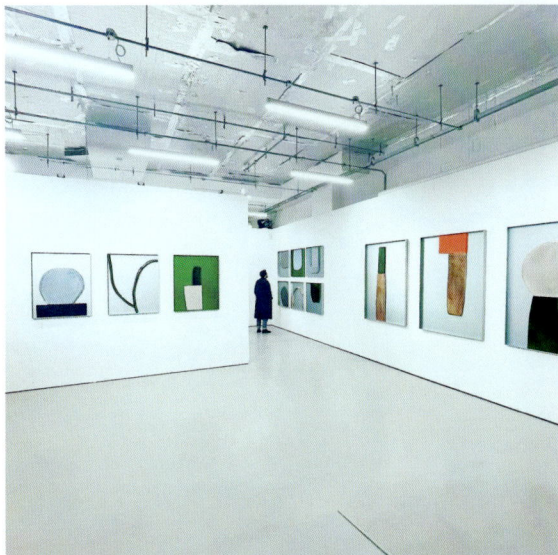

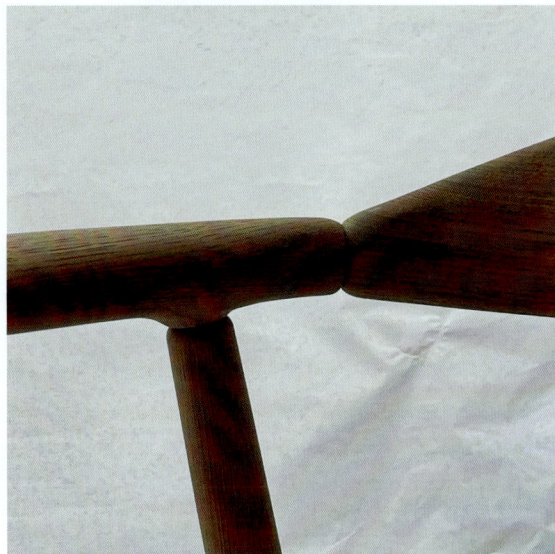

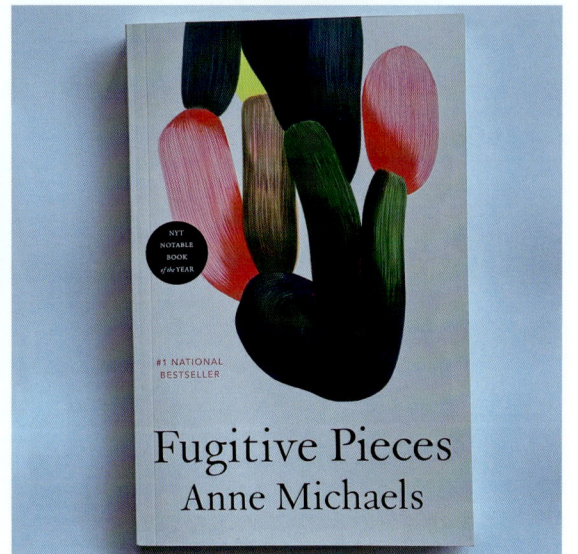

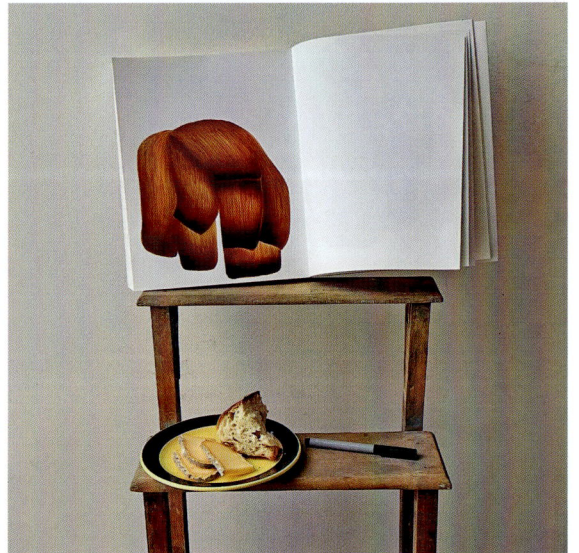

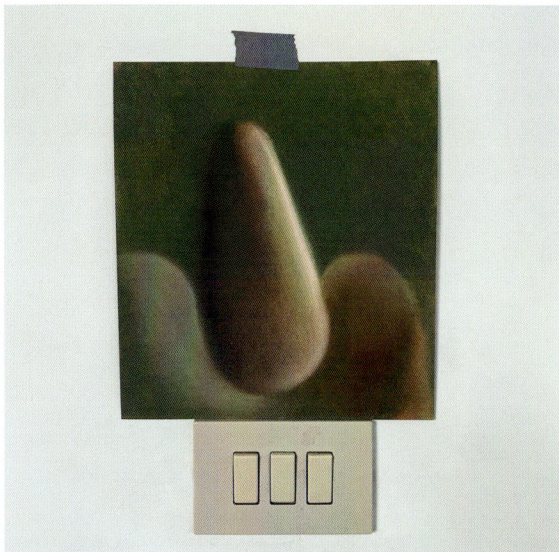
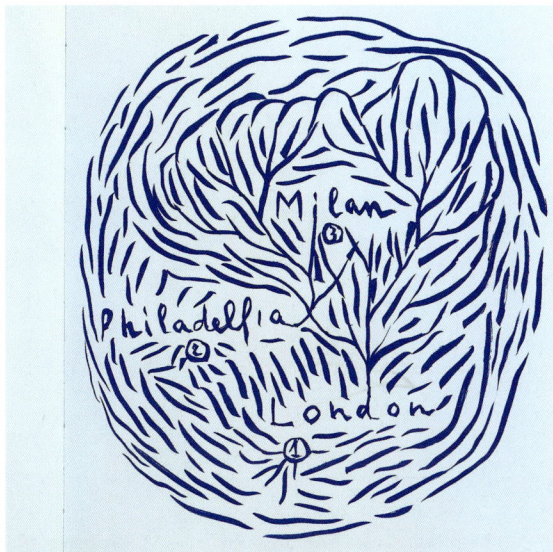

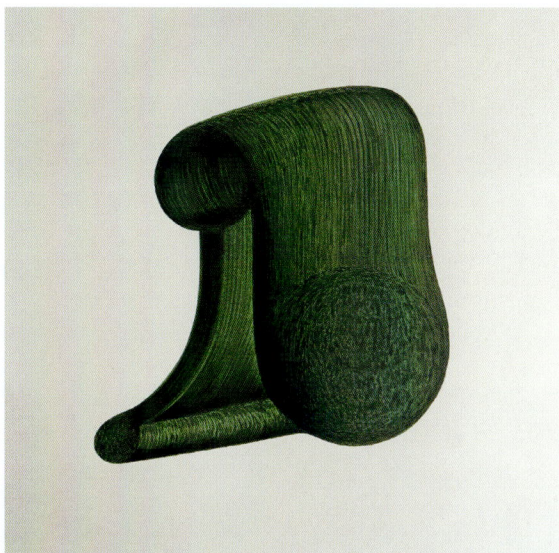
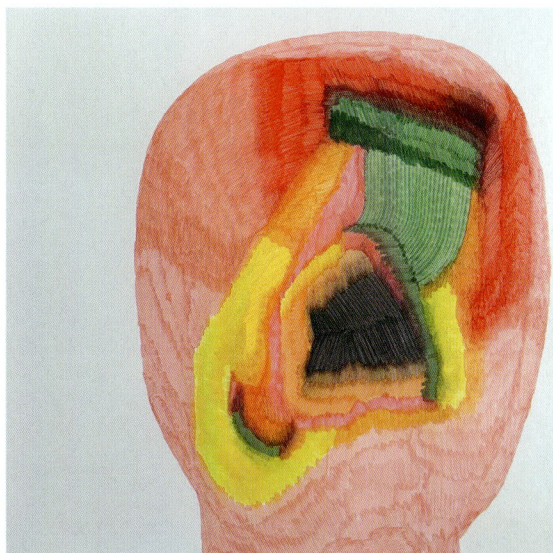

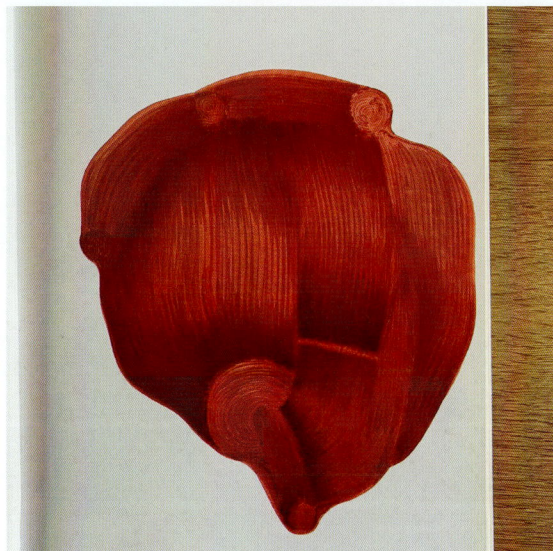

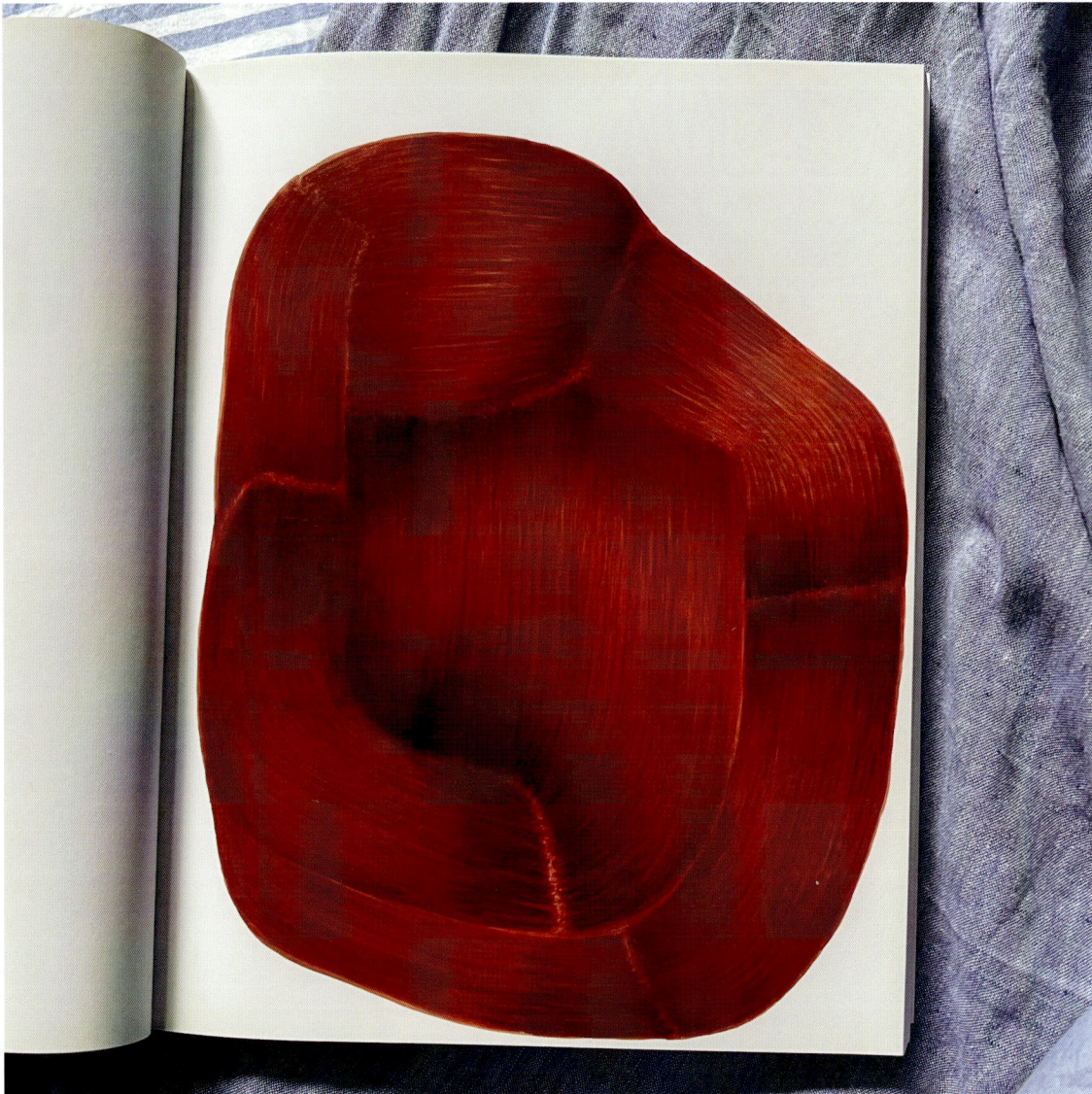

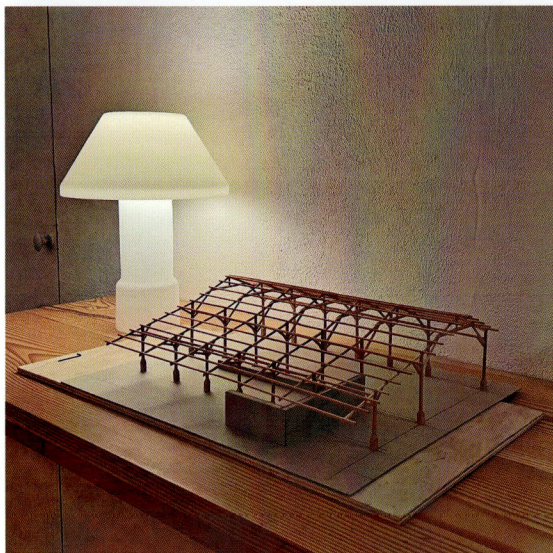

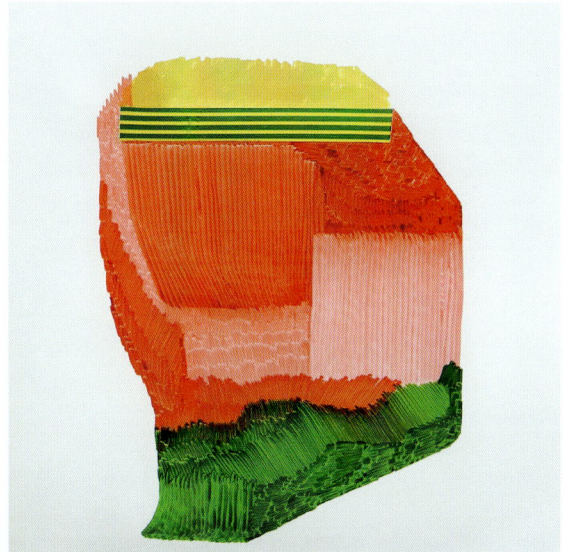

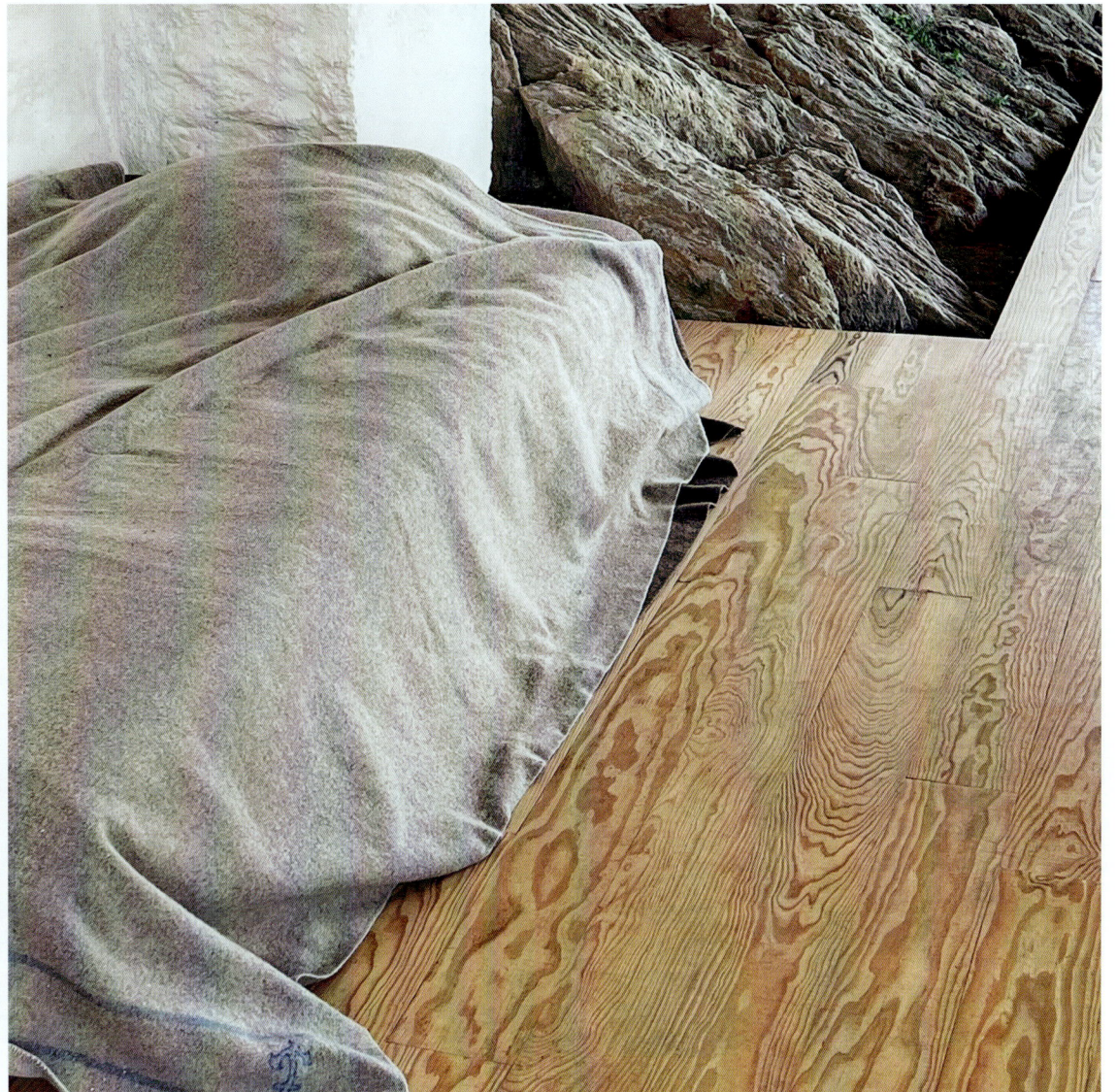

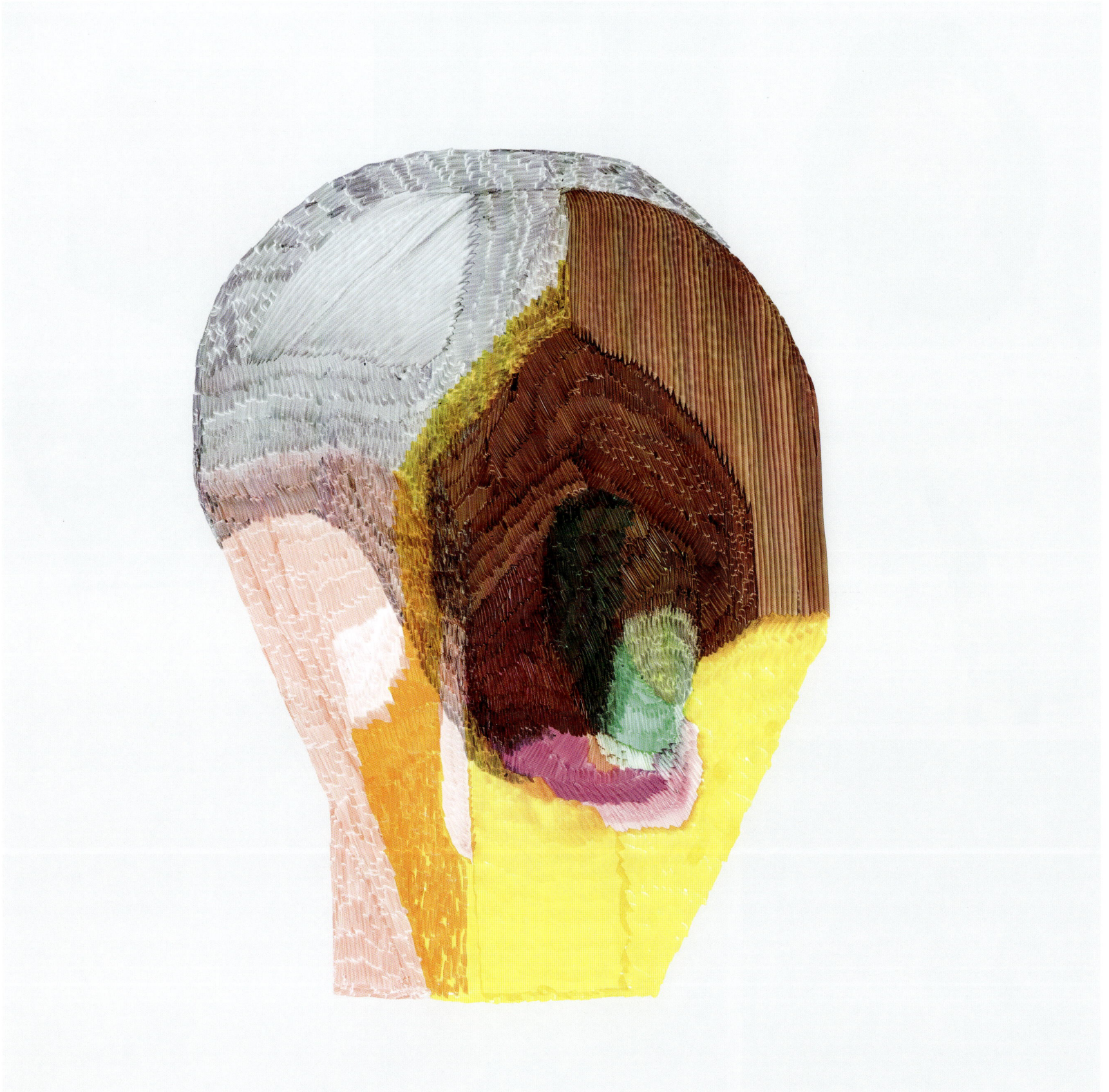

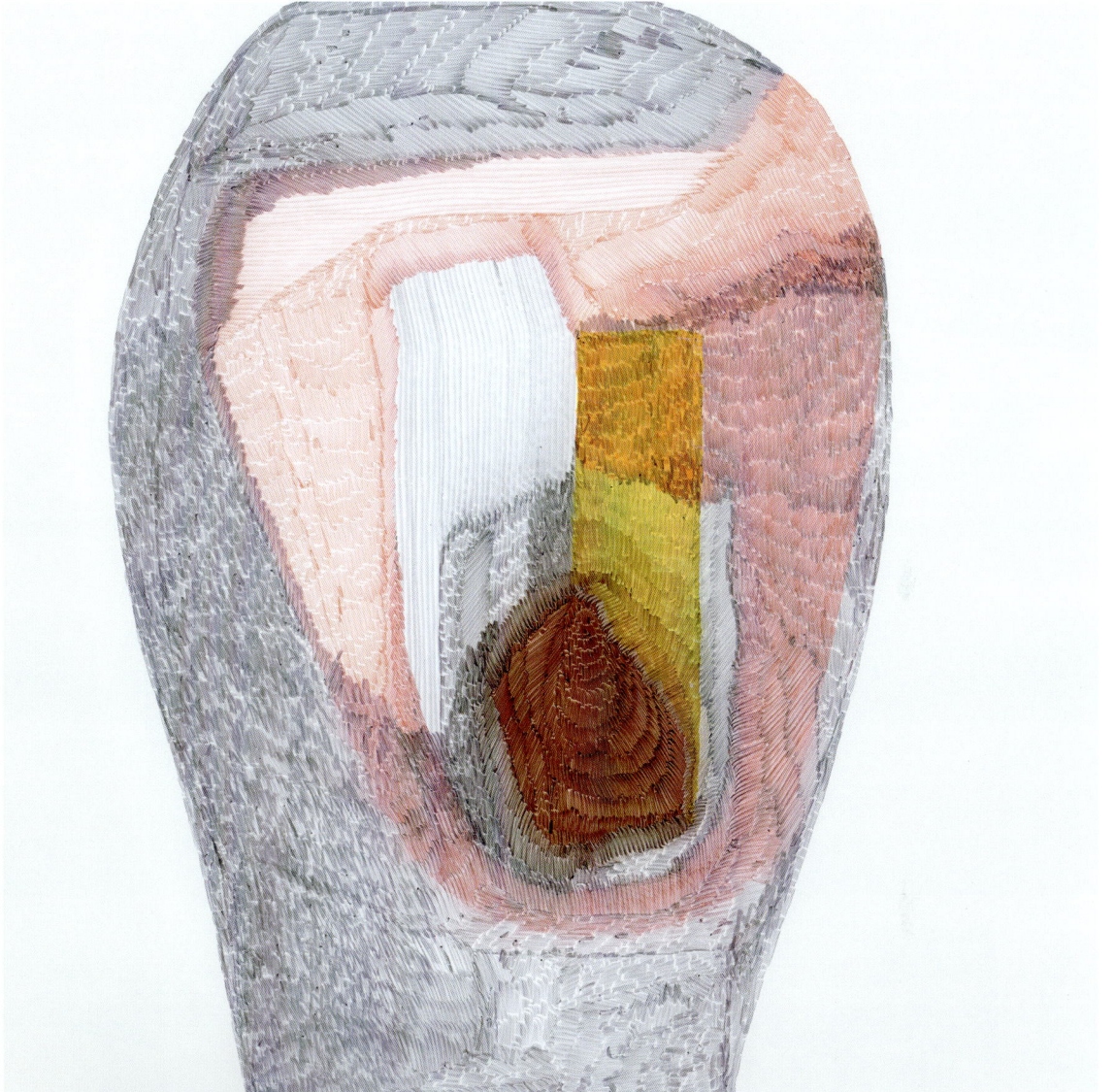

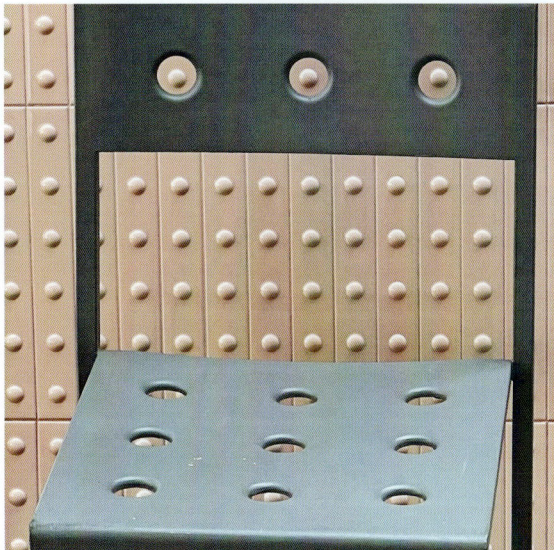

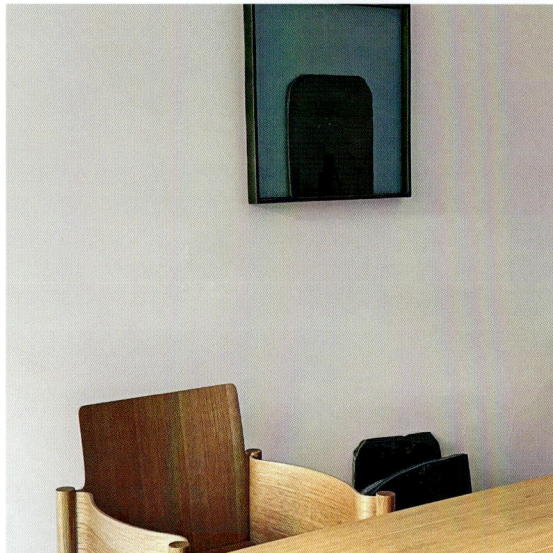

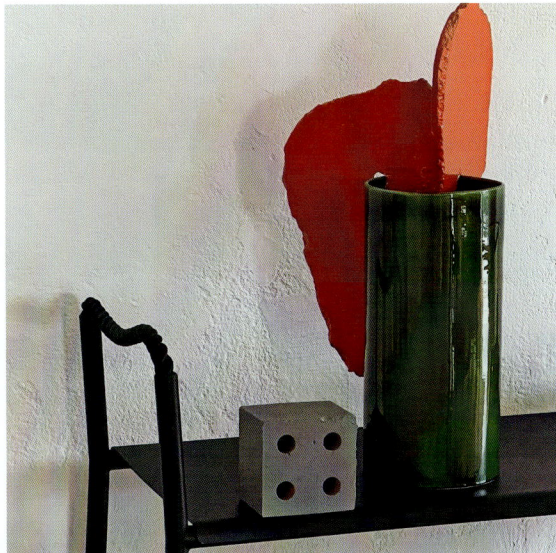
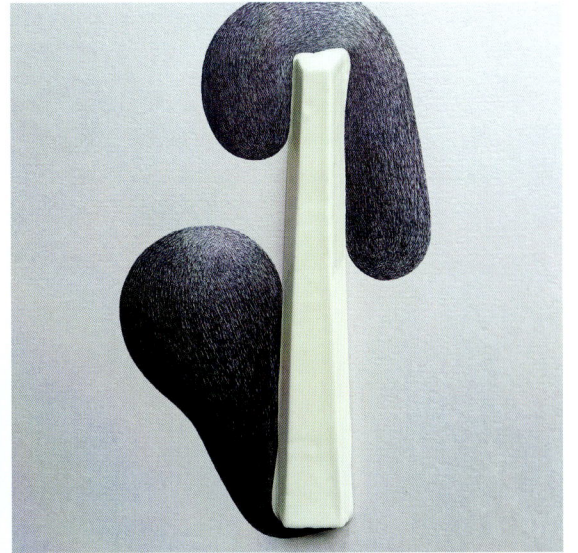

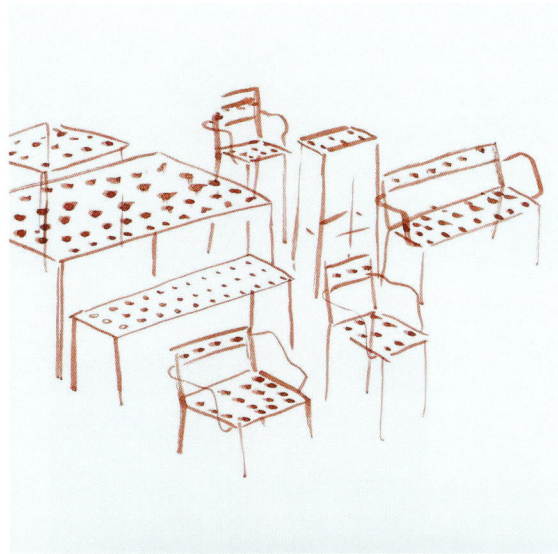

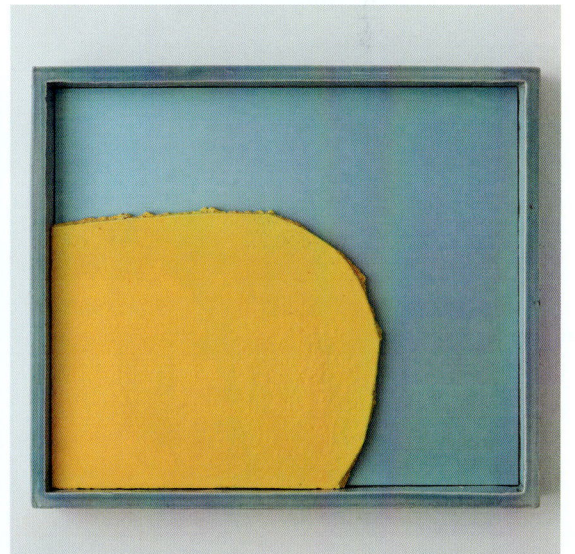

Ronan Bouroullec
The Sound
of My Left Hand

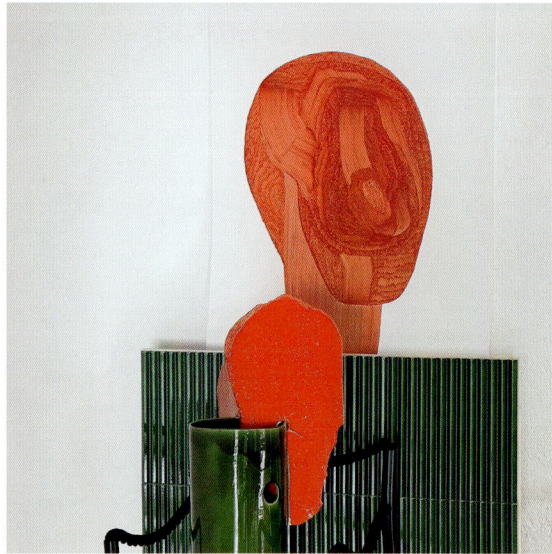

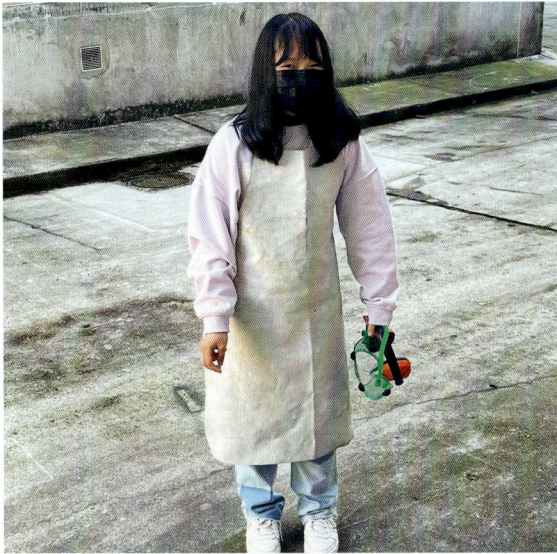
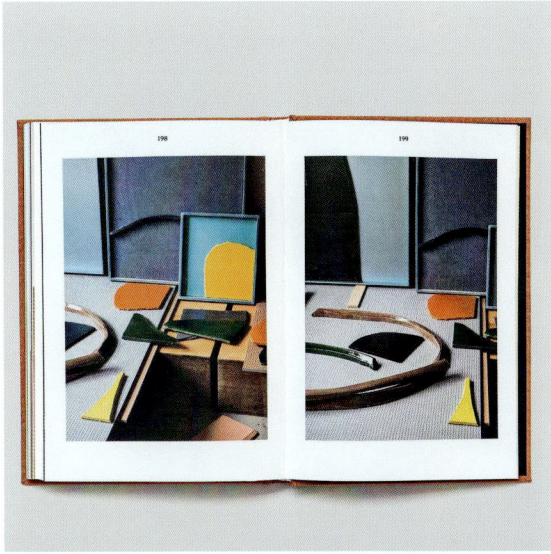

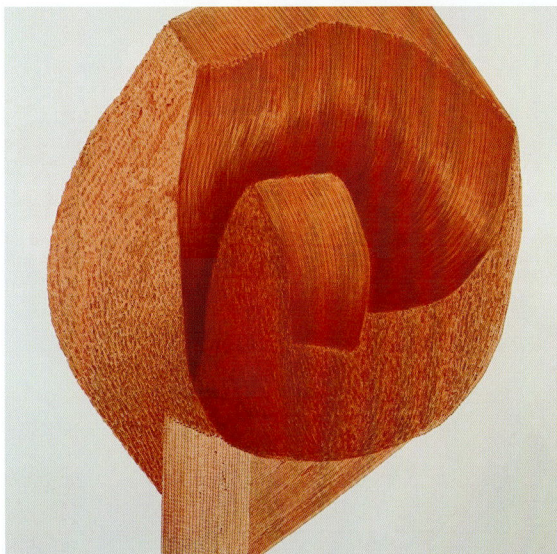

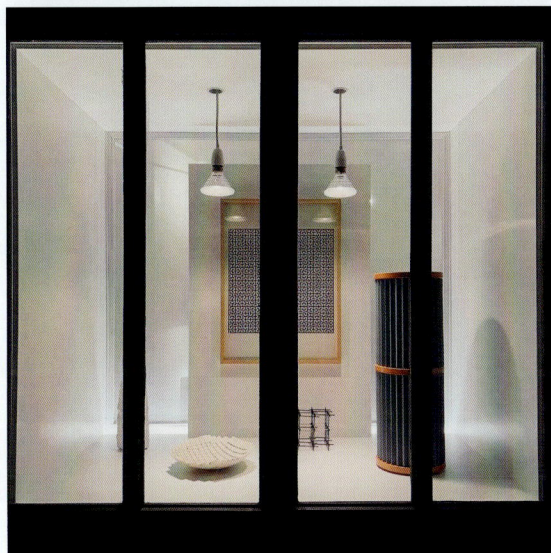

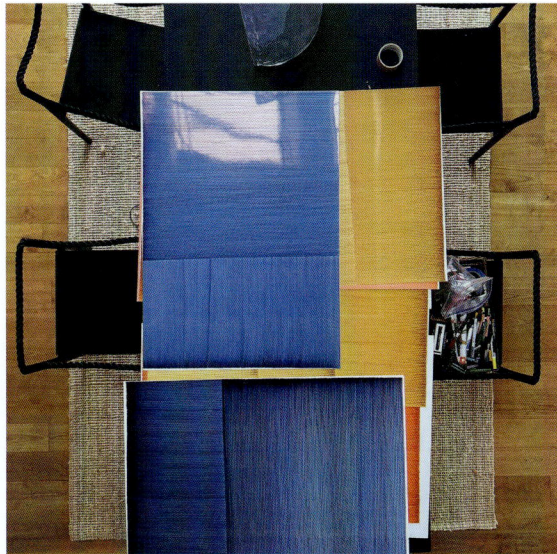

  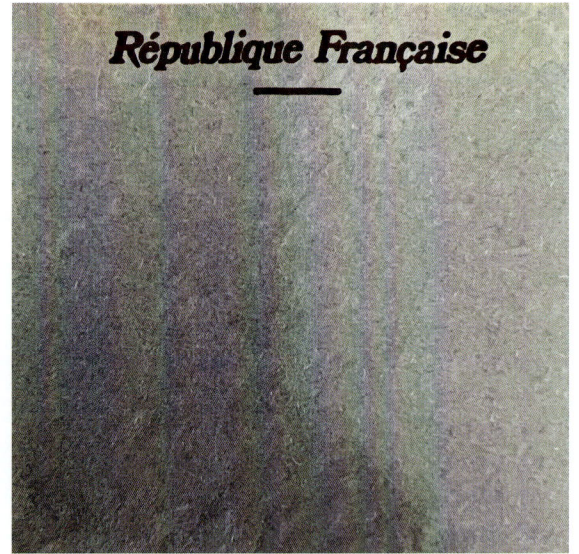

ronan bouroullec   giorgio mastinu   in collaborazione con Mutina
aprile-giugno 2022   calle malipiero
san marco 3160
30124 venezia

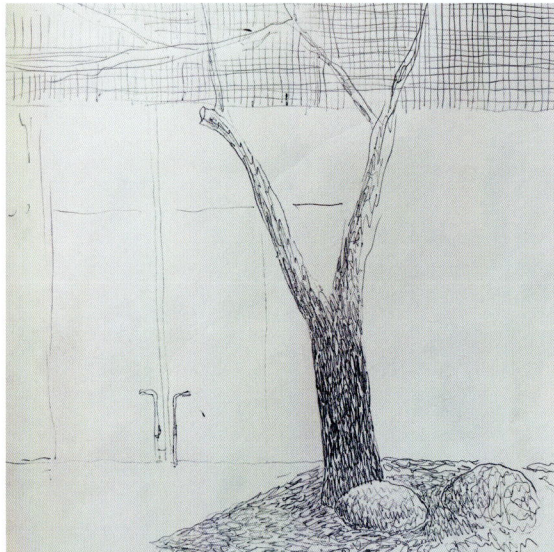

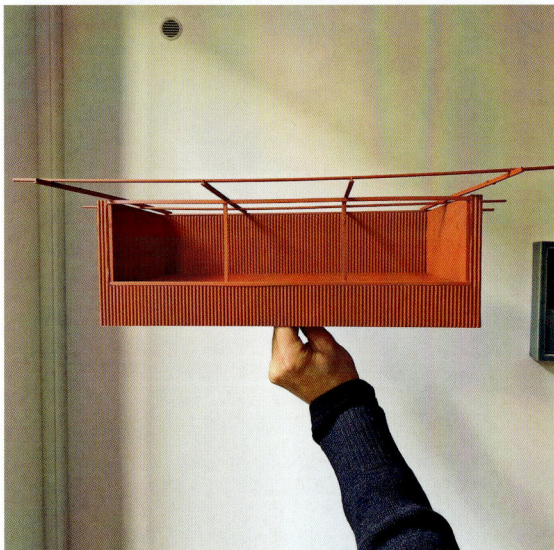

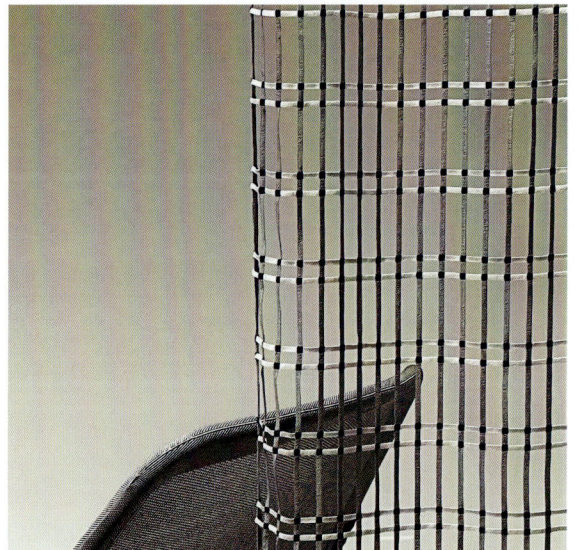

cafesrichard.fr

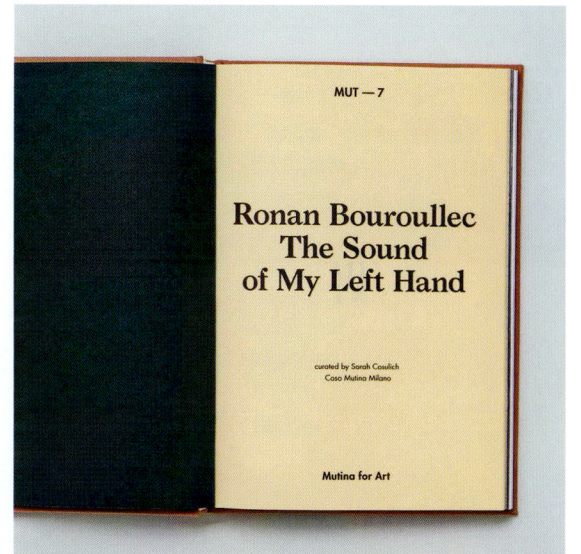

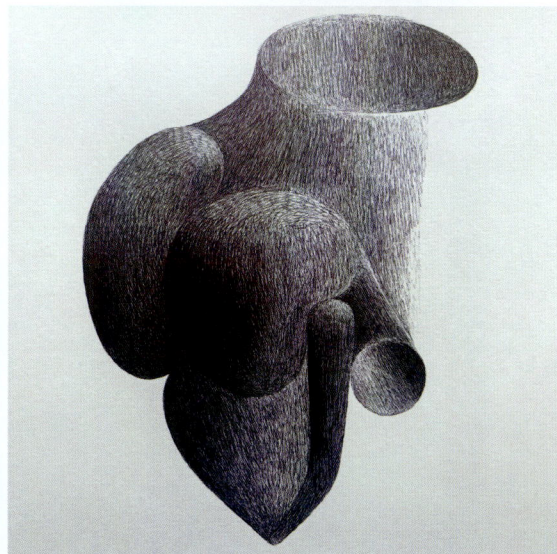
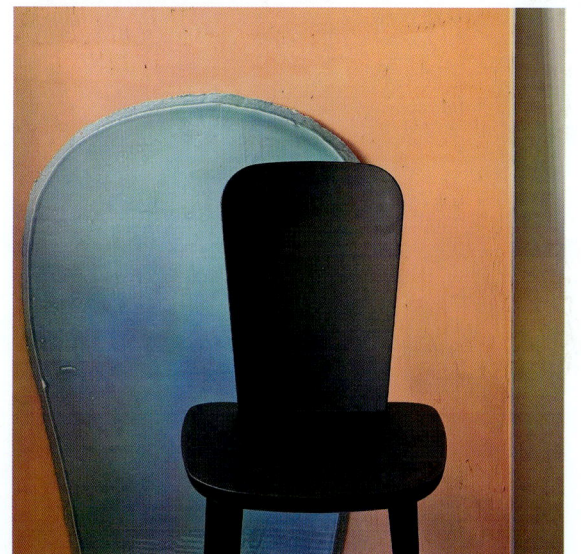
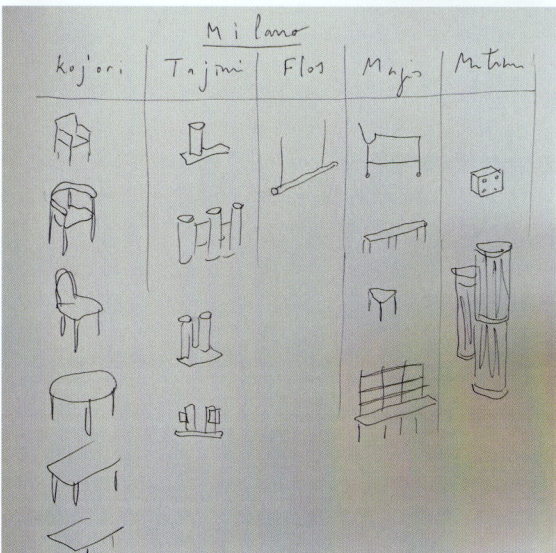

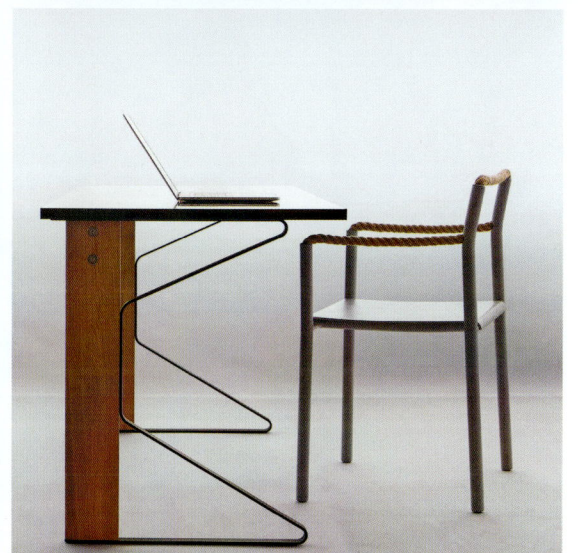

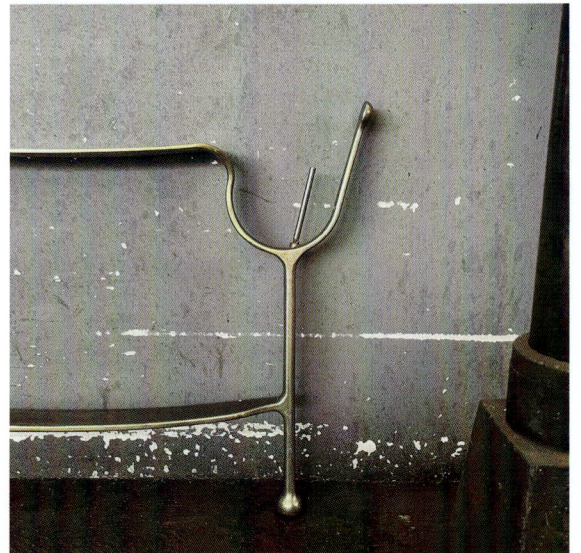

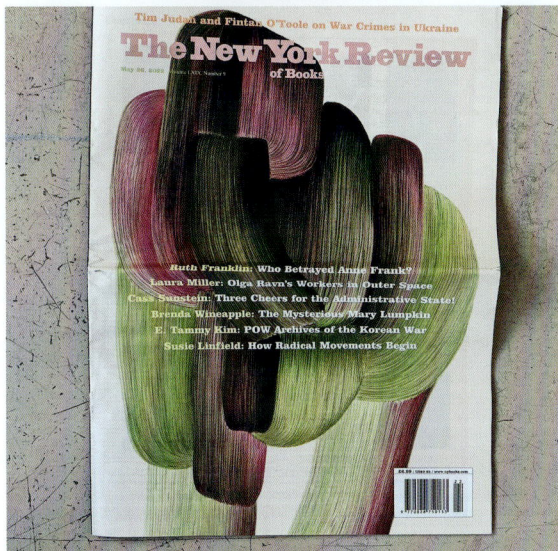

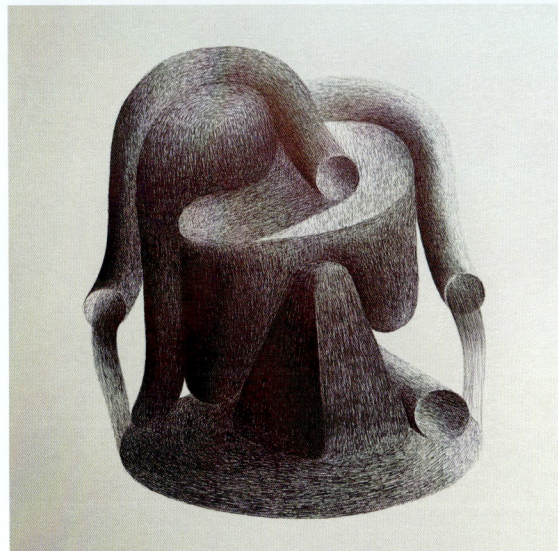

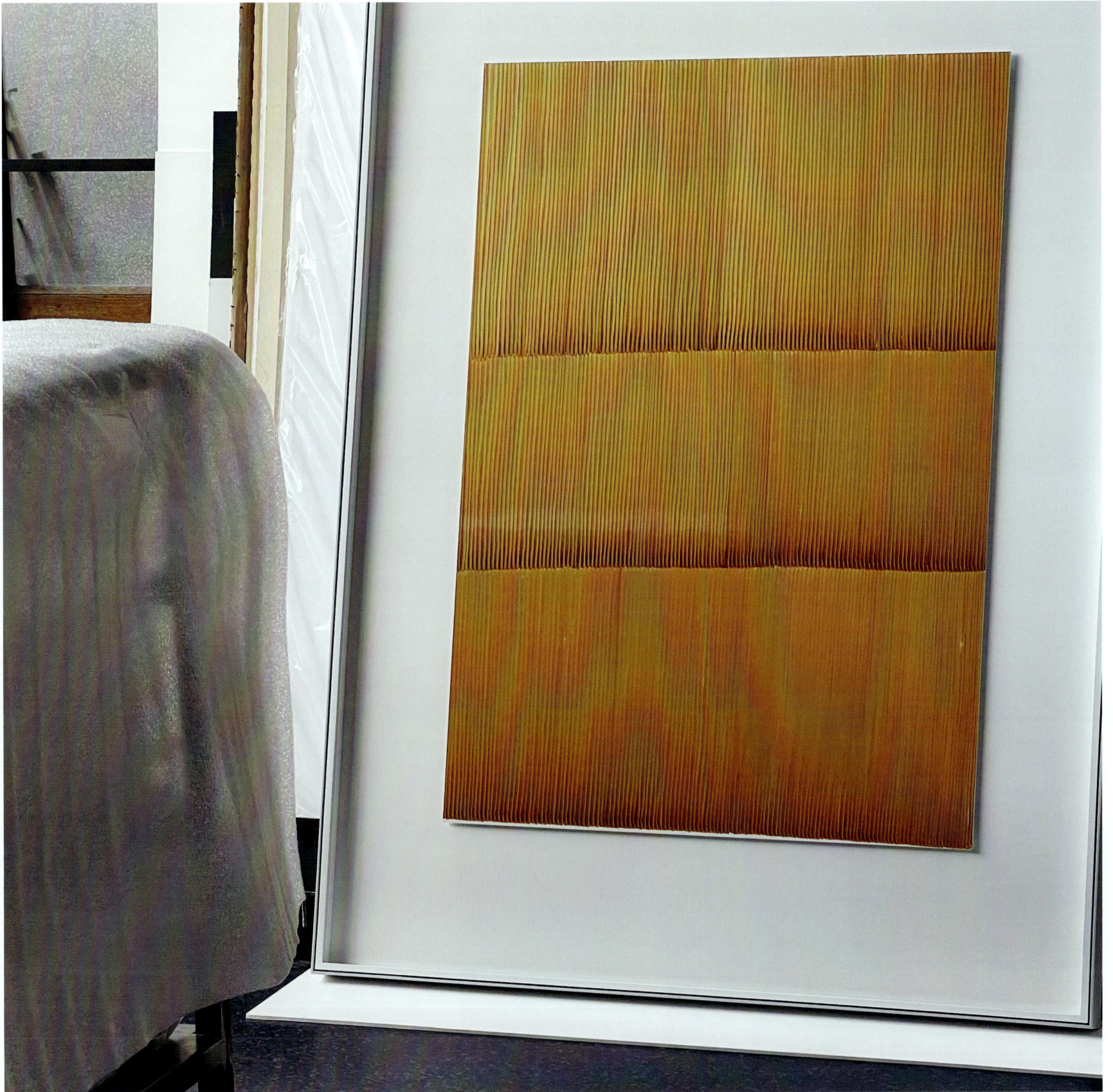

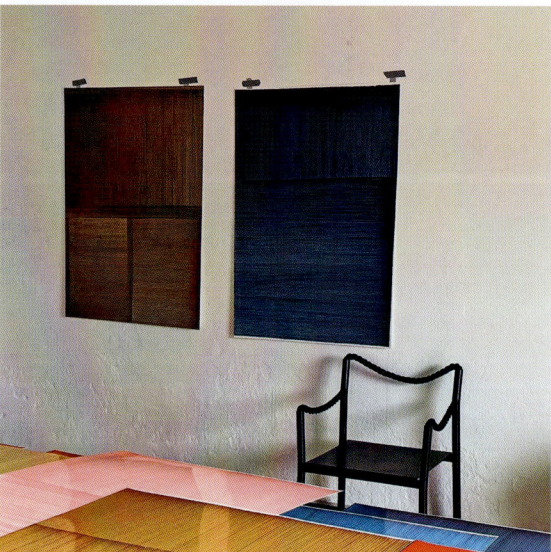

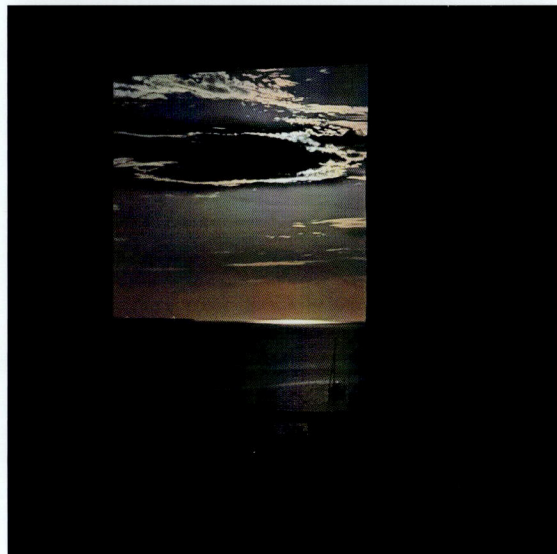

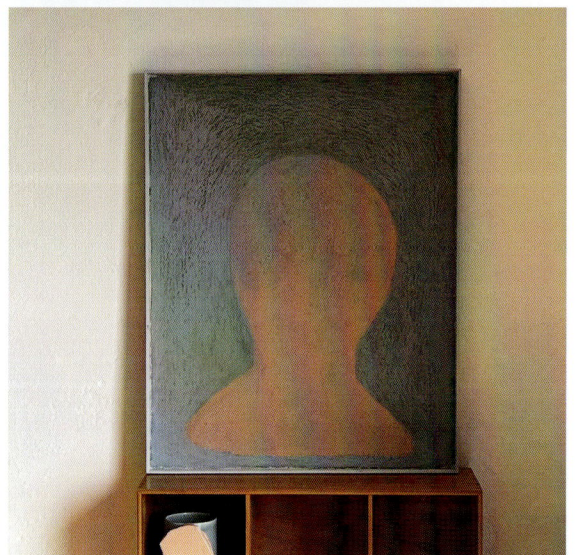

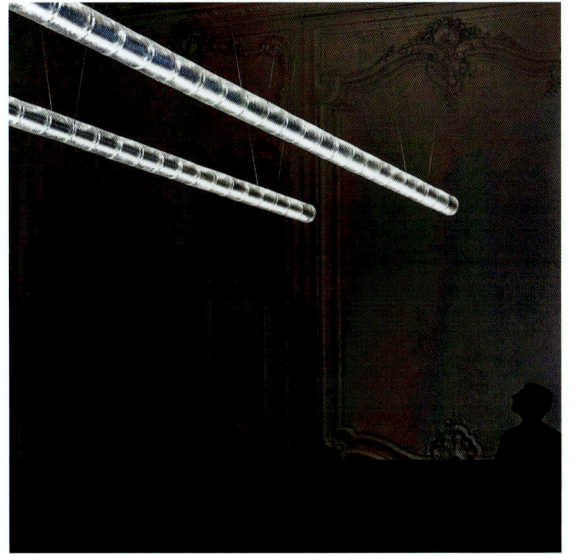

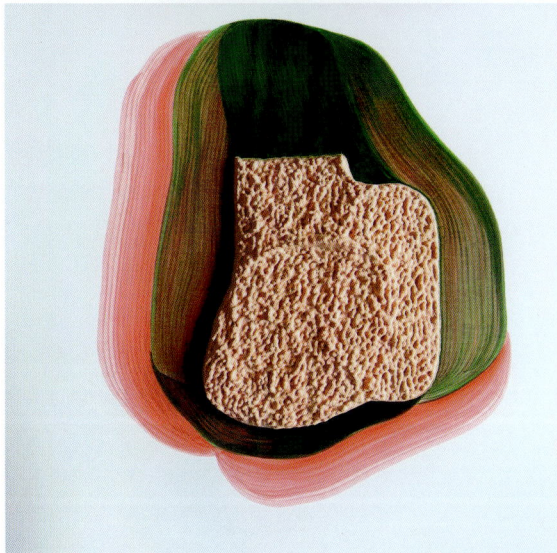

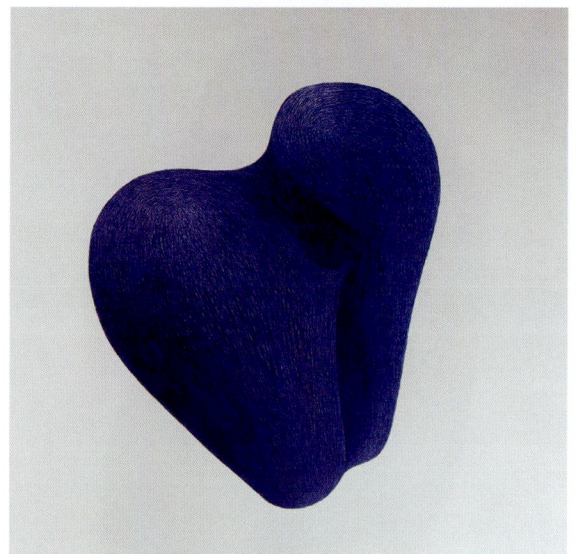
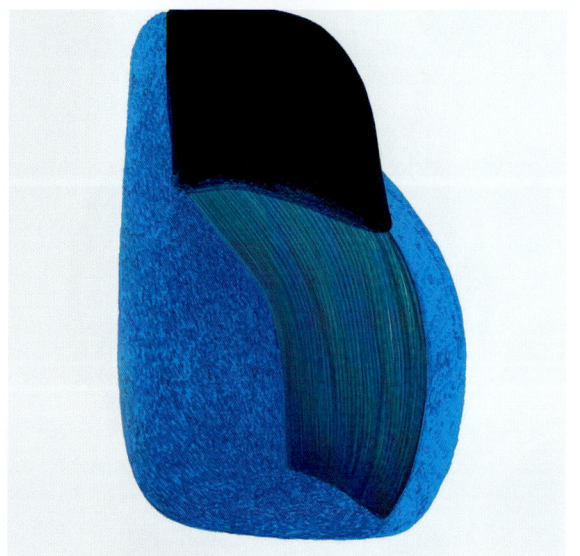

From left to right, top to bottom

2014/October

PAGE 8

Ink on paper

'Momentary' exhibition, Musée des Arts Décoratifs, Paris

Research for an installation at the Victoria and Albert Museum, London

Research for an installation at the Victoria and Albert Museum, London

Ink on paper

3D printed model of a spiral staircase

Spiral staircase

Mette hanging on the stairs

Ink on paper

2014/November

PAGE 9

Inga going up the stairs

Ink on paper

Ink on aluminium foil

Ballpoint pen on paper

Ink on paper

Ink on wood

2014/December

PAGE 10

Studio, Brittany, France

Ink on paper and kayak in the studio, Brittany, France

Ruutu vases, Iittala, in front of my window, Paris

Wall in the house, Brittany, France

Studio wall, Paris

Research collage for the 'Bivouac' exhibition catalogue, Centre Pompidou-Metz, France

PAGE 11

Algue, Seaweed and *Twigs*, Vitra, La Pelota, Milan

Floating House, collaboration with architects Jean-Marie Finot and Denis Daversin, Chatou, France

Sailing the *Floating House*, collaboration with architects Jean-Marie Finot and Denis Daversin, Chatou, France

Floating House, collaboration with architects Jean-Marie Finot and Denis Daversin, Chatou, France

Ink on paper

3D printed Christmas tree for *Disegno* magazine

3D printed Christmas tree for *Disegno* magazine

Ink on paper

Clouds, Kvadrat, and *Steelwood* chair, Magis

2015/January

PAGE 12

Clouds, Kvadrat

Ink on aluminium foil

Ink on paper

Table and wall in the house, Brittany, France

Ink on paper

Ink on aluminium foil

2015/February

PAGE 13

Ink on aluminium foil

Ink on paper

Sketch, *Kaari* shelf, Artek

Ink on aluminium foil

Ink on aluminium foil

Ink on aluminium foil

House, Brittany, France

Ink on aluminium foil

Ink on gold paper

PAGE 14

Coloured pencil on paper

PAGE 15

Ink on wood

Ink on paper

Ballpoint pen on paper

Ink on paper

Ink on paper

Ink on aluminium foil

Ink on paper

Graphite on paper

w103 lamp, Wästberg and *Trame* mirror by Inga Sempé, Domestic; ink on paper and wood

2015/March

PAGE 16

Print on paper, The Wrong

Shop, studio, Paris

Ink on paper

Box of drawings

Aluminium anodization tests and ink on aluminium foil

House, Brittany, France

Ink on aluminium foil

Ink and adhesive tape on aluminium foil

Ink on paper

Ink on aluminium foil

2015/April

PAGE 17

Nuage vase, ceramic, limited edition

Ink on paper

Preparatory drawing for the *Kaari* collection, Artek

Programme of the Salone del Mobile, Milan

3D printed model, *Nuage* vases

Clouds screen, Kvadrat, Copenhagen

2015/August

PAGE 18

Shadow of Joshua carrying a *Palissade* chair, HAY

2015/September

PAGE 19

Prototype of the *Palissade* armchair, HAY, Brittany, France

Cat on *The Serif* TV, Samsung

Ink and graphite on wood

Studio, Paris

Research in Guipure

Rombini wall ceramic, Mutina

2015/October

PAGE 20

Preparatory drawing for the *Kaari* collection, Artek

Palissade chair, HAY, and *Rombini* wall ceramic, Mutina

Kiosk, Emerige and Galerie kreo, Jardin des Tuileries, Paris

Kiosk, Emerige and Galerie kreo, Jardin des Tuileries, Paris

Colour test, enamel on ceramic

Photo shoot for the 'Seventeen Screens' exhibition, Tel Aviv Museum of Art, Israel

PAGE 21

Palissade chairs, HAY, studio courtyard, Paris

2015/November

PAGE 22

Rennes screen, 'Seventeen Screens' exhibition, Tel Aviv Museum of Art, Israel

Installation of the 'Seventeen Screens' exhibition, Tel Aviv Museum of Art, Israel

'Seventeen Screens' exhibition, Tel Aviv Museum of Art, Israel

Preparatory drawing on photograph, 'Seventeen Screens' exhibition, Tel Aviv Museum of Art, Israel

Paint on paper

Detail, screen, 'Seventeen Screens' exhibition, Tel Aviv Museum of Art, Israel

Detail, screen, 'Seventeen Screens' exhibition, Tel Aviv Museum of Art, Israel

Paint and ink on paper

Embroidered screen, 'Seventeen Screens' exhibition, Tel Aviv Museum of Art, Israel

PAGE 23

'Seventeen Screens' exhibition, Tel Aviv Museum of Art, Israel

Detail, screen, 'Seventeen Screens', Tel Aviv Museum of Art, Israel

'Seventeen Screens' exhibition, Tel Aviv Museum of Art, Israel

Detail, screen, 'Seventeen Screens', Tel Aviv Museum of Art, Israel

'Seventeen Screens' exhibition, Tel Aviv Museum of Art, Israel

Detail, screen, 'Seventeen Screens', Tel Aviv Museum of Art, Israel

PAGE 24

Twigs, Vitra

Ink on wood

'Seventeen Screens' exhibition, Tel Aviv Museum of Art, Israel

Ink on aluminium foil

Preparatory drawing, 'Seventeen Screens' exhibition, Tel Aviv Museum of Art, Israel

Preparatory drawing, 'Seventeen Screens' exhibition, Tel Aviv Museum of Art, Israel

2015/December

PAGE 25

Detail, 'Seventeen Screens' exhibition, Tel Aviv Museum of Art, Israel

'Seventeen Screens' exhibition, Tel Aviv Museum of Art, Israel

13 November 2015

Detail, screen, 'Seventeen Screens' exhibition, Tel Aviv Museum of Art, Israel

'Seventeen Screens' exhibition, Tel Aviv Museum of Art, Israel

Palissade collection, HAY, in the snow

PAGE 26

Ink on paper

Embroidery

Ruutu vases, Iittala

'Seventeen Screens' exhibition, Tel Aviv Museum of Art, Israel

Detail, screen, 'Seventeen Screens' exhibition, Tel Aviv Museum of Art, Israel

Clouds, Kvadrat, 'Bivouac' exhibition, Museum of Contemporary Art, Chicago

Research, 'Urban Reveries' exhibition

Rombini ceramic tiles, Mutina

Rombini ceramic tiles, Mutina

PAGE 27

Studio, Paris

LIST OF WORKS

2016/January

PAGE 28
Ink on paper
Lighthouse lamp, Venini blown glass, Established & Sons
'Momentary' exhibition, Musée des Arts Décoratifs, Paris
Municipal poster for the new year, city of Rennes, France
'Bivouac' exhibition, Museum of Contemporary Art, Chicago
Studio, Paris
Production, *Palissade* chairs, HAY
Print on paper, The Wrong Shop, studio, Paris
'Bivouac' exhibition, Museum of Contemporary Art, Chicago

PAGE 29
Manufacturing, *Kiosk*, Emerige and Galerie kreo
Kiosk, Emerige and Galerie kreo, Jardin des Tuileries, Paris
Lattice rug, Nanimarquina
Lattice rug, Nanimarquina
'Seventeen Screens' exhibition, Tel Aviv Museum of Art, Israel
Lattice rug, Nanimarquina, and *Palissade* sofa, HAY

PAGE 30
Studio, Paris
Ronan & Erwan Bouroullec: Drawing, JRP|Editions
Ink on paper
Research, 'Urban Reveries' exhibition
Rombini ceramic tiles, Mutina
Ink on paper

PAGE 31
House, Brittany, France

PAGE 32
Mette, studio, Brittany, France
House, Brittany, France
Research, studio, Paris
Research, 'Urban Reveries' exhibition
Collapse of research at the studio, Paris
Rombini ceramic tiles, Mutina

2016/February

PAGE 33
Unexpected
Officina candle holder, Magis
Detail, *Officina* candle holder, Magis
Elements of the models, 'Urban Reveries' exhibition
Marquee model
Rombini ceramic tiles, Mutina

PAGE 34
Rombini ceramic tiles, Mutina Studio, Paris
Ballpoint pen and watercolour on paper
Ink on paper
Ronan & Erwan Bouroullec: Drawing, JRP|Editions
Print on paper, The Wrong Shop, studio, Paris
Dark night
Passion for sea kayaking
The lighthouse

PAGE 35
Rombini ceramic tiles, Mutina

PAGE 36
Aluminium anodization for models, 'Urban Reveries' exhibition
Aluminium anodization for models, 'Urban Reveries' exhibition
Aluminium anodization for models, 'Urban Reveries' exhibition
Ink on paper
Kaari shelving unit, Artek
Kaari shelving unit, Artek

2016/March

PAGE 37
Photography studio, Copenhagen
Me taking a photo in Copenhagen
Copenhagen chair and table, HAY
Kaari desk, Artek
Studio, Paris
Palissade bench, *Copenhagen* chairs and tables, HAY, photography studio, Copenhagen

'Seventeen Screens' exhibition, Frac Bretagne, Rennes, France
Detail, screen, 'Seventeen Screens' exhibition, Frac Bretagne, Rennes, France
Suspended tray, 'Urban Reveries' exhibition, Les Champs Libres, Rennes, France

PAGE 38
Parasols project, 'Urban Reveries' exhibition
Seaweed drying in progress
Seaweed drying in progress
House, Brittany, France
Disaster
Installation, *Chains*, ceramics, Frac Bretagne, Rennes, France

PAGE 39
'Seventeen Screens' exhibition, Frac Bretagne, Rennes, France
'Seventeen Screens' exhibition, Frac Bretagne, Rennes, France
Invitation card for the 4 Breton exhibitions, Rennes, France
Invitation card for the 4 Breton exhibitions, Rennes, France
Invitation card for the 4 Breton exhibitions, Rennes, France
'Seventeen Screens' exhibition, Frac Bretagne, Rennes, France
Installation, *Chains*, ceramic, Frac Bretagne, Rennes, France
'Retrospective' exhibition, Frac Bretagne, Rennes, France
'Seventeen Screens' exhibition, Frac Bretagne, Rennes, France

PAGE 40
'Retrospective' exhibition, Frac Bretagne, Rennes, France
'Urban Reveries' exhibition, Les Champs Libres, Rennes, France
'Retrospective' exhibition, Frac Bretagne, Rennes, France
Crane, *Kiosk*, Emerige and Galerie kreo, courtyard of the Parliament of Brittany,

Rennes, France
Crane, *Kiosk*, Emerige and Galerie kreo, courtyard of the Parliament of Brittany, Rennes, France
Landing, *Kiosk*, Emerige and Galerie kreo, courtyard of the Parliament of Brittany, Rennes, France
Fountain *Slide* project, 'Urban Reveries' exhibition
Lianes project, 'Urban Reveries' exhibition
Municipal poster for the new year, Rennes, France

PAGE 41
'Seventeen Screens' exhibition, Frac Bretagne, Rennes, France
'Seventeen Screens' exhibition, Frac Bretagne, Rennes, France
Clouds pergola project, 'Urban Reveries' exhibition
Tree and Rocks roof project, 'Urban Reveries' exhibition
'Retrospective' exhibition, Frac Bretagne, Rennes, France
'Urban Reveries' exhibition, Les Champs Libres, Rennes, France

PAGE 42
Lianes project, 'Urban Reveries' exhibition

2016/April

PAGE 43
'Retrospective' exhibition, Frac Bretagne, Rennes, France
'Seventeen Screens' exhibition, Frac Bretagne, Rennes, France
'Retrospective' exhibition, Frac Bretagne, Rennes, France
Ink and adhesive tape, notepad from Hotel Okura, Tokyo
'Seventeen Screens' exhibition, Frac Bretagne, Rennes, France
'Seventeen Screens' exhibition, Frac Bretagne, Rennes, France
Mattéo lighting the *Officina* candle holder, Magis

Ink on aluminium foil
Ink on paper

PAGE 44
'Seventeen Screens' exhibition, Frac Bretagne, Rennes, France
'Seventeen Screens' exhibition, Frac Bretagne, Rennes, France
'Seventeen Screens' exhibition, Frac Bretagne, Rennes, France
'Seventeen Screens' exhibition, Frac Bretagne, Rennes, France
'Seventeen Screens' exhibition, Frac Bretagne, Rennes, France
Poster for HAY, Salone del Mobile, Milan
Wooden Side Table, Vitra
Can sofa, HAY
Programme, Salone del Mobile, Milan

PAGE 45
Officina candle holders and coat racks, Magis
Photo shoot, *Copenhagen* tables, HAY
Officina coat rack and valet stand, Magis
Cast glass tables, Glas Italia
'Seventeen Screens' exhibition, Frac Bretagne, Rennes, France
Detail, cast glass table, Glas Italia

PAGE 46
Cast glass table, Glas Italia
Officina coat rack, Magis
Photography studio, Copenhagen
'Seventeen Screens' exhibition, Frac Bretagne, Rennes, France
Palissade chair and footstool, HAY
Ink on paper
Ink on paper
Ink on aluminium foil
Ink on aluminium foil

PAGE 47
Kaari shelves, Artek
Ink on aluminium foil

Ink on aluminium foil
Can sofa, HAY
Aluminium anodization for the
models, 'Urban Reveries'
exhibition
'Urban Reveries' exhibition,
Les Champs Libres, Rennes,
France

PAGE 48
Long Fountain project, 'Urban
Reveries' exhibition

PAGE 49
Studio, Paris
Detail, *Officina* base, Magis
Ink and wood on paper
Kaari collection, Artek
Palissade collection, HAY
Studio, Paris
Aluminium extrusion, *Nuage*
vase, Vitra
Long Fountain project, 'Urban
Reveries' exhibition
Studio, Paris

2016/May

PAGE 50
Ink and wood on paper
House, Héricy, France
Ink on aluminium foil
Night drawings
Colour test at Ufacto, *Hole*
chair, Cappellini
Kiosk, Emerige and Galerie
kreo, courtyard of the
Parliament of Brittany,
Rennes, France

PAGE 51
TV vase, Galerie kreo

PAGE 52
Ink and paint on paper
Ink and paint on paper
Ink and paint on paper
Hole chairs, Cappellini
Rain screen, ceramic
Studio, Paris
Ring bench project, 'Urban
Reveries' exhibition
Necklace, ceramic, *Torique*
collection
Ballpoint pen on magazine

PAGE 53
Cabane and polystyrene shelf

Brick, Galerie kreo
Cabin, Galerie kreo
Research, *Pergola* project,
'Urban Reveries' exhibition
Detail, ceramic piece,
'Seventeen Screens'
exhibition, Frac Bretagne,
Rennes, France
Ink on paper
'Seventeen Screens'
exhibition, Frac Bretagne,
Rennes, France

PAGE 54
'Seventeen Screens'
exhibition, Frac Bretagne,
Rennes, France
Graphite on a Japanese hotel
envelope
Roof project, 'Urban Reveries'
exhibition
Nuage vases, Vitra
Detail, screen, 'Seventeen
Screens' exhibition, Frac
Bretagne, Rennes, France
Ink and adhesive tape on
paper

PAGE 55
Roof project, 'Urban Reveries'
exhibition
Seated project, 'Urban
Reveries' exhibition
'Seventeen Screens'
exhibition, Frac Bretagne,
Rennes, France
*Ronan & Erwan Bouroullec:
Drawing*, JRP|Editions
Ink and paint on paper and
ballpoint pen on magazine
Ink on aluminium foil

PAGE 56
Lattice rug, Nanimarquina

PAGE 57
Research, 'Urban Reveries'
exhibition
Parts, *Pergola*
Pergola project, 'Urban
Reveries' exhibition
Pergola project, 'Urban
Reveries' exhibition
Research, 'Urban Reveries'
exhibition
Copenhagen chair and table,
HAY

PAGE 58
Kiosk, Emerige and Galerie
kreo, courtyard of the
Parliament of Brittany,
Rennes, France
Ink and adhesive tape on paper
Ink and adhesive tape on paper
Ink and adhesive tape on paper
Ink and adhesive tape on paper
'Retrospective' exhibition, Frac
Bretagne, Rennes, France
Ink on paper
Ink on paper
Ink on paper

PAGE 59
Ink, paint and adhesive tape
on paper

2016/June

PAGE 60
Ink on paper
Ballpoint pen on paper
Ink and adhesive tape on
paper
Model, *Palissade* project, HAY
Graphite on paper
Ink on paper
Palissade collection, HAY
'Seventeen Screens'
exhibition, Frac Bretagne,
Rennes, France
Wrought iron structure,
Officina chair, Magis

PAGE 61
The anvil and hammer
Officina chair and table, Magis
Ink on paper
Detail, *Uncino* chair, Mattiazzi
Stock, wrought iron
structure, *Officina* chair,
Magis
Ink, sticker and adhesive tape
on paper
Ink, sticker and adhesive tape
on paper
Detail, *Uncino* chair, Mattiazzi
Ink, sticker and adhesive tape
on paper

PAGE 62
Nuage vase, Vitra
Paint and adhesive tape on
paper
Ink on paper
House, Brittany, France

Cast glass tables, Glas Italia,
house, Brittany, France
Stampa Chair, Kettal

PAGE 63
Plant detail

PAGE 64
Ink on paper
Nuage vase, Vitra
Rolf Fehlbaum, installation
tribute to Zaha Hadid, fire
station, Vitra campus, Weil
am Rhein, Germany
Ink on paper
Mette, studio, Brittany, France
Design drawing

PAGE 65
Floating House, collaboration
with architects Jean-Marie
Finot and Denis Daversin,
Chatou, France
Rombini ceramic tiles, Mutina
'Seventeen Screens' exhibition,
Frac Bretagne, Rennes,
France
Ink on paper
Ink on paper
Ink on paper
Ballpoint pen on paper
Installation, *Kiosk*, Emerige and
Galerie kreo, *Palissade* chairs
and benches, HAY, Jardin
des Tuileries, Paris
Ink on paper

2016/July

PAGE 66
Model and *The Serif* TV,
Samsung, studio, Paris
My table, studio, Paris
Around Manhattan on an
America's Cup boat, New
York
House, Brittany, France
House, Brittany, France
House, Brittany, France
Ink on paper
Ink on paper
Photo shoot, *Nuage* vases,
Vitra, studio, Paris

PAGE 67
Nuage vases, Vitra

PAGE 68
Ink on paper
Ink on paper
Ink on paper
Officina chairs, Magis
Research, *Long Fountain*
project, 'Urban Reveries'
exhibition
Rombini ceramic tiles, Mutina
Nuage vase, Vitra
Ink on paper
Officina candle holder, Magis

PAGE 69
Ink on paper
Ink on paper
Ink on paper
Ink on paper
Ink on paper
Ink on paper

PAGE 70
Ink on paper
Coloured pencil on paper
Coloured pencil on paper
Officina chairs, Magis
Model, half chair in front of
a mirror
3D model, *Palissade* chair, HAY

PAGE 71
Model of the *Bird*, Vitra, and
model of *Roche* shelf, Galerie
kreo, studio, Paris
Model, *Osso* chair, Mattiazzi
Ink on paper
Osso chair, Mattiazzi
Studio, Brittany, France
Studio, Brittany, France

2016/August

PAGE 72
Ink on paper
Ink on paper
Wall, studio, Brittany, France
Rooftop terrace, Brittany,
France
House, Brittany, France
Stampa chair, Kettal
Officina base, Magis
Shadow, *Palissade* chair, HAY
Shadow and base, *Officina*
candle holder, Magis

PAGE 73
Ink on paper
Mette, rooftop terrace,

LIST OF WORKS

Brittany, France
Rooftop terrace, Brittany,
  France
Studio, Brittany, France
Detail, *Striped* chair, Magis
Detail and shadow, *Striped*
  chair, Magis
Striped chair, Magis, trunk and
  children's chair
Pila chair, Magis
Lattice rug, Nanimarquina

PAGE 74
Officina candle holder, Magis

PAGE 75
Walls, studio, Brittany, France
Studio, Brittany, France
Theca sideboard, Magis
Ink on aluminium foil and crab
Palissade bench, HAY
Ink on paper
Drawing by Mette
Mette and me in kayaks
CD cover, The Wire magazine

PAGE 76
Drawing on the iPad
Pila chair, Magis, house,
  Brittany, France
Crane, *Kiosk*, Emerige and
  Galerie kreo, courtyard of
  the Parliament of Brittany,
  Rennes, France
Pila chair, Magis
Ink on paper, walls, studio,
  Brittany, France
Ink on paper
Production, *Palissade* chairs,
  HAY
Ink and adhesive tape on paper
Poster published by ECAL

2016/September

PAGE 77
Installation, *Nuage* vases, Vitra,
  studio courtyard, Paris

PAGE 78
Ink and adhesive tape on paper
'Seventeen Screens' exhibition,
  Tel Aviv Museum of Art,
  Israel
Installation, *Nuage* vases, studio
  courtyard, Paris
Installation, *Nuage* vases, studio
  courtyard, Paris

Officina trestle table, Magis,
  studio courtyard, Paris
Ink, adhesive tape and coloured
  cellophane on paper

PAGE 79
Nuage vase, Vitra

PAGE 80
Ink, adhesive tape and
  coloured cellophane on
  paper
Ink, adhesive tape and
  coloured cellophane on
  paper
Ink on paper
Ink on paper
Ink on paper
Production, very large *Ruutu*
  vases, Iittala
Wooden side table, Vitra, and
  trunk
Torique vase, ceramic, turned
  in Vallauris
Ink on paper

PAGE 81
Nuage vases, Vitra, in front of
  a painting by Erwan, studio,
  Paris
Y-122 table, Galerie kreo
I proudly carry a very large
  Ruutu vase, Iittala
Very large *Ruutu* vases, Iittala,
  Galerie kreo
Production, very large *Ruutu*
  vase, Iittala
Very large *Ruutu* vases, Iittala,
  Galerie kreo

PAGE 82
Y-122 table, Galerie kreo
Y-122 table, Galerie kreo
Ink on paper
Ink on paper
Ink and adhesive tape on paper
Ink on paper
Ink on paper
Copenhagen collection, HAY
Officina chair, Magis

PAGE 83
Ink on paper
Research drawing, *Ring* bench
Ink on paper
My table, studio, Paris
Nuage vases, Vitra, studio, Paris
Ink on paper

PAGE 84
Very large *Ruutu* vases, Iittala,
  Galerie kreo, London

PAGE 85
Cornelius, rooftop terrace,
  Brittany, France
Y-122 table, studio, Paris
Officina coat rack, Magis
Ink on paper
Clémence Krzentowski
  carrying a large *Ruutu* vase,
  Iittala, Galerie kreo
Clémence Krzentowski behind
  two very large *Ruutu* vases,
  Iittala, Galerie kreo

PAGE 86
Ink on paper
Michel carrying a large *Ruutu*
  vase, Iittala, Galerie kreo
Prototype, *Blur* rug,
  Nanimarquina
Very large *Ruutu* vases, Iittala,
  Galerie kreo
Coloured pencil on paper
Ink on paper
Ink on paper
Ink on paper
Striped chair, Magis

2016/October

PAGE 87
Ink on paper
Ink on paper
Ink on paper
'Urban Reveries' exhibition,
  Vitra Design Museum, Weil
  am Rhein, Germany
'Urban Reveries' exhibition,
  Vitra Design Museum,
  Weil am Rhein, Germany
Ink on paper
'Urban Reveries' exhibition,
  Vitra Design Museum,
  Weil am Rhein, Germany
Ink on paper
Ink on paper

PAGE 88
Ink on paper
Cyl table, Vitra
Detail, *Y-122* table, Galerie kreo
Ink and adhesive tape on paper
Ink on paper
Ink on paper
Ink on paper

Cyl table and *Belleville* chair,
  Vitra
Cyl table, Vitra

PAGE 89
Ink on paper
Graphite on paper
Ink on paper
'Seventeen Screens'
  exhibition, Frac Bretagne,
  Rennes, France
Very large *Ruutu* vases, Iittala,
  Galerie kreo
'Seventeen Screens'
  exhibition, Frac Bretagne,
  Rennes, France

PAGE 90
Cyl table and *Belleville* chair,
  Vitra
Nuage vases, Vitra
Aluminium extrusion, *Nuage*
  vase, Vitra
Cyl collection, Vitra
Cyl collection, Vitra
Coloured pencil on paper

PAGE 91
Cyl sofa, Vitra
Ink and adhesive tape on
  paper
Shadow, *Stampa* chair, Kettal
Stampa chair, Kettal
Osso chair, Mattiazzi, house,
  Brittany, France
Palissade bench, HAY, terrace,
  Brittany, France
Cyl collection, Vitra
Ring benches, Orgatec Trade
  Fair, Cologne, Germany
Ring benches, Orgatec Trade
  Fair, Cologne, Germany

PAGE 92
Luminous object, Galerie kreo,
  and Didier Krzentowski
  going down the stairs
Model, *Ring* bench
Parrot on my shoulder
Ink on paper
Didier Krzentowski and
  Chains, ceramic, Galerie
  kreo, Paris
Ink on paper

PAGE 93
Chains, aluminium, Galerie
  kreo, Paris

2016/November

PAGE 94
Ink on paper
Ink on paper
Chains, plaster, Galerie kreo,
  Paris
Invitation 'Chains' exhibition,
  Galerie kreo, Paris
Ink and adhesive tape on paper
Setting up 'Chains' exhibition,
  Galerie kreo, Paris
Ink and adhesive tape on paper
Ink and adhesive tape on paper
Ink on paper

PAGE 95
Ink on paper
Ink on paper
Puzzle
Ink on paper
Model in pieces, *Pila* chair, Magis
Ink and adhesive tape on paper
Wrought iron detail
Detail, *Officina* collection, Magis
Ink and adhesive tape on paper

PAGE 96
Ink on paper
Ink on paper
Ink on paper
Ink on paper
Invitation, 'Chains' exhibition,
  Galerie kreo, London
'Chains' exhibition, Galerie kreo,
  London

PAGE 97
Sketch
Officina chair and table, Magis
Ink and coloured cellophane on
  paper
Ink and paint on paper
Ink, adhesive tape and coloured
  cellophane on paper
Ink, adhesive tape and coloured
  stickers on paper
Ink, adhesive tape and coloured
  cellophane on paper
Officina valet stand, Magis
Photo shoot, *Cyl* collection, Vitra

PAGE 98
Ink and coloured cellophane on
  paper
Gabriel chandelier, Swarovski
  crystal, Palace of Versailles,
  France

Setting up *Gabriel* chandelier, Swarovski crystal, Palace of Versailles, France
Setting up *Gabriel* chandelier, Swarovski crystal, Palace of Versailles, France
Setting up, *Gabriel* chandelier, Swarovski crystal, Palace of Versailles, France
Pearl necklace, jasper, Galerie kreo
Pearl necklace, Carrara marble, Galerie kreo
Ink, adhesive tape and coloured cellophane on paper
Ink, adhesive tape and coloured cellophane on paper

PAGE 99
Research drawing, *Gabriel* chandelier

PAGE 100
Research, bright marquee
The Bird series, Vitra
Adhesive tape, coloured cellophane and sticker on paper
Lianes hanging lights, Galerie kreo
Conques, Galerie kreo
Adhesive tape, coloured cellophane and ink on paper

PAGE 101
Production, *Lianes* hanging lights, Galerie kreo
Ink and coloured cellophane on paper
Ink, adhesive tape, coloured cellophane and stickers on paper
Sketch
Model, *Gabriel* chandelier
Ink, adhesive tape and coloured cellophane on paper

PAGE 102
Ballpoint pen, adhesive tape, coloured cellophane and stickers on paper
Ballpoint pen, adhesive tape and coloured cellophane on paper
Ballpoint pen, adhesive tape and coloured cellophane on paper
Lunch break
Researching patterns
Uncino chairs, Mattiazzi

2016/December

PAGE 103
Adhesive tape and coloured cellophane on paper
Kiosk, Emerige and Galerie kreo, Jardin des Tuileries, Paris
A gift for Rolf Fehlbaum
Patterns, *Rivi* fabric, Artek
Research, patterns, *Rivi* fabric, Artek
Ballpoint pen and adhesive tape on paper
Ballpoint pen, adhesive tape and stickers on paper
Ballpoint pen, adhesive tape and stickers on paper
Ballpoint pen, adhesive tape and stickers on paper

PAGE 104
Officina bench, Magis
With Rolf, *Palissade* collection, HAY
Ink and coloured cellophane on paper
Research, marquee on the water
Prototype, *Rennes* curtains, Kvadrat, studio, Paris
Model, *Palissade* chair, HAY
Colour tests, *The Bird*, ceramic, Vitra
Palissade bench, HAY
Palissade chair, HAY

PAGE 105
One of the first models, *Palissade* collection, HAY

PAGE 106
Officina candle holder, Magis
Ink on paper
In the morning, Brittany, France
Surfing session, Brittany, France
Brittany, France
Officina coat rack, Magis, studio, Brittany, France
Sketch
Landscape, Brittany, France
My work desk, studio, Paris

PAGE 107
Wall, studio, Paris
Stampa chair, Kettal, studio, Brittany, France

Research, 'Urban Reveries' exhibition
Graphite, adhesive tape, stickers and aluminium on paper
Colony of *Bird*, ceramic, Vitra
'Seventeen Screens' exhibition, Tel Aviv Museum of Art, Israel
The Bird, Vitra
The Bird with broken head, Vitra
Greeting card, city of Rennes, France

2017/January

PAGE 108
Ink, stickers and thread on paper
Ink, stickers and thread on paper
Ink and adhesive tape on paper
Ronan & Erwan Bouroullec: Drawing, JRP|Editions
Ink, stickers and thread on paper
Rivi fabric, Artek
Rivi fabric, Artek
I photograph the *Bird*, ceramic, Vitra
Ballpoint pen on paper

PAGE 109
Ink on paper
Full moon
Ink on paper
Ronan & Erwan Bouroullec: Drawing, JRP|Editions
Graphite on paper
Ronan & Erwan Bouroullec: Drawing, JRP|Editions
Ronan & Erwan Bouroullec: Drawing, JRP|Editions
Sketch, *Quindici* chair and lounge chair, Mattiazzi
Ink on paper

PAGE 110
Studio, Paris
Rivi fabric, Artek
Stack of *Pila* chairs, Magis
Ready-made curtain system, Kvadrat
Production, *Stampa* chairs, Kettal
Ballpoint pen, hotel notepad
Ink on paper

Ink and adhesive tape on paper
Ballpoint pen on paper

PAGE 111
Rivi fabric, Artek
Graphite and coloured cellophane on paper
Ink, adhesive tape and coloured cellophane on paper
Ink and adhesive tape on paper
Ink on paper
Frame, *Officina* sofa, Magis

PAGE 112
Work meeting at Magis
Officina bench, Magis
Officina sofa, Magis
Officina sofa, Magis
Work meeting at Magis
Frame detail, *Officina* chair, Magis
Officina stools, Magis
Palissade chair, HAY, *Rombini* ceramic tiles, Mutina
Diapositive desk, Glas Italia

PAGE 113
Theca storage unit, Magis, studio, Paris
Sketch, marquee
Ink and adhesive tape on paper
Model, *Long Fountain* project, 'Urban Reveries' exhibition
Graphite on paper
Ink and adhesive tape on paper

2017/February

PAGE 114
Ink and adhesive tape on paper
Ink on paper
Ink on paper
Ink on paper
Ink and adhesive tape on paper
Detail, *Osso* chair, Mattiazzi
Ink and stickers on paper
Palissade bench, HAY
Photo shoot, *Palissade* collection, HAY

PAGE 115
Palissade chair, HAY

PAGE 116
Graphite on paper
Bells lamp and coffee table, Galerie kreo

Ink and paint on paper
Detail, *Officina* collection, Magis
Model studio, Paris
Preparatory collage, 'Seventeen Screens' exhibition, Tel Aviv Museum of Art, Israel

PAGE 117
Preparatory collage, 'Seventeen Screens' exhibition, Tel Aviv Museum of Art, Israel
Preparatory drawing on photo, 'Seventeen Screens' exhibition, Tel Aviv Museum of Art, Israel
Chains, plaster, Galerie kreo, Paris
Palissade bench, HAY
Ink and paint on paper
Lampalumina lamps, Bitossi
Lampalumina lamps, Bitossi
Assembly, Galerie kreo
Paint on paper

PAGE 118
Model, *Quindici* lounge chair, Mattiazzi

PAGE 119
Ink and adhesive tape on paper
Paint and coloured stickers on paper
Paint, adhesive tape and stickers on paper
Moving in, Brittany, France
Ink, paint and adhesive tape on paper
Model, *Quindici* lounge chair, Mattiazzi
At Cassina
Ink on paper
Ink, adhesive tape and gold card on paper

PAGE 120
Detail, *Uncino* chair, Mattiazzi
Ink, adhesive tape and gold card on paper
Uncino chair, Mattiazzi
Kaari shelf and desk, Artek
Detail, *Officina* chair, Magis
Ink on paper
Officina sofa, Magis
Officina chair, Magis
Officina chair and armchair, Magis

LIST OF WORKS

PAGE 121
Eugenio Perazza's office
Archive, drawings
Archive, ink on paper
Ink on paper
Officina chair, Magis
Ink on paper

PAGE 122
Archive, ink on wood
Ruutu vase, Iittala
Designer of the Year Exhibition,
Architecture & Wohnen,
Kölnischer Kunstverein,
Cologne, Germany
Prototype, *Quindici* lounge
chair, Mattiazzi
Quindici lounge chair, Mattiazzi
Quindici armchair, Mattiazzi

2017/March

PAGE 123
Quindici armchair, Mattiazzi
Quindici lounge chair, Mattiazzi
Ruutu vase, Iittala, and collage
on my window, Paris
Rains screen
'Bivouac' exhibition, Centre
Pompidou-Metz, France
'Steps' exhibition, Villa Noailles,
Hyères, France
Pencil shavings
Drawings, house, Paris
Studio, Paris

PAGE 124
Ink and adhesive tape on paper

PAGE 125
Flowers
Pencil, coloured cellophane and
adhesive tape on paper
'Seventeen Screens' exhibition,
Frac Bretagne, Rennes,
France
Sketch, *Semis* rug, Kvadrat
Semis rug, Kvadrat
Detail, *Slow Chair* armchair, Vitra

PAGE 126
Rennes curtains, Kvadrat
Graphite on paper
Uncino stool, Mattiazzi
Coloured pencil on paper
Softshell chairs, Vitra
Photo shoot, *Softshell* chair,
Vitra

PAGE 127
Ink on paper and net bag for
oranges
Photomontage, *Luce Verticale*
suspension lights, Flos
Uncino stool, Mattiazzi
Detail, *Uncino* chair, Mattiazzi
Detail, *Uncino* chair, Mattiazzi
Quindici armchair, Mattiazzi
At Cassina, *Warning: sit with
caution, the joints are not
glued.*
Ink and adhesive tape on paper
Ink on paper

PAGE 128
Ballpoint pen on paper
Kaari desk, Artek, and *Stool 60*
stool by Alvar Aalto, Artek
Article on my Instagram
account, *Surface* magazine
Officina bench, Magis
Building site, Brittany, France
Quindici armchair and lounge
chair, Mattiazzi

PAGE 129
Ink on paper
Ink on paper
Detail, *Quindici* armchair,
Mattiazzi
Detail, *Uncino* chair, Mattiazzi
Detail, *Uncino* stool, Mattiazzi
Programme, Salone del Mobile,
Milan
Programme, Salone del Mobile,
Milan
Graphite on paper
Coloured pencil and graphite
on paper

2017/April

PAGE 130
Ink on paper

PAGE 131
Detail, *Luce Verticale*
suspension light, Flos
Detail, cast glass table, Glas
Italia
Cast glass table, Glas Italia
Cast glass table, Glas Italia
Quindici armchair, Mattiazzi
Installation, *Luce Verticale*
suspension light, Salone del
Mobile, Milan
Ink on paper

Research, *Semis* rugs, Kvadrat
Semis rugs, Kvadrat

PAGE 132
Ink on paper
Luce Verticale suspension
light, Flos
Luce Verticale suspension light,
Flos
Ink on paper
Ballpoint pen on paper
Photomontage, *Luce Verticale*
suspension light, Flos
Paint, ink and adhesive tape on
paper
Detail, *Semis* rug, Kvadrat
Ballpoint pen on paper

PAGE 133
Ballpoint pen on paper
Détail, *Semis* rugs, Kvadrat
Ruutu vase, Iittala, studio,
Brittany, France
Ruutu vase, Iittala, studio,
Brittany, France
Ruutu vase, Iittala, studio,
Brittany, France
Ink on paper

PAGE 134
Ink on paper
Ink on paper
Ink on paper
Ink on TGV paper napkins
Studio, Brittany, France
Ink on paper
Plate for American Airlines,
Alessi
Ink on paper
House, Paris

PAGE 135
Ink on paper
Ready-made curtain system,
Kvadrat, house, Paris
Ink on paper
Graphite on paper
Ink on paper
Ink on paper
Ink on paper
Ink on paper
Ink on Norwegian Airline
sickness bag

PAGE 136
Production, *Ring* bench
Palissade bench, HAY
Prototypes, *Losange* vases,

ceramic, Galerie kreo
'Album' exhibition, Arc en
rêve centre d'architecture,
Bordeaux, France
Ink on Norwegian Airline
sick bag
'Bivouac' exhibition, Centre
Pompidou-Metz, France

PAGE 137
Ink on paper
Clouds screen, Kvadrat
Ink on paper
'Bivouac' exhibition, Centre
Pompidou-Metz, France
'Bivouac' exhibition, Centre
Pompidou-Metz, France
Ink on paper

2017/May

PAGE 138
Ink on paper
Cut-out, *Ronan & Erwan
Bouroullec: Drawing*,
JRP|Editions, installation,
Cologne, Germany
Model of *Ring* bench
Ring bench, *OUI* installation,
Kunsthal Aarhus Park,
Denmark
Palissade bench, HAY, and
Ring bench, *OUI* installation,
Kunsthal Aarhus Park,
Denmark
Wall and desk, house, Brittany,
France
Ink and gold card on paper
Ink, paint and adhesive tape
on paper
Striped armchair, Magis

PAGE 139
Palissade chair in galvanized
steel, HAY
Installation test, *Gabriel*
chandelier, Swarovski,
Wattens, Austria
Gabriel chandelier, Swarovski
crystal, Palace of Versailles,
France
Ink on paper
Ink on paper
Ink on paper
Ink and paint on paper
Ink and paint on paper
Cut-out pages, *Ronan & Erwan
Bouroullec: Drawing*,

JRP|Editions, installation,
Cologne, Germany

PAGE 140
Ink on paper, house, Paris
Ink, paint and adhesive tape
on paper
Ink on paper
Detail, *Pila* chair, Magis
Ink on paper
Ring bench, *OUI* installation,
Kunsthal Aarhus Park,
Denmark

PAGE 141
Ring fireplace bench, *OUI*
installation, Kunsthal Aarhus
Park, Denmark
Installation, *Ring* bench, *OUI*
installation, Kunsthal Aarhus
Park, Denmark
Prototypes, *Semis* rugs,
Kvadrat
Ink on paper
Ink and paint on paper
Ink and paint on paper
Ink and paint on paper
Ink and paint on paper
Ring bench, *OUI* installation,
Kunsthal Aarhus Park,
Denmark

PAGE 142
Ballpoint pen on paper
Ink and adhesive tape, hotel
notepad
Research, *Lianes* project,
'Urban Reveries' exhibition
Scale 1 test passed,
revegetation of ropes
Research, *Lianes* project,
'Urban Reveries' exhibition
Scale 1 test passed,
revegetation of ropes
Research, *Lianes* project,
and Trunk bench, 'Urban
Reveries' exhibition
Badge, jury member, Brest
Surf Film Festival, France
Drawing for the inauguration,
OUI installation, Kunsthal
Aarhus Park, Denmark

PAGE 143
House, Brittany, France

2017/June

PAGE 144
Sketches, benches and
marquees
Detail, *Ring* bench, *OUI*
installation, Kunsthal
Aarhus Park, Denmark
Ink on paper
Ink on paper
Ink on paper
Ring bench, *OUI* installation,
Kunsthal Aarhus Park,
Denmark
Ring bench, *OUI* installation,
Kunsthal Aarhus Park,
Denmark
Ring bench, *OUI* installation,
Kunsthal Aarhus Park,
Denmark
Collage on accounts from the
1990s

PAGE 145
Invitation card, talk with Rolf
HAY, Copenhagen
Copenhagen chairs, HAY,
before the public arrive
Ink on paper
Ink on paper
Ink on paper
Ink on paper

PAGE 146
Ink on paper
Drawings in front of the Seine,
Héricy, France
Drawing on the iPad
Ink on paper
Ink on paper
Ink on paper
Ink on paper
Lighthouse lamp, Established
& Sons
Very large *Ruutu* vases, littala,
Galerie kreo, London

PAGE 147
Drawing in a studio
Research, *Tourniquets*
project, 'Urban Reveries'
exhibition
Installation, *Nuage* vases,
Vitra, studio courtyard,
Paris
Prototype, ink on silk
Sketches, suspension lights
Ink on paper and book

Test, coloured glass in the sun
Test, coloured glass in the sun
Ink on paper

PAGE 148
Ink on paper, terrace, Villa
Noailles, Hyères, France
Nuage vase, Vitra, ink on wood
and portrait in the mirror
Ink on paper, house, Paris
Semis rug, Kvadrat
Graphite and adhesive tape on
paper
Graphite, ink, paint and
adhesive tape on paper

PAGE 149
Ink and paint on paper
Semis rugs, Kvadrat
w103 pendant lights by Inga
Sempé, Wästberg, Villa
Noailles, Hyères, France
Ink on paper
Drawing on skateboard
Archive label on a notebook

PAGE 150
Ruutu vase, ceramic, littala
Quindici lounge chair, Mattiazzi
Ink on paper
Ink on paper
Ink, paint and adhesive tape on
paper
'Seventeen Screens' exhibition,
Frac Bretagne, Rennes,
France
Chains, aluminium, Galerie kreo
Very large *Ruutu* vase, littala,
Galerie kreo
Ink on paper

2017/July

PAGE 151
Ink and adhesive tape on paper

PAGE 152
Chains, ceramic, Galerie kreo
Ink on paper
Kiosk, Emerige and Galerie kreo
Detail, *Striped* chair, Magis
Ink on paper
Ink and paint on paper
Research, *Piano* ceramic tiles,
Mutina
Research, *Piano* ceramic tiles,
Mutina
Ink on paper

PAGE 153
Ink on paper
Ink on paper
Rombini ceramic tiles, Mutina
Me photographing *Piano*
ceramic tiles, Mutina
Ballpoint pen on paper
Research, marquee
Ink on paper
Ink on paper
Ink on paper

PAGE 154
Pico ceramic tiles, Mutina
With Massimo Orsini
Archive, drawings
Ink on paper
Ink and paint on paper
Ink on paper

PAGE 155
Jean-Marie's ceramics studio,
Burgundy, France
Ink on paper
Research, floating square
Semis rug, Kvadrat
Semis rug, Kvadrat
Luce Verticale suspension light,
Flos
Semis rug, Kvadrat
Invitation poster, 'Bivouac'
exhibition, Centre Pompidou-
Metz, France
Coloured pencil on paper

PAGE 156
Ink on paper

PAGE 157
Ink on paper
Studio, Brittany, France
Ink on paper
Ink on paper
Ink on paper
Ink on paper
Ink on paper
Ink on paper
Losange vases, Galerie kreo

2017/August

PAGE 158
Shadow, *Stampa* chair, Kettal
Rock, studio, Brittany, France
Ink on paper
Ink on paper
Chainette curtain, Kvadrat
Ink on paper

Wall, studio, Brittany, France
Rock, studio, Brittany, France
'Momentary' exhibition, Musée
des Arts Décoratifs, Paris

PAGE 159
Sun, house, Brittany, France
Walls, studio, Brittany, France
Ink on paper
Ink and adhesive tape on paper
Ink on paper
Ink and adhesive tape on paper

PAGE 160
Ink on paper
Ink on paper
Ink on paper
Ink, adhesive tape and paint on
paper
Ink on paper and *Officina*
candle holder, Magis
Ink and adhesive tape on paper
Ink and adhesive tape on paper
Ink on paper
Ink and adhesive tape on paper

PAGE 161
Pila chair, Magis, terrace,
Brittany, France
Detail, *Palissade* chair, HAY
Palissade chair, HAY, terrace,
Brittany, France
Ink and adhesive tape on paper
Ink and adhesive tape on paper
Ink and adhesive tape on paper
Ready-made curtain system,
Kvadrat
Ink on paper
Rennes curtains, Kvadrat

2017/September

PAGE 162
Model, *Promenade Nuage*,
Miami

PAGE 163
Detail, *Pila* chair, Magis
Guipure embroidery
Quindici armchair and its
cushion, Mattiazzi
Inga going up the stairs, house,
Paris
Ink and oil pastel on paper
Mette, studio, Brittany, France
Staircase, house, Paris
Ink and oil pastel on paper
Oil pastel on wood

PAGE 164
Ink, adhesive tape and coloured
cellophane on paper
'Seventeen Screens' exhibition,
Frac Bretagne, Rennes,
France
Scenography, 'Retrospective'
exhibition, Frac Bretagne,
Rennes, France
Shadow, *Palissade* chair, HAY
Detail, *Belleville* chair, Vitra
Officina valet stand, Magis

PAGE 165
Ink on paper
Ink on paper
Detail, frame, Corian
Slow Chair, Vitra
Research, textile
Ink on paper
Losange rug, Nanimarquina
Scenography, 'Retrospective'
exhibition, Frac Bretagne,
Rennes, France
Ink on paper

PAGE 166
Ink on paper
At Mutina
Piano ceramic tiles, Mutina
Ink and paint on paper
Emi hangs drawings, studio,
Paris
Emi, studio, Paris
On the train
Steelwood chair, Magis
Piano ceramic tiles, Mutina

2017/October

PAGE 167
Clémence Krzentowski
carrying a very large *Ruutu*
vase, littala, Galerie kreo

PAGE 168
Pastel, graphite and adhesive
tape on wood
Ink and adhesive tape on paper
Pastel, graphite and adhesive
tape on wood
Pastel, graphite and adhesive
tape on wood
Ink and pastel on paper
Installation, *Kiosk*, Emerige and
Galerie kreo, garden, Mexico
City
Ink on TGV paper napkin

LIST OF WORKS

Conference, Théâtre du
   Capitole, Toulouse, France
Conference, Théâtre du
   Capitole, Toulouse, France

PAGE 169
Ink on paper
Wall, house, Paris
Ink on paper
Exhibition, *Torique* collection,
   Gilles Peyroulet & Cie
   Gallery, Paris
At Claude Aïello's, Vallauris,
   France
At Claude Aïello's, Vallauris,
   France
Cast glass element, *Luce
   Orizzontale* suspension light,
   Flos
Pastel on wood, pink living
   room, Villa Noailles, Hyères,
   France
Studio, Paris

PAGE 170
Ink on paper
Ink on paper
Print on paper, The Wrong
   Shop, studio, Paris
Me photographing *Piano*
   ceramic tiles, Mutina
Coloured pencil on paper
Detail, cast glass table, Glas
   Italia
Textile Field installation, Victoria
   and Albert Museum, London
Nuage vase, ceramic, limited
   edition
Paint on paper

PAGE 171
Coloured pencil on paper
Ballpoint pen on paper
Sketch, kiosk, Rennes, France
Ballpoint pen, sticker and
   adhesive tape on paper
Ink on paper
Ink on paper

PAGE 172
Palissade bench, HAY
Detail, *Osso* chair, Mattiazzi
Softshell chair, Vitra
Nuage vase, Vitra
Digital image, kiosk on the
   water, Rennes, France
Graphite, adhesive tape and oil
   pastel on wood

Brittany, France
Studio, Brittany, France
Officina candle holder, studio,
   Brittany, France

2017/November

PAGE 173
Sketch, kiosk on the water

PAGE 174
Chainette curtain, Kvadrat
Studio, Brittany, France
Exhibition of *Losange* vases,
   Galerie kreo, Paris
Ink on paper
Ink on paper
Exhibition of *Losange* vases,
   Galerie kreo, Paris
Exhibition of *Losange* vases,
   Galerie kreo, Paris
Exhibition of *Losange* vases,
   Galerie kreo, Paris
Ruutu vases, Iittala

PAGE 175
Ink on paper
Ink on paper
Studio, Brittany, France
Banana tree, *w103* lamp by
   Inga Sempé, Wästberg, and
   drawing on the wall, house,
   Paris
Ink on paper
Guipure embroidery

PAGE 176
Promenade Nuage project,
   'Urban Reveries' exhibition
Manufacturing, *Promenade
   Nuage*, Miami
Manufacturing, *Promenade
   Nuage*, Miami
Ink on paper
Manufacturing, *Promenade
   Nuage*, Miami
Model, *Promenade Nuage*, Miami
Ink, paint and coloured
   cellophane on paper
Textile Field installation, Victoria
   and Albert Museum, London
Greetings poster, Vitra

PAGE 177
Invitation card, exhibition of
   Losange vases, Galerie kreo,
   Paris

Prototype, *Nuage* vase,
   ceramic, Vitra
Ink on paper
Ink on paper
Ink on paper
Model, *Promenade Nuage*,
   Miami
With Erwan, studio, Paris
Losange vases, Galerie kreo
Sketch, kiosk on the water,
   Rennes, France

2017/December

PAGE 178
Nuage vase, ceramic, Vitra
Model, *Promenade Nuage*,
   Miami
Promenade Nuage, Miami
Nuage vase, Vitra, and ink on
   paper
Promenade Nuage, Miami
Promenade Nuage, Miami
Ink on paper
Promenade Nuage, Miami
Promenade Nuage, Miami

PAGE 179
Promenade Nuage, Miami
Model, *Promenade Nuage*,
   Miami
Ink on paper
Ink on paper
Clouds, textile, Kvadrat
Promenade Nuage, Miami

PAGE 180
Ink on paper
Ink on paper
Promenade Nuage, Miami
Ink on paper
Ink on paper
Ink on paper
Ink on paper
Ruutu vases, Iittala
Rennes curtains, Kvadrat

PAGE 181
Rennes curtains, Kvadrat
Ink on paper
Original sketch, *Algue*, Vitra
Technical plan, *Algue*, Vitra
Algue, Vitra
'Momentary' exhibition, Musée
   des Arts Décoratifs, Paris
'Momentary' exhibition, Musée
   des Arts Décoratifs, Paris

Ink on paper
Ink on paper

PAGE 182
Ink on paper
Tree and Rocks roof project,
   'Urban Reveries' exhibition
Floating House, collaboration
   with architects Jean-Marie
   Finot and Denis Daversin,
   Chatou, France
Ink on paper
Ruutu vase, Iittala
Ink on paper

PAGE 183
Ink on paper
Ink on paper
Ink on paper
Digital image, kiosk on the
   water, Rennes, France
Ink on paper
Michel carrying a very large
   Ruutu vase, Iittala, Galerie
   kreo
Very large *Ruutu* vases, Iittala,
   Galerie kreo
Very large *Ruutu* vases, Iittala,
   Galerie kreo
Ink on paper

2018/January

PAGE 184
House, Paris
Walls, house, Paris
Installation tribute to Zaha
   Hadid, fire station, Vitra
   campus, Weil am Rhein,
   Germany
Ink on paper
Ballpoint pen, adhesive tape
   and stickers on paper
Rennes curtain, Kvadrat
Rennes curtain, Kvadrat
Ink on paper
Quindici lounge chair, Mattiazzi

PAGE 185
Promenade Nuage, Miami

PAGE 186
Conques, Galerie kreo
Cast glass table, Glas Italia
Clutch bag, Prada
Sketch, *Clutch bag*
Collaboration with Prada
Clutch bag, Prada

Research, *Vegetal Marquee*
   project, 'Urban Reveries'
   exhibition
'Seventeen Screens' exhibition,
   Frac Bretagne, Rennes,
   France
Ink on paper

PAGE 187
Ink on paper
Ink on paper
Ink and adhesive tape on paper
Mette on the *Cassette* sofa,
   Established & Sons
Ink and adhesive tape on paper
Graphite on paper
Model studio, Paris
Parasols project, 'Urban
   Reveries' exhibition
Sketch, *The Fountains of the
   Champs-Élysées*, Paris

PAGE 188
Ink on paper
Chainette curtains, Kvadrat
Ink on paper
Ink on paper
Ink on paper
Clouds, textile, Kvadrat

PAGE 189
Prototypes, *Rennes* curtain,
   Kvadrat showroom,
   Copenhagen

PAGE 190
Detail, *Chainette* curtain,
   Kvadrat
'Seventeen Screens' exhibition,
   Tel Aviv Museum of Art,
   Israel
Ink on aluminium foil
Prototypes, *Rennes* curtain,
   Kvadrat showroom,
   Copenhagen
Prototypes, *Rennes* curtain,
   Kvadrat showroom,
   Copenhagen
Ink on paper

2018/February

PAGE 191
Digital image, *Belvédère*
   project, Rennes, France
Rennes and *Chainette* curtains,
   Kvadrat showroom,
   Stockholm

Chainette curtain, Kvadrat
    showroom, Stockholm
Coloured pencil on digital
    image, Belvédère project,
    Rennes, France
Ink on paper
Preparation of a book, Nieves
    editions
Detail, Élémentaire chair, HAY
Ballpoint pen, hotel notepad
Ballpoint pen, hotel notepad

PAGE 192
Pond bench, Promenade Nuage,
    Miami
Ink on paper napkin
Drawings archive
Model, Ring bench
Formwork mould, pond bench,
    Promenade Nuage, Miami
Drawings archive

PAGE 193
Kvadrat showroom, Stockholm
Metal Side tables, Vitra
Losange vase, ceramic, Galerie
    kreo
Ink on paper
Ink on paper
Officina bench, Magis
Detail, Cassette sofa,
    Established & Sons
End of the night
Model, The Fountains of the
    Champs-Élysées, Paris

PAGE 194
Archive of drawings and
    notebooks

PAGE 195
Nuage vases, Vitra
Rain in the studio, Brittany,
    France
Studio, Brittany, France
Ink on paper
Ink on paper
Ink on paper
Prototype, Blur rug,
    Nanimarquina
Rayures screen, Glas Italia
Research, Ruutu vases, Iittala

2018/March

PAGE 196
Belleville chair and Cyl desk,
    Vitra

Research, floating marquee
'Urban Reveries' exhibition,
    EPFL, Lausanne, Switzerland
Detail, Cyl table, Vitra
Shadow of Alcova vases,
    WonderGlass
Blur rug, Nanimarquina
Ink on paper
Studio, Brittany, France
Hole chair, Cappellini

PAGE 197
Rayures screen, Glas Italia
Ink on paper
Palissade armchair, galvanized
    steel, HAY
Blur rug, Nanimarquina
Blur rug, Nanimarquina
Detail, Blur rug, Nanimarquina

PAGE 198
Artek table prototype
Detail, Cotone chair, Cassina
Ink on paper
Conference on the 'Urban
    Reveries' exhibition
'Urban Reveries' exhibition,
    EPFL, Lausanne, Switzerland
Research, Ring and Roof bench,
    'Urban Reveries' exhibition
Research, Trunk bench, 'Urban
    Reveries' exhibition
Ink on paper
Blur rug, Nanimarquina

PAGE 199
Blur rug, Nanimarquina, and
    Quindici armchair, Mattiazzi

PAGE 200
Alcova vases, WonderGlass
Photo shoot, Alcova vases,
    WonderGlass, Veneto, Italy
Photo shoot, Alcova vases,
    WonderGlass, Veneto, Italy
Alcova vase, WonderGlass
Print test for a book, Nieves
    editions
Print test for a book, Nieves
    editions
At WonderGlass, Veneto, Italy
Research, illuminated marquee
Graphite on wood

2018/April

PAGE 201
Ink on paper

Ink on paper
Ink on paper
Seat prototype for Vitra
Ink on paper
Studio, Paris
Ink on paper
Three Élémentaire chairs, HAY
Élémentaire chairs, HAY

PAGE 202
Drawing on digital image
Ergonomics test model,
    Élémentaire chair, HAY
Cardboard model, Élémentaire
    chair, HAY
With Pierre Keller
Élémentaire chair, HAY
Palissade bench, galvanized
    steel, HAY

PAGE 203
Collage, vase project
Programme, Salone del Mobile,
    Milan
Élémentaire chairs and
    Copenhagen table, HAY
Alcova vases, WonderGlass
Seat, Vitra Typecasting
    installation, La Pelota, Milan
Palissade collection, HAY,
    courtyard of Palazzo Clerici,
    Milan
Seat, Vitra Typecasting
    installation, La Pelota, Milan
Cotone chair, Cassina
Rayures screen, Glas Italia

PAGE 204
Alcova vases, WonderGlass
Alcova vases, WonderGlass
Cotone chair, Cassina
Rayures screen, Glas Italia
Alcova vases, WonderGlass
Studio, Brittany, France
Rayures screen, Glas Italia
Production, Alcova vases,
    WonderGlass
Production, Alcova vases,
    WonderGlass

PAGE 205
Quindici lounge chair, Mattiazzi
Juillet book, Nieves editions
Ink on paper
Ink on paper
Ink on paper
Ergonomics test model,
    Élémentaire chair, HAY

Ink on paper
Gears, The Fountains of the
    Champs-Élysées, Paris
Cotone table and chairs,
    Cassina

2018/May

PAGE 206
Cotone table and chair, Cassina

PAGE 207
Shadow of models, The
    Fountains of the Champs-
    Élysées, Paris
Palissade collection, galvanized
    steel, HAY
Pico ceramic tiles, Mutina
Prototype, Élémentaire chair,
    HAY
Juillet book, Nieves editions
Sketch on a wooden table,
    Belvédère project, Rennes,
    France
Ink on paper
Research, marquee
Ink on paper

PAGE 208
Model, Rayures screen, Glas
    Italia
Ink and adhesive tape on paper
Ink and adhesive tape on paper
Model, Élémentaire chair, HAY,
    and Losange vases, Galerie
    kreo
Ink and adhesive tape on paper
Ink on paper
Model, Élémentaire chair, HAY
Ink, adhesive tape and coloured
    cellophane on paper
Blur rug, Nanimarquina, and
    Quindici chair, Mattiazzi

PAGE 209
Ink, adhesive tape and coloured
    cellophane on paper
Poster, exhibition, Giorgio
    Mastinu Gallery, Venice
Poster, exhibition, Giorgio
    Mastinu Gallery, Venice
Rayures screen, Glas Italia
Ink on paper
Ink and adhesive tape on paper
Ink and paint on paper
Blur rug, Nanimarquina
Models, Belvédère project,
    Rennes, France

PAGE 210
Ink and gold card on paper
Ink, stickers and graphite on
    paper
Promenade Nuage, Miami
Article, exhibition of drawings,
    Giorgio Mastinu Gallery,
    Venice
Ink on paper
Ink on paper
Production, Stream, Vitra
    campus, Portugal
Objects Drawings Models book,
    Archibooks
Detail, Steelwood shelving unit,
    Magis

PAGE 211
Installation, Stream, Vitra
    campus, Weil am Rhein,
    Germany
Graphite on paper
Ink on paper
Ink, adhesive tape and paint on
    paper
Ink on paper
Ink on paper
Ink on paper
Blur rug, Nanimarquina, studio
    courtyard, Paris
Polyptych, ink on paper

2018/June

PAGE 212
Polyptych, ink on paper
Palissade collection, galvanized
    steel, HAY
Rombini ceramic tiles, Mutina
Losange vases, Galerie kreo,
    and Stampa chair, Kettal
Sketch, mobile on the Garonne
Detail, Cotone chair, Cassina
Giorgio Mastinu Gallery, Venice
Exhibition, Vitra, Chicago
Ink on paper napkin

PAGE 213
Ruisseau, Vitra campus, Weil
    am Rhein, Germany
Ruisseau and Ring bench, Vitra
    campus, Weil am Rhein,
    Germany
Ruisseau and Ring bench, Vitra
    campus, Weil am Rhein,
    Germany
Ink on paper
Ink on paper

Ink on paper
Ink and paint on paper
Ink on paper
Ink on paper

PAGE 214
Alcova vase, WonderGlass
Ruisseau, Vitra campus, Weil
   am Rhein, Germany
Ink on paper
Ink on paper
Digital image, *Belvédère*
   project, Rennes, France
Digital image, *Belvédère*
   project, Rennes, France

PAGE 215
Night drawing
Ink on paper
Print on paper, The Wrong
   Shop
Use of drawings, poster, Frieze
   Art Fair, London
Hanging, studio, Paris
Ink on paper
Ink on paper
Ballpoint pen on paper napkin
Samples, *Rennes* and *Chainette*
   curtains, Kvadrat

2018/July

PAGE 216
Rayures screen, Glas Italia
Ink and adhesive tape on paper
Ring bench, Vitra campus, Weil
   am Rhein, Germany
Palissade bench, HAY
Portrait for article, *Intramuros*
   magazine, about 1995
Rolf Fehlbaum

PAGE 217
'Seventeen Screens' exhibition,
   Frac Bretagne, Rennes,
   France
Palissade armchair, galvanized
   steel, HAY, studio courtyard,
   Paris
First research, exterior design,
   Bourse de Commerce –
   Pinault Collection, Paris
Samples, *Chainette* curtain,
   Kvadrat
Greetings poster, Vitra
Studio, Paris
'Bivouac' exhibition, Centre
   Pompidou-Metz, France

Clouds, textile, Kvadrat
Manufacturing, *The Fountains
   of the Champs-Élysées*, Paris

PAGE 218
Sketch on paper napkin
Palissade chairs, galvanized
   steel, studio courtyard,
   Paris
Ink and adhesive tape
   on paper
Studio, Brittany, France
Research, green pavilion
Polyptych, ink on paper
Research, green pavilion
Ink on paper
Officina chair and table, Magis

PAGE 219
Ink on paper
House, Brittany, France
Officina chair, Magis
Palissade bench, HAY, rooftop
   terrace, Brittany, France
Studio, Brittany, France
Houpette

2018/August

PAGE 220
Detail, *Palissade* chair,
   galvanized steel, HAY
Terrace, Brittany, France
Ink on paper
Officina bench, Magis
Palissade chairs, galvanized
   steel, HAY, terrace,
   Brittany, France
Quindici armchair, Mattiazzi
Studio, Brittany, France
Detail, *Quindici* lounge chair,
   Mattiazzi
Houpette

PAGE 221
Prototype, chair
Quindici lounge chair,
   Mattiazzi
Detail, *Palissade* bench, HAY
Drawing, terrace, Brittany,
   France
Palissade chairs, galvanized
   steel, HAY, terrace,
   Brittany, France
Losange vases, Galerie kreo,
   and *Steelwood* chair, Magis,
   house, Brittany, France
Nuage vase, Vitra

Prototype, chair
Ink on paper

PAGE 222
Ink on paper
Ink on paper
Palissade chair, galvanized
   steel, HAY
Studio, Brittany, France
Cat assistant
Ink on paper
Ink on paper
Ink on paper
Studio, Brittany, France

PAGE 223
Studio, Brittany, France

PAGE 224
Poster, The Wrong Shop
Drawing for poster, Frieze Art
   Fair, London
Drawing for poster, Frieze Art
   Fair, London
Drawing for poster, Frieze Art
   Fair, London
Studio, Paris
The Bird, terrace, Brittany,
   France
Ink on paper
Drawings and *Pila* chair, Magis
Ink on paper

2018/September

PAGE 225
Ink on paper
Ink on paper
Giorgio Mastinu
Detail, *Cotone* chair, Cassina
Alcova vase, WonderGlass
Ink and paint on paper
Bouroullec Pasta
Collage
Giorgio Mastinu Gallery,
   Venice

PAGE 226
Ink on paper
Stock of polyurethane
   injections, *Softshell* chair,
   Vitra
Ink on paper
Ink on paper and *Österlen*
   chair by Inga Sempé,
   Gärsnas
Graphite on paper
Blur rug, Nanimarquina

PAGE 227
Print tests, posters, The
   Wrong Shop
Officina chair, Magis
Officina chair and table, Magis
Ink on paper
Officina stools and table, Magis
Ink and paint on paper
Bouroullec Pasta
Ink and paint on paper
Ink and paint on paper

2018/October

PAGE 228
Ink on paper
Drawings, studio, Paris
Nitouche
Poster for a conference
Ink on paper
Cloud screen, 'Bivouac'
   exhibition, Museum of
   Contemporary Art, Chicago
Ink on paper
Ballpoint pen on paper
Ink on paper

PAGE 229
Bouroullec Pasta
Ink on paper
Pastel on wood
Ink on paper
Ink on paper
Nuage vase, Vitra
Ink on paper
Studio, Paris
Print on paper, The Wrong
   Shop

PAGE 230
'Seventeen Screens'
   exhibition, Frac Bretagne,
   Rennes, France
Chains, plaster, Galerie kreo
Models, *Belvédère* project,
   Rennes, France
Clouds, textile, Kvadrat
Rennes curtain, Kvadrat
Rennes curtain, Kvadrat
Lunch break
'Urban Reveries' exhibition,
   Hong Kong Design Institute
'Urban Reveries' exhibition,
   Hong Kong Design Institute

PAGE 231
Poster, The Wrong Shop
Clouds, Kvadrat, *Palissade*

chair, HAY, and ink on paper
Ink on paper
House, Brittany, France
Ink on paper
Palissade chair, galvanized
   steel, HAY
Ink on paper
House, Brittany, France
Quindici lounge chair,
   Mattiazzi

2018/November

PAGE 232
Ink on paper

PAGE 233
W153 Île lamp, Wästberg, by
   Inga Sempé, and *Nuage*
   vase, Vitra
Test prints, The Wrong Shop
Detail, *Élémentaire* chair, HAY,
   and *Rivi* textile, Artek
Printing at Charles's, The
   Wrong Shop
Ink on paper
Poster, The Wrong Shop
Nuage vase, Vitra
Ink on paper napkin
Ink on paper napkin

PAGE 234
Clouds, Kvadrat, and ink on
   paper
Poster, conference
Model, *Belvédère* project,
   Rennes, France
Ink on paper
Ink on paper
Ink on paper
'Bivouac' exhibition, Centre
   Pompidou-Metz, France
Ink and paint on paper
Ink on paper

PAGE 235
Conference, Théâtre de Liège,
   Belgium
Ink and paint on paper
Belleville chair and *Cyl* desk,
   Vitra
Lighthouse lamp, Established
   & Sons
Chains, aluminium, Galerie
   kreo
Hanging test, *Gabriel*
   chandelier
Ink on paper

Ink on paper
Ink on paper

2018/December

PAGE 236
Ink on paper
Rubbish
Manufacturing, *The Fountains of the Champs-Élysées*, Paris
Ink on paper
Ink on paper
Ink on paper
Manufacturing, *The Fountains of the Champs-Élysées*, Paris
Graphite, hotel notepad
'Retrospective' exhibition, Frac Bretagne, Rennes, France

PAGE 237
Graphite on paper
Ink on paper
Graphite on paper
Graphite on wood
Preparation, exhibition of drawings, Galerie kreo, Paris
Preparation, exhibition of drawings, Galerie kreo, Paris

PAGE 238
Ink on paper
Ink on paper
Night drawings, house, Paris
Welding tests
Ink on aluminium foil
Shadow of models, *The Fountains of the Champs-Élysées*, studio courtyard, Paris
Swarovski crystal, *The Fountains of the Champs-Élysées*, Paris
Swarovski crystal, *The Fountains of the Champs-Élysées*, Paris
House, Brittany, France

PAGE 239
Preparation, exhibition of drawings, Galerie kreo, Paris
Chains, plaster, Galerie kreo
Installation tribute to Zaha Hadid, fire station, Vitra campus, Weil am Rhein, Germany
Palissade chair, galvanized steel, HAY
Ink on paper
Ink on paper

2019/January

PAGE 240
Ink on paper
Kaari shelf-desk, Artek
Kaari table, Artek
Ink on paper
Ink on paper
Ink on paper
Ink on paper
Alcova vases, WonderGlass
Ink on paper

PAGE 241
Jean-Marie's ceramics studio, Burgundy, France

PAGE 242
Ink on paper
Model, interior design, Bourse de Commerce – Pinault Collection, Paris
Ink on paper
Assembly of Swarovski crystal, *The Fountains of the Champs-Élysées*, Paris
Assembly of Swarovski crystal, *The Fountains of the Champs-Élysées*, Paris
Preparation, exhibition of drawings, Galerie kreo, Paris
Digital drawing by Erwan
Models, *The Fountains of the Champs-Élysées*, Paris
Sketch, *The Fountains of the Champs-Élysées*, Paris

PAGE 243
Ink on paper
Ink on paper
Ink on paper
Cupro-aluminium tubes, *The Fountains of the Champs-Élysées*, Paris
Palissade armchairs, HAY, in the snow
Hotel, Innsbruck, Austria
Swarovski industrial site, Wattens, Austria
Preparation, exhibition of drawings, Galerie kreo, Paris
Pre-assembly, *The Fountains of the Champs-Élysées*, Paris

2019/February

PAGE 244
Drawing table and stool, house, Paris
Studio, Paris
Model, exhibition of drawings, Galerie kreo
House, Brittany, France
Studio, Brittany, France
Photomontage, interior design, La Halle aux Grains restaurant, Bourse de Commerce – Pinault Collection, Paris
At the framer's
At the framer's
At the framer's

PAGE 245
Pre-assembly, *The Fountains of the Champs-Élysées*, Paris
Selection, exhibition of drawings, Galerie kreo, Paris
Guipure test
Chainette curtain, Kvadrat, studio, Paris
Alcova vase, WonderGlass
Ink on paper
Hanging, exhibition of drawings, Galerie kreo, Paris
Hanging, exhibition of drawings, Galerie kreo, Paris
Guipure test

PAGE 246
Models, *The Fountains of the Champs-Élysées*, Paris
Hanging, exhibition of drawings, Galerie kreo, Paris
Collage
Sketch, marquee
Circular Roof project, 'Urban Reveries' exhibition
The masts, *The Fountains of the Champs-Élysées*, Atelier blam, Nantes, France

PAGE 247
Exhibition of drawings, Galerie kreo, Paris
Exhibition of drawings, Galerie kreo, Paris
Exhibition of drawings, Galerie kreo, Paris
Exhibition of drawings, Galerie kreo, Paris
Sketch, *The Fountains of the*

Champs-Élysées, Paris
Coloured pencil on a photograph of a model of a fountain
Alcova vase, WonderGlass
Exhibition of drawings, Galerie kreo, Paris
Installation, *The Fountains of the Champs-Élysées*, Paris

2019/March

PAGE 248
The Fountains of the Champs-Élysées, Paris
Assembly of Swarovski crystal, *The Fountains of the Champs-Élysées*, Paris
Découpage vases
Engine for rotation, *The Fountains of the Champs-Élysées*, Paris
The Fountains of the Champs-Élysées, Paris
Detail, *The Fountains of the Champs-Élysées*, Paris
A gift for Rolf
Sketch, *Belvédère* project, Rennes, France
Casting of the tubes before manufacturing the masts, *The Fountains of the Champs-Élysées*, Paris

PAGE 249
The Fountains of the Champs-Élysées, Paris
Ink on paper
Pre-assembly, *The Fountains of the Champs-Élysées*, Atelier blam, Nantes, France
Ink on paper
The Fountains of the Champs-Élysées, Paris
Ink on paper

PAGE 250
Quindici lounge chair, Mattiazzi
Ink on paper
Jean-Marie's ceramics studio, Burgundy, France
Exhibition of drawings, Galerie kreo, Paris
Portrait by Inga
Découpage vases

2019/April

PAGE 251
Models, *Belvédère* project, Rennes, France
Programme, Salone del Mobile, Milan
Découpage vases
Vitra stand, Salone del Mobile, Milan
Belt suspension light, Flos
Carved and polychrome wood pieces made by craftsmen, Wakabayashi edition, Kyoto
Découpage vase
Découpage vase
Découpage vase

PAGE 252
Ink on paper
Ink on paper
Ink on paper
Ink on paper
Models, *Belvédère* project, Rennes, France
Quindici armchair, Mattiazzi

PAGE 253
Composition, *Découpage* vase

PAGE 254
Detail, *Palissade* chair, galvanized steel, HAY
House, Brittany, France
W153 Île lamp, Wästberg, by Inga Sempé, *Nuage* vase, Vitra, and oil on canvas
Palissade chair, galvanized steel, HAY
Patterns, *Rivi* fabric, Artek
Rolf and *Ring* bench, Vitra campus, Weil am Rhein, Germany
18, Nieves editions
18, Nieves editions
Shelter project, 'Urban Reveries' exhibition

2019/May

PAGE 255
'Urban Reveries' exhibition, Les Champs Libres, Rennes, France
Algae installation, Vitra, Seoul, South Korea
Ballpoint pen on paper
Graphite on paper

LIST OF WORKS

Sailing the *Floating House*, collaboration with architects Jean-Marie Finot and Denis Daversin, Chatou, France
Graphite on paper

PAGE 256
Ink and paint on paper
Roof project, 'Urban Reveries' exhibition
Studio, Brittany, France
Palissade chair, galvanized steel, HAY
Hidden model
Ink on paper

PAGE 257
Ink on paper
Exhibition of drawings, Galerie kreo, Paris
Rombini ceramic tiles, Mutina
Ink on paper
Model, exterior design, Bourse de Commerce – Pinault Collection, Paris
Safety helmet
Portrait in the studio
Découpage vase
Kilim test by Nanimarquina and *Palissade* chair, HAY

2019/June

PAGE 258
Drawing on digital image, *Belvédère* project, Rennes, France
Sketch on a wooden table, *Belvédère* project, Rennes, France
Model, *Gabriel* chandelier, Palace of Versailles, France
Ink on hotel notepad
Model, interior design, Bourse de Commerce – Pinault Collection, Paris
Ink on paper
Ink on paper
Drawings
Ballpoint pen on paper

PAGE 259
Ink, paint, coloured cellophane and adhesive tape on paper
Chains, plaster, Galerie kreo
Research collage, *Rayures* screen, Glas Italia
Ballpoint pen, adhesive tape

and stickers on paper
Découpage vase and ink on paper
Guipure curtain
Drawing, Giorgio Mastinu Gallery, Venice
Ink on paper
Tests, mobiles, Atelier blam, Nantes, France

PAGE 260
Ink on paper
Promenade Nuage, Miami
Crate, 'Album' exhibition
Ink on paper
Secret project
The team with Aurélien, Atelier blam, Nantes, France
Prototypes, *Rennes* curtain, Kvadrat
Officina candle holder, Magis
Graphite on paper

2019/July

PAGE 261
Ink on paper
Ink on paper
Ink on paper
Studio, Paris
Drawing at sea
Ink and paint on paper

2019/August

PAGE 262
Studio, Brittany, France
Ink on paper
Matin lamp, HAY, by Inga Sempé, house, Brittany, France
Ink on paper
Painting, WANC studio, house, Brittany, France
Ink on paper
Nap time
Officina coat rack, Magis
Quindici lounge chair, Mattiazzi

PAGE 263
Ink on paper
Ink on paper
Cats in the shade
Studio, Brittany, France
Studio, Brittany, France
Pila chair, Magis, and *Screen 100* room divider by Alvar Aalto

Good catch with Bernard
Ink on paper
Ink on paper

PAGE 264
Ink on paper
Studio, Brittany, France
Ink and adhesive tape on paper
Mette, studio, Brittany, France
Cats nap in the *Slow Chair*, Vitra
Models, *Belvédère* project, Rennes, France, on my table, studio, Paris
Ballpoint pen on paper
Ink on paper
Ink on paper

2019/September

PAGE 265
Studio, Brittany, France

PAGE 266
Sign, conference in Quimperlé, France
Ink on paper
Ink on paper
Ink on paper
Scale 1 model swaddled, rock, Bourse de Commerce – Pinault Collection, Paris
With Michel Bras, studio, Paris
Ink on paper
Ink on paper
Ink-black night

PAGE 267
Surf session
Model, chandelier, hall, Bourse de Commerce – Pinault Collection, Paris
With Clémence and Didier in London
Découpage vase on table by Alvar Aalto and W153 Île lamp, Wästberg, by Inga Sempé
Model, hall, Bourse de Commerce – Pinault Collection, Paris
Ink on paper

2019/October

PAGE 268
Ink on paper
Collaboration with Virgil Abloh and Off-White

Catalogue, 'Surrealism and Design' exhibition, Vitra Design Museum, Weil am Rhein, Germany
Conference
Ink on paper
Manufacture, mould for the formwork of the base, *Belvédère* project
With Erwan, about 2002
W153 Île lamp, Wästberg, by Inga Sempé, and *Nuage* vase, Vitra
Fenêtre vases, Maison Matisse

PAGE 269
Ink on paper
Secret project
Ink and paint on paper
Polyptych, ink on paper, and *Cotone* chair, Cassina
Fenêtre vases, Maison Matisse
Exhibition, Giorgio Mastinu Gallery, Venice
Studio, Brittany, France
W103 lamp, Wästberg, by Inga Sempé, and *Nuage* vase, Vitra
Ink on paper

PAGE 270
Ink on paper

PAGE 271
Découpage vases
Ink on paper
Ink on paper
Prototypes, chair
Alcova vases, WonderGlass
Well secured
Pearl necklace, Carrara marble, Galerie kreo
Ink on paper
Ink on paper

2019/November

PAGE 272
Ink on paper
Collage
Collage
Ink on paper
Research, bas-relief
Ink on paper

PAGE 273
Découpage vases
Découpage vases

Jean-Marie's ceramics studio, Burgundy, France
Enthusiasm for a new project
Digital image, *Belvédère* project, Rennes, France
'Retrospective' exhibition, Frac Bretagne, Rennes, France
Model, quarter of *Élémentaire* chair, HAY
Detail, *Élémentaire* chair, HAY
Being hindered

PAGE 274
Ring bench, Place Charles VII, Poitiers, France
Ink and adhesive tape on paper
Ink and adhesive tape on paper
Installation, stake, *Belvédère* project, Rennes, France
Digital image, *Belvédère* project, Rennes, France
Signature, limited editions, The Wrong Shop

PAGE 275
Model, *Belvédère* project, Rennes, France

PAGE 276
Ink and adhesive tape on paper
Ink and adhesive tape on paper
Ink on paper
Carved and polychrome wood piece made by craftsmen, Wakabayashi edition, Kyoto
Sketch on hotel notebook
Ink and adhesive tape on paper

2019/December

PAGE 277
Ink on paper napkin
Models, *Sugata* glasses, Jins
On a trip to Kyoto
Architectural sketch, Kyoto
Notebook, Kyoto
Thermal protection of plants, Kyoto

PAGE 278
Carved and polychrome wood piece made by craftsmen, Wakabayashi edition, Kyoto

PAGE 279
Garden, Kyoto
Rayures screen, Glas Italia
Bottom, *Ruutu* vase, ceramic,

Iittala
Ink on paper
Nitouche coming down the
    stairs
One of the first models,
    Palissade chair, HAY
Ballpoint pen on paper
Sketch
Preparation, casting of
    concrete, *Belvédère* project,
    Rennes, France

PAGE 280
Fleurs, Iittala
Studio, Brittany, France
Ink and adhesive tape on paper
Studio, Brittany, France
Ink and adhesive tape on paper
Ink on paper, Brittany, France

PAGE 281
Prototype, chair
Ink and adhesive tape on paper
Ink and adhesive tape on paper
Ink and adhesive tape on paper
Brittany, France
Drawing table, house, Brittany,
    France
Thorns
Bramble
Studio, Brittany, France

2020/January

PAGE 282
Models, *Belvédère* project,
    Rennes, on my table, studio,
    Paris
Ballpoint pen on paper
Ink, adhesive tape and sticker
    on paper
Officina armchair, Magis
Ink and adhesive tape on paper
Bending of an element,
    Belvédère project, Rennes,
    France
Didier and *Luminous object*,
    Galerie kreo
Studio, Paris
Dedication to Jesper who
    worked at HAY

PAGE 283
Rope Chair, Artek
Detail, *Rope Chair*, Artek
Detail, *Rope Chair*, Artek
Erkkeri vase, Iittala
Ink and adhesive tape on paper

Ink on paper, house, Paris
Ink and adhesive tape on paper
Ink on paper, house, Paris
Fleurs, Iittala, and *Erkkeri* vases,
    Iittala

PAGE 284
The large storage room, studio,
    Paris
Kaari desk, Artek, and *Rope
    Chair*, Artek
Rope Chair, Artek, studio,
    Brittany, France
Model, *Belvédère* project,
    Rennes, France
Blown glass tests, lighting,
    Belvédère project, Rennes,
    France
Tupla wall hook, Artek

2020/February

PAGE 285
Erkkeri vases, Iittala
Poster, 'Imperfections'
    exhibition, Stockholm
Rope Chair, Artek
'Imperfections' exhibition,
    Stockholm
Fleurs, Iittala, and *Ruutu* vase,
    Iittala
'Imperfections' exhibition,
    Stockholm
Graphite on kraft paper
Ink and adhesive tape on paper
Ink and adhesive tape on paper

PAGE 286
Model, *Belvédère* project,
    Rennes, France
Digital image, *Belvédère*
    project, Rennes, France
Studio, Paris
Ink and adhesive tape on paper
Ink and adhesive tape on paper
Ink and adhesive tape on paper
My table, studio, Paris
Model, rock, exterior design,
    Bourse de Commerce –
    Pinault Collection, Paris
Test, *Guipure* curtain,
    restaurant, Bourse de
    Commerce – Pinault
    Collection, Paris

PAGE 287
*The Fountains of the Champs-
    Élysées*, Paris

PAGE 288
Photo shoot, *Rope Chair*, Artek
Model of layout on the river
    Vilaine, *Belvédère* project,
    Rennes, France
Pastel and adhesive tape on
    kraft paper
Pastel and adhesive tape on
    kraft paper
Rope Chair, Artek, rotunda,
    Bourse de Commerce –
    Pinault Collection, Paris
Rope Chair, Artek, waiting to be
    deployed, rotunda, Bourse
    de Commerce – Pinault
    Collection, Paris
Pastel, adhesive tape and
    graphite on kraft paper
Model, exterior design, Bourse
    de Commerce – Pinault
    Collection, Paris
Ink and adhesive tape on paper

2020/March

PAGE 289
Model, rock, exterior design,
    Bourse de Commerce-
    Pinault Collection, Paris
Detail, mobile, *Belvédère*
    project, Rennes, France
Ink on paper
Nuage vase, ceramic, limited
    edition
Découpage vase
Ink and adhesive tape on paper
Hanging of drawings
Ink and adhesive tape on paper
Ink and adhesive tape on paper

PAGE 290
View from my apartment
    window of the school open
    for children of caregivers
    during the first lockdown
Ink and adhesive tape on paper
Drawing table, house, Paris
Walls and drawing table, house,
    Paris
Ink and adhesive tape on paper
Walls and drawing table, house,
    Paris

PAGE 291
Tribute to bakers working
    during the Covid-19
    pandemic

Wall and drawing table, house,
    Paris
Support for key workers
    during lockdown
Hanging of drawings, house,
    Paris
Support for key workers
    during lockdown
Ink and adhesive tape on paper
Support for key workers
    during lockdown
Hanging of drawings
House, Paris

PAGE 292
Ink and adhesive tape on paper
Taking down
Sketch, house on stilts
Ink on paper
The Serif TV, Samsung, and
    Armoire Souple, Moustache,
    by Inga Sempé, house, Paris
Ink on paper
Ink on paper
Ink on paper
Ink on paper

2020/April

PAGE 293
My portrait by Mette
Ink on paper
Ink on paper
Research, marquee on the
    water
Roof and Rocks project, 'Urban
    Reveries' exhibition
Hanging and drawing table,
    house, Paris
Hanging and *Steelwood* chair,
    Magis, house, Paris
Charcoal on paper
Drawing, kitchen, Paris

PAGE 294
Découpage vases, Vitra
Collage and ballpoint pen on
    paper
Collage and ballpoint pen on
    paper
Découpage vase, Vitra
Drawing of Inga sewing cloth
    face masks
Ink on paper
The cat and *The Bird*, Vitra
Inga going up the stairs, house,
    Paris
Découpage vases, Vitra

2020/May

PAGE 295
Découpage vases, Vitra

PAGE 296
Sketch
Drawings taped to the wall,
    house, Paris
Ink on paper
Ink on paper
Still life
Ink on paper

PAGE 297
Hanging, house, Paris
Hanging, house, Paris
Portrait in front of the
    drawing table
Graphite on paper
Hanging, house, Paris
Graphite on paper
Graphite on paper
Graphite on paper and
    Steelwood chair, Magis
Graphite on paper

PAGE 298
Graphite on paper
Ink on paper
Ink on paper
Ink and adhesive tape on
    paper
Graphite on paper
Ballpoint pen on paper

PAGE 299
Ballpoint pen on paper
Ink on paper
Ballpoint pen on paper
Ballpoint pen on wood
Hanging and drawing table,
    house, Paris
Framed drawings

PAGE 300
Last day of lockdown

PAGE 301
Return to the studio, Paris
Hanging, house, Paris
Hanging, house, Paris
Ink on paper
Coloured pencil on paper
Studio, Paris
First trip out of Paris after
    weeks of lockdown
Ink on paper

LIST OF WORKS

Standing on *Palissade* chairs,
HAY

2020/June

PAGE 302
Black Lives Matter
Palissade chairs and table,
HAY
Nuage vase, Vitra, and Daisy
Hello
Graphite on paper
My table, studio, Paris

PAGE 303
Meeting room in the
courtyard, studio, Paris
Palissade chair, HAY
Pastel and graphite on paper
Ink on paper
Hanging, house, Paris
Fleurs, Iittala
Hanging, house, Paris
Shadow, *Palissade* chair and
table, HAY
Erkkeri vase, Iittala

PAGE 304
Nuage vase, Vitra, and fern,
house, Brittany, France
Ink on paper
Ink on paper
Ink on paper
Ink on paper
Jean-Marie's ceramics studio,
Burgundy, France
Ink on paper
Découpage vase and fern,
house, Brittany, France
Quindici lounge chair,
Mattiazzi, and *Officina*
candleholder, Magis

PAGE 305
Greetings poster, city of
Rennes, studio, Paris
Print on paper, The Wrong
Shop
Vegetal chair, Vitra
Research, bronze chair
Ink on paper
Découpage vase and
Rope Chair, Artek
Hanging, house, Paris
Ink on paper
Ink on paper

2020/July

PAGE 306
Rope Chair, Artek, rotunda,
Bourse de Commerce –
Pinault Collection, Paris

PAGE 307
Cloud, polystyrene, studio,
Brittany, France
Erkkeri vases, Iittala
Wind mobile, *Belvédère* project,
Atelier blam, Nantes, France
Ink and adhesive tape on paper
Découpage vases, Vitra, and
poster, The Wrong Shop
Print on paper, The
Wrong Shop
Ink on paper
Découpage vase, Vitra, in front
of a poster by Ellsworth Kelly
Poster, The Wrong Shop

PAGE 308
Model, rock, exterior design,
Bourse de Commerce –
Pinault Collection, Paris
Ink on paper
Ink on paper
Detail, *Quindici* lounge chair,
Matiazzi
Detail, *Hole* chair, Cappellini
Ink on paper
Algues, Vitra
Découpage vase, Vitra, and
Rope Chair, Artek
Ink on paper

PAGE 309
Promenade Nuage, Miami
Sketch on a wooden table,
Belvédère project, Rennes,
France
Corolla and stake, *Belvédère*
project, Rennes, France
Detail, assembly of the stays
to the main structure,
Belvédère project, Rennes,
France
Model of layout on the river
Vilaine, *Belvédère* project,
Rennes, France
Découpage vases, Vitra

PAGE 310
Palissade chairs and table,
galvanized steel, HAY

Jean-Marie's ceramics studio,
Burgundy, France
Wine label for Château Marsau
Clay scraps
Rolf and *Ring* bench, Vitra
campus, Weil am Rhein,
Germany
Model of layout, chandelier,
hall, Bourse de Commerce –
Pinault Collection, Paris
Functional test of an element,
chandelier, hall, Bourse
de Commerce – Pinault
Collection, Paris
House, Brittany, France
Palissade lounge chair, HAY

2020/August

PAGE 311
Palissade lounge chair, HAY, in
the fog
Palissade lounge chair and
armchair, HAY
Ink on paper
Detail, *Rope Chair*, Artek, and
ceramics, unknown artist
Ink on paper
Notebook on the rock
Ink on paper
Rope Chair, Artek
Ink and adhesive tape on paper

PAGE 312
Ink on paper
Erkkeri vase, Iittala
Rope Chair, Artek, roof terrace,
Brittany, France
Palissade lounge chair, HAY
Portrait in the studio, Brittany,
France
Ink on paper
Ink on paper
Detail, studio, Brittany, France
House, Brittany, France

PAGE 313
Ink on paper

PAGE 314
Découpage vase, Vitra, and
banc Corde
Palissade lounge chair, HAY
Two vertebrae
Graphite on paper
House, Brittany, France
Nitouche and *Piani* lamp, Flos
My father's wooden spoons

Ink on paper
Ink on paper

PAGE 315
Ink on paper
Ink on paper
Ink on paper
Découpage vase, Vitra
Model, *Belvédère* project,
Rennes, France
Detail, *Uncino* chair, Mattiazzi

2020/September

PAGE 316
Poster, The Wrong Shop
Diptych, ink on paper
Ink on paper
Rope Chair, Artek, framed
drawing and *Flou* mirror,
Galerie kreo, studio, Paris
Print test, The Wrong Shop
Ring bench, Kvadrat
headquarters, Ebeltoft,
Denmark
Ring bench, Kvadrat
headquarters, Ebeltoft,
Denmark
Studio, Brittany, France
Receipt of ceramics that I cut in
Burgundy, studio, Paris

PAGE 317
Belvédère project, Rennes,
France
Model, *Belvédère* project,
Rennes, France
Belvédère project, Rennes,
France
Belvédère project, Rennes,
France
Reflection in the river Vilaine,
Belvédère project, Rennes,
France
Belvédère project, Rennes,
France

PAGE 318
New wrought iron railing,
house, Brittany, France
Terrace, Brittany, France
Detail, wrought iron railing,
house, Brittany, France
Rope Chair, Artek, and *Rope*
bench, terrace, Brittany,
France
Ink on paper
Hydrangea

Ink on paper
Bronze rock before polishing,
exterior design, Bourse
de Commerce – Pinault
Collection, Paris
Mould, bronze rock,
exterior design, Bourse
de Commerce – Pinault
Collection, Paris

PAGE 319
Reflection in the river Vilaine,
Belvédère project, Rennes,
France

PAGE 320
Alcova vase, WonderGlass
Studio, Paris
Studio, Brittany, France
Print test, The Wrong Shop
Print on paper, The Wrong
Shop
Ink on paper
Tribute to Enzo Mari
Models, *Belvédère* project,
Rennes, France
Sign, conference

2020/October

PAGE 321
Rope Chair, Artek, and ink on
paper, exhibition, Piacé Le
Radieux art centre, Piacé,
France
Coat on hidden chair
Découpage vase, Vitra, *Nuage*
vase, Vitra, and *Rope Chair*,
Artek
Ink on paper
Ink on paper and *Steelwood*
chair, Magis
Ink on paper and adhesive tape
Ink on paper and adhesive tape
Detail, bronze rock before
patina, exterior design,
Bourse de Commerce –
Pinault Collection, Paris
Palissade lounge chairs, HAY,
terrace, Brittany, France

PAGE 322
Printing of posters, The Wrong
Shop
Assembly, *Gabriel* chandelier,
Swarovski crystal, Palace of
Versailles, France
Wine label for Château Marsau

Ink on paper
Ring bench and fireplace, *OUI* installation, Kunsthal Aarhus Park, Denmark
Ink on paper
Ink on paper
Ink on paper
Crayon-Pinceau book, Nieves editions

2020/November

PAGE 323
Cloud screen, 'Bivouac' exhibition, Museum of Contemporary Art, Chicago
White American Flag, *New York Times*
Packaging, *Découpage* vases, Vitra
Research for a new version of the *Ring* bench
Poster, The Wrong Shop
Around Manhattan on an America's Cup boat, New York

PAGE 324
Poster, The Wrong Shop
Print on an Enzo Mari card holder
Rope Chair, Artek, under tarpaulin
Installation, bench, exterior design, Bourse de Commerce – Pinault Collection, Paris
Ink on paper
Ink on paper
Thank you card
Ink on paper
Ink on paper

PAGE 325
Ink on paper
Crayon-Pinceau book, Nieves editions
Ink on paper
Ink on paper
Ink on paper
Poster, The Wrong Shop Studio, Paris
Ink on paper
Rope Chair, Artek

PAGE 326
Cast glass pieces, chandelier, hall, Bourse de Commerce –

Pinault Collection, Paris
Prototype of lamp and *Flou* mirror, Galerie kreo, La Halle aux Grains restaurant, Bourse de Commerce – Pinault Collection, Paris
Detail, chandelier, hall, Bourse de Commerce – Pinault Collection, Paris
Ink on paper
Ink on paper
Ink on paper
Ink on paper
Découpage vase, Vitra, and anodized aluminium sheet
Party

2020/December

PAGE 327
Hanging, house, Paris

PAGE 328
Ink on paper
Palissade lounge chair, HAY, in the mist, Brittany, France
Ink on paper
Ink on paper
Rope Chair, Artek, rotunda, Bourse de Commerce – Pinault Collection, Paris
Model of layout, *Luce Orizzontale* suspension lights, hall, Bourse de Commerce – Pinault Collection, Paris
Model of layout, *Luce Orizzontale* suspension lights, hall, Bourse de Commerce – Pinault Collection, Paris
Cotone bench, Cassina, *Rope Chair*, Artek, and *banc Corde*, rotunda, Bourse de Commerce – Pinault Collection, Paris
Drawings

PAGE 329
Taped drawings, house, Paris
La Halle aux Grains restaurant, Bourse de Commerce – Pinault Collection, Paris
Studio, Brittany, France
Ink on paper
Model, exterior design, Bourse de Commerce – Pinault Collection, Paris
Belvédère project, Rennes, France

PAGE 330
Model, bench, rock and flag, exterior design, Bourse de Commerce – Pinault Collection, Paris
Erkkeri vase, Iittala, house, Brittany, France
Ink-black night, Brittany, France
Crayon-Pinceau book, Nieves editions
Palissade lounge chair, HAY, rooftop terrace, Brittany, France
Découpage vase, house, Brittany, France

2021/January

PAGE 331
Detail, *Cotone* bench, Cassina, hall, Bourse de Commerce – Pinault Collection, Paris
Model, rock, exterior design, Bourse de Commerce – Pinault Collection, Paris
Framed drawing, photo and *Diapositive* bench, Glas Italia, house, Brittany, France
Detail, *Flou* mirror, Galerie kreo, and *Alcova* vase, WonderGlass
The Fountains of the Champs-Élysées, Paris
Ink on paper
Ink on paper
Ink on paper
Rope Chair, Artek, Bourse de Commerce – Pinault Collection, Paris

PAGE 332
Forecourt, Bourse de Commerce – Pinault Collection, Paris

PAGE 333
Forecourt, Bourse de Commerce – Pinault Collection, Paris
Ballpoint pen on paper
Ballpoint pen on paper
Detail, bench and rock, forecourt, Bourse de Commerce – Pinault Collection, Paris
Belvédère project, Rennes, France
Ballpoint pen on paper

Bench, forecourt, Bourse de Commerce – Pinault Collection, Paris
Ballpoint pen on paper
Ballpoint pen on paper

PAGE 334
Model, flag and rock, Bourse de Commerce – Pinault Collection, Paris
Wilton rug, woven, Galerie kreo, *Cotone* bench and table, Cassina, interior design, Bourse de Commerce – Pinault Collection, Paris
Model, flag, Bourse de Commerce – Pinault Collection, Paris
Detail, *Wilton* rug, woven, Galerie kreo, Bourse de Commerce – Pinault Collection, Paris
Photomontage, benches and rugs, Bourse de Commerce – Pinault Collection, Paris
Model, pavilion

2021/Febuary

PAGE 335
Model, pavilion for a permanent installation of the *Lincoln* sculpture by Pascal Rivet
Ink on paper
Ink on paper
Ink on paper
Ballpoint pen on paper
Chance encounter

PAGE 336
Detail, flag, Bourse de Commerce – Pinault Collection, Paris
Reflection in the river Vilaine, *Belvédère* project, Rennes, France
Ballpoint pen on paper
Model, exterior design, Bourse de Commerce – Pinault Collection, Paris
Model, exterior design, Bourse de Commerce – Pinault Collection, Paris
Ballpoint pen on paper
Ballpoint pen and coloured ink on paper
Ballpoint pen and coloured ink on paper

Ballpoint pen and coloured ink on paper

PAGE 337
Scale 1 model, bench, rock and flag, Bourse de Commerce – Pinault Collection, Paris
Ballpoint pen on paper
Ballpoint pen and coloured ink on paper
Photo shoot, *The Bird*, Vitra, workshop, Paris
House, Brittany, France
Ballpoint pen and coloured ink on paper

PAGE 338
Detail, flag, Bourse de Commerce – Pinault Collection, Paris

PAGE 339
Framed drawing
Ballpoint pen on paper
Ballpoint pen and coloured ink on paper
Framed drawing in its shipping box
Ink on paper
Ink on paper
Detail, *Filo* chair, Mattiazzi
Ballpoint pen on paper
Ballpoint pen on paper

PAGE 340
Ballpoint pen and coloured ink on paper
Ballpoint pen and coloured ink on paper
Printed drawing, Artek showroom, Helsinki
Drawings, wall, house, Paris
Profile, *Filo* chair, Mattiazzi
Exhibition of drawings, Licht Gallery, Tokyo

PAGE 341
Model, tired chair
Ballpoint pen on paper
Lighthouse lamp, Established & Sons, ballpoint pen and coloured ink on paper
Ballpoint pen and coloured ink on paper
Framed drawings, studio, Paris
Ballpoint pen and coloured ink on paper

LIST OF WORKS

2021/March

PAGE 342
Rope Chair, Artek, and ink on paper, exhibition, Piacé Le Radieux Art Centre, Piacé, France
Ballpoint pen and coloured ink on paper
The cherry thief
My drawing board, Paris
Ballpoint pen and coloured ink on paper
Model, bench, rock and flag, Bourse de Commerce – Pinault Collection, Paris

PAGE 343
Print tests
Print test
Ruutu vase, Iittala, window, studio, Paris
Ink on paper
Ink on paper
Collage
Article, *Purple Magazine*
Detail, *Osso* chair, Mattiazzi
Full moon, Brittany, France

PAGE 344
Erkkeri vase, Iittala, *Rope Chair*, Artek, and *Vitrail* mirror, Magis, by Inga Sempé
Ink on paper
Découpage vase, Vitra, and *banc Corde*
Algae
Floating House, collaboration with architects Jean-Marie Finot and Denis Daversin, Chatou, France
Floating House, collaboration with architects Jean-Marie Finot and Denis Daversin, Chatou, France
Ink and adhesive tape on paper
Ballpoint pen and coloured ink on paper
Ballpoint pen and coloured ink on paper

2021/April

PAGE 345
Ballpoint pen and coloured ink on paper

PAGE 346
Ink on paper, studio, Brittany, France

PAGE 347
Studio, Paris
Hangar
Palissade armchair and lounge chair, HAY
Forecourt, Bourse de Commerce – Pinault Collection, Paris
Rope Chair, Artek, rotunda, Bourse de Commerce – Pinault Collection, Paris
Colour sequencing for print test
Colour sequencing for print test
Ink and adhesive tape on paper
The original and the reproduction

PAGE 348
Detail, *Rope Chair*, Artek
Hanging, house, Paris
Hanging, house, Paris
Ink on paper
Nuage vase, Vitra, Brittany, France
Ballpoint pen and coloured ink on paper

PAGE 349
Palissade lounge chairs, HAY
Research sketch, *Palissade* lounge chair, HAY
Rope Chair, Artek, Brittany, France
Detail, wrought iron railing and armrest of the *Quindici* lounge chair, Mattiazzi
Palissade lounge chairs, HAY
banc Corde

2021/May

PAGE 350
Hanging, house, Paris
Hanging, house, Paris
Ink on paper
Rolf and *Ring* bench, Vitra campus, Weil am Rhein, Germany
Filo chair, Mattiazzi
Slow Chair, Vitra

PAGE 351
Ink on paper

PAGE 352
Posters, The Wrong Shop
Ink on paper
Ink on paper
Poster, The Wrong Shop
Mette, terrace, Brittany, France
Skeleton at the window

PAGE 353
Ring bench and *Long Fountain*, Piet Oudolf Garden, Vitra Campus, Weil am Rhein, Germany
Showroom for Vitra miniatures, Vitra Design Museum, Weil am Rhein, Germany
Sketch, Vitra miniatures showroom, Vitra Design Museum, Weil am Rhein, Germany
Photomontage
Chandelier, Flos, Bourse de Commerce – Pinault Collection, Paris
Flag, Bourse de Commerce – Pinault Collection, Paris
Chandelier, Flos, Bourse de Commerce – Pinault Collection, Paris
Rock and bench, exterior design, Bourse de Commerce – Pinault Collection, Paris
Interior design, Bourse de Commerce – Pinault Collection, Paris

PAGE 354
Bench, forecourt, Bourse de Commerce – Pinault Collection, Paris
Photomontage, rugs and benches, interior design, Bourse de Commerce – Pinault Collection, Paris
Graphite on paper
Chandelier, Flos, Bourse de Commerce – Pinault Collection, Paris
Graphite and ink on paper
Rope Chair, Artek

PAGE 355
Flag, exterior, Bourse de Commerce – Pinault Collection, Paris

PAGE 356
Posters, The Wrong Shop

PAGE 357
Bench, forecourt, Bourse de Commerce – Pinault Collection, Paris
Poster, The Wrong Shop
Ink and adhesive tape on paper
Palissade lounge chairs, HAY
Palissade chairs and table, galvanized steel, HAY, terrace, Brittany, France
Hole chair, Cappellini
Children's drawings, *Belvédère* project, Rennes, France
Children's drawings, *Belvédère* project, Rennes, France
Hanging, house, Paris

2021/June

PAGE 358
Publication
Print test, The Wrong Shop
Ink on paper
My corner of the studio, Paris
Ballpoint pen on card
La Halle aux Grains restaurant, Bourse de Commerce – Pinault Collection, Paris

PAGE 359
Guipure curtain and *Luce Verticale* suspension lights, Flos, La Halle aux Grains restaurant, Bourse de Commerce – Pinault Collection, Paris
Signing of editions, The Wrong Shop
La Halle aux Grains restaurant, Bourse de Commerce – Pinault Collection, Paris
House, Brittany, France
Editions, The Wrong Shop
Filo chair, Mattiazzi

PAGE 360
Studio, Paris
Palissade armchair and lounge chair, HAY
Studio, Paris
Research, assembly
Model, bench, rock and flag, Bourse de Commerce – Pinault Collection, Paris

Painting on wood
Publication
At the framer's, Paris
Research model, wind mobiles

2021/July

PAGE 361
Ring bench, Kvadrat headquarters, Ebeltoft, Denmark

PAGE 362
Graphite on paper
Research, platform, exterior design, Bourse de Commerce – Pinault Collection, Paris
Research, pond, exterior design, Bourse de Commerce – Pinault Collection, Paris
Watercolour
Punto ceramic tiles, Mutina Edition, The Wrong Shop, and *Rope Chair*, Artek

PAGE 363
Hydrangeas and *Nuage* vase, Vitra
Palissade armchair, HAY, roof terrace, Brittany, France
Edition, The Wrong Shop
Coloured pencil on paper
Hydrangeas and *Nuage* vase, Vitra, Brittany, France
10 years of projects with Mutina, terrace, Brittany, France
Rombini ceramic tiles, Mutina
Signing of editions, The Wrong Shop
Ink on paper

PAGE 364
Punto ceramic tiles, Mutina, and *Nuage* vase, Vitra

PAGE 365
Ink on paper
Hanging test, exhibition of drawings and bas-reliefs
Cover drawing, *TLmag*
Hanging test, exhibition of drawings and bas-reliefs
Rocks, Brittany, France
Hanging test, exhibition of drawings and bas-reliefs

2021/August

PAGE 366
House, Brittany, France
Drawings, terrace, Brittany,
France
Ballpoint pen and coloured ink
on paper
Ink on paper
Ballpoint pen on paper
Palissade armchair, HAY,
terrace, Brittany, France
Découpage vase, house,
Brittany, France
Ballpoint pen on paper
Ink on paper

PAGE 367
Palissade lounge chair and
armchair, HAY
Ink on paper
Filo chair, Mattiazzi, and
Aggregato lamp by Enzo Mari
Ink on paper
Studio, Brittany, France
Ink on paper

PAGE 368
Rombini ceramic tile, *Block*
brick, Mutina, and
banc Corde
Drawing on the water
Ink on paper
Studio, Brittany, France
Uncino chair, Mattiazzi
Ballpoint pen on paper
Punto ceramic tiles, Mutina,
and *Découpage* vase
Ink on paper
Ink on paper

PAGE 369
Studio, Brittany, France

2021/September

PAGE 370
Filo chair, Mattiazzi
House, Brittany, France
Filo chair, Mattiazzi, *Rope
Chair*, Artek, and edition,
The Wrong Shop
Punto ceramic tiles, Mutina
Punto ceramic tiles, Mutina
Ink on paper
Ink on paper
Filo chair, Mattiazzi
Block brick, Mutina

PAGE 371
Jean-Marie's ceramics studio,
Burgundy
Studio, Paris
Hanging test, exhibition of
drawings and bas-reliefs
Block bricks, Mutina
My shadow and ink on paper
Block bricks, Mutina

PAGE 372
Janvier and *Stylo-Bille* books,
Nieves editions

PAGE 373
Ink on paper
Filo chair, Mattiazzi, and *Block*
bricks, Mutina
Ink on paper
Ink on paper
Palissade chairs and tables,
HAY, terrace, Solomon R.
Guggenheim Museum,
New York
Ink on paper
Block bricks, Mutina
Ring bench and *Long Fountain*,
Piet Oudolf Garden, Vitra
Campus, Weil am Rhein,
Germany
Belvédère project, Rennes,
France

PAGE 374
Reflection in the river Vilaine,
Belvédère project, Rennes,
France
'Ensemble' exhibition, Mutina,
Sassuolo, Italy
'Ensemble' exhibition, Mutina,
Sassuolo, Italy
Rombini vases, Mutina
Ink on paper
Block bricks, Mutina
'Ensemble' exhibition, Mutina,
Sassuolo, Italy
Alcova vases, WonderGlass
Hanging test, exhibition
of drawings and bas-reliefs

2021/October

PAGE 375
Prototype, chair
Exhibition, Licht Gallery, Tokyo
Ink on paper
Rombini vases, *Block* bricks and
Rombini ceramic tiles, Mutina

Ink on paper
Rombini vase, Mutina

PAGE 376
Exhibition, Licht Gallery, Tokyo
Chains suspension lights,
plaster, Galerie kreo
Exhibition, Licht Gallery, Tokyo
'Ensemble' exhibition, Mutina,
Sassuolo, Italy
Ink on paper
Rombini vase and *Punto* ceramic
tiles, Mutina
On the cover, *T, le magazine
du Temps*
Exhibition, Licht Gallery, Tokyo
Composition, bas-relief, studio,
Paris

PAGE 377
Studio, Brittany, France

PAGE 378
Presentation of the first studies,
exterior design, Bourse
de Commerce – Pinault
Collection, Paris
Gabriel chandelier, Palace of
Versailles, France
Palissade Park bench, HAY
Palissade Park bench, HAY
Poster, 'The Sound of My
Left Hand' exhibition, Casa
Mutina, Milan
Poster, 'The Sound of My
Left Hand' exhibition, Casa
Mutina, Milan
Posters, 'The Sound of My
Left Hand' exhibition, Casa
Mutina, Milan
Jean-Marie's ceramics studio,
Burgundy
Ceramics, bas-reliefs,
courtyard, studio, Paris

2021/November

PAGE 379
Composition, bas-reliefs, studio,
Paris

PAGE 380
Ink on paper
Bas-relief and *Osso* chair,
Mattiazzi
Small bas-relief
Composition, bas-reliefs, studio,
Paris

'Circus' exhibition, Philadelphia
Museum of Art, Philadelphia
Bas-relief and *Filo* chair,
Mattiazzi

PAGE 381
Posters, 'The Sound of My
Left Hand' exhibition, Casa
Mutina, Milan
Bas-reliefs
'23 bas-reliefs' exhibition,
Galerie kreo, London
'23 bas-reliefs' exhibition,
Galerie kreo, London
Small bas-relief and *Filo* chair,
Mattiazzi
'23 bas-reliefs' exhibition,
Galerie kreo, London
Studio, Brittany, France
Detail, *Musubi* chair, Koyori
Cover drawing, *Fugitive Pieces*,
Anne Michaels, Penguin
Random House Canada

2021/December

PAGE 382
Small bas-reliefs
Ink on paper
Bas-reliefs, studio, Paris
Detail, *Musubi* chair, Koyori
Studio, Paris
Portrait, studio, Paris

PAGE 383
Model, *Musubi* chair, Koyori

PAGE 384
Small bas-relief
Cornelius, house, Brittany,
France
House, Brittany, France
Ballpoint pen, pastel and tape
on paper
Palissade Park bench, HAY
Ink on paper
Ink on paper
Ink on paper
Drawing and light lunch

PAGE 385
Pastel on paper
Ink on paper
'23 bas-reliefs' exhibition,
Galerie kreo, London
Ink on paper
Ink on paper
Palissade armchair, HAY, in

the snow, Paris
Ink on paper
Ink on paper
Brittany, France

PAGE 386
Ink on paper
Ink on paper
Brittany, France
Model, framework, hangar, and
Lampyre lamp, Wästberg by
Inga Sempé
Detail, *Musubi* chair, Koyori
House, Brittany, France

PAGE 387
Ink on paper
Quindici lounge chair, Mattiazzi,
house, Brittany, France
Ink and adhesive tape on
paper
Detail, *Shaku* chair, Koyori
Studio, Brittany, France
Brittany, France

2022/January

PAGE 388
Ink on paper

PAGE 389
Ink and adhesive tape on paper
Ink on paper
Detail, *Musubi* chair, Koyori, and
poster, The Wrong Shop
Detail, *Balcony* table, HAY
Balcony chair, HAY, and *Punto*
ceramic tiles, Mutina
Ink on paper

PAGE 390
Palissade Park bench, HAY
House, Brittany, France
Model, '23 bas-reliefs' exhibition,
Galerie kreo, London
House, Brittany, France
Kawara chair, Koyori, and bas-
relief
Découpage vase, Vitra, and
Shaku chair, Koyori
Ink on paper
Palissade Park bench, HAY
Palissade Park bench, HAY

PAGE 391
Balcony chairs and table, HAY
Découpage vase, *Block* brick,
Mutina, and *banc Corde*

Ballpoint pen and
    thermoforming on paper
Balcony chair and table, HAY
Balcony chair, HAY, ink and
    adhesive tape on paper
Balcony armchair, HAY

2022/February

PAGE 392
    A drawing in support of Ukraine

PAGE 393
    Detail, *Shaku* chair, Koyori
    Sketch, *Balcony* collection, HAY
    Ink on paper
    'The Sound of My Left Hand'
        exhibition, Casa Mutina, Milan
    Ink on paper
    Bas-relief
    Poster, The Wrong Shop
    Poster in support of Ukraine,
        The Wrong Shop, and bas-
        relief
    Kawara chair, Koyori

2022/March

PAGE 394
    Catalogue, 'The Sound of My
        Left Hand' exhibition, Mutina
        editions
    Découpage vase, *Rope Chair*,
        Artek, *Rombini* ceramic tiles,
        Mutina, and ink on paper
    Palissade lounge chairs, HAY,
        terrace, Alvar Aalto's Paimio
        sanatorium, Finland
    Ink on paper
    Ink on paper
    Detail, *Kawara* chair, Koyori

PAGE 395
    Cassandra, a Year 10 student
        welcomed for a week at
        the studio thanks to the
        ViensVoirMonTaf association
    Catalogue, 'The Sound of My
        Left Hand' exhibition, Mutina
        editions
    Prototype, *Palissade* armchair,
        HAY
    Ink on paper
    Ceramics, bas-reliefs,
        courtyard, studio, Paris
    Ink on paper
    Bas-reliefs, studio, Paris
    Rombini vase, Mutina, Giorgio

Mastinu Gallery, Venice
Copenhagen chair and desk,
    HAY

PAGE 396
    Ink on paper and *Rope Chair*,
        Artek

PAGE 397
    Drawings, house, Brittany,
        France
    Drawings, house, Brittany,
        France
    Brittany, France
    Brittany, France
    Flag, Bourse de Commerce –
        Pinault Collection, Paris
    'The Sound of My Left Hand'
        exhibition, Casa Mutina, Milan
    Special edition, *Copenhagen*
        tables, HAY, and *Piani* lamps,
        Flos
    Model, courtyard, studio, Paris
    Graphite, pastel and adhesive
        tape on paper

2022/April

PAGE 398
    Portrait by Inga
    Kawara chairs, Koyori, and
        drawings, Licht Gallery, Tokyo
    Voting day
    Studio, Paris
    Poster, exhibition, Giorgio
        Mastinu Gallery, Venice
    Shaku chair, Koyori and drawing,
        Licht Gallery, Tokyo

PAGE 399
    Palissade collection, HAY,
        terrace, John Lautner's
        House, Los Angeles
    Exhibition, Giorgio Mastinu
        Gallery, Venice
    Block brick, Mutina
    Studio, Brittany, France
    Assembly, *Sosei* vases, Tajimi,
        Paris
    Ink on paper

PAGE 400
    Model, frame, hangar, Brittany,
        France
    Palissade Park bench, HAY
    Sosei vase, Tajimi
    'Circus' exhibition, Philadelphia
        Museum of Art, Philadelphia

Noguchi Museum Park, New
    York, ballpoint pen on paper
Model, *Lincoln Pavilion*
Model, *Lincoln Pavilion*
'Circus' exhibition, Philadelphia
    Museum of Art, Philadelphia
'Circus' exhibition, Philadelphia
    Museum of Art, Philadelphia

2022/May

PAGE 401
    New York

PAGE 402
    Paris

PAGE 403
    Studio, Paris
    Ink on paper
    Catalogue, 'The Sound of My
        Left Hand' exhibition, Mutina
        editions
    Bernard, the lobsters'
        nightmare
    Ballpoint pen on paper
    Shaku chair, Koyori, and bas-
        relief
    Summary of the projects
        presented, Salone del Mobile
        in Milan
    Balcony chair, galvanized steel,
        HAY
    Kaari desk, Artek, and *Rope
        Chair*, Artek

PAGE 404
    Studio, Brittany, France
    Valiant fleabanes
    Ink on paper
    Studio, Brittany, France
    Musubi chair, Koyori
    Permanent installation, *Lincoln*
        sculpture by Pascal Rivet,
        Lincoln Pavilion, Piacé, France
    Permanent installation, *Lincoln*
        sculpture by Pascal Rivet,
        Lincoln Pavilion, Piacé, France
    Model, *Lincoln Pavilion*
    Detail, base, bronze, *Riace*
        sofa, Magis

PAGE 405
    Riace sofa, Magis
    Lincoln Pavilion, Piacé, France
    Sosei vase, Tajimi
    On the cover, *The New York
        Review of Books*

Ballpoint pen on paper
Passerelle table, HAY, and
    Élementaire chair, HAY

2022/June

PAGE 406
    Bas-relief
    Lithograph, limited edition,
        Centre Pompidou-Metz,
        France
    Ciel ladder, Galerie kreo
    Signature, editions, The
        Wrong Shop
    Palissade chair, HAY
    Ink and adhesive tape on paper

2022/July

PAGE 407
    At the framer's

PAGE 408
    Ink on paper
    Lincoln Pavilion, Piacé, France
    Balcony Chair, HAY
    House, Brittany, France
    Ink on paper
    Studio, Brittany, France

PAGE 409
    Assembly, bas-reliefs, hangar,
        Brittany, France
    Assembly, bas-reliefs, hangar,
        Brittany, France
    Watercolour on paper
    Hangar, Brittany, France
    Brittany, France
    Model, frame, hangar, Brittany,
        France
    Kawara chair and table, Koyori
    Brittany, France
    Brittany, France

2022/August

PAGE 410
    Rope Chair, Artek, and bas-relief
    François
    Small bas-relief, fireplace,
        Brittany, France
    View, studio, Brittany, France
    banc Corde, *Alcova* alcove,
        WonderGlass, and sculpture
        of Saint Anne, ceramic,
        Henriot-Quimper
    A-Poc shop, Issey Miyake
    Brittany, France

Detail, small bas-relief
House, Brittany, France

PAGE 411
    Nuage vase, Vitra, studio,
        Brittany, France

PAGE 412
    Palissade chairs and tables,
        galvanized steel, HAY
    House, Brittany, France
    Ink on paper
    Brittany, France
    Kawara chair, Koyori, and
        Erkkeri vase, littala
    Metal Side Tables, galvanized
        steel, Vitra
    Bas-relief and *Balcony* chair,
        HAY
    Pastel in wooden frame
    Pastel in wooden frame

2022/September

PAGE 413
    My table, studio, Paris
    Shaku chair, Koyori, and table,
        Koyori
    Luce Orizzontale suspension
        lights, unique piece
    Ink on paper
    Balcony chair, galvanized steel,
        HAY
    Ciel ladder and shelf, Galerie
        kreo
    Ink and 3D printing on paper
    Ruutu vase and *Fleurs*, littala
    My table, studio, Paris

PAGE 414
    Balcony bench, HAY
    Installation, *Rombini* vases,
        Mutina, Fiorano Modenese,
        Italy
    Installation, *Block* bricks, Mutina,
        Fiorano Modenese, Italy
    My space, studio, Paris
    Ballpoint pen on paper
    Ink on paper

2022/October

PAGE 415
    My portrait by Inga

PAGE 416
    Ink on paper

De gauche à droite, de haut en bas :

2014/Octobre

PAGE 8
Encre sur papier
Exposition « Momentanée »,
    musée des Arts décoratifs,
    Paris
Recherches pour une
    installation, Victoria and
    Albert Museum, Londres
Recherches pour une
    installation, Victoria and
    Albert Museum, Londres
Encre sur papier
Maquette en impression 3D,
    escalier hélicoïdal
Escalier hélicoïdal
Mette suspendue à l'escalier
Encre sur papier

2014/Novembre

PAGE 9
Inga montant l'escalier
Encre sur papier
Encre sur papier aluminium
Stylo-bille sur papier
Encre sur papier
Encre sur bois

2014/Décembre

PAGE 10
Atelier, Bretagne, France
Encre sur papier et kayak,
    atelier, Bretagne, France
Vases *Ruutu,* Iittala, devant ma
    fenêtre, Paris
Mur, maison, Bretagne, France
Mur, atelier, Paris
Collage de recherche,
    catalogue, exposition
    « Bivouac », Centre
    Pompidou-Metz, France

PAGE 11
Algues et *Twigs,* Vitra,
    La Pelota, Milan
Maison flottante, conçue avec
    Jean-Marie Finot et Denis
    Daversin, architectes,
    Chatou, France
Navigation de la *Maison
    flottante,* conçue avec
    Jean-Marie Finot et Denis
    Daversin, architectes

Maison flottante, conçue avec
    Jean-Marie Finot et Denis
    Daversin, architectes,
    Chatou, France
Encre sur papier
Sapin de Noël, impression 3D,
    revue *Disegno*
Sapin de Noël, impression 3D,
    revue *Disegno*
Encre sur papier
Clouds, Kvadrat et chaise
    Steelwood, Magis

2015/Janvier

PAGE 12
Clouds, Kvadrat
Encre sur papier aluminium
Encre sur papier
Table et mur, maison, Bretagne,
    France
Encre sur papier
Encre sur papier aluminium

2015/Février

PAGE 13
Encre sur papier aluminium
Encre sur papier
Croquis, étagère *Kaari,* Artek
Encre sur papier aluminium
Encre sur papier aluminium
Maison, Bretagne, France
Encre sur papier aluminium
Encre sur papier doré

PAGE 14
Crayon de couleur sur papier

PAGE 15
Encre sur bois
Encre sur papier
Stylo-bille sur papier
Encre sur papier
Encre sur papier
Encre sur papier aluminium
Encre sur papier
Graphite sur papier
Lampe *w103,* Wästberg et
    miroir *Trame,* Domestic,
    d'Inga Sempé, encre sur
    papier et bois

2015/Mars

PAGE 16
Impression sur papier,

The Wrong Shop, atelier,
    Paris
Encre sur papier
Boîte de dessins
Tests d'anodisation
    d'aluminium et encre
    sur papier aluminium
Maison, Bretagne, France
Encre sur papier aluminium
Encre et ruban adhésif
    sur papier aluminium
Encre sur papier
Encre sur papier aluminium

2015/Avril

PAGE 17
Vase *Cloud,* céramique,
    édition limitée
Encre sur papier
Dessin préparatoire, collection
    Kaari, Artek
Programme, Salone del Mobile
    de Milan
Maquette en impression 3D,
    vases *Cloud*
Paroi *Clouds,* Kvadrat,
    Copenhague

2015/Août

PAGE 18
Ombre de Joshua portant
    une chaise *Palissade,* HAY

2015/Septembre

PAGE 19
Fauteuil *Palissade,* prototype,
    HAY, Bretagne, France
Chat sur téléviseur *The Serif,*
    Samsung
Encre et graphite
    sur bois
Atelier, Paris
Recherches de guipure
Céramique murale *Rombini,*
    Mutina

2015/Octobre

PAGE 20
Dessin préparatoire, collection
    Kaari, Artek
Chaise *Palissade,* HAY
    et céramique murale
    Rombini, Mutina
Kiosque, Emerige et Galerie

kreo, jardin des Tuileries,
    Paris
Kiosque, Emerige et Galerie
    kreo, jardin des Tuileries,
    Paris
Test de couleurs, émail
    sur céramique
Séance photo, exposition
    « Seventeen Screens »,
    musée d'Art de Tel-Aviv, Israël

PAGE 21
Chaises *Palissade,* HAY, cour
    de l'atelier, Paris

2015/Novembre

PAGE 22
Paroi *Rennes,* exposition
    « Seventeen Screens »,
    musée d'Art de Tel-Aviv,
    Israël
Installation, exposition
    « Seventeen Screens »,
    musée d'Art de Tel-Aviv,
    Israël
Exposition « Seventeen
    Screens », musée d'Art
    de Tel-Aviv, Israël
Dessin préparatoire sur
    photographie, exposition
    « Seventeen Screens »,
    musée d'Art de Tel-Aviv,
    Israël
Peinture sur papier
Détail, paroi, exposition
    « Seventeen Screens »,
    musée d'Art de Tel-Aviv,
    Israël
Détail, paroi, exposition
    « Seventeen Screens »,
    musée d'Art de Tel-Aviv,
    Israël
Peinture et encre sur papier
Paroi brodée, exposition
    « Seventeen Screens »,
    musée d'Art de Tel-Aviv,
    Israël

PAGE 23
Exposition « Seventeen
    Screens », musée d'Art
    de Tel-Aviv, Israël
Détail, paroi, « Seventeen
    Screens », musée d'Art
    de Tel-Aviv, Israël
Exposition « Seventeen
    Screens », musée d'Art

de Tel-Aviv, Israël
Détail, paroi, « Seventeen
    Screens », musée d'Art
    de Tel-Aviv, Israël
Exposition « Seventeen
    Screens », musée d'Art
    de Tel-Aviv, Israël
Détail, paroi, « Seventeen
    Screens », musée d'Art
    de Tel-Aviv, Israël

PAGE 24
Twigs, Vitra
Encre sur bois
Exposition « Seventeen
    Screens », musée d'Art
    de Tel-Aviv, Israël
Encre sur papier aluminium
Dessin préparatoire, exposition
    « Seventeen Screens »,
    musée d'Art de Tel-Aviv,
    Israël
Dessin préparatoire, exposition
    « Seventeen Screens »,
    musée d'Art de Tel-Aviv,
    Israël

2015/Décembre

PAGE 25
Détail, exposition « Seventeen
    Screens », musée d'Art
    de Tel-Aviv, Israël
Exposition « Seventeen
    Screens », musée d'Art
    de Tel-Aviv, Israël
13 novembre 2015
Détail, paroi, exposition
    « Seventeen Screens »,
    musée d'Art de Tel-Aviv, Israël
Exposition « Seventeen
    Screens », musée d'Art
    de Tel-Aviv, Israël
Palissade, HAY, sous la neige

PAGE 26
Encre sur papier
Broderie
Vases *Ruutu,* Iittala
Exposition « Seventeen
    Screens », musée d'Art
    de Tel-Aviv, Israël
Détail, paroi, exposition
    « Seventeen Screens »,
    musée d'Art de Tel-Aviv, Israël
Clouds, Kvadrat, exposition
    « Bivouac », Museum of
    Contemporary Art, Chicago

435

LISTE DES ŒUVRES

Recherches, exposition
« Rêveries urbaines »
Céramique *Rombini*, Mutina
Céramique *Rombini*, Mutina

PAGE 27
Atelier, Paris

2016/Janvier

PAGE 28
Encre sur papier
Verre soufflé Venini, lampe
Lighthouse, Established
& Sons
Exposition « Momentanée »,
musée des Arts décoratifs,
Paris
Affichage municipal pour
la nouvelle année, ville
de Rennes, France
Exposition « Bivouac »,
Museum of Contemporary
Art, Chicago
Atelier, Paris
Production, *Palissade*, HAY
Impression sur papier, The
Wrong Shop, atelier, Paris
Exposition « Bivouac »,
Museum of Contemporary
Art, Chicago

PAGE 29
Fabrication, *Kiosque*, Emerige
et Galerie kreo
Kiosque, Emerige et Galerie
kreo, jardin des Tuileries, Paris
Tapis *Lattice*, Nanimarquina
Tapis *Lattice*, Nanimarquina
Exposition « Seventeen
Screens », musée d'Art
de Tel-Aviv, Israël
Tapis *Lattice*, Nanimarquina
et canapé *Palissade*, HAY

PAGE 30
Atelier, Paris
Livre *Ronan & Erwan
Bouroullec: Drawing*,
JRP|Editions
Encre sur papier
Recherches, exposition
« Rêveries urbaines »
Céramique *Rombini*, Mutina
Encre sur papier

PAGE 31
Maison, Bretagne, France

PAGE 32
Mette, atelier, Bretagne, France
Maison, Bretagne, France
Recherches, atelier, Paris
Recherches, exposition
« Rêveries urbaines »
Effondrement de recherches
à l'atelier, Paris
Céramique *Rombini*, Mutina

2016/Février

PAGE 33
Inattendu
Bougeoir *Officina*, Magis
Détail, bougeoir *Officina*, Magis
Éléments des maquettes,
exposition « Rêveries
urbaines »
Maquette de chapiteau
Céramique *Rombini*, Mutina

PAGE 34
Céramique *Rombini*, Mutina
Atelier, Paris
Stylo-bille et aquarelle
sur papier
Encre sur papier
Livre *Ronan & Erwan
Bouroullec: Drawing*,
JRP|Editions
Impression sur papier, The
Wrong Shop, atelier, Paris
Nuit noire
Passion kayak de mer
Le phare

PAGE 35
Céramique *Rombini*, Mutina

PAGE 36
Anodisation d'aluminium pour
les maquettes, exposition
« Rêveries urbaines »
Anodisation d'aluminium pour
les maquettes, exposition
« Rêveries urbaines »
Anodisation d'aluminium pour
les maquettes, exposition
« Rêveries urbaines »
Encre sur papier
Étagère *Kaari*, Artek
Étagère *Kaari*, Artek

2016/Mars

PAGE 37
Studio photo, Copenhague

Je prends une photo
à Copenhague
Chaise et table *Copenhague*, HAY
Bureau *Kaari*, Artek
Atelier, Paris
Banc *Palissade*, chaises et
tables *Copenhague*, HAY,
Studio photo, Copenhague
Exposition « Seventeen
Screens », Frac Bretagne,
Rennes, France
Détail, paroi, exposition
« Seventeen Screens », Frac
Bretagne, Rennes, France
Plateau suspendu, exposition
« Rêveries urbaines »,
Les Champs libres, Rennes,
France

PAGE 38
Projet *Parasols*, exposition
« Rêveries urbaines »
Séchage des algues en cours
Séchage des algues en cours
Maison, Bretagne, France
Catastrophe
Installation, *Chaînes*,
céramique, Frac Bretagne,
Rennes, France

PAGE 39
Exposition « Seventeen
Screens », Frac Bretagne,
Rennes, France
Exposition « Seventeen
Screens », Frac Bretagne,
Rennes, France
Carton d'invitation pour les
4 expositions bretonnes,
Rennes, France
Carton d'invitation pour les
4 expositions bretonnes,
Rennes, France
Carton d'invitation pour les
4 expositions bretonnes,
Rennes, France
Exposition « Seventeen
Screens », Frac Bretagne,
Rennes, France
Installation, *Chaînes*,
céramique, Frac Bretagne,
Rennes, France
Exposition « Rétrospective »,
Frac Bretagne, Rennes,
France
Exposition « Seventeen
Screens », Frac Bretagne,
Rennes, France

PAGE 40
Exposition « Rétrospective »,
Frac Bretagne, Rennes,
France
Exposition « Rêveries
urbaines », Les Champs
libres, Rennes,
France
Exposition « Rétrospective »,
Frac Bretagne, Rennes,
France
Grutage, *Kiosque*,
Emerige et Galerie kreo,
cour du Parlement de
Bretagne, Rennes,
France
Grutage, *Kiosque*,
Emerige et Galerie kreo,
cour du Parlement de
Bretagne, Rennes,
France
Atterrissage, *Kiosque*,
Emerige et Galerie kreo,
cour du Parlement de
Bretagne, Rennes,
France
Projet fontaine *Toboggan*,
exposition « Rêveries
urbaines »
Projet *Lianes*, exposition
« Rêveries urbaines »
Affiche municipale pour la
nouvelle année, Rennes,
France

PAGE 41
Exposition « Seventeen
Screens », Frac Bretagne,
Rennes, France
Exposition « Seventeen
Screens », Frac Bretagne,
Rennes, France
Projet pergola *Clouds*,
exposition « Rêveries
urbaines »
Projet toit *Arbre et Rochers*,
exposition « Rêveries
urbaines »
Exposition « Rétrospective »,
Frac Bretagne, Rennes,
France
Exposition « Rêveries
urbaines », Les Champs
libres, Rennes, France

PAGE 42
Projet *Lianes*, exposition
« Rêveries urbaines »

2016/Avril

PAGE 43
Exposition « Rétrospective »,
Frac Bretagne, Rennes,
France
Exposition « Seventeen
Screens », Frac Bretagne,
Rennes, France
Exposition « Rétrospective »,
Frac Bretagne, Rennes,
France
Encre et ruban adhésif,
bloc-notes de l'hôtel Okura,
Tokyo
Exposition « Seventeen
Screens », Frac Bretagne,
Rennes, France
Exposition « Seventeen
Screens », Frac Bretagne,
Rennes, France
Mattéo allumant le bougeoir
Officina, Magis
Encre sur papier aluminium
Encre sur papier

PAGE 44
Exposition « Seventeen
Screens », Frac Bretagne,
Rennes, France
Exposition « Seventeen
Screens », Frac Bretagne,
Rennes, France
Exposition « Seventeen
Screens », Frac Bretagne,
Rennes, France
Exposition « Seventeen
Screens », Frac Bretagne,
Rennes, France
Affiche pour HAY, Salone del
Mobile de Milan
Wooden Side Table, Vitra
Canapé *Can*, HAY
Programme, Salone del Mobile
de Milan

PAGE 45
Bougeoirs et portemanteau
Officina, Magis
Séance photo, tables
Copenhague, HAY
Portemanteau et valet *Officina*,
Magis
Tables en verre coulé, Glas
Italia

Exposition « Seventeen
  Screens », Frac Bretagne,
  Rennes, France
Détail, table en verre coulé,
  Glas Italia

PAGE 46
Table en verre coulé, Glas Italia
Portemanteau Officina, Magis
Studio photo, Copenhague
Exposition « Seventeen
  Screens », Frac Bretagne,
  Rennes, France
Fauteuil et repose-pieds
  Palissade, HAY
Encre sur papier
Encre sur papier
Encre sur papier aluminium
Encre sur papier aluminium

PAGE 47
Étagère Kaari, Artek
Encre sur papier aluminium
Encre sur papier aluminium
Canapé Can, HAY
Anodisation d'aluminium pour
  les maquettes, exposition
  « Rêveries urbaines »
Exposition « Rêveries
  urbaines », Les Champs
  libres, Rennes, France

PAGE 48
Projet Fontaine longue,
  exposition « Rêveries
  urbaines »

PAGE 49
Atelier, Paris
Détail, piètement Officina,
  Magis
Encre et bois sur papier
Collection Kaari, Artek
Collection Palissade, HAY
Atelier, Paris
Extrusion d'aluminium, vase
  Nuage, Vitra
Projet Fontaine longue,
  exposition « Rêveries
  urbaines »
Atelier, Paris

2016/Mai

PAGE 50
Encre et bois sur papier
Maison, Héricy, France
Encre sur papier aluminium

Dessins de nuit
Test de couleurs chez Ufacto,
  chaise Hole, Cappellini
Kiosque, Emerige et Galerie
  kreo, cour du Parlement de
  Bretagne, Rennes, France

PAGE 51
Vase Télé, Galerie kreo

PAGE 52
Encre et peinture sur papier
Encre et peinture sur papier
Encre et peinture sur papier
Chaises Hole, Cappellini
Paroi Pluie, céramique
Atelier, Paris
Projet banc Ring, exposition
  « Rêveries urbaines »
Collier, céramique, collection
  Torique
Stylo-bille sur page de magazine

PAGE 53
Cabane et étagère polystyrène
  Brick, Galerie kreo
Cabane, Galerie kreo
Recherche, projet Pergola,
  exposition « Rêveries
  urbaines »
Détail, pièce en céramique,
  exposition « Seventeen
  Screens », Frac Bretagne,
  Rennes, France
Encre sur papier
Exposition « Seventeen
  Screens », Frac Bretagne,
  Rennes, France

PAGE 54
Exposition « Seventeen
  Screens », Frac Bretagne,
  Rennes, France
Graphite sur enveloppe
  d'un hôtel japonais
Projet Toit, exposition
  « Rêveries urbaines »
Vases Nuage, Vitra
Détail, paroi, exposition
  « Seventeen Screens »,
  Frac Bretagne, Rennes,
  France
Encre et ruban adhésif
  sur papier

PAGE 55
Projet Toit, exposition
  « Rêveries urbaines »

Projet Assise, exposition
  « Rêveries urbaines »
Exposition « Seventeen
  Screens », Frac Bretagne,
  Rennes, France
Livre Ronan & Erwan
  Bouroullec: Drawing,
  JRP|Editions
Encre et peinture sur papier
  et stylo-bille sur page
  de magazine
Encre sur papier aluminium

PAGE 56
Tapis Lattice, Nanimarquina

PAGE 57
Recherches, exposition
  « Rêveries urbaines »
Pièces, Pergola
Projet Pergola, exposition
  « Rêveries urbaines »
Projet Pergola, exposition
  « Rêveries urbaines »
Recherches, exposition
  « Rêveries urbaines »
Chaise et table Copenhague,
  HAY

PAGE 58
Kiosque, Emerige et Galerie
  kreo, cour du Parlement de
  Bretagne, Rennes, France
Encre et ruban adhésif
  sur papier
Encre et ruban adhésif
  sur papier
Encre et ruban adhésif
  sur papier
Encre et ruban adhésif
  sur papier
Exposition « Rétrospective »,
  Frac Bretagne, Rennes,
  France
Encre sur papier
Encre sur papier
Encre sur papier

PAGE 59
Encre, peinture
  et ruban adhésif
  sur papier

2016/Juin

PAGE 60
Encre sur papier
Stylo-bille sur papier

Encre et ruban adhésif
  sur papier
Maquette, projet Palissade,
  HAY
Graphite sur papier
Encre sur papier
Collection Palissade, HAY
Exposition « Seventeen
  Screens », Frac Bretagne,
  Rennes, France
Structure en fer forgé, chaise
  Officina, Magis

PAGE 61
L'enclume et le marteau
Chaise et table Officina, Magis
Encre sur papier
Détail, chaise Uncino,
  Mattiazzi
Stock, structure en fer forgé,
  chaise Officina, Magis
Encre, gommette et ruban
  adhésif sur papier
Encre, gommette et ruban
  adhésif sur papier
Détail, chaise Uncino, Mattiazzi
Encre, gommette et ruban
  adhésif sur papier

PAGE 62
Vase Nuage, Vitra
Peinture et ruban adhésif
  sur papier
Encre sur papier
Maison, Bretagne, France
Tables en verre coulé,
  Glas Italia, maison,
  Bretagne, France
Chaise Stampa, Kettal

PAGE 63
Détail végétal

PAGE 64
Encre sur papier
Vase Nuage, Vitra
Rolf Fehlbaum, installation en
  hommage à Zaha Hadid,
  caserne de pompiers,
  campus Vitra, Weil am Rhein,
  Allemagne
Encre sur papier
Mette, atelier, Bretagne, France
Dessin d'étude

PAGE 65
Maison flottante, conçue avec
  Jean-Marie Finot et Denis

Daversin, architectes,
  Chatou, France
Céramique Rombini, Mutina
Exposition « Seventeen
  Screens », Frac Bretagne,
  Rennes, France
Encre sur papier
Encre sur papier
Encre sur papier
Stylo-bille sur papier
Installation, Kiosque,
  Emerige et Galerie kreo,
  chaises et bancs Palissade,
  HAY, jardin des Tuileries,
  Paris
Encre sur papier

2016/Juillet

PAGE 66
Maquette et téléviseur
  The Serif, Samsung,
  atelier, Paris
Ma table, atelier, Paris
Autour de Manhattan sur
  un bateau de la Coupe
  de l'America, New York
Maison, Bretagne, France
Maison, Bretagne, France
Maison, Bretagne, France
Encre sur papier
Encre sur papier
Séance photo, vases Nuage,
  Vitra, atelier, Paris

PAGE 67
Vases Nuage, Vitra

PAGE 68
Encre sur papier
Encre sur papier
Encre sur papier
Chaises Officina, Magis
Recherches, projet Fontaine
  longue, exposition « Rêveries
  urbaines »
Céramique Rombini, Mutina
Vase Nuage, Vitra
Encre sur papier
Bougeoir Officina, Magis

PAGE 69
Encre sur papier
Encre sur papier
Encre sur papier
Encre sur papier
Encre sur papier
Encre sur papier

LISTE DES ŒUVRES

PAGE 70
Encre sur papier
Crayon de couleur sur papier
Crayon de couleur sur papier
Chaises *Officina*, Magis
Maquette, demi-chaise devant
un miroir
Modèle 3D, fauteuil *Palissade*,
HAY

PAGE 71
Maquette, *L'Oiseau*, Vitra et
maquette, étagère *Roche*,
Galerie kreo, atelier, Paris
Maquette, fauteuil *Osso*,
Mattiazzi
Encre sur papier
Chaise *Osso*, Mattiazzi
Atelier, Bretagne, France
Atelier, Bretagne, France

2016/Août

PAGE 72
Encre sur papier
Encre sur papier
Mur, atelier, Bretagne, France
Toit-terrasse, Bretagne, France
Maison, Bretagne, France
Chaise *Stampa*, Kettal
Piètement *Officina*, Magis
Ombre, fauteuil *Palissade*, HAY
Ombre et piètement, bougeoir
Officina, Magis

PAGE 73
Encre sur papier
Mette, toit-terrasse, Bretagne,
France
Toit-terrasse, Bretagne, France
Atelier, Bretagne, France
Détail, chaise *Striped*, Magis
Détail et ombre, chaise *Striped*,
Magis
Chaise *Striped*, Magis, tronc
et chaise d'enfant
Chaise *Pila*, Magis
Tapis *Lattice*, Nanimarquina

PAGE 74
Bougeoir *Officina*, Magis

PAGE 75
Murs, atelier, Bretagne, France
Atelier, Bretagne, France
Meuble *Theca*, Magis
Encre sur papier aluminium
et crabe

Banc *Palissade*, HAY
Encre sur papier
Dessin de Mette
Mette et moi en kayak
Pochette de CD, magazine
The Wire

PAGE 76
Dessin à l'iPad
Chaise *Pila*, Magis, maison,
Bretagne, France
Grutage, *Kiosque*, Emerige
et Galerie kreo, cour du
Parlement de Bretagne,
Rennes, France
Chaise *Pila*, Magis
Encre sur papier, murs, atelier,
Bretagne, France
Encre sur papier
Production, fauteuils *Palissade*,
HAY
Encre et ruban adhésif
sur papier
Poster édité par l'ECAL

2016/Septembre

PAGE 77
Installation, vases *Nuage*, Vitra,
cour de l'atelier, Paris

PAGE 78
Encre et ruban adhésif
sur papier
Exposition « Seventeen
Screens », musée d'Art
de Tel-Aviv, Israël
Installation, vases *Nuage*,
cour de l'atelier, Paris
Installation, vases *Nuage*,
cour de l'atelier, Paris
Tréteau *Officina*, Magis,
cour de l'atelier, Paris
Encre, ruban adhésif et
cellophane coloré sur papier

PAGE 79
Vase *Nuage*, Vitra

PAGE 80
Encre, ruban adhésif
et cellophane coloré
sur papier
Encre, ruban adhésif et
cellophane coloré sur papier
Encre sur papier
Encre sur papier
Encre sur papier

Production, très grands vases
Ruutu, littala
Wooden side table, Vitra,
et tronc
Vase *Torique*, céramique,
tourné à Vallauris
Encre sur papier

PAGE 81
Vases *Nuage*, Vitra devant une
peinture d'Erwan, atelier,
Paris
Table *Y-122*, Galerie kreo
Je porte fièrement un très
grand vase *Ruutu*, littala
Très grands vases *Ruutu*, littala,
Galerie kreo
Production, très grand vase
Ruutu, littala
Très grands vases *Ruutu*, littala,
Galerie kreo

PAGE 82
Table *Y-122*, Galerie kreo
Table *Y-122*, Galerie kreo
Encre sur papier
Encre sur papier
Encre et ruban adhésif sur papier
Encre sur papier
Encre sur papier
Collection *Copenhague*, HAY
Chaise *Officina*, Magis

PAGE 83
Encre sur papier
Dessin de recherche, banc *Ring*
Encre sur papier
Ma table, atelier, Paris
Vases *Nuage*, Vitra, atelier, Paris
Encre sur papier

PAGE 84
Très grands vases *Ruutu*, littala,
Galerie kreo, Londres

PAGE 85
Cornelius, toit-terrasse,
Bretagne, France
Table *Y-122*, atelier, Paris
Portemanteau *Officina*, Magis
Encre sur papier
Clémence Krzentowski portant
un grand vase *Ruutu*, littala,
Galerie kreo
Clémence Krzentowski
derrière deux très grands
vases *Ruutu*, littala,
Galerie kreo

PAGE 86
Encre sur papier
Michel portant un grand vase
Ruutu, littala, Galerie kreo
Prototype, tapis *Blur*,
Nanimarquina
Très grands vases *Ruutu*, littala,
Galerie kreo
Crayon de couleur sur papier
Encre sur papier
Encre sur papier
Encre sur papier
Fauteuil *Striped*, Magis

2016/Octobre

PAGE 87
Encre sur papier
Encre sur papier
Encre sur papier
Exposition « Rêveries
urbaines », Vitra Design
Museum, Weil am Rhein,
Allemagne
Exposition « Rêveries
urbaines », Vitra Design
Museum, Weil am Rhein,
Allemagne
Encre sur papier
Exposition « Rêveries
urbaines », Vitra Design
Museum, Weil am Rhein,
Allemagne
Encre sur papier
Encre sur papier

PAGE 88
Encre sur papier
Table *Cyl*, Vitra
Détail, table *Y-122*, Galerie kreo
Encre et ruban adhésif
sur papier
Encre sur papier
Encre sur papier
Encre sur papier
Table *Cyl* et chaise *Belleville*,
Vitra
Table *Cyl*, Vitra

PAGE 89
Encre sur papier
Graphite sur papier
Encre sur papier
Exposition « Seventeen
Screens », Frac Bretagne,
Rennes, France
Très grands vases *Ruutu*, littala,
Galerie kreo

Exposition « Seventeen
Screens », Frac Bretagne,
Rennes, France

PAGE 90
Table *Cyl* et chaise *Belleville*,
Vitra
Vases *Nuage*, Vitra
Extrusion aluminium,
vase *Nuage*, Vitra
Collection *Cyl*, Vitra
Collection *Cyl*, Vitra
Crayon de couleur sur papier

PAGE 91
Canapé *Cyl*, Vitra
Encre et ruban adhésif
sur papier
Ombre, chaise *Stampa*, Kettal
Chaise *Stampa*, Kettal
Chaise *Osso*, Mattiazzi, maison,
Bretagne, France
Banc *Palissade*, HAY, terrasse,
Bretagne, France
Collection *Cyl*, Vitra
Bancs *Ring*, foire Orgatec,
Cologne, Allemagne
Bancs *Ring*, foire Orgatec,
Cologne, Allemagne

PAGE 92
Objet lumineux, Galerie kreo
et Didier Krzentowski
descendant l'escalier
Maquette, banc *Ring*
Perroquet sur mon épaule
Encre sur papier
Didier Krzentowski et *Chaînes*,
céramique, Galerie kreo,
Paris
Encre sur papier

PAGE 93
Chaînes, aluminium, Galerie
kreo, Paris

2016/Novembre

PAGE 94
Encre sur papier
Encre sur papier
Chaînes, plâtre, Galerie kreo,
Paris
Invitation, exposition
« Chaînes », Galerie kreo,
Paris
Encre et ruban adhésif
sur papier

Montage, exposition
« Chaînes », Galerie kreo,
Paris
Encre et ruban adhésif
sur papier
Encre et ruban adhésif
sur papier
Encre sur papier

PAGE 95
Encre sur papier
Encre sur papier
Énigme
Encre sur papier
Maquette en morceaux,
chaise Pila, Magis
Encre et ruban adhésif
sur papier
Détail en fer forgé
Détail, collection Officina, Magis
Encre et ruban adhésif
sur papier

PAGE 96
Encre sur papier
Encre sur papier
Encre sur papier
Encre sur papier
Invitation, exposition « Chaînes »,
Galerie kreo, Londres
Exposition « Chaînes »,
Galerie kreo, Londres

PAGE 97
Croquis
Chaise et table Officina, Magis
Encre et cellophane coloré
sur papier
Encre et peinture sur papier
Encre, ruban adhésif et
cellophane coloré sur papier
Encre, ruban adhésif et
gommettes sur papier
Encre, ruban adhésif et
cellophane coloré sur papier
Valet Officina, Magis
Séance photo, collection Cyl,
Vitra

PAGE 98
Encre et cellophane coloré
sur papier
Lustre Gabriel, cristal
Swarovski, château
de Versailles, France
Montage, lustre Gabriel, cristal
Swarovski, château
de Versailles, France

Montage, lustre Gabriel,
cristal Swarovski, château
de Versailles, France
Montage, lustre Gabriel,
cristal Swarovski, château
de Versailles, France
Collier Perles, jaspe, Galerie
kreo
Collier Perles, marbre de
Carrare, Galerie kreo
Encre, ruban adhésif et
cellophane coloré sur papier
Encre, ruban adhésif et
cellophane coloré sur papier

PAGE 99
Dessin de recherche, lustre
Gabriel

PAGE 100
Recherches, chapiteau
lumineux
Série L'Oiseau, Vitra
Ruban adhésif, cellophane
coloré et gommette
sur papier
Lianes, Galerie kreo
Conques, Galerie kreo
Ruban adhésif, cellophane
coloré et encre sur papier

PAGE 101
Production, Lianes,
Galerie kreo
Encre et cellophane coloré
sur papier
Encre, ruban adhésif,
cellophane coloré et
gommettes sur papier
Croquis
Maquette, lustre Gabriel
Encre, ruban adhésif
et cellophane coloré
sur papier

PAGE 102
Stylo-bille, ruban adhésif,
cellophane coloré
et gommettes sur papier
Stylo-bille, ruban adhésif
et cellophane coloré
sur papier
Stylo-bille, ruban adhésif
et cellophane coloré
sur papier
Pause déjeuner
Recherches de motifs
Chaises Uncino, Mattiazzi

2016/Décembre

PAGE 103
Ruban adhésif et cellophane
coloré sur papier
Kiosque, Emerige et Galerie
kreo, jardin des Tuileries,
Paris
Un cadeau pour Rolf Fehlbaum
Motifs, tissu Rivi, Artek
Recherches, motifs, tissu Rivi,
Artek
Stylo-bille et ruban adhésif
sur papier
Stylo-bille, ruban adhésif
et gommettes sur papier
Stylo-bille, ruban adhésif
et gommettes sur papier
Stylo-bille, ruban adhésif
et gommettes sur papier

PAGE 104
Banc Officina, Magis
Avec Rolf, collection Palissade,
HAY
Encre et cellophane coloré
sur papier
Recherches, chapiteau sur l'eau
Prototype, rideaux Rennes,
Kvadrat, atelier, Paris
Maquette, fauteuil Palissade,
HAY
Tests de couleurs, L'Oiseau,
céramique, Vitra
Banc Palissade, HAY
Fauteuil Palissade, HAY

PAGE 105
Une des premières maquettes,
collection Palissade, HAY

PAGE 106
Bougeoir Officina, Magis
Encre sur papier
Le matin, Bretagne, France
Session surf, Bretagne, France
Bretagne, France
Portemanteau Officina,
Magis, atelier, Bretagne,
France
Croquis
Paysage, Bretagne, France
Ma table de travail, atelier, Paris

PAGE 107
Mur, atelier, Paris
Chaise Stampa, Kettal, atelier,
Bretagne, France

Recherches, exposition
« Rêveries urbaines »
Graphite, ruban adhésif,
gommettes et aluminium
sur papier
Colonie d'Oiseau, céramique,
Vitra
Exposition « Seventeen
Screens », musée d'Art
de Tel-Aviv, Israël
L'Oiseau, Vitra
L'Oiseau à la tête cassée, Vitra
Carte de vœux, ville de Rennes,
France

2017/Janvier

PAGE 108
Encre, gommettes et fil
sur papier
Encre, gommettes et fil
sur papier
Encre et ruban adhésif
sur papier
Livre Ronan & Erwan
Bouroullec: Drawing,
JRP|Editions
Encre, gommettes et fil
sur papier
Tissu Rivi, Artek
Tissu Rivi, Artek
Je photographie les Oiseau,
céramique, Vitra
Stylo-bille sur papier

PAGE 109
Encre sur papier
Pleine lune
Encre sur papier
Livre Ronan & Erwan
Bouroullec: Drawing,
JRP|Editions
Graphite sur papier
Livre Ronan & Erwan
Bouroullec: Drawing,
JRP|Editions
Livre Ronan & Erwan
Bouroullec: Drawing,
JRP|Editions
Croquis, fauteuil et chaise
longue Quindici, Mattiazzi
Encre sur papier

PAGE 110
Atelier, Paris
Tissu Rivi, Artek
Empilement, chaises Pila,
Magis

Système de rideau Ready made
curtain, Kvadrat
Production, chaises Stampa,
Kettal
Stylo-bille, bloc-notes d'hôtel
Encre sur papier
Encre et ruban adhésif
sur papier
Stylo-bille sur papier

PAGE 111
Tissu Rivi, Artek
Graphite et cellophane coloré
sur papier
Encre, ruban adhésif et
cellophane coloré sur papier
Encre et ruban adhésif
sur papier
Encre sur papier
Structure, canapé Officina,
Magis

PAGE 112
Séance de travail chez Magis
Banc Officina, Magis
Canapé Officina, Magis
Canapé Officina, Magis
Séance de travail chez Magis
Détail de la structure,
chaise Officina, Magis
Tabourets Officina, Magis
Chaise Palissade, HAY,
Céramique Rombini, Mutina
Bureau Diapositive, Glas Italia

PAGE 113
Rangement Theca, Magis,
atelier, Paris
Croquis, chapiteau
Encre et ruban adhésif
sur papier
Maquette, projet Fontaine
longue, exposition « Rêveries
urbaines »
Graphite sur papier
Encre et ruban adhésif
sur papier

2017/Février

PAGE 114
Encre et ruban adhésif
sur papier
Encre sur papier
Encre sur papier
Encre sur papier
Encre et ruban adhésif
sur papier

LISTE DES ŒUVRES

Détail, chaise *Osso*, Mattiazzi
Encre et gommettes sur papier
Banc *Palissade*, HAY
Séance photo, collection
    Palissade, HAY

PAGE 115
Chaise *Palissade*, HAY

PAGE 116
Graphite sur papier
Lampe et table basse *Bells*,
    Galerie kreo
Encre et peinture sur papier
Détail, collection *Officina*, Magis
Atelier de maquettes, Paris
Collage préparatoire,
    exposition « Seventeen
    Screens », musée d'Art
    de Tel-Aviv, Israël

PAGE 117
Collage préparatoire,
    exposition « Seventeen
    Screens », musée d'Art
    de Tel-Aviv, Israël
Dessin préparatoire sur photo,
    exposition « Seventeen
    Screens », musée d'Art
    de Tel-Aviv, Israël
Chaînes, plâtre, Galerie kreo,
    Paris
Banc *Palissade*, HAY
Encre et peinture sur papier
Lampes *Lampalumina*, Bitossi
Lampes *Lampalumina*, Bitossi
Assemblage, Galerie kreo
Peinture sur papier

PAGE 118
Maquette, chaise longue
    Quindici, Mattiazzi

PAGE 119
Encre et ruban adhésif
    sur papier
Peinture et gommettes
    sur papier
Peinture, ruban adhésif
    et gommettes sur papier
Emménagement, Bretagne,
    France
Encre, peinture et ruban
    adhésif sur papier
Maquette, chaise longue
    Quindici, Mattiazzi
Chez Cassina
Encre sur papier

Encre, ruban adhésif et carton
    doré sur papier

PAGE 120
Détail, chaise *Uncino*, Mattiazzi
Encre, ruban adhésif et carton
    doré sur papier
Chaise *Uncino*, Mattiazzi
Étagère et bureau *Kaari*, Artek
Détail, chaise *Officina*, Magis
Encre sur papier
Canapé *Officina*, Magis
Chaise *Officina*, Magis
Chaise et fauteuil *Officina*,
    Magis

PAGE 121
Le bureau d'Eugenio Perazza
Archive, dessins
Archive, encre sur papier
Encre sur papier
Chaise *Officina*, Magis
Encre sur papier

PAGE 122
Archive, encre sur bois
Vase *Ruutu*, Iittala
Exposition des designers
    de l'année, Architecture
    & Wohnen, Kölnischer
    Kunstverein, Cologne,
    Allemagne
Prototype, chaise longue
    Quindici, Mattiazzi
Chaise longue *Quindici*,
    Mattiazzi
Fauteuil *Quindici*, Mattiazzi

2017/Mars

PAGE 123
Fauteuil *Quindici*, Mattiazzi
Chaise longue *Quindici*,
    Mattiazzi
Vase *Ruutu*, Iittala et collage
    sur ma fenêtre, Paris
Paroi *Rains*
Exposition « Bivouac », Centre
    Pompidou-Metz, France
Exposition « Étapes », villa
    Noailles, Hyères, France
Pelures de crayon
Dessins, maison, Paris
Atelier, Paris

PAGE 124
Encre et ruban adhésif
    sur papier

PAGE 125
Fleurs
Crayon, cellophane coloré et
    ruban adhésif sur papier
Exposition « Seventeen
    Screens », Frac Bretagne,
    Rennes, France
Croquis, tapis *Semis*, Kvadrat
Tapis *Semis*, Kvadrat
Détail, fauteuil *Slow Chair*, Vitra

PAGE 126
Rideau *Rennes*, Kvadrat
Graphite sur papier
Tabouret *Uncino*, Mattiazzi
Crayon de couleur sur papier
Chaises *Softshell*, Vitra
Séance photo, chaise *Softshell*,
    Vitra

PAGE 127
Encre sur papier et filet
    d'oranges
Photomontage, suspension
    Luce verticale, Flos
Tabouret *Uncino*, Mattiazzi
Détail, chaise *Uncino*, Mattiazzi
Détail, chaise *Uncino*, Mattiazzi
Fauteuil *Quindici*, Mattiazzi
Chez Cassina, *Attention :
    s'asseoir prudemment,
    les joints ne sont pas collés.*
Encre et ruban adhésif
    sur papier
Encre sur papier

PAGE 128
Stylo-bille sur papier
Bureau *Kaari*, Artek
    et tabouret *Stool 60*, Artek,
    d'Alvar Aalto
Article sur mon compte
    Instagram, *Surface Magazine*
Banc *Officina*, Magis
Chantier, Bretagne, France
Fauteuil et chaise longue
    Quindici, Mattiazzi

PAGE 129
Encre sur papier
Encre sur papier
Détail, fauteuil *Quindici*,
    Mattiazzi
Détail, chaise *Uncino*, Mattiazzi
Détail, tabouret *Uncino*,
    Mattiazzi
Programme, Salone del Mobile
    de Milan

Programme, Salone del Mobile
    de Milan
Graphite sur papier
Crayon de couleur et graphite
    sur papier

2017/Avril

PAGE 130
Encre sur papier

PAGE 131
Détail, suspension *Luce
    verticale*, Flos
Détail, table en verre coulé,
    Glas Italia
Table en verre coulé, Glas Italia
Table en verre coulé, Glas Italia
Fauteuil *Quindici*, Mattiazzi
Installation, suspension *Luce
    verticale*, Salone del Mobile,
    Milan
Encre sur papier
Recherches, tapis *Semis*,
    Kvadrat
Tapis *Semis*, Kvadrat

PAGE 132
Encre sur papier
Suspension *Luce verticale*, Flos
Suspension *Luce verticale*, Flos
Encre sur papier
Stylo-bille sur papier
Photomontage, suspension
    Luce verticale, Flos
Peinture, encre et ruban
    adhésif sur papier
Détail, tapis *Semis*, Kvadrat
Stylo-bille sur papier

PAGE 133
Stylo-bille sur papier
Détail, tapis *Semis*, Kvadrat
Vase *Ruutu*, Iittala, atelier,
    Bretagne, France
Vase *Ruutu*, Iittala, atelier,
    Bretagne, France
Vase *Ruutu*, Iittala, atelier,
    Bretagne, France
Encre sur papier

PAGE 134
Encre sur papier
Encre sur papier
Encre sur papier
Encre sur serviettes en papier
    du TGV
Atelier, Bretagne, France

Encre sur papier
Assiette pour American
    Airlines, Alessi
Encre sur papier
Maison, Paris

PAGE 135
Encre sur papier
Système de rideau *Ready
    made curtain*, Kvadrat,
    maison, Paris
Encre sur papier
Graphite sur papier
Encre sur papier
Encre sur papier
Encre sur papier
Encre sur papier
Encre sur sachet vomitif
    de Norwegian Airlines

PAGE 136
Production, banc *Ring*
Banc *Palissade*, HAY
Prototypes, vases *Losange*,
    céramique, Galerie kreo
Exposition « Album »,
    Arc en rêve centre
    d'architecture,
    Bordeaux, France
Encre sur sachet vomitif
    de Norwegian Airlines
Exposition « Bivouac »,
    Centre Pompidou-Metz,
    France

PAGE 137
Encre sur papier
Paroi *Clouds*, Kvadrat
Encre sur papier
Exposition « Bivouac », Centre
    Pompidou-Metz, France
Exposition « Bivouac », Centre
    Pompidou-Metz, France
Encre sur papier

2017/Mai

PAGE 138
Encre sur papier
Pages découpées, livre
    *Ronan & Erwan Bouroullec:
    Drawing*, JRP|Editions,
    installation, Cologne,
    Allemagne
Maquette du banc *Ring*
Banc *Ring*, installation *OUI*,
    parc du Kunsthal Aarhus,
    Danemark

LISTE DES ŒUVRES

Encre et ruban adhésif
    sur papier
Encre sur papier
Encre et ruban adhésif
    sur papier

PAGE 161
Chaise *Pila*, Magis, terrasse,
    Bretagne, France
Détail, chaise *Palissade*, HAY
Chaise *Palissade*, HAY, terrasse,
    Bretagne, France
Encre et ruban adhésif
    sur papier
Encre et ruban adhésif
    sur papier
Encre et ruban adhésif
    sur papier
Système de rideau *Ready made
    curtain*, Kvadrat
Encre sur papier
Rideaux *Rennes*, Kvadrat

2017/Septembre

PAGE 162
Maquette *Promenade Nuage*,
    Miami

PAGE 163
Détail, chaise *Pila*, Magis
Broderie *Guipure*
Fauteuil *Quindici* et son coussin,
    Mattiazzi
Inga montant l'escalier, maison,
    Paris
Encre et pastel gras sur papier
Mette, atelier, Bretagne, France
Escalier, maison, Paris
Encre et pastel gras sur papier
Pastel gras sur bois

PAGE 164
Encre, ruban adhésif et
    cellophane coloré sur papier
Exposition « Seventeen
    Screens », Frac Bretagne,
    Rennes, France
Scénographie, exposition
    « Rétrospective », Frac
    Bretagne, Rennes, France
Ombre, chaise *Palissade*, HAY
Détail, fauteuil *Belleville*, Vitra
Valet *Officina*, Magis

PAGE 165
Encre sur papier
Encre sur papier

Détail, cadre, Corian
Fauteuil *Slow Chair*, Vitra
Recherches, textile
Encre sur papier
Tapis *Losange*, Nanimarquina
Scénographie, exposition
    « Rétrospective », Frac
    Bretagne, Rennes, France
Encre sur papier

PAGE 166
Encre sur papier
Chez Mutina
Céramique *Piano*, Mutina
Encre et peinture sur papier
Emi accroche des dessins,
    atelier, Paris
Emi, atelier, Paris
Dans le train
Chaise *Steelwood*, Magis
Céramique *Piano*, Mutina

2017/Octobre

PAGE 167
Clémence Krzentowski portant
    un très grand vase *Ruutu*,
    Iittala, Galerie kreo

PAGE 168
Pastel, graphite et ruban
    adhésif sur bois
Encre et ruban adhésif
    sur papier
Pastel, graphite et ruban
    adhésif sur bois
Pastel, graphite et ruban
    adhésif sur bois
Encre et pastel sur papier
Installation, *Kiosque*, Emerige
    et Galerie kreo, jardin,
    Mexico City
Encre sur serviette en papier
    de TGV
Conférence, théâtre du
    Capitole, Toulouse, France
Conférence, théâtre du
    Capitole, Toulouse, France

PAGE 169
Encre sur papier
Mur, maison, Paris
Encre sur papier
Exposition, collection *Torique*,
    galerie Gilles Peyroulet
    & Cie, Paris
Chez Claude Aïello, Vallauris,
    France

Chez Claude Aïello, Vallauris,
    France
Élément en verre coulé,
    suspension *Luce orizzontale*,
    Flos
Pastel sur bois, salon rose,
    villa Noailles, Hyères, France
Atelier, Paris

PAGE 170
Encre sur papier
Encre sur papier
Impression sur papier, The
    Wrong Shop, atelier, Paris
Je photographie la céramique
    Piano, Mutina
Crayon de couleur sur papier
Détail, table en verre coulé,
    Glas Italia
Installation *Textile Field*,
    Victoria and Albert Museum,
    Londres
Vase *Cloud*, céramique,
    édition limitée
Peinture sur papier

PAGE 171
Crayon de couleur sur papier
Stylo-bille sur papier
Croquis, kiosque, Rennes,
    France
Stylo-bille, gommette et ruban
    adhésif sur papier
Encre sur papier
Encre sur papier

PAGE 172
Banc *Palissade*, HAY
Détail, chaise *Osso*, Mattiazzi
Chaise *Softshell*, Vitra
Vase *Nuage*, Vitra
Image numérique, kiosque
    sur l'eau, Rennes, France
Graphite, ruban adhésif
    et pastel gras sur bois
Bretagne, France
Atelier, Bretagne, France
Bougeoir *Officina*, atelier,
    Bretagne, France

2017/Novembre

PAGE 173
Croquis, kiosque sur l'eau

PAGE 174
Rideau *Chainette*, Kvadrat
Atelier, Bretagne, France

Exposition des vases *Losange*,
    Galerie kreo, Paris
Encre sur papier
Encre sur papier
Exposition des vases *Losange*,
    Galerie kreo, Paris
Exposition des vases *Losange*,
    Galerie kreo, Paris
Exposition des vases *Losange*,
    Galerie kreo, Paris
Vases *Ruutu*, Iittala

PAGE 175
Encre sur papier
Encre sur papier
Atelier, Bretagne, France
Bananier, lampe *w103*,
    Wästberg, d'Inga Sempé
    et dessin au mur, maison,
    Paris
Encre sur papier
Broderie *Guipure*

PAGE 176
Projet, *Promenade Nuage*,
    exposition « Rêveries
    urbaines »
Fabrication, *Promenade Nuage*,
    Miami
Fabrication, *Promenade Nuage*,
    Miami
Encre sur papier
Fabrication, *Promenade Nuage*,
    Miami
Maquette, *Promenade Nuage*,
    Miami
Encre, peinture et cellophane
    coloré sur papier
Installation *Textile Field*,
    Victoria and Albert Museum,
    Londres
Poster de vœux, Vitra

PAGE 177
Carton d'invitation, exposition
    des vases *Losange*,
    Galerie kreo, Paris
Prototype, vase *Cloud*,
    céramique, Vitra
Encre sur papier
Encre sur papier
Encre sur papier
Maquette, *Promenade Nuage*,
    Miami
Avec Erwan, atelier, Paris
Vases *Losange*, Galerie kreo
Croquis, kiosque sur l'eau,
    Rennes, France

2017/Décembre

PAGE 178
Vase *Nuage*, céramique,
    Vitra
Maquette, *Promenade Nuage*,
    Miami
Promenade Nuage, Miami
Vase *Nuage*, Vitra et encre
    sur papier
Promenade Nuage, Miami
Promenade Nuage, Miami
Encre sur papier
Promenade Nuage, Miami
Promenade Nuage, Miami

PAGE 179
Promenade Nuage, Miami
Maquette, *Promenade Nuage*,
    Miami
Encre sur papier
Encre sur papier
Clouds, textile, Kvadrat
Promenade Nuage, Miami

PAGE 180
Encre sur papier
Encre sur papier
Promenade Nuage, Miami
Encre sur papier
Encre sur papier
Encre sur papier
Encre sur papier
Vases *Ruutu*, Iittala
Rideaux *Rennes*, Kvadrat

PAGE 181
Rideaux *Rennes*, Kvadrat
Encre sur papier
Croquis original, *Algue*, Vitra
Plan technique, *Algue*, Vitra
Algue, Vitra
Exposition « Momentanée »,
    musée des Arts décoratifs,
    Paris
Exposition « Momentanée »,
    musée des Arts décoratifs,
    Paris
Encre sur papier
Encre sur papier

PAGE 182
Encre sur papier
Projet toit *Arbre et Rochers*,
    exposition « Rêveries
    urbaines »
Maison flottante, conçue avec
    Jean-Marie Finot et

Denis Daversin, architectes,
Chatou, France
Encre sur papier
Vase *Ruutu*, Iittala
Encre sur papier

PAGE 183
Encre sur papier
Encre sur papier
Encre sur papier
Image numérique, kiosque
sur l'eau, Rennes,
France
Encre sur papier
Michel portant un très grand
vase *Ruutu*, Iittala,
Galerie kreo
Très grand vase *Ruutu*, Iittala,
Galerie kreo
Très grand vase *Ruutu*, Iittala,
Galerie kreo
Encre sur papier

2018/Janvier

PAGE 184
Maison, Paris
Murs, maison, Paris
Installation en hommage à
Zaha Hadid, caserne des
pompiers, campus Vitra,
Weil am Rhein, Allemagne
Encre sur papier
Stylo-bille, ruban adhésif
et gommettes
sur papier
Rideau *Rennes*, Kvadrat
Rideau *Rennes*, Kvadrat
Encre sur papier
Chaise longue *Quindici*, Matiazzi

PAGE 185
Promenade Nuage, Miami

PAGE 186
Conques, Galerie kreo
Table en verre coulé, Glas Italia
Pochette, Prada
Croquis, *Pochette*
Collaboration avec Prada
Pochette, Prada
Recherches, projet *Chapiteau
végétal*, exposition « Rêveries
urbaines »
Exposition « Seventeen
Screens », Frac Bretagne,
Rennes, France
Encre sur papier

PAGE 187
Encre sur papier
Encre sur papier
Encre et ruban adhésif
sur papier
Mette sur le canapé *Cassette*,
Established & Sons
Encre et ruban adhésif
sur papier
Graphite sur papier
Atelier de maquettes, Paris
Projet *Parasols*, exposition
« Rêveries urbaines »
Croquis, *Les Fontaines des
Champs-Élysées*, Paris

PAGE 188
Encre sur papier
Rideaux *Chainette*, Kvadrat
Encre sur papier
Encre sur papier
Encre sur papier
Clouds, textile, Kvadrat

PAGE 189
Prototypes, rideau *Rennes*,
showroom de Kvadrat,
Copenhague

PAGE 190
Détail, rideau *Chainette*,
Kvadrat
Exposition « Seventeen
Screens », musée d'Art
de Tel-Aviv, Israël
Encre sur papier aluminium
Prototypes, rideau *Rennes*,
showroom de Kvadrat,
Copenhague
Prototypes, rideau *Rennes*,
showroom de Kvadrat,
Copenhague
Encre sur papier

2018/Février

PAGE 191
Image numérique, projet
Belvédère, Rennes, France
Rideaux *Rennes* et *Chainette*,
showroom Kvadrat,
Stockholm
Rideau *Chainette*, showroom
Kvadrat, Stockholm
Crayon de couleur sur image
numérique, projet *Belvédère*,
Rennes, France
Encre sur papier

Préparation d'un livre, éditions
Nieves
Détail, chaise *Élémentaire*, HAY
Stylo-bille, bloc-notes d'hôtel
Stylo-bille, bloc-notes d'hôtel

PAGE 192
Banc bassin, *Promenade Nuage*,
Miami
Encre sur serviette en papier
Archive des dessins
Maquette, banc *Ring*
Moule de coffrage, banc
bassin, *Promenade Nuage*,
Miami
Archive des dessins

PAGE 193
Showroom Kvadrat, Stockholm
Metal Side Tables, Vitra
Vase *Losange*, céramique,
Galerie kreo
Encre sur papier
Encre sur papier
Banc *Officina*, Magis
Détail, canapé *Cassette*,
Established & Sons
Fin de soirée
Maquette, *Les Fontaines
des Champs-Élysées*, Paris

PAGE 194
Archive des dessins
et des carnets

PAGE 195
Vases *Nuage*, Vitra
Pluie dans l'atelier, Bretagne,
France
Atelier, Bretagne, France
Encre sur papier
Encre sur papier
Encre sur papier
Prototype, tapis *Blur*,
Nanimarquina
Paravent *Rayures*, Glas Italia
Recherches, vases *Ruutu*, Iittala

2018/Mars

PAGE 196
Chaise *Belleville* et bureau *Cyl*,
Vitra
Recherche, chapiteau flottant
Exposition « Rêveries
urbaines », EPFL,
Lausanne, Suisse
Détail, table *Cyl*, Vitra

Ombre des vases *Alcova*,
WonderGlass
Tapis *Blur*, Nanimarquina
Encre sur papier
Atelier, Bretagne, France
Chaise *Hole*, Cappellini

PAGE 197
Paravent *Rayures*, Glas Italia
Encre sur papier
Fauteuil *Palissade*, acier
galvanisé, HAY
Tapis *Blur*, Nanimarquina
Tapis *Blur*, Nanimarquina
Détail, tapis *Blur*, Nanimarquina

PAGE 198
Prototype de table Artek
Détail, chaise *Cotone*, Cassina
Encre sur papier
Conférence sur l'exposition
« Rêveries urbaines »
Exposition « Rêveries
urbaines », EPFL, Lausanne,
Suisse
Recherches, banc *Ring* et *Toit*,
exposition « Rêveries urbaines »
Recherches, banc *Tronc*,
exposition « Rêveries
urbaines »
Encre sur papier
Tapis *Blur*, Nanimarquina

PAGE 199
Tapis *Blur*, Nanimarquina et
fauteuil *Quindici*, Mattiazzi

PAGE 200
Vases *Alcova*, WonderGlass
Séance photo, vases *Alcova*,
WonderGlass, Vénétie, Italie
Séance photo, vases *Alcova*,
WonderGlass, Vénétie, Italie
Vase *Alcova*, WonderGlass
Test d'impression pour un livre,
éditions Nieves
Test d'impression pour un livre,
éditions Nieves
Chez WonderGlass, Vénétie,
Italie
Recherches, chapiteau lumineux
Graphite sur bois

2018/Avril

PAGE 201
Encre sur papier
Encre sur papier

Encre sur papier
Prototype d'assise pour Vitra
Encre sur papier
Atelier, Paris
Encre sur papier
Trois chaises *Élémentaire*, HAY
Chaises *Élémentaire*, HAY

PAGE 202
Dessin sur image numérique
Maquette de test d'ergonomie,
chaise *Élémentaire*, HAY
Maquette carton, chaise
Élémentaire, HAY
Avec Pierre Keller
Chaise *Élémentaire*, HAY
Banc *Palissade*, acier galvanisé,
HAY

PAGE 203
Collage, projet de vase
Programme, Salone del Mobile
de Milan
Chaises *Élémentaire* et table
Copenhague, HAY
Vases *Alcova*, WonderGlass
Assise, installation *Vitra
Typecasting*, La Pelota, Milan
Collection *Palissade*, HAY, cour
du Palazzo Clerici, Milan
Assise, installation *Vitra
Typecasting*, La Pelota, Milan
Chaise *Cotone*, Cassina
Paravent *Rayures*, Glas Italia

PAGE 204
Vases *Alcova*, WonderGlass
Vases *Alcova*, WonderGlass
Chaise *Cotone*, Cassina
Paravent *Rayures*, Glas Italia
Vases *Alcova*, WonderGlass
Atelier, Bretagne, France
Paravent *Rayures*, Glas Italia
Production, vases *Alcova*,
WonderGlass
Production, vases *Alcova*,
WonderGlass

PAGE 205
Chaise longue *Quindici*,
Mattiazzi
Livre *Juillet*, éditions Nieves
Encre sur papier
Encre sur papier
Encre sur papier
Maquette de test d'ergonomie,
chaise *Élémentaire*, HAY
Encre sur papier

LISTE DES ŒUVRES

Engrenages, *Les Fontaines des Champs-Élysées*, Paris
Table et chaises *Cotone*, Cassina

2018/Mai

PAGE 206
Table et chaise *Cotone*, Cassina

PAGE 207
Ombre des maquettes, *Les Fontaines des Champs-Élysées*, Paris
Collection *Palissade*, acier galvanisé, HAY
Céramique *Pico*, Mutina
Prototype, chaise *Élémentaire*, HAY
Livre *Juillet*, éditions Nieves
Croquis sur une table en bois, projet *Belvédère*, Rennes, France
Encre sur papier
Recherches, chapiteau
Encre sur papier

PAGE 208
Maquette, paravent *Rayures*, Glas Italia
Encre et ruban adhésif sur papier
Encre et ruban adhésif sur papier
Maquette, chaise *Élémentaire*, HAY et vases *Losange*, Galerie kreo
Encre et ruban adhésif sur papier
Encre sur papier
Maquette, chaise *Élémentaire*, HAY
Encre, ruban adhésif et cellophane coloré sur papier
Tapis *Blur*, Nanimarquina et chaise *Quindici*, Mattiazzi

PAGE 209
Encre, ruban adhésif et cellophane coloré sur papier
Affiche, exposition, galerie Giorgio Mastinu, Venise
Affiche, exposition, galerie Giorgio Mastinu, Venise
Paravent *Rayures*, Glas Italia
Encre sur papier
Encre et ruban adhésif sur papier

Encre et peinture sur papier
Tapis *Blur*, Nanimarquina
Maquettes, projet *Belvédère*, Rennes, France

PAGE 210
Encre et carton doré sur papier
Encre, gommette et graphite sur papier
Promenade Nuage, Miami
Article, exposition de dessins, galerie Giorgio Mastinu, Venise
Encre sur papier
Encre sur papier
Production, *Ruisseau*, campus Vitra, Portugal
Livre *Objets Dessins Maquettes*, Archibooks
Détail, étagère *Steelwood*, Magis

PAGE 211
Installation, *Ruisseau*, campus Vitra, Weil am Rhein, Allemagne
Graphite sur papier
Encre sur papier
Encre, ruban adhésif et peinture sur papier
Encre sur papier
Encre sur papier
Encre sur papier
Tapis *Blur*, Nanimarquina, cour de l'atelier, Paris
Polyptyque, encre sur papier

2018/Juin

PAGE 212
Polyptyque, encre sur papier
Collection *Palissade*, acier galvanisé, HAY
Céramique *Rombini*, Mutina
Vases *Losange*, Galerie kreo et chaise *Stampa*, Kettal
Croquis, mobile sur la Garonne
Détail, chaise *Cotone*, Cassina
Galerie Giorgio Mastinu, Venise
Exposition, Vitra, Chicago
Encre sur serviette en papier

PAGE 213
Ruisseau, campus Vitra, Weil am Rhein, Allemagne
Ruisseau et banc *Ring*, campus Vitra, Weil am Rhein, Allemagne

Ruisseau et banc *Ring*, campus Vitra, Weil am Rhein, Allemagne
Encre sur papier
Encre sur papier
Encre sur papier
Encre et peinture sur papier
Encre sur papier
Encre sur papier

PAGE 214
Vase *Alcova*, WonderGlass
Ruisseau, campus Vitra, Weil am Rhein, Allemagne
Encre sur papier
Encre sur papier
Image numérique, projet *Belvédère*, Rennes, France
Image numérique, projet *Belvédère*, Rennes, France

PAGE 215
Dessin de nuit
Encre sur papier
Impression sur papier, The Wrong Shop
Utilisation des dessins, affiche, Frieze Art Fair, Londres
Accrochage, atelier, Paris
Encre sur papier
Encre sur papier
Stylo-bille sur serviette en papier
Échantillons, rideaux *Rennes* et *Chainette*, Kvadrat

2018/Juillet

PAGE 216
Paravent *Rayures*, Glas Italia
Encre et ruban adhésif sur papier
Banc *Ring*, campus Vitra, Weil am Rhein, Allemagne
Banc *Palissade*, HAY
Portrait pour article, revue *Intramuros*, vers 1995
Rolf Fehlbaum

PAGE 217
Exposition « Seventeen Screens », Frac Bretagne, Rennes, France
Fauteuil *Palissade*, acier galvanisé, HAY, cour de l'atelier, Paris

Première recherche, aménagement des extérieurs, Bourse de commerce – Pinault Collection, Paris
Échantillons, rideau *Chainette*, Kvadrat
Poster de vœux, Vitra
Atelier, Paris
Exposition « Bivouac », Centre Pompidou-Metz, France
Clouds, textile, Kvadrat
Fabrication, *Les Fontaines des Champs-Élysées*, Paris

PAGE 218
Croquis sur serviette en papier
Chaises *Palissade*, acier galvanisé, cour de l'atelier, Paris
Encre et ruban adhésif sur papier
Atelier, Bretagne, France
Recherches, pavillon végétalisé
Polyptyque, encre sur papier
Recherches, pavillon végétalisé
Encre sur papier
Chaise et table *Officina*, Magis

PAGE 219
Encre sur papier
Maison, Bretagne, France
Chaise *Officina*, Magis
Banc *Palissade*, HAY, toit-terrasse, Bretagne, France
Atelier, Bretagne, France
Houpette

2018/Août

PAGE 220
Détail, chaise *Palissade*, acier galvanisé, HAY
Terrasse, Bretagne, France
Encre sur papier
Banc *Officina*, Magis
Chaises *Palissade*, acier galvanisé, HAY, terrasse, Bretagne, France
Fauteuil *Quindici*, Mattiazzi
Atelier, Bretagne, France
Détail, chaise longue *Quindici*, Mattiazzi
Houpette

PAGE 221
Prototype, chaise
Chaise longue *Quindici*, Mattiazzi

Détail, banc *Palissade*, HAY
Dessin, terrasse, Bretagne, France
Chaises *Palissade*, acier galvanisé, HAY, terrasse, Bretagne, France
Vases *Losange*, Galerie kreo et chaise *Steelwood*, Magis, maison, Bretagne, France
Vase *Nuage*, Vitra
Prototype, chaise
Encre sur papier

PAGE 222
Encre sur papier
Encre sur papier
Chaise *Palissade*, acier galvanisé, HAY
Atelier, Bretagne, France
Chat assistant
Encre sur papier
Encre sur papier
Atelier, Bretagne, France

PAGE 223
Atelier, Bretagne, France

PAGE 224
Poster, The Wrong Shop
Dessin pour l'affiche, Frieze Art Fair, Londres
Dessin pour l'affiche, Frieze Art Fair, Londres
Dessin pour l'affiche, Frieze Art Fair, Londres
Atelier, Paris
L'Oiseau, terrasse, Bretagne, France
Encre sur papier
Dessins et chaise *Pila*, Magis
Encre sur papier

2018/Septembre

PAGE 225
Encre sur papier
Encre sur papier
Giorgio Mastinu
Détail, chaise *Cotone*, Cassina
Vase *Alcova*, WonderGlass
Encre et peinture sur papier
Bouroullec Pasta
Collage
Galerie Giorgio Mastinu, Venise

PAGE 226
Encre sur papier

Stock des injections
de polyuréthane,
chaise *Softshell*, Vitra
Encre sur papier
Encre sur papier et chaise
Österlen d'Inga Sempé,
Gärsnas
Graphite sur papier
Tapis *Blur*, Nanimarquina

PAGE 227
Tests d'impression, posters,
The Wrong Shop
Chaise *Officina*, Magis
Chaise et table *Officina*, Magis
Encre sur papier
Tabourets et table *Officina*,
Magis
Encre et peinture sur papier
Bouroullec Pasta
Encre et peinture sur papier
Encre et peinture sur papier

2018/Octobre

PAGE 228
Encre sur papier
Dessins, atelier, Paris
Nitouche
Affiche pour une conférence
Encre sur papier
Paroi *Cloud*, exposition
« Bivouac », Museum of
Contemporary Art, Chicago
Encre sur papier
Stylo-bille sur papier
Encre sur papier

PAGE 229
Bouroullec Pasta
Encre sur papier
Pastel sur bois
Encre sur papier
Encre sur papier
Vase *Nuage*, Vitra
Encre sur papier
Atelier, Paris
Impression sur papier,
The Wrong Shop

PAGE 230
Exposition « Seventeen
Screens », Frac Bretagne,
Rennes, France
Chaînes, plâtre, Galerie kreo
Maquettes, projet *Belvédère*,
Rennes, France
Clouds, textile, Kvadrat

Rideau *Rennes*, Kvadrat
Rideau *Rennes*, Kvadrat
Pause déjeuner
Exposition « Rêveries
urbaines », Hong Kong
Design Institute
Exposition « Rêveries
urbaines », Hong Kong
Design Institute

PAGE 231
Poster, The Wrong Shop
Clouds, Kvadrat, chaise
Palissade, HAY et encre
sur papier
Encre sur papier
Maison, Bretagne, France
Encre sur papier
Chaise *Palissade*, acier
galvanisé, HAY
Encre sur papier
Maison, Bretagne, France
Chaise longue *Quindici*,
Mattiazzi

2018/Novembre

PAGE 232
Encre sur papier

PAGE 233
Lampe *W153 Île*, Wästberg,
d'Inga Sempé et vase *Nuage*,
Vitra
Tirages test, The Wrong Shop
Détail, chaise *Élémentaire*, HAY
et textile *Rivi*, Artek
Impression chez Charles,
The Wrong Shop
Encre sur papier
Poster, The Wrong Shop
Vase *Nuage*, Vitra
Encre sur serviette en papier
Encre sur serviette en papier

PAGE 234
Clouds, Kvadrat et encre
sur papier
Affiche, conférence
Maquette, projet *Belvédère*,
Rennes, France
Encre sur papier
Encre sur papier
Encre sur papier
Exposition « Bivouac », Centre
Pompidou-Metz, France
Encre et peinture sur papier
Encre sur papier

PAGE 235
Conférence, théâtre de Liège,
Belgique
Encre et peinture sur papier
Chaise *Belleville* et bureau *Cyl*,
Vitra
Lampe *Lighthouse*,
Established & Sons
Chaînes, aluminium, Galerie kreo
Test d'accrochage, lustre *Gabriel*
Encre sur papier
Encre sur papier
Encre sur papier

2018/Décembre

PAGE 236
Encre sur papier
Poubelle
Fabrication, *Les Fontaines
des Champs-Élysées*, Paris
Encre sur papier
Encre sur papier
Encre sur papier
Fabrication, *Les Fontaines
des Champs-Élysées*, Paris
Graphite, bloc-notes d'hôtel
Exposition « Rétrospective »,
Frac Bretagne, Rennes,
France

PAGE 237
Graphite sur papier
Encre sur papier
Graphite sur papier
Graphite sur bois
Préparation, exposition de
dessins, Galerie kreo, Paris
Préparation, exposition de
dessins, Galerie kreo, Paris

PAGE 238
Encre sur papier
Encre sur papier
Dessins de nuit, maison, Paris
Tests de soudure
Encre sur papier aluminium
Ombre des maquettes,
*Les Fontaines des Champs-
Élysées*, cour de l'atelier,
Paris
Cristal Swarovski,
*Les Fontaines des Champs-
Élysées*, Paris
Cristal Swarovski,
*Les Fontaines des Champs-
Élysées*, Paris
Maison, Bretagne, France

PAGE 239
Préparation, exposition de
dessins, Galerie kreo, Paris
Chaînes, plâtre, Galerie kreo
Installation en hommage à
Zaha Hadid, caserne des
pompiers, campus Vitra,
Weil am Rhein, Allemagne
Chaise *Palissade*, acier
galvanisé, HAY
Encre sur papier
Encre sur papier

2019/Janvier

PAGE 240
Encre sur papier
Bureau-étagère *Kaari*, Artek
Table *Kaari*, Artek
Encre sur papier
Encre sur papier
Encre sur papier
Vases *Alcova*, WonderGlass
Encre sur papier

PAGE 241
Atelier céramique de Jean-
Marie, Bourgogne, France

PAGE 242
Encre sur papier
Maquette, aménagement
des intérieurs, Bourse
de commerce – Pinault
Collection, Paris
Encre sur papier
Assemblage du cristal
Swarovski, *Les Fontaines
des Champs-Élysées*, Paris
Assemblage du cristal
Swarovski, *Les Fontaines
des Champs-Élysées*, Paris
Préparation, exposition de
dessins, Galerie kreo, Paris
Dessin numérique d'Erwan
Maquettes, *Les Fontaines
des Champs-Élysées*, Paris
Croquis, *Les Fontaines
des Champs-Élysées*, Paris

PAGE 243
Encre sur papier
Encre sur papier
Encre sur papier
Tubes en cupro-aluminium,
*Les Fontaines des Champs-
Élysées*, Paris

Fauteuils *Palissade*, HAY,
sous la neige
Hôtel, Innsbruck, Autriche
Site industriel Swarovski,
Wattens, Autriche
Préparation, exposition de
dessins, Galerie kreo, Paris
Prémontage, *Les Fontaines
des Champs-Élysées*, Paris

2019/Février

PAGE 244
Table à dessin et tabouret,
maison, Paris
Atelier, Paris
Maquette, exposition de
dessins, Galerie kreo
Maison, Bretagne, France
Atelier, Bretagne, France
Photomontage, aménagement,
restaurant La Halle
aux grains, Bourse de
commerce – Pinault
Collection, Paris
Chez l'encadreur
Chez l'encadreur
Chez l'encadreur

PAGE 245
Prémontage, *Les Fontaines
des Champs-Élysées*, Paris
Sélection, exposition de
dessins, Galerie kreo, Paris
Test de guipure
Rideau *Chainette*, Kvadrat,
atelier, Paris
Vase *Alcova*, WonderGlass
Encre sur papier
Accrochage, exposition de
dessins, Galerie kreo, Paris
Accrochage, exposition de
dessins, Galerie kreo, Paris
Test de guipure

PAGE 246
Maquettes, *Les Fontaines
des Champs-Élysées*, Paris
Accrochage, exposition
de dessins, Galerie kreo,
Paris
Collage
Croquis, chapiteau
Projet *Toit circulaire*, exposition
« Rêveries urbaines »
Les mâts, *Les Fontaines des
Champs-Élysées*, Atelier
blam, Nantes, France

LISTE DES ŒUVRES

PAGE 247
Exposition de dessins, Galerie kreo, paris
Exposition de dessins, Galerie kreo, paris
Exposition de dessins, Galerie kreo, paris
Exposition de dessins, Galerie kreo, paris
Croquis, *Les Fontaines des Champs-Élysées*, Paris
Crayon de couleur sur une photographie de maquette d'une fontaine
Vase *Alcova*, WonderGlass
Exposition de dessins, Galerie kreo, Paris
Installation, *Les Fontaines des Champs-Élysées*, Paris

2019/Mars

PAGE 248
Les Fontaines des Champs-Élysées, Paris
Assemblage du cristal Swarovski, *Les Fontaines des Champs-Élysées*, Paris
Vases *Découpage*
Moteur pour la rotation, *Les Fontaines des Champs-Élysées*, Paris
Les Fontaines des Champs-Élysées, Paris
Détail, *Les Fontaines des Champs-Élysées*, Paris
Un cadeau pour Rolf
Croquis, projet *Belvédère*, Rennes, France
Fonte des tubes avant usinage des mâts, *Les Fontaines des Champs-Élysées*, Paris

PAGE 249
Les Fontaines des Champs-Élysées, Paris
Encre sur papier
Prémontage, *Les Fontaines des Champs-Élysées*, Atelier blam, Nantes, France
Encre sur papier
Les Fontaines des Champs-Élysées, Paris
Encre sur papier

PAGE 250
Chaise longue *Quindici*, Mattiazzi
Encre sur papier
Atelier céramique de Jean-Marie, Bourgogne, France
Exposition de dessins, Galerie kreo, Paris
Portrait par Inga
Vases *Découpage*

2019/Avril

PAGE 251
Maquettes, projet *Belvédère*, Rennes, France
Programme, Salone del Mobile de Milan
Vases *Découpage*
Stand Vitra, Salone del Mobile de Milan
Suspension *Belt*, Flos
Pièces en bois sculpté et polychrome réalisées par les artisans, édition Wakabayashi, Kyoto
Vase *Découpage*
Vase *Découpage*
Vase *Découpage*

PAGE 252
Encre sur papier
Encre sur papier
Encre sur papier
Encre sur papier
Maquettes, projet *Belvédère*, Rennes, France
Fauteuil *Quindici*, Mattiazzi

PAGE 253
Composition, vase *Découpage*

PAGE 254
Détail, chaise *Palissade*, acier galvanisé, HAY
Maison, Bretagne, France
Lampe *W153 Île*, Wästberg, d'Inga Sempé, vase *Nuage*, Vitra et huile sur toile
Chaise *Palissade*, acier galvanisé, HAY
Motifs, tissu *Rivi*, Artek
Rolf et banc *Ring*, campus Vitra, Weil am Rhein, Allemagne
Livre *18*, éditions Nieves
Livre *18*, éditions Nieves

Projet *Abris*, exposition « Rêveries urbaines »

2019/Mai

PAGE 255
Exposition « Rêveries urbaines », Les Champs Libres, Rennes, France
Installation, *Algues*, Vitra, Séoul, Corée du Sud
Stylo-bille sur papier
Graphite sur papier
Navigation de la *Maison flottante*, conçue avec Jean-Marie Finot et Denis Daversin, architectes
Graphite sur papier

PAGE 256
Encre et peinture sur papier
Projet *Toit*, exposition « Rêveries urbaines »
Atelier, Bretagne, France
Chaise *Palissade*, acier galvanisé, HAY
Maquette secrète
Encre sur papier

PAGE 257
Encre sur papier
Exposition de dessins, Galerie kreo, Paris
Céramique *Rombini*, Mutina
Encre sur papier
Maquette, aménagement des extérieurs, Bourse de commerce – Pinault Collection, Paris
Casque de chantier
Portrait dans l'atelier
Vase *Découpage*
Test de kilim par Nanimarquina et chaise *Palissade*, HAY

2019/Juin

PAGE 258
Dessin sur image numérique, projet *Belvédère*, Rennes, France
Croquis sur une table en bois, projet *Belvédère*, Rennes, France
Maquette, lustre *Gabriel*, château de Versailles, France
Encre sur bloc-notes d'hôtel
Maquette, aménagement des intérieurs, Bourse

de commerce – Pinault Collection, Paris
Encre sur papier
Encre sur papier
Dessins
Stylo-bille sur papier

PAGE 259
Encre, peinture, cellophane coloré et ruban adhésif sur papier
Chaînes, plâtre, Galerie kreo
Collage de recherche, paravent *Rayures*, Glas Italia
Stylo-bille, ruban adhésif et gommettes sur papier
Vase *Découpage* et encre sur papier
Rideau *Guipure*
Dessin, galerie de Giorgio Mastinu, Venise
Encre sur papier
Tests, mobiles, Atelier blam, Nantes, France

PAGE 260
Encre sur papier
Promenade Nuage, Miami
Caisse, exposition « Album »
Encre sur papier
Projet secret
L'équipe avec Aurélien, Atelier blam, Nantes, France
Prototypes, rideau *Rennes*, Kvadrat
Bougeoir *Officina*, Magis
Graphite sur papier

2019/Juillet

PAGE 261
Encre sur papier
Encre sur papier
Encre sur papie
Atelier, Paris
Dessin en mer
Encre et peinture sur papier

2019/Août

PAGE 262
Atelier, Bretagne, France
Encre sur papier
Lampe *Matin*, HAY, d'Inga Sempé, maison, Bretagne, France
Encre sur papier
Peinture, atelier WANC, maison, Bretagne, France

Encre sur papier
Sieste
Portemanteau *Officina*, Magis
Chaise longue *Quindici*, Mattiazzi

PAGE 263
Encre sur papier
Encre sur papier
Les chats à l'ombre
Atelier, Bretagne, France
Atelier, Bretagne, France
Chaise *Pila*, Magis et paravent *Screen 100* d'Alvar Aalto
Bonne pêche avec Bernard
Encre sur papier
Encre sur papier

PAGE 264
Encre sur papier
Atelier, Bretagne, France
Encre et ruban adhésif sur papier
Mette, atelier, Bretagne, France
Les chats font la sieste dans la *Slow Chair*, Vitra
Maquettes, projet *Belvédère*, Rennes, France, sur ma table, atelier, Paris
Stylo-bille sur papier
Encre sur papier
Encre sur papier

2019/Septembre

PAGE 265
Atelier, Bretagne, France

PAGE 266
Annonce, conférence à Quimperlé, France
Encre sur papier
Encre sur papier
Encre sur papier
Maquette échelle 1 emmaillotée, rocher, Bourse de commerce – Pinault Collection, Paris
Avec Michel Bras, atelier, Paris
Encre sur papier
Encre sur papier
Nuit d'encre

PAGE 267
Session surf
Maquette, lustre, vestibule, Bourse de commerce – Pinault Collection, Paris

Avec Clémence et Didier
   à Londres
Vase *Découpage* sur table
   d'Alvar Aalto et
   lampe *W153 Île*,
   Wästberg, d'Inga Sempé
Maquette, vestibule, Bourse
   de commerce – Pinault
   Collection, Paris
Encre sur papier

2019/Octobre

PAGE 268
Encre sur papier
Collaboration avec Virgil Abloh
   et Off-White
Catalogue, exposition
   « Surrealism and Design »,
   Vitra Design Museum,
   Weil am Rhein, Allemagne
Conférence
Encre sur papier
Fabrication, moule pour
   le coffrage de la base,
   projet *Belvédère*
Avec Erwan, vers 2002
Lampe *W153 Île*, Wästberg,
   d'Inga Sempé et vase *Nuage*,
   Vitra
Vases *Fenêtre*, maison Matisse

PAGE 269
Encre sur papier
Projet secret
Encre et peinture sur papier
Polyptyque, encre sur papier
   et fauteuil *Cotone*, Cassina
Vases *Fenêtre*, Maison Matisse
Exposition, galerie de Giorgio
   Mastinu, Venise
Atelier, Bretagne, France
Lampe *W103*, Wästberg, d'Inga
   Sempé et vase *Nuage*, Vitra
Encre sur papier

PAGE 270
Encre sur papier

PAGE 271
Vases *Découpage*
Encre sur papier
Encre sur papier
Prototypes, chaise
Vases *Alcova*, WonderGlass
Bien amarré
Collier *Perles*, marbre de
   Carrare, Galerie kreo

Encre sur papier
Encre sur papier

2019/Novembre

PAGE 272
Encre sur papier
Collage
Collage
Encre sur papier
Recherches, bas-relief
Encre sur papier

PAGE 273
Vases *Découpage*
Vases *Découpage*
Atelier de céramique de
   Jean-Marie, Bourgogne,
   France
L'enthousiasme d'un nouveau
   projet
Image numérique, projet
   Belvédère, Rennes, France
Exposition « Rétrospective »,
   Frac Bretagne, Rennes,
   France
Maquette, quart de chaise
   Élémentaire, HAY
Détail, chaise *Élémentaire*, HAY
Être empêché

PAGE 274
Banc *Ring*, place Charles-VII,
   Poitiers, France
Encre et ruban adhésif
   sur papier
Encre et ruban adhésif
   sur papier
Installation, pieu, projet
   Belvédère, Rennes, France
Image numérique, projet
   Belvédère, Rennes, France
Signature, éditions limitées,
   The Wrong Shop

PAGE 275
Maquette, projet *Belvédère*,
   Rennes, France

PAGE 276
Encre et ruban adhésif
   sur papier
Encre et ruban adhésif
   sur papier
Encre et ruban adhésif
   sur papier
Encre sur papier
Pièce en bois sculpté
   et polychrome réalisés
   par les artisans, édition

Wakabayashi, Kyoto
Croquis sur bloc-notes d'hôtel
Encre et ruban adhésif
   sur papier

2019/Décembre

PAGE 277
Encre sur serviette en papier
Maquettes, lunettes *Sugata*,
   Jins
En voyage à Kyoto
Croquis architectural, Kyoto
Carnet, Kyoto
Protection thermique
   des végétaux, Kyoto

PAGE 278
Pièce en bois sculpté et
   polychrome réalisés
   par les artisans, édition
   Wakabayashi, Kyoto

PAGE 279
Jardin, Kyoto
Paravent *Rayures*, Glas Italia
Dessous, vase *Ruutu*,
   céramique, littala
Encre sur papier
Nitouche descendant l'escalier
Une des premières maquettes,
   chaise *Palissade*, HAY
Stylo-bille sur papier
Croquis
Préparation, coulée du béton,
   projet *Belvédère*, Rennes,
   France

PAGE 280
Fleurs, littala
Atelier, Bretagne, France
Encre et ruban adhésif
   sur papier
Atelier, Bretagne, France
Encre et ruban adhésif
   sur papier
Encre sur papier, Bretagne,
   France

PAGE 281
Prototype, chaise
Encre et ruban adhésif
   sur papier
Encre et ruban adhésif
   sur papier
Encre et ruban adhésif
   sur papier
Encre et ruban adhésif
   sur papier
Bretagne, France

Table à dessin, maison,
   Bretagne, France
Épines
Ronce
Atelier, Bretagne, France

2020/Janvier

PAGE 282
Maquettes, projet *Belvédère*,
   Rennes, sur ma table, atelier,
   Paris
Stylo-bille sur papier
Encre, ruban adhésif et
   gommette sur papier
Fauteuil *Officina*, Magis
Encre et ruban adhésif
   sur papier
Cintrage d'un élément, projet
   Belvédère, Rennes, France
Didier et *Objet lumineux*,
   Galerie kreo
Atelier, Paris
Dédicace à Jesper qui
   travaillait chez HAY

PAGE 283
Rope Chair, Artek
Détail, *Rope Chair*, Artek
Détail, *Rope Chair*, Artek
Vase *Erkkeri*, littala
Encre et ruban adhésif
   sur papier
Encre sur papier, maison, Paris
Encre et ruban adhésif
   sur papier
Encre sur papier, maison, Paris
Fleurs, littala et vases *Erkkeri*,
   littala

PAGE 284
Le grand débarras, atelier,
   Paris
Bureau *Kaari*, Artek et *Rope
   Chair*, Artek
Rope Chair, Artek, atelier,
   Bretagne, France
Maquette, projet *Belvédère*,
   Rennes, France
Tests de verre soufflé,
   luminaires, projet *Belvédère*,
   Rennes, France
Portemanteau *Tupla*, Artek

2020/Février

PAGE 285
Vases *Erkkeri*, littala

Affiche, exposition
   « Imperfections », Stockholm
Rope Chair, Artek
Exposition « Imperfections »,
   Stockholm
Fleurs, littala et vase *Ruutu*,
   littala
Exposition « Imperfections »,
   Stockholm
Graphite sur papier kraft
Encre et ruban adhésif
   sur papier
Encre et ruban adhésif
   sur papier

PAGE 286
Maquette, projet *Belvédère*,
   Rennes, France
Image numérique, projet
   Belvédère, Rennes, France
Atelier, Paris
Encre et ruban adhésif
   sur papier
Encre et ruban adhésif
   sur papier
Encre et ruban adhésif
   sur papier
Ma table, atelier, Paris
Maquette, rocher,
   aménagement des
   extérieurs, Bourse de
   commerce – Pinault
   Collection, Paris
Test, rideau *Guipure*,
   restaurant, Bourse de
   commerce – Pinault
   Collection, Paris

PAGE 287
*Les Fontaines des Champs-
   Élysées*, Paris

PAGE 288
Séance photo, *Rope Chair*,
   Artek
Maquette d'implantation sur
   la Vilaine, projet *Belvédère*,
   Rennes, France
Pastel et ruban adhésif
   sur papier kraft
Pastel et ruban adhésif
   sur papier kraft
Rope Chair, Artek, rotonde,
   Bourse de commerce –
   Pinault Collection, Paris
Rope Chair, Artek, en attente
   d'être déployées,
   rotonde, Bourse de

LISTE DES ŒUVRES

commerce – Pinault
Collection, Paris
Pastel, ruban adhésif et
graphite sur papier kraft
Maquette, aménagement
des extérieurs, Bourse
de commerce – Pinault
Collection, Paris
Encre et ruban adhésif
sur papier

2020/Mars

PAGE 289
Maquette, rocher,
aménagement des
extérieurs, Bourse de
commerce – Pinault
Collection, Paris
Détail, mobile, projet *Belvédère*,
Rennes, France
Encre sur papier
Vase *Cloud*, céramique,
édition limitée
Vase *Découpage*
Encre et ruban adhésif
sur papier
Accrochage de dessins
Encre et ruban adhésif
sur papier
Encre et ruban adhésif
sur papier

PAGE 290
Vue de la fenêtre de mon
appartement sur l'école
ouverte pour les enfants
des soignants pendant le
premier confinement
Encre et ruban adhésif
sur papier
Table à dessin, maison, Paris
Murs et table à dessin, maison,
Paris
Encre et ruban adhésif
sur papier
Murs et table à dessin, maison,
Paris

PAGE 291
Hommage aux boulangers
travaillant pendant la
pandémie de Covid-19
Mur et table à dessin, maison,
Paris
Soutien aux professions
mobilisées pendant
le confinement

Accrochage de dessins,
maison, Paris
Soutien aux professions
mobilisées pendant
le confinement
Encre et ruban adhésif
sur papier
Soutien aux professions
mobilisées pendant
le confinement
Accrochage de dessins
Maison, Paris

PAGE 292
Encre et ruban adhésif
sur papier
Décrochage
Croquis, Maison sur pilotis
Encre sur papier
Téléviseur *The Serif*, Samsung
et *Armoire souple*,
Moustache, d'Inga Sempé,
maison, Paris
Encre sur papier
Encre sur papier
Encre sur papier
Encre sur papier

2020/Avril

PAGE 293
Mon portrait par Mette
Encre sur papier
Encre sur papier
Recherches, chapiteau sur l'eau
Projet *Toit et Rochers*,
exposition « Rêveries
urbaines »
Accrochage et table à dessin,
maison, Paris
Accrochage et chaise
Steelwood, Magis, maison,
Paris
Fusain sur papier
Dessin, cuisine, Paris

PAGE 294
Vases *Découpage*, Vitra
Collage et stylo-bille
sur papier
Collage et stylo-bille
sur papier
Vase *Découpage*, Vitra
Dessin d'Inga cousant des
masques en tissu
Encre sur papier
Le chat et *L'Oiseau*, Vitra
Inga montant l'escalier,

maison, Paris
Vases *Découpage*, Vitra

2020/Mai

PAGE 295
Vases *Découpage*, Vitra

PAGE 296
Croquis
Dessins scotchés au mur,
maison, Paris
Encre sur papier
Encre sur papier
Nature morte
Encre sur papier

PAGE 297
Accrochage, maison, Paris
Accrochage, maison, Paris
Portrait devant la table à dessin
Graphite sur papier
Accrochage, maison, Paris
Graphite sur papier
Graphite sur papier
Graphite sur papier et chaise
Steelwood, Magis
Graphite sur papier

PAGE 298
Graphite sur papier
Encre sur papier
Encre sur papier
Encre et ruban adhésif
sur papier
Graphite sur papier
Stylo-bille sur papier

PAGE 299
Stylo-bille sur papier
Encre sur papier
Stylo-bille sur papier
Stylo-bille sur bois
Accrochage et table à dessin,
maison, Paris
Dessins encadrés

PAGE 300
Dernier jour de confinement

PAGE 301
Le retour à l'atelier, Paris
Accrochage, maison, Paris
Accrochage, maison, Paris
Encre sur papier
Crayon de couleur sur papier
Atelier, Paris
Première sortie de Paris

après des semaines
de confinement
Encre sur papier
Debout sur les chaises
Palissade, HAY

2020/Juin

PAGE 302
Black Lives Matter
Chaises et table *Palissade*, HAY
Vase *Nuage*, Vitra et
pâquerette
Bonjour
Graphite sur papier
Ma table, atelier, Paris

PAGE 303
Salle de réunion dans la cour,
atelier, Paris
Chaise *Palissade*, HAY
Pastel et graphite sur papier
Encre sur papier
Accrochage, maison, Paris
Fleurs, littala
Accrochage, maison, Paris
Ombre, chaise et table
Palissade, HAY
Vase *Erkkeri*, littala

PAGE 304
Vase *Nuage*, Vitra et fougère,
maison, Bretagne, France
Encre sur papier
Encre sur papier
Encre sur papier
Encre sur papier
Atelier de céramique
de Jean-Marie, Bourgogne,
France
Encre sur papier
Vase *Découpage* et fougère,
maison, Bretagne, France
Chaise longue *Quindici*,
Mattiazzi et bougeoir
Officina, Magis

PAGE 305
Poster de vœux, ville de
Rennes, atelier, Paris
Impression sur papier,
The Wrong Shop
Chaise *Végétal*, Vitra
Recherches, chaise
en bronze
Encre sur papier
Vase *Découpage* et *Rope Chair*,
Artek

Accrochage, maison, Paris
Encre sur papier
Encre sur papier

2020/Juillet

PAGE 306
Rope Chair, Artek, rotonde,
Bourse de commerce –
Pinault Collection, Paris

PAGE 307
Cloud, polystyrène, atelier,
Bretagne, France
Vases *Erkkeri*, littala
Mobile éolien, projet
Belvédère, Atelier blam,
Nantes, France
Encre et ruban adhésif
sur papier
Vases *Découpage*, Vitra
et poster, The Wrong Shop
Impression sur papier,
The Wrong Shop
Encre sur papier
Vase *Découpage*, Vitra
devant une affiche
d'Ellsworth Kelly
Poster, The Wrong Shop

PAGE 308
Maquette, rocher,
aménagement des
extérieurs, Bourse de
commerce – Pinault
Collection, Paris
Encre sur papier
Encre sur papier
Détail, chaise longue *Quindici*,
Matiazzi
Détail, chaise *Hole*, Cappellini
Encre sur papier
Algues, Vitra
Vase *Découpage*, Vitra
et *Rope Chair*, Artek
Encre sur papier

PAGE 309
Promenade Nuage, Miami
Croquis sur une table en bois,
projet *Belvédère*, Rennes,
France
Corolle et pieu, projet
Belvédère, Rennes, France
Détail, assemblage des
haubans à la structure
principale, projet *Belvédère*,
Rennes, France

Maquette d'implantation sur la Vilaine, projet *Belvédère*, Rennes, France
Vases *Découpage*, Vitra

PAGE 310
Chaises et table *Palissade*, acier galvanisé, HAY
Atelier de céramique de Jean-Marie, Bourgogne, France
Étiquette de vin pour Château Marsau
Chutes d'argile
Rolf et banc *Ring*, campus Vitra, Weil am Rhein, Allemagne
Maquette d'implantation, lustre, vestibule, Bourse de commerce – Pinault Collection, Paris
Test de fonctionnement d'un élément, lustre, vestibule, Bourse de commerce – Pinault Collection, Paris
Maison, Bretagne, France
Chaise longue *Palissade*, HAY

2020/Août

PAGE 311
Chaise longue *Palissade*, HAY, dans le brouillard
Chaise longue et fauteuil *Palissade*, HAY
Encre sur papier
Détail, *Rope Chair*, Artek et céramique, auteur inconnu
Encre sur papier
Carnet sur le rocher
Encre sur papier
Rope Chair, Artek
Encre et ruban adhésif sur papier

PAGE 312
Encre sur papier
Vase *Erkkeri*, Iitala
Rope Chair, Artek, toit-terrasse, Bretagne, France
Chaise longue *Palissade*, HAY
Portrait dans l'atelier, Bretagne, France
Encre sur papier
Encre sur papier
Détail, atelier, Bretagne, France
Maison, Bretagne, France

PAGE 313
Encre sur papier

PAGE 314
Vase *Découpage*, Vitra et banc *Corde*
Chaise longue *Palissade*, HAY
Deux vertèbres
Graphite sur papier
Maison, Bretagne, France
Nitouche et lampe *Piani*, Flos
Les cuillères en bois de mon père
Encre sur papier
Encre sur papier

PAGE 315
Encre sur papier
Encre sur papier
Encre sur papier
Vase *Découpage*, Vitra
Maquette, projet *Belvédère*, Rennes, France
Détail, chaise *Uncino*, Mattiazzi

2020/Septembre

PAGE 316
Poster, The Wrong Shop
Diptyque, encre sur papier
Encre sur papier
Rope Chair, Artek, dessin encadré et miroir *Flou*, Galerie kreo, atelier, Paris
Test d'impression, The Wrong Shop
Banc *Ring*, siège de Kvadrat, Ebeltoft, Danemark
Banc *Ring*, siège de Kvadrat, Ebeltoft, Danemark
Atelier, Bretagne, France
Réception de céramique que j'ai découpée en Bourgogne, atelier, Paris

PAGE 317
Projet *Belvédère*, Rennes, France
Maquette, projet *Belvédère*, Rennes, France
Projet *Belvédère*, Rennes, France
Projet *Belvédère*, Rennes, France
Reflet dans la Vilaine, projet *Belvédère*, Rennes, France
Projet *Belvédère*, Rennes, France

PAGE 318
Nouvelle rambarde en fer forgé,

maison, Bretagne, France
Terrasse, Bretagne, France
Détail, rambarde en fer forgé, maison, Bretagne, France
Rope Chair, Artek, et banc *Corde*, terrasse, Bretagne, France
Encre sur papier
Hortensia
Encre sur papier
Rocher bronze avant polissage, aménagement des extérieurs, Bourse de commerce – Pinault Collection, Paris
Moule, rocher bronze, aménagement des extérieurs, Bourse de commerce – Pinault Collection, Paris

PAGE 319
Reflet dans la Vilaine, projet *Belvédère*, Rennes, France

PAGE 320
Vase *Alcova*, WonderGlass
Atelier, Paris
Atelier, Bretagne, France
Test d'impression, The Wrong Shop
Impression sur papier, The Wrong Shop
Encre sur papier
Encre sur papier
Hommage à Enzo Mari
Maquettes, projet *Belvédère*, Rennes, France
Annonce, conférence

2020/Octobre

PAGE 321
Rope Chair, Artek et encre sur papier, exposition, centre d'art Piacé Le Radieux, Piacé, France
Manteau sur chaise secrète
Vase *Découpage*, Vitra, vase *Nuage*, Vitra et *Rope Chair*, Artek
Encre sur papier
Encre sur papier et chaise *Steelwood*, Magis
Encre sur papier et ruban adhésif
Encre sur papier et ruban adhésif

Détail, rocher bronze avant patine, aménagement des extérieurs, Bourse de commerce – Pinault Collection, Paris
Chaises longues *Palissade*, HAY, terrasse, Bretagne, France

PAGE 322
Impression des posters, The Wrong Shop
Assemblage, lustre *Gabriel*, cristal Swarovski, château de Versailles, France
Étiquette de vin pour Château Marsau
Encre sur papier
Banc et cheminée *Ring*, installation *OUI*, parc du Kunsthal Aarhus, Danemark
Encre sur papier
Encre sur papier
Encre sur papier
Livre *Crayon-Pinceau*, éditions Nieves

2020/Novembre

PAGE 323
Paroi *Cloud*, exposition « Bivouac », Museum of Contemporary Art, Chicago
Drapeau américain blanc, *New York Times*
Emballages, vases *Découpage*, Vitra
Recherches pour une nouvelle version du banc *Ring*
Poster, The Wrong Shop
Autour de Manhattan sur un bateau de la Coupe de l'America, New York

PAGE 324
Poster, The Wrong Shop
Impression sur un porte-cartes d'Enzo Mari
Rope Chair, Artek, sous bâche
Installation, banc, aménagement des extérieurs, Bourse de commerce – Pinault Collection, Paris
Encre sur papier
Encre sur papier
Carte de remerciements
Encre sur papier
Encre sur papier

PAGE 325
Encre sur papier
Livre *Crayon-Pinceau*, éditions Nieves
Encre sur papier
Encre sur papier
Encre sur papier
Poster, The Wrong Shop
Atelier, Paris
Encre sur papier
Rope Chair, Artek

PAGE 326
Pièces en verre coulé, lustre, vestibule, Bourse de commerce – Pinault Collection, Paris
Prototype de lampe et miroir *Flou*, Galerie kreo, restaurant La Halle aux grains, Bourse de commerce – Pinault Collection, Paris
Détail, lustre, vestibule, Bourse de commerce – Pinault Collection, Paris
Encre sur papier
Encre sur papier
Encre sur papier
Encre sur papier
Vase *Découpage*, Vitra et tôle d'aluminium anodisé
Soirée

2020/Décembre

PAGE 327
Accrochage, maison, Paris

PAGE 328
Encre sur papier
Chaise longue *Palissade*, HAY, dans la brume, Bretagne, France
Encre sur papier
Encre sur papier
Rope Chair, Artek, rotonde, Bourse de commerce – Pinault Collection, Paris
Maquette d'implantation, suspension *Luce orizzontale*, vestibule, Bourse de commerce – Pinault Collection, Paris
Maquette d'implantation, suspension *Luce orizzontale*, vestibule, Bourse de commerce

LISTE DES ŒUVRES

– Pinault Collection, Paris
Banc *Cotone*, Cassina, *Rope Chair*, Artek et banc *Corde*, rotonde, Bourse de commerce – Pinault Collection, Paris
Des dessins

PAGE 329
Dessins scotchés, maison, Paris
Restaurant La Halle aux grains, Bourse de commerce – Pinault Collection, Paris
Atelier, Bretagne, France
Encre sur papier
Maquette, aménagement des extérieurs, Bourse de commerce – Pinault Collection, Paris
Projet *Belvédère*, Rennes, France

PAGE 330
Maquette, banc, rocher et drapeau, aménagement des extérieurs, Bourse de commerce – Pinault Collection, Paris
Vase *Erkkeri*, Iittala, maison, Bretagne, France
Nuit d'encre, Bretagne, France
Livre *Crayon-Pinceau*, éditions Nieves
Chaise longue *Palissade*, HAY, toit-terrasse, Bretagne, France
Vase *Découpage*, maison, Bretagne, France

2021/Janvier

PAGE 331
Détail, banquette *Cotone*, Cassina, vestibule, Bourse de commerce – Pinault Collection, Paris
Maquette, rocher, aménagement des extérieurs, Bourse de commerce – Pinault Collection, Paris
Dessin encadré, photo et banc *Diapositive*, Glas Italia, maison, Bretagne, France
Détail, miroir *Flou*, Galerie kreo et vase *Alcova*, WonderGlass
Les Fontaines des Champs-Élysées, Paris

Encre sur papier
Encre sur papier
Encre sur papier
Rope Chair, Artek, Bourse de commerce – Pinault Collection, Paris

PAGE 332
Parvis, Bourse de commerce – Pinault Collection, Paris

PAGE 333
Parvis, Bourse de commerce – Pinault Collection, Paris
Stylo-bille sur papier
Stylo-bille sur papier
Détail, banc et rocher, parvis, Bourse de commerce – Pinault Collection, Paris
Projet *Belvédère*, Rennes, France
Stylo-bille sur papier
Banc, parvis, Bourse de commerce – Pinault Collection, Paris
Stylo-bille sur papier
Stylo-bille sur papier

PAGE 334
Maquette, drapeau et rocher, Bourse de commerce – Pinault Collection, Paris
Tapis *Wilton*, tissé, Galerie kreo, banc et table *Cotone*, Cassina, aménagement des intérieurs, Bourse de commerce – Pinault Collection, Paris
Maquette, drapeau, Bourse de commerce – Pinault Collection, Paris
Détail, tapis *Wilton*, tissé, Galerie kreo, Bourse de commerce – Pinault Collection, Paris
Photomontage, banquettes et tapis, Bourse de commerce – Pinault Collection, Paris
Maquette, pavillon

2021/Février

PAGE 335
Maquette, pavillon pour une installation permanente de la sculpture *Lincoln* de Pascal Rivet
Encre sur papier

Encre sur papier
Encre sur papier
Stylo-bille sur papier
Rencontre fortuite

PAGE 336
Détail, drapeau, Bourse de commerce – Pinault Collection, Paris
Reflet dans la Vilaine, projet *Belvédère*, Rennes, France
Stylo-bille sur papier
Maquette, aménagement des extérieurs, Bourse de commerce – Pinault Collection, Paris
Maquette, aménagement des extérieurs, Bourse de commerce – Pinault Collection, Paris
Stylo-bille sur papier
Stylo-bille et encre colorée sur papier
Stylo-bille et encre colorée sur papier
Stylo-bille et encre colorée sur papier

PAGE 337
Maquette échelle 1, banc, rocher et drapeau, Bourse de commerce – Pinault Collection, Paris
Stylo-bille sur papier
Stylo-bille et encre colorée sur papier
Séance photo, *L'Oiseau*, Vitra, atelier, Paris
Maison, Bretagne, France
Stylo-bille et encre colorée sur papier

PAGE 338
Détail, drapeau, Bourse de commerce – Pinault Collection, Paris

PAGE 339
Dessin encadré
Stylo-bille sur papier
Stylo-bille et encre colorée sur papier
Dessin encadré dans sa boîte d'expédition
Encre sur papier
Encre sur papier
Détail, chaise *Filo*, Mattiazzi

Stylo-bille sur papier
Stylo-bille sur papier

PAGE 340
Stylo-bille et encre colorée sur papier
Stylo-bille et encre colorée sur papier
Dessin imprimé, showroom Artek, Helsinki
Dessins, mur, maison, Paris
Profil, chaise *Filo*, Mattiazzi
Exposition de dessins, Licht Gallery, Tokyo

PAGE 341
Maquette, chaise fatiguée
Stylo-bille sur papier
Lampe *Lighthouse*, Established & Sons, stylo-bille et encre colorée sur papier
Stylo-bille et encre colorée sur papier
Dessins encadrés, atelier, Paris
Stylo-bille et encre colorée sur papier

2021/Mars

PAGE 342
Rope Chair, Artek et encre sur papier, exposition, centre d'art Piacé Le Radieux, Piacé, France
Stylo-bille et encre colorée sur papier
Le voleur de cerises
Ma table à dessin, Paris
Stylo-bille et encre colorée sur papier
Maquette, banc, rocher et drapeau, Bourse de commerce – Pinault Collection, Paris

PAGE 343
Tests d'impression
Test d'impression
Vase *Ruutu*, Iittala, fenêtre, atelier, Paris
Encre sur papier
Encre sur papier
Collage
Article, *Purple Magazine*
Détail, chaise *Osso*, Mattiazzi
Pleine lune, Bretagne, France

PAGE 344
Vase *Erkkeri*, Iittala, *Rope Chair*,

Artek et miroir *Vitrail*, Magis, d'Inga Sempé
Encre sur papier
Vase *Découpage*, Vitra et banc *Corde*
Algues
Maison flottante, Chatou, conçue avec Jean-Marie Finot et Denis Daversin, architectes
Maison flottante, Chatou, conçue avec Jean-Marie Finot et Denis Daversin, architectes
Encre et ruban adhésif sur papier
Stylo-bille et encre colorée sur papier
Stylo-bille et encre colorée sur papier

2021/Avril

PAGE 345
Stylo-bille et encre colorée sur papier

PAGE 346
Encre sur papier, atelier, Bretagne, France

PAGE 347
Atelier, Paris
Hangar
Fauteuil et chaise longue *Palissade*, HAY
Parvis, Bourse de commerce – Pinault Collection, Paris
Rope Chair, Artek, rotonde, Bourse de commerce – Pinault Collection, Paris
Séquençage des couleurs pour test d'impression
Séquençage des couleurs pour test d'impression
Encre et ruban adhésif sur papier
L'original et la reproduction

PAGE 348
Détail, *Rope Chair*, Artek
Accrochage, maison, Paris
Accrochage, maison, Paris
Encre sur papier
Vase *Nuage*, Vitra, Bretagne, France

Stylo-bille et encre colorée
	sur papier

PAGE 349
	Chaises longues *Palissade*, HAY
	Croquis de recherche, chaise
		longue *Palissade*, HAY
	Rope Chair, Artek, Bretagne,
		France
	Détail, rambarde en fer forgé
		et accoudoir de la chaise
		longue *Quindici*, Mattiazzi
	Chaises longues *Palissade*, HAY
	Banc *Corde*

2021/Mai

PAGE 350
	Accrochage, maison, Paris
	Accrochage, maison, Paris
	Encre sur papier
	Rolf et banc *Ring*, campus Vitra,
		Weil am Rhein, Allemagne
	Chaise *Filo*, Mattiazzi
	Slow Chair, Vitra

PAGE 351
	Encre sur papier

PAGE 352
	Posters, The Wrong Shop
	Encre sur papier
	Encre sur papier
	Poster, The Wrong Shop
	Mette, terrasse, Bretagne,
		France
	Squelette à la fenêtre

PAGE 353
	Banc *Ring* et *Fontaine longue*,
		jardin de Piet Oudolf,
		campus Vitra, Weil am Rhein,
		Allemagne
	Salle d'exposition pour
		miniatures Vitra, Vitra
		Design Museum, Weil am
		Rhein, Allemagne
	Croquis, salle d'exposition
		miniatures Vitra, Vitra
		Design Museum, Weil am
		Rhein, Allemagne
	Photomontage
	Lustre, Flos, Bourse de
		commerce – Pinault
		Collection, Paris
	Drapeau, Bourse
		de commerce – Pinault
		Collection, Paris

Lustre, Flos, Bourse de
	commerce – Pinault
	Collection, Paris
Rocher et banc, aménagement
	des extérieurs, Bourse
	de commerce – Pinault
	Collection, Paris
Aménagement des intérieurs,
	Bourse de commerce –
	Pinault Collection, Paris

PAGE 354
	Banc, parvis, Bourse de
		commerce – Pinault
		Collection, Paris
	Photomontage, tapis et
		banquettes, aménagement
		des intérieurs, Bourse de
		commerce – Pinault
		Collection, Paris
	Graphite sur papier
	Lustre, Flos, Bourse de
		commerce – Pinault
		Collection, Paris
	Graphite et encre sur papier
	Rope Chair, Artek

PAGE 355
	Drapeau, aménagement
		des extérieurs, Bourse
		de commerce – Pinault
		Collection, Paris

PAGE 356
	Posters, The Wrong Shop

PAGE 357
	Banc, parvis, Bourse de
		commerce – Pinault
		Collection, Paris
	Poster, The Wrong Shop
	Encre et ruban adhésif sur
		papier
	Chaises longues *Palissade*, HAY
	Chaises et table *Palissade*, acier
		galvanisé, HAY, terrasse,
		Bretagne, France
	Chaise *Hole*, Cappellini
	Dessins d'enfants, projet
		Belvédère, Rennes, France
	Dessins d'enfants, projet
		Belvédère, Rennes, France
	Accrochage, maison, Paris

2021/Juin

PAGE 358
	Parution

Test d'impression,
	The Wrong Shop
Encre sur papier
Mon coin d'atelier, Paris
Stylo-bille sur carton
Restaurant La Halle aux grains,
	Bourse de commerce
	– Pinault Collection, Paris

PAGE 359
	Rideau *Guipure* et suspension
		Luce verticale, Flos,
		restaurant La Halle aux
		grains, Bourse de commerce
		– Pinault Collection, Paris
	Signature des éditions,
		The Wrong Shop
	Restaurant La Halle aux grains,
		Bourse de commerce –
		Pinault Collection, Paris
	Maison, Bretagne, France
	Éditions, The Wrong Shop
	Chaise *Filo*, Mattiazzi

PAGE 360
	Atelier, Paris
	Fauteuil et chaise longue
		Palissade, HAY
	Atelier, Paris
	Recherches, assemblage
	Maquette, banc, rocher
		et drapeau, Bourse de
		commerce – Pinault
		Collection, Paris
	Peinture sur bois
	Publication
	Chez l'encadreur, Paris
	Maquette de recherche,
		mobiles éoliens

2021/Juillet

PAGE 361
	Banc *Ring*, siège de Kvadrat,
		Ebeltoft, Danemark

PAGE 362
	Graphite sur papier
	Recherches, estrade,
		aménagement des
		extérieurs, Bourse de
		commerce – Pinault
		Collection, Paris
	Recherches, bassin,
		aménagement des
		extérieurs, Bourse de
		commerce – Pinault
		Collection, Paris

Aquarelle
Céramique *Punto*, Mutina
Édition, The Wrong Shop
	et *Rope Chair*, Artek

PAGE 363
	Hortensias et vase *Nuage*, Vitra
	Fauteuil *Palissade*, HAY,
		toit-terrasse, Bretagne,
		France
	Édition, The Wrong Shop
	Crayon de couleur sur papier
	Hortensias et vase *Nuage*,
		Vitra, Bretagne, France
	10 années de projets avec
		Mutina, terrasse, Bretagne,
		France
	Céramique *Rombini*, Mutina
	Signature des éditions,
		The Wrong Shop
	Encre sur papier

PAGE 364
	Céramique *Punto*, Mutina
		et vase *Nuage*, Vitra

PAGE 365
	Encre sur papier
	Essai d'accrochage, exposition
		de dessins et bas-reliefs
	Dessin en couverture, *TLmag*
	Essai d'accrochage, exposition
		de dessins et bas-reliefs
	Rochers, Bretagne, France
	Essai d'accrochage, exposition
		de dessins et bas-reliefs

2021/Août

PAGE 366
	Maison, Bretagne, France
	Dessins, terrasse, Bretagne,
		France
	Stylo-bille et encre colorée
		sur papier
	Encre sur papier
	Stylo-bille sur papier
	Fauteuil *Palissade*, HAY,
		terrasse, Bretagne, France
	Vase *Découpage*, maison,
		Bretagne, France
	Stylo-bille sur papier
	Encre sur papier

PAGE 367
	Chaise longue et fauteuil
		Palissade, HAY
	Encre sur papier

Chaise *Filo*, Mattiazzi et lampe
	Aggregato d'Enzo Mari
Encre sur papier
Atelier, Bretagne, France
Encre sur papier

PAGE 368
	Céramique *Rombini*, brique
		Bloc, Mutina et banc *Corde*
	Dessin sur l'eau
	Encre sur papier
	Atelier, Bretagne, France
	Chaise *Uncino*, Mattiazzi
	Stylo-bille sur papier
	Céramique *Punto*, Mutina
		et vase *Découpage*
	Encre sur papier
	Encre sur papier

PAGE 369
	Atelier, Bretagne, France

2021/Septembre

PAGE 370
	Chaise *Filo*, Mattiazzi
	Maison, Bretagne, France
	Chaise *Filo*, Mattiazzi, *Rope
		Chair*, Artek et édition,
		The Wrong Shop
	Céramique *Punto*, Mutina
	Céramique *Punto*, Mutina
	Encre sur papier
	Encre sur papier
	Chaise *Filo*, Mattiazzi
	Brique *Bloc*, Mutina

PAGE 371
	Atelier de céramique
		de Jean-Marie, Bourgogne
	Atelier, Paris
	Essai d'accrochage, exposition
		de dessins et bas-reliefs
	Briques *Bloc*, Mutina
	Mon ombre portée et encre
		sur papier
	Briques *Bloc*, Mutina

PAGE 372
	Livres *Janvier* et *Stylo-Bille*,
		éditions Nieves

PAGE 373
	Encre sur papier
	Chaise *Filo*, Mattiazzi, et
		briques *Bloc*, Mutina
	Encre sur papier
	Encre sur papier

Chaises et tables *Palissade*, HAY,
  terrasse, musée Solomon R.
  Guggenheim, New York
Encre sur papier
Briques *Bloc*, Mutina
Banc *Ring* et *Fontaine longue*,
  jardin de Piet Oudolf,
  campus Vitra, Weil am Rhein,
  Allemagne
Projet *Belvédère*, Rennes,
  France

PAGE 374
Reflet dans la Vilaine, projet
  Belvédère, Rennes, France
Exposition « Ensemble »,
  Mutina, Sassuolo, Italie
Exposition « Ensemble »,
  Mutina, Sassuolo, Italie
Vases *Rombini*, Mutina
Encre sur papier
Briques *Bloc*, Mutina
Exposition « Ensemble »,
  Mutina, Sassuolo, Italie
Vases *Alcova*, WonderGlass
Essai d'accrochage, exposition
  de dessins et bas-reliefs

2021/Octobre

PAGE 375
Prototype, chaise
Exposition, Licht Gallery, Tokyo
Encre sur papier
Vases *Rombini*, briques *Bloc* et
  céramique *Rombini*, Mutina
Encre sur papier
Vase *Rombini*, Mutina

PAGE 376
Exposition, Licht Gallery,
  Tokyo
Suspension *Chaînes*, plâtre,
  Galerie kreo
Exposition, Licht Gallery, Tokyo
Exposition « Ensemble »,
  Mutina, Sassuolo, Italie
Encre sur papier
Vase *Rombini* et céramique
  Punto, Mutina
En couverture, *T, le magazine
  du Temps*
Exposition, Licht Gallery, Tokyo
Composition, bas-relief, atelier,
  Paris

PAGE 377
Atelier, Bretagne, France

PAGE 378
Présentation des premières
  études, aménagement
  des extérieurs, Bourse
  de commerce – Pinault
  Collection, Paris
Lustre *Gabriel*, château de
  Versailles, France
Banc *Palissade Park*, HAY
Banc *Palissade Park*, HAY
Affiche, exposition « The Sound
  of My Left Hand », Casa
  Mutina, Milan
Affiche, exposition « The Sound
  of My Left Hand », Casa
  Mutina, Milan
Affiche, exposition « The Sound
  of My Left Hand », Casa
  Mutina, Milan
Atelier de céramique
  de Jean-Marie, Bourgogne
Céramiques, bas-reliefs, cour,
  atelier, Paris

2021/Novembre

PAGE 379
Composition, bas-reliefs,
  atelier, Paris

PAGE 380
Encre sur papier
Bas-relief et chaise *Osso*,
  Mattiazzi
Petit bas-relief
Composition, bas-reliefs,
  atelier, Paris
Exposition « Circus »,
  Philadelphia Museum of Art,
  Philadelphie
Bas-relief et chaise *Filo*,
  Mattiazzi

PAGE 381
Affiches, exposition
  « The Sound of My Left
  Hand », Casa Mutina,
  Milan
Bas-reliefs
Exposition « 23 bas-reliefs »,
  Galerie kreo, Londres
Exposition « 23 bas-reliefs »,
  Galerie kreo, Londres
Petit bas-relief et chaise *Filo*,
  Mattiazzi
Exposition « 23 bas-reliefs »,
  Galerie kreo, Londres
Atelier, Bretagne, France

Détail, chaise *Musubi*, Koyori
Dessin de couverture, livre
  Fugitive Pieces,
  Anne Michaels, Penguin
  Random House Canada

2021/Décembre

PAGE 382
Petits bas-reliefs
Encre sur papier
Bas-reliefs, atelier, Paris
Détail, chaise *Musubi*, Koyori
Atelier, Paris
Portrait, atelier, Paris

PAGE 383
Maquette, chaise *Musubi*, Koyori

PAGE 384
Petit bas-relief
Cornelius, maison, Bretagne,
  France
Maison, Bretagne, France
Stylo-bille, pastel et scotch
  sur papier
Banc *Palissade Park*, HAY
Encre sur papier
Encre sur papier
Encre sur papier
Dessin et déjeuner frugal

PAGE 385
Pastel sur papier
Encre sur papier
Exposition « 23 bas-reliefs »,
  Galerie kreo, Londres
Encre sur papier
Encre sur papier
Fauteuil *Palissade*, HAY,
  sous la neige, Paris
Encre sur papier
Encre sur papier
Bretagne, France

PAGE 386
Encre sur papier
Encre sur papier
Bretagne, France
Maquette, charpente, hangar
  et lampe *Lampyre*, Wästberg
  d'Inga Sempé
Détail, chaise *Musubi*,
  Koyori
Maison, Bretagne, France

PAGE 387
Encre sur papier

Chaise longue *Quindici*,
  Mattiazzi, maison,
  Bretagne, France
Encre et ruban adhésif sur
  papier
Détail, chaise *Shaku*, Koyori
Atelier, Bretagne, France
Bretagne, France

2022/Janvier

PAGE 388
Encre sur papier

PAGE 389
Encre et ruban adhésif
  sur papier
Encre sur papier
Détail, chaise *Musubi*, Koyori
  et poster, The Wrong Shop
Détail, table *Balcony*, HAY
Chaise *Balcony*, HAY et
  céramique *Punto*, Mutina
Encre sur papier

PAGE 390
Banc *Palissade Park*, HAY
Maison, Bretagne, France
Maquette, exposition
  « 23 bas-reliefs », Galerie
  kreo, Londres
Maison, Bretagne, France
Chaise *Kawara*, Koyori
  et bas-relief
Vase *Découpage*, Vitra et
  chaise *Shaku*, Koyori
Encre sur papier
Banc *Palissade Park*, HAY
Banc *Palissade Park*, HAY

PAGE 391
Chaises et table *Balcony*, HAY
Vase *Découpage*, brique *Block*,
  Mutina et banc *Corde*
Stylo-bille et thermoformage
  sur papier
Chaise et table *Balcony*, HAY
Chaise *Balcony*, HAY, encre et
  ruban adhésif sur papier
Fauteuil *Balcony*, HAY

2022/Février

PAGE 392
Un dessin en soutien à l'Ukraine

PAGE 393
Détail, chaise *Shaku*, Koyori

Croquis, collection *Balcony*,
  HAY
Encre sur papier
Exposition « The Sound
  of My Left Hand », Casa
  Mutina, Milan
Encre sur papier
Bas-relief
Poster, The Wrong Shop
Poster en soutien à l'Ukraine,
  The Wrong Shop
  et bas-relief
Chaise *Kawara*, Koyori

2022/Mars

PAGE 394
Catalogue, exposition
  « The Sound of My Left
  Hand », éditions Mutina
Vase *Découpage*, *Rope Chair*,
  Artek, céramique *Rombini*,
  Mutina et encre sur papier
Chaises longues *Palissade*, HAY,
  terrasse, sanatorium Paimio
  d'Alvar Aalto, Finlande
Encre sur papier
Encre sur papier
Détail, chaise *Kawara*, Koyori

PAGE 395
Cassandra, une élève de
  troisième accueillie
  une semaine à l'atelier
  grâce à l'association
  ViensVoirMonTaf
Catalogue, exposition
  « The Sound of My Left
  Hand », éditions Mutina
Prototype, fauteuil *Palissade*,
  HAY
Encre sur papier
Céramiques, bas-reliefs, cour,
  atelier, Paris
Encre sur papier
Bas-reliefs, atelier, Paris
Vase *Rombini*, Mutina, galerie
  de Giorgio Mastinu, Venise
Chaise et bureau *Copenhague*,
  HAY

PAGE 396
Encre sur papier et *Rope Chair*,
  Artek

PAGE 397
Dessins, maison, Bretagne,
  France

Dessins, maison, Bretagne,
France
Bretagne, France
Bretagne, France
Drapeau, Bourse de commerce
– Pinault Collection, Paris
Exposition « The Sound of My
Left Hand », Casa Mutina,
Milan
Edition spéciale, tables
Copenhague, HAY et lampes
Piani, Flos
Maquette, cour, atelier, Paris
Graphite, pastel et ruban
adhésif sur papier

2022/Avril

PAGE 398
Portrait par Inga
Chaises *Kawara*, Koyori
et dessins, Licht Gallery,
Tokyo
Jour de vote
Atelier, Paris
Affiche, exposition, galerie de
Giorgio Mastinu, Venise
Chaise *Shaku*, Koyori, et dessin,
Licht Gallery, Tokyo

PAGE 399
Collection *Palissade*, HAY,
terrasse, maison de John
Lautner, Los Angeles
Exposition, galerie de Giorgio
Mastinu, Venise
Brique *Bloc*, Mutina
Atelier, Bretagne, France
Assemblage, vases *Sosei*,
Tajimi, Paris
Encre sur papier

PAGE 400
Maquette, charpente, hangar,
Bretagne, France
Banc *Palissade Park*, HAY
Vase *Sosei*, Tajimi
Exposition « Circus »,
Philadelphia Museum of Art,
Philadelphie
Parc du musée Noguchi,
New York, stylo-bille
sur papier
Maquette, *Lincoln Pavilion*
Maquette, *Lincoln Pavilion*
Exposition « Circus »,
Philadelphia Museum of Art,
Philadelphie

Exposition « Circus »,
Philadelphia Museum of Art,
Philadelphie

2022/Mai

PAGE 401
New York

PAGE 402
Paris

PAGE 403
Atelier, Paris
Encre sur papier
Catalogue, exposition
« The Sound of My Left
Hand », éditions Mutina
Bernard, le cauchemar
des homards
Stylo-bille sur papier
Chaise *Shaku*, Koyori
et bas-relief
Résumé des projets
présentés, Salone del
Mobile de Milan
Chaise *Balcony*, acier
galvanisé, HAY
Bureau *Kaari*, Artek et *Rope
Chair*, Artek

PAGE 404
Atelier, Bretagne, France
Valeureux érigérons
Encre sur papier
Atelier, Bretagne, France
Chaise *Musubi*, Koyori
Installation permanente,
sculpture *Lincoln* de Pascal
Rivet, *Lincoln Pavilion*, Piacé,
France
Installation permanente,
sculpture *Lincoln* de Pascal
Rivet, *Lincoln Pavilion*, Piacé,
France
Maquette, *Lincoln Pavilion*
Détail, piétement, bronze,
canapé *Riace*, Magis

PAGE 405
Canapé *Riace*, Magis
Lincoln Pavilion, Piacé, France
Vase *Sosei*, Tajimi
En couverture, *The New York
Review of Books*
Stylo-bille sur papier
Table *Passerelle*, HAY et
chaise *Élementaire*, HAY

2022/Juin

PAGE 406
Bas-relief
Lithographie, édition limitée,
Centre Pompidou-Metz,
France
Échelle *Ciel*, Galerie kreo
Signature, éditions, The Wrong
Shop
Fauteuil *Palissade*, HAY
Encre et ruban adhésif sur
papier

2022/Juillet

PAGE 407
Chez l'encadreur

PAGE 408
Encre sur papier
Lincoln Pavilion, Piacé,
France
Chaise *Balcony*, HAY
Maison, Bretagne, France
Encre sur papier
Atelier, Bretagne, France

PAGE 409
Assemblage, bas-reliefs,
hangar, Bretagne, France
Assemblage, bas-reliefs,
hangar, Bretagne, France
Aquarelle sur papier
Hangar, Bretagne, France
Bretagne, France
Maquette, charpente, hangar,
Bretagne, France
Chaise et table *Kawara*, Koyor
Bretagne, France
Bretagne, France

2022/Août

PAGE 410
Rope Chair, Artek et bas-relief
François
Petit bas-relief, cheminée,
Bretagne, France
Vue, atelier, Bretagne, France
Banc *Corde*, alcove *Alcova*,
WonderGlass et sculpture
de sainte Anne, céramique,
Henriot-Quimper
Boutique *A-Poc*, Issey Miyake
Bretagne, France
Détail, petit bas-relief
Maison, Bretagne, France

PAGE 411
Vase *Nuage*, Vitra, atelier,
Bretagne, France

PAGE 412
Chaises et tables *Palissade*,
acier galvanisé, HAY
Maison, Bretagne, France
Encre sur papier
Bretagne, France
Chaise *Kawara*, Koyori
et vase *Erkkeri*, Iittala
Metal Side Tables, acier
galvanisé, Vitra
Bas-relief et chaise *Balcony*,
HAY
Pastel dans cadre en bois
Pastel dans cadre en bois

2022/Septembre

PAGE 413
Ma table, atelier, Paris
Chaise *Shaku*, Koyori et table,
Koyori
Suspension *Luce orizzontale*,
pièce unique
Encre sur papier
Chaise *Balcony*, acier galvanisé,
HAY
Échelle et étagère *Ciel*,
Galerie kreo
Encre et impression 3D
sur papier
Vase *Ruutu* et *Fleurs*, Iittala
Ma table, atelier, Paris

PAGE 414
Banc *Balcony*, HAY
Installation, vases *Rombini*,
Mutina, Fiorano Modenese,
Italie
Installation, briques *Bloc*,
Mutina, Fiorano Modenese,
Italie
Mon espace, atelier, Paris
Stylo-bille sur papier
Encre sur papier

2022/Octobre

PAGE 415
Mon portrait par Inga

PAGE 416
Encre sur papier

All photographs by Ronan Bouroullec, unless noted below.

t – top,   m – middle,   b – bottom, l – left,
c – centre and r – right.

Alexis Armanet: 376br. Artek: 254mc; 340tr. Atelier blam: 168mr; 176mr; 178tc; 206bc; 217br; 238ml; 246br; 248ml; 274tl, ml; 282mr; 289mc; 309ml, bl. Juriaan Booij: 61tl. Erwan Bouroullec: 242bl. Mette Bouroullec: 149br; 222ml, mc, br; 256tr; 261br; 291br; 293tl; 312mc; 368tc. Studio Bouroullec: 11mr; 17tl; 18tc, br; 20tr; 22tr, mr, bl; 23; 24tr; 25tl, tr, bl, bm; 26tr, ml, mc, mr; 28mc, br; 29tc, bl, mr, br; 30br; 35; 36bl; 37tc, ml, mr; 38tr, mr; 43tl, tc, tr, mc; 44tl, tc, tr, ml, bl, bc; 45br; 46ml; 47tl, ml; 49ml; 50br; 52mc; 53br; 54tl; 56; 57bl, br; 58tl; 60bc; 70ml, bl; 76ml; 79; 81bl; 82tl, tc, bc; 84; 85bl, br; 86tc, mr; 87bl; 88tc, bm, br; 89bc; 90tl, tr, ml; 91tl; 92tr; 93; 94tr; 98tc, tr, ml, mc, mr, bl; 100tl, bl, bc; 101tl, br; 104mr; 105; 107mr; 108mr, bl; 110ml; 114bc; 115; 117tr, ml, mr, bl; 120ml; 122mr, br; 123tl, ml, mc, mr; 125br; 126bc; 127tr, ml, mc; 128tc; 129ml, mc; 131bl; 139tr; 146br; 149tc; 150mr, bl, bc; 152tr; 154tl; 155tr, ml, mc, bl; 158br; 164tm; 165bl; 166bc; 167; 170bl, bc; 172mc; 174br; 179tc; 180bc; 181mc, mr, bl; 182bc; 183ml, mr, bl, bc; 186tl; 190tc; 191tl, ml; 194; 195br; 196tl, tr, ml; 197tr, mr, bl, br; 198br; 199; 200bc; 201bc, br; 202tl; 203tr; 204tc, ml, mc, bl, bc, br; 207tc, tr; 208br; 209bc; 212tc; 214bc, br; 215tr; 217tl; 218mc, bl; 225br; 226r; 227bl; 229tl, mr; 235mc, tr; 238bl; 240tr; 241; 244mr; 247mr; 248tr; 250bl, tr; 251mc, bl, bc, br; 254br; 258tl, tr; 259tr; 267tr, ml; 271ml, bl; 273tc, tr, mc; 274bl, br; 289ml; 293ml; 305tc; 310tc; 316bl; 317tl; 322tc, mc; 323tc, bl; 325br; 328mr, bl; 334bl, mc; 337bl; 343ml; 349br; 354tr; 371tl; 373br; 395br; 413mr. DSL: 397mr. Enrico Fiorese: 399tc. Established & Sons: 235ml. Flos: 310bl. Albrecht Fuchs: 257bl. Morgane Le Gall: 50bc; 51; 52ml, bc; 53tl, tr; 165ml; 169ml, mc, mr; 174mr, bl, bc; 177bm; 193tr; 247tl, tc, tr, ml, bc; 410mr. Galerie kreo: 177tl. Giulio Ghirardi: 225mc; 240bc. Glas Italia: 45ml, bl; 131tc, tr, mr. Philippe Grohe: 66tr; 323br. HAY: 46mc; 49mc; 60bl; 76bl; 104tc, bc; 301br; 373tc; 399tr; 400tc. Elizabeth Heltoft: 316mr; 361. Iittala: 80mr; 81br; 250br; 285mr. Hiroshi Iwasaki: 386bc. Gerhardt Kellermann: 129tr; 131mc; 343bc; 370bc; 375br; 376mr. Kettal: 110mc. Kvadrat: 190bl; 231tc; 234tl; 325tc. Claire Lavabre: 8tc; 26bl; 36tl; 38tl; 47bl, br; 48; 49bc; 52bl; 53mr; 54ml; 55tl, tc; 57tl, tr, ml; 113ml; 176tl; 182tr; 186bl; 187bc; 200tl; 203ml, br; 209ml; 214tl; 216tl; 236bl, tr; 242tl, tr; 243ml, br; 246mc; 247bl; 248tc, mr, br; 249tr, br; 253; 254tl; 256tc; 268br; 269mc; 271mc; 279tr; 280tl; 282tl, tc, tr; 284tc, bl, br; 285tl, tr; 287; 293mc; 303mr; 304ml; 305; 306tc, tl; 309br; 315bl; 326tr; 329br; 330tl; 331br; 332; 338; 340ml; 345; 347mc; 353mc, mr, br; 354tl, br; 355; 358br; 359ml; 373tc; 374bc; 378br, bc; 379; 380tc, tr, bl, mr, br; 381tc, mc; 382br; 391bl; 393mr, br; 397mc; 398bl, mr; 399br; 400tr; 403br; 404mr; 405tr, ml, br; 406tl; 408tr; 413tc, tr, bc; 414tl. Julien Lanoo: 64tr; 184tr; 213tl, tc, tr; 239ml. Verona Libri: 322tl. Licht Gallery: 340br; 375tc; 376tl, tr, bc; 378tl, tr; 398tc, br. lightfilms: 331mc.

Magis: 404br. Giorgio Mastinu: 212bl; 225br; 259bl; 269mr; 395bc. Mattiazzi: 102br. Mutina: 395tc. Nieves: 330bl. Hans-Ulrich Obrist: 202ml. Massimo Orsini: 153ml; 166tc. David Perreau: 28ml; 142ml, mc, mr; 147tc; 268mr. Charles Pétillon: 219tl; 232; 233ml; 240br; 242tl, tr; 248mc; 249tl; 293tc; 308mr; 359tr; 406ml. Yann Peucat: 317mr; 319; 333mc; 336tc; 374tl. Piacé le radieux: 321tl; 342tl. Leon Ransmeier: 394tr. Julien Renault: 193bc; 326br. Samsung: 177bl. Tommaso Sartori: 353bl; 354bl; 359tl. Inga Sempé: 75bc; 320br; 398tl; 415. Paul Tahon and R & E Bouroullec: 11tr, tc, tl, ml, br; 12tr; 17br; 24tl; 40br, bc; 41tr, ml, bl; 65tl; 117bc; 125bl; 136br; 137tr, br, bc; 178tr, mc, mr, bc, br; 179bl, br; 180tr; 182mr; 185; 188br; 192tl; 193tc; 210tr; 217bl, bc; 254br; 260tc; 308bl; 344mr. Vincent Thibert: 216br. UH5: 408tl. Vitra: 212bc; 253tl; 373bc. Till Weber: 226tr.

Every effort has been made to secure all permissions prior to publication. Phaidon apologizes for any inadvertent errors or omissions. If notified, the publisher will endeavour to correct these at the earliest opportunity.

Bourse de Commerce
Courtesy Bourse de Commerce – Pinault Collection
© Ronan & Erwan Bouroullec
© Tadao Ando Architect & Associates, NeM / Niney & Marca Architectes, Agence Pierre-Antoine Gatier

With the exception of the drawings, bas-reliefs and some personal research and installations by Ronan Bouroullec, all the creations reproduced in this book are creations by Ronan and Erwan Bouroullec.

À l'exception des dessins, des bas-reliefs et de certaines recherches et installations personnelles de Ronan Bouroullec, l'ensemble des créations reproduites dans ce livre sont des créations de Ronan et Erwan Bouroullec.

I'm very grateful to Emilia Terragni at Phaidon for offering me the opportunity to make this book, Caitlin Arnell Argles, the people at Phaidon, Claire Lavabre from Bouroullec Studio who worked on this project and Martin Béthenod.

I would like to thank Erwan and all the designers and members of the Bouroullec studio who have been working with me since 2014: Montserrat Alvarez, Sybille Berger, Joschua Brunn, Py Cha, Marie Cornil, Emillie Desegaulx, Camille Donias, Salomé Drouet, Jean-Baptiste Fastrez, Quentin Frichet, Michel Giesbrecht, Claire Lavabre, Valérie Lopin, Cyrille Mariën, Jorinel Monday, Hiroyuki Morita, Sacha Parent, Natacha Poutoux, Felipe Ribon, Martin Schenk, Christian Spiess, Philippe Thibault, Paul Tubiana, Emi Yatsuzaki and Alexandre Willaume.

And special thanks are due to Inga, Mette and Cornelius.

Phaidon
55, rue Traversière
75012 Paris

Dépôt légal septembre 2023

Phaidon Press Limited
2 Cooperage Yard
London E15 2QR

Phaidon Press Inc.
65 Bleecker Street
New York, NY 10012

phaidon.com

First published 2023
© 2023 Phaidon Press Limited

ISBN 978 1 83866 689 7
ISBN 978 1 83866 751 1 (Signed edition)

A CIP catalogue record for this book is available from
the British Library and the Library of Congress.

Commissioning Editor: Emilia Terragni
Project Editor (English): Caitlin Arnell Argles
Project Editor (French): Baptiste Roque-Genest
Production Controller: Lily Rodgers
Design: Cantina

Printed in China

The publisher would like to thank James Brown, Hélène
Gallois Montbrun, Anne Heining, Sophie Hodgkin, Lucie
Nédellec, Camilla Rockwood, Kim Scott, Clara Soupart and
Phoebe Stephenson for their contributions to this book.